THE POLITICS OF RETRIBUTION

THE POLITICS OF RETRIBUTION IN EUROPE

WORLD WAR II AND
ITS AFTERMATH

Edited by

István Deák, Jan T. Gross, and Tony Judt

PRINCETON UNIVERSITY PRESS   PRINCETON, NEW JERSEY

Library of Congress Catalog Card Number 99-0694-00

ISBN 0-691-00953-8 (cloth : alk. paper)
ISBN 0-691-00954-6 (paper : alk. paper)

The essay entitled "The Criminal Justice System as a
Political Actor in Regime Transitions: The Case of
Belgium (1944–50)" is copyrighted, 2000, by Luc Huyse.

This book has been composed in Sabon

The paper used in this publication meets the minimum
requirements of ANSI/NISO Z39.48-1992 (R 1997)
(*Permanence of Paper*)

www.pup.princeton.edu

Printed in the United States of America

10 9 8 7 6 5 4 3 2 1

10 9 8 7 6 5 4 3 2 1
(pbk.)

Contents

Preface

Tony Judt

IT USED to be easy to write contemporary European history. World War II came to an end in 1945, and with it ended a thirty-year crisis. Between 1913 and 1945 relations between European states, relations within most European states, economic and other forms of commerce between European states, all suffered traumatic changes. Revolutions—radical and reactionary—shifted power away from the old ruling elites. Massive upheaval and collapse within the capitalist economy brought an end to the stability of nineteenth-century life and introduced radical changes in social relations. Violence in every sphere—war, civil war, domestic instability, state violence against opponents—became endemic. All of this, so the story ran, came to a head in the appalling experience of World War II, itself symbolized by the policies and practices of a genocidal state at the heart of Europe.

In the conventional story as thus told, everything changed after 1945. The rapid shift of allegiance, from the anti-Nazi alliance to the divisions of the Cold War, institutionalized the military division of Europe to the point where, forty years after the death of Hitler, the division of the continent seemed part of the natural order of things. In Eastern Europe, Soviet hegemony seemed to be the logical product of the upheavals of the first half of the century, while in Western Europe progressive moves toward economic and political union—and the two decades of postwar prosperity—appeared to have resolved definitively the problems that had seemed so insoluble before 1939. European history, in short, had come to an end and this was all to the good.

In order for history to have resolved itself in this convenient way, it was necessary for memory to conform. From 1945 through the mid-1960s at least, the experience of the first half of the European twentieth century in general and the war years in particular was blurred: it suited almost everyone to forget what they or their parents did, to forget what was done to them, to forget what they saw and to forget what they knew. This psychologically and politically convenient convergence of historic renewal and collective amnesia was well reflected in the conventional histories of Europe after World War II and as recently as the 1980s. Most histories of post–World War II Europe treated either Eastern Europe or Western Europe but only very rarely the two together.

Furthermore, most such histories began in 1945, as though the desire on the part of many Europeans to being afresh in 1945 could also be treated as a rational, objective perspective on their history. Even where the war itself was incorporated into accounts of the reconstruction of Europe in its aftermath, that war was normally understood as a prelude, the moment of utter collapse preceding the rebirth. The very suggestion that the war might in certain important ways not have ended, or that its aftermath could yet prove fragile or temporary, was unwelcome and usually denied.

In the course of the 1990s all of this has changed in ways that now make the postwar historiography of Europe curiously outdated almost before the ink has dried. In the first place, and obviously of great importance, the collapse of the Soviet Empire in Europe has meant that one crucial pillar of the old story—the permanence of the postwar divisions—has crumpled. If the division of Europe into East and West on military, economic, and ideological lines was but a temporary (albeit forty-year-long) hiatus in a longer European story, then the history of the postwar era has to be rethought.

Secondly, and intimately related to the events of 1989 and afterward, there has been the now widely debated "revival of memory." This did not begin in 1989. From the mid-1960s in Germany, and a little later in France, Italy, and elsewhere, younger generations began to ask not only what happened in the war, but also what happened after the war? Why was so much of the horrific recent history of contemporary Europe so obscured by the well-meaning amnesia of the 1950s? The center of gravity of such questioning has understandably been the Shoah, the Nazi attempt to exterminate the Jews of Europe. Bu around that fundamental horror there orbit other questions. What was collaboration? Who—in France, Belgium, the Netherlands, Italy, and so on—helped the Nazis achieve their goals and why? What was the resistance? What did it mean to resist and how far can we still give credit to the heroic if self-serving tales that came out of the war in much of Western Europe and served as the moral cement with which postwar democracies reconstructed themselves.

A third element in the remaking of recent history has been the related question of justice—or more accurately, retribution. On and off from the 1960s through the 1980s, West European jurists and historians have debated the nature and limits of the way in which punishment for wartime crimes was meted out after 1945. Since 1989 and the pressing need in former communist countries to address analogous questions concerning crimes committed under Stalinist auspices, the debate about postwar, or posttotalitarian retribution has grown, One reason for this is simply the practical difficulty faced in former communist countries in dealing with crimes and criminals from earlier decades; another, of course, concerns the definition of political crime itself.

And these debates in post-1989 Europe not only throw light (sometimes) on the decisions and actions of 1956–46; they also, of course, open up a very different order of questions largely neglected before 1989 for political or ideological reasons in East and West alike. These concern the legal, moral, and political context in which communism itself came to power in the aftermath of Nazism. What happened in Eastern Europe between 1944 and 1949, who did what to whom and with whose help; these are hard questions—because they raise for Eastern Europe the same painful issues as those facing West European students of the same period: what did the Nazi era bring in Eastern Europe and who benefited or suffered under it? But they also point to distinctively local dilemmas: was the history of Eastern Europe after 1945 something imported from the East in the baggage train of the Red Army, or does it have its own roots further back in the troubled and insecure history of the region?

Even so superficial a listing of the intricately interwoven issues of history, politics, and memory in the recent European past will suffice to illustrate how much has changed since the history writing of the pre-1989 decades. Not only do we now pay more attention to questions about political justice, collective memory, the gray zone between resistance and collaboration, the long-term social and political consequences of war, and so forth, but we are also much more sensitive to different chronological perspectives. It is no longer self-evident that European history can be divided into convenient blocks: pre-1913, 1913–45, post-1945. The decade 1938–48, in Central and Eastern Europe at least, has a historical logic of its own, in the sense that much of what we think of as the important features of Nazi domination began before the outbreak of war between Germany and Poland, and did not end until long after the fall of Hitler.

Similarly, the decade 1945–56 might usefully be understood now as "postwar" in the sense that the unresolved business of the war itself—with respect to economic damage, social disruption, political score settling, and so on—was still the dominant feature. And analogously, the turning point of 1989–90 reveals how much of the unfinished business of the pre-1945 era remains, indeed, unfinished—in former Yugoslavia, most obviously, but elsewhere as well. We are now also able to see, in a way that we preferred to ignore before 1989, just how fragile the West European postwar settlement truly was—prosperity and economic unity, to be sure, but both of them fragile and in the case of prosperity, at least, not destined to endure indefinitely. None of this suggests that East and West European history have now converged; nor does it require of us as historians that we insist upon a common history from 1945 onward, where clearly the paths of the two halves of the continent forcefully diverged. Nonetheless, the time for rethinking the whole history of twentieth-century Europe, and especially the postwar era, is clearly upon us.

The collaborative research project that gave rise to the essays in this book entitled *The Politics of Retribution*, was centered on three distinct themes, all of which are echoed here and lie at the heart of contemporary debates on the recent European past. Our first concern was to focus on the question of collaboration and resistance during the war itself. What do we now understand by these terms (particularly in the light of their use and abuse in debates about post-1989 Eastern Europe)? How did the experience of collaboration and resistance differ between countries across Europe? In this part of our project, as with everything that followed, it was crucial to our purposes that Europe be understood as a whole, that the history of Western Europe and Eastern Europe be incorporated into a single story, that the experience of countries like France, Czechoslovakia, Hungary, and the Netherlands be compared and contrasted rather than written about in separate, isolated ways.

The second area of emphasis in this project concerned the issue of political justice. Here we encouraged scholars not only to ask once again, and this time in the light of newly opened archives and other sources, what sort of justice was meted out in different parts of Europe at the end of World War II, but also to reflect upon how we might understand the limits and constraints upon retributive justice in a postwar situation, especially in light of our renewed appreciation of the difficulties of such legal resolution as observed in postcommunist Eastern Europe. Our third concern, and the last of our research emphases, was on the ways in which Europe "overcame" the experience of war in the decade that followed. Here we were particularly interested in encouraging discussion of the uses that were made of wartime memories and myths in the construction of postwar states, both pluralist and authoritarian.

One striking outcome of this five-year project has been the degree to which the important questions about wartime and postwar European history emerge as fundamentally similar from country to country. Superficially the history of Belgium or France looks utterly different from that of Poland or Czechoslovakia. In certain important respects, of course, these differences remain salient. But it is noteworthy how much one may learn from asking questions about resistance and collaboration, about postwar score settling and forms of punishment, about the use of myths of "antifascism" or small country "heroism" in the reconstruction of shattered societies.

One common element in much recent work on contemporary European history is the fascinating account of the freezing and unfreezing of national and political identities. We are familiar with the notion that from 1949 to 1989 Eastern Europe was "frozen" into place, forced to tell itself a story of fraternal relations, common and heroic resistance to fascism, and the successful overcoming of ethnic and other forms of interstate and intrastate division. What is perhaps less readily recognized is the degree to which Western Europe experienced an analogous glacis. The story of Western Europe from 1945 through the 1980s is after all also a story of overcoming the past—overcoming Franco-German conflict, overcoming the past—overcoming Franco-German conflict, overcoming extreme political movements and their disruptive effects, and overcoming war and civil war.

Yet in Western Europe, too, the most important development of the last two decades has been not the growing movement for European unity, but the escalating collapse of old established national states. Just as Yugoslavia and Czechoslovakia imploded after 1989, so Belgium, Italy, and in less dramatic ways Spain and the United Kingdom have seen sectional and geographically defined efforts to break up the authority of the unitary states. Here, too, the myth and memory of World War II and the need for postwar stability and tranquillity—facilitated by unparalleled prosperity—tended to obscure this process until quite recently. But looking back we can now see that the breakup of nineteenth-century European states into smaller units, a process set in motion before World War I and escalated in the aftermath of imperial collapse, has begun again.

This reference to long-term processes is a reminder that one of the defects of European historiography, as it reflected the post–war World War II settlement, was a marked inclination to separate the past from the present, as though 1945 was a true Year Zero and nothing that had gone before counted in the experience of what would come after. We can now see that this was patently false, albeit convenient and perhaps even helpful in the rebuilding of the continent. One might debate interminably about the longer and shorter term causes of the breakup of various European states, just as it is a matter of scholarly argument whether the divisions between East and West Europe or the Stalinist imposition of communism after 1945 in the Eastern half were inscribed in longer historical processes.

What is clear, however, is that nothing started altogether from zero in 1945. Even the curious "memory hole" into which collective awareness of the crimes of the past was to fall in the postwar decades has its own, longer, history. The conflicts of World War II, which we too easily package as "collaboration" and "resistance," were themselves echoes and transpositions of political, ideological, religious, local, and ethnic disagreements and disputes whose roots lay variously in interwar politics, post–World War I state making, pre–World War I small wars, and even (e.g., in the Italian or Belgian cases) the imperfect and incomplete forms of state making of the earlier nineteenth century.

These European pasts lie folded over one another like tectonic plates. Some move frequently and violently, others in longer waves and with less obvious disruptive impact. But none of them came to a stop in 1945 or first came into being then. What Henry Rousso in France has called the Vichy syndrome—the way in which postwar France denied, misremembered, incorporate, rejected, accepted, or abused the memory of the wartime regime—only makes sense if we set it in a larger and longer context, the history of French political and social conflict.

Every country has its Vichy Syndrome. In Poland it concerns Polish-Jewish relations, whose wartime apotheosis and postwar nemesis make no sense when divorced from the history that preceded them. The same applies, mutatis mutandis, to the subterranean histories of Czechoslovakia, Belgium, Hungary, and so on. And in each case these conjoined stories—what happened before 1939, what happened between 1939 (or 1938) and 1945, and how the memory of those events was adapted or distorted or occluded after 1945—have only recently begun to be unravelled and interwoven by scholars. In formerly Communist lands the availability of newly released archives has played a major role in this renewal of national historiographies, but in West and East alike it is the revised public perspective brought to bear upon the postwar decades that has played the most important role.

This project was based at the Institute for Human Sciences in Vienna, where a number of senior and junior scholars from the United States and Europe were fortunate enough to be able to spend time pursuing their research in a congenial and supportive environment. The editors wish to express their appreciation to the staff of the Institute, and its director Professor Kristof Michalski, for their unstinting hospitality. We also wish to express our appreciation to Jair Kessler and her staff at the Remarque Institute at New York University, where the third of our conferences took place, and who provided administrative assistance, logistical advice, and much else besides.

The editors would like to thank participants in those conferences for permission to publish their papers in this collection; a few of these papers have already appeared in the journal *Eastern European Politics and Societies*, whose former editor Jan Gross is also coeditor of the present volume. We would also like to express our deepest appreciation to the various foundations, public and private, that have made possible the conferences and this book, which derives from them. These include the Joint Committee on Eastern Europe of the American Council of Learned Societies and the Social Science Research Council; the Andrew W. Mellon Foundation; the Volkswagen Foundation of the Federal Republic of German; and the Remarque Institute at New York University.

Part I

PRELIMINARIES

Introduction

CONQUERING ARMIES over the centuries have always found willing collaborators in the countries they occupy, and, if sufficiently oppressive and brutal, they have also met with civilian resistance. Following occupation, those who had given aid and comfort to the enemy were often hunted down and punished. In the annals of history, however, never have so many people been caught up in the process of collaboration, resistance, and retribution as in Europe during and after the Second World War. True, even then, active collaborators and active resisters were but a small minority among the many who just wanted to get by, but the impact of collaboration and resistance was so great as to affect nearly everyone's life.

Postwar purges, part of a brutal and sweeping pattern of retribution, produced an enormous demographic upheaval—especially in Central and Eastern Europe—one whose long-range consequences we are still unable to fathom. Moreover, an extraordinary number of individuals were prosecuted, after the war, for collaboration and war crimes. This is not to say that all the guilty were actually punished. Far from it—some of the most obnoxious traitors and war criminals escaped retribution altogether.[1] It is to say only that all across what once had been Hitler's Europe, an attempt at retribution frightened or, alternately, exhilarated vast sections of the population.

What motivated the postwar antifascist regimes was, primarily, rightful indignation over the many acts of cruelty and treason committed by the collaborators. There were other motives as well: the desire to place the blame on specific individuals for what had been, in reality, a large scale, popular accommodation with the enemy, and the perceived need to eliminate, or at least to reduce, the influence of social, political, and ethnic groups that might stand in the way of the creation of a new society and state.

Just as accommodation to the wishes of the occupier had been popular in most occupied countries, so now did the prosecution of collaborators meet with widespread public approval. It was as if the Europeans hoped to rid themselves of the memory of their compromises and crimes by decimating their own ranks.

It is nearly impossible to calculate the total number of persons targeted by postwar retribution, but, even by the most conservative estimates, they numbered several million, that is, 2 or 3 percent of the population formerly under German occupation. Because educated adult males constituted the majority of those purged, this segment of the population was even more seriously affected. In some countries, such as France, actors, actresses, cabaret singers, journalists, writers, poets, and philosophers were especially singled out by the prosecutors.

Punishment of the guilty ranged from lynchings during the last months of the war to postwar death sentencing, imprisonment, or hard labor. Added to those harsh punishments were condemnation to national dishonor, the loss of civic rights, and/or monetary fines as well as such administrative measures as expulsion, police supervision, loss of the right to travel or to live in certain desirable places, dismissal, and the loss of pension rights. It is one of the great paradoxes of the postwar era that in all of Europe, the smallest percentage of former Nazis was executed or imprisoned in Western Germany. On the other hand, Western Germany made a greater effort than any other country in Europe to atone collectively for its past.

To the bewildering array of persons who were charged by the national courts for what was alternately, or often simultaneously, termed collaboration with the enemy, treason, and war crimes should be added those who were not charged individually but belonged to one or another group held collectively responsible for what had taken place during the war. These groups included, among others, the thirteen to fifteen million Volksdeutsche, German-speaking inhabitants of Poland, Czechoslovakia, Hungary, Yugoslavia, Russia, and the three Baltic countries, who were charged collectively with war crimes and treason by the governments of their own countries and by the leaders of the three great Allied powers meeting at Potsdam in June 1945. These Germans were either killed or expelled to what remained of Germany after the war.[2]

Collective punishment targeted more than just the Volksdeutsche. Other ethnic groups, such as the Hungarians in Czechoslovakia, the Poles in the Ukraine, the Ukrainians in Poland, and the Albanians in Greece, were also held collectively responsible for the horrors of the war. Persons belonging to these groups were killed, imprisoned, driven from their homelands, or officially degraded to second-class citizens as, for example, in the case of the Hungarians in Czechoslovakia. Add to this the organizations whose membership were pronounced guilty either by the International Military Tribunal at Nuremberg or by the national courts after the war. These included the SS with all its branches, the Leadership Corps of the German National Socialist Party, the German Security Police, and the Gestapo. Outside Germany, diverse national courts indicted such organi-

zations as the Hungarian gendarmes, the Serbian Chetnik guerrillas, all
Soviet citizens in German service, all Soviet soldiers who had surrendered
to the Germans, and many others. Members of these groups had to prove
their innocence in court, rather than the court having to demonstrate their
individual guilt, although it must be admitted that at least in the American, British, and French zones of occupied Germany the verdicts of the
Nuremberg Court pertaining to such institutions were barely, if at all,
enforced. On the other hand in Hungary, former members of the notori-
ously brutal gendarmes were automatically imprisoned, and in Yugoslavia mere membership in the Serbian Chetnik forces or in the Croatian
Ustashas was frequently sufficient grounds for a death sentence.[3] An analogous situation obtained in Greece, as Mark Mazower explains in this
book, with the difference, however, that it was membership in the Communist anti-Nazi resistance that could easily lead to execution by the
postwar anti-Communist authorities there.[4]

The wholesale expulsion of the Germans from Central and Eastern
Europe as well as the massive transfer of other ethnic minorities came on
the heels of gigantic purges in the region during the war. The primary
victims of the wartime slaughter were, of course, the more than five million European Jews who perished at the hands of the Nazis and their,
mostly East European, helpers.[5] Yet the Jews were not alone in falling
victim to the principle and practice of collective responsibility. The Polish
intelligentsia, for example, was charged in German-occupied Poland with
conspiring against German-, and in Soviet-occupied Poland, against Soviet interests and, as a result, was nearly annihilated. Other groups, such
as the Serbian Orthodox in wartime Croatia, the so-called kulaks and
their offspring in the Soviet Union, as well as several ethnic groups in that
country, were held collectively guilty of anti-state behavior and dealt with
accordingly.

The primary purpose of this book is not to discuss the problems of
collective responsibility and ethnic or racial cleansing. The goal is, rather,
to analyze different facets of wartime resistance and collaboration as well
as, to a much larger extent, to treat the diverse aspects of postwar judicial
retribution. In other words, contributors to this book are primarily analyzing the actions of individuals who were able to make political choices
during the war and could, therefore, be held personally accountable for
their actions after the war. Still, it seems to me necessary to place the case
of these individuals in the larger, and more terrible, context of wartime
and postwar racial and ethnic purification. The captured and deported
French resister Charlotte Delbos, a poet and a writer, found herself in a
sea of tortured humanity at Auschwitz: Jews, Gypsies, German asocials,
homosexuals, Jehovah's Witnesses, Soviet and other prisoners of war,
only a fraction of whom were there for actions taken against Nazi rule.[6]

Similarly, in the Gulag archipelago, Soviet citizens who had given assistance to or had fought on the side of the Germans during the war shared their bunks with a much larger number of individuals who were not guilty of any anti-Soviet or criminal activity.

Admittedly, it is not always easy to separate those punished in the name of collective responsibility from those held accountable individually. Even in a model democracy such as Norway, all women who had worked as Red Cross nurses in German military hospitals were considered guilty. Similarly, all members of the Nasjonal Samling, the minuscule Norwegian fascist party, were automatically indicted, even those who had belonged to the party before the war, when its existence was undoubtedly legal. In fact, prewar party membership, presumably motivated by ideological convictions, was judged more harshly in the Norwegian courts than wartime membership, best explained by opportunism.[7]

Scanning the essays in this or other books on wartime Europe, one is struck by the similarities between the behavior of the occupied peoples and their occupiers. Everywhere, the comportment of the occupied population was "occupier-driven," to use a term aptly coined by Jan Gross. This means that generally the population did not spontaneously formulate its own behavior toward the occupier but rather reacted to the behavior of the German, Soviet, and other occupying powers. Where the Germans behaved correctly, as was the case, at least initially, in Western Europe, the populace also tended to behave correctly toward the Germans, irrespective of the presence or absence of any racial affinity with the Germans. In occupied Denmark the German army felt so confident of popular and official compliance that within a few weeks of the country's invasion in April 1940, it reduced the number of occupation forces to half of an infantry division, less than ten thousand men. This was far less than the total number of Danish army and armed police forces in the country, both of which the German occupiers had allowed to continue to function.[8] Similarly, in France, certainly not a fellow "Nordic country," German police forces in mid-1942 consisted only of three battalions, some 2,500 or 3,000 men, far too few to be able to maintain order or carry out the deportation of the Jews.[9] These functions were performed by the French police on behalf of the Germans. On the other hand, in Yugoslavia, where the Germans' Croatian fascist Ustasha allies unleashed a reign of utter terror, there was almost immediate massive armed resistance. At the end of 1943, fourteen German divisions and five divisions of non-Germans under German command, well over 200,000 men, fought—in vain—against Tito's Communist Partisan army.[10]

In occupied Europe a sharp distinction existed between those regions that the German leadership envisaged as future venues of direct German settlement and colonization, and all other regions, with the inhabitants of the former being subjected to considerably worse treatment. The areas of new German settlement, and hence, most onerous occupation, were concentrated in Eastern Europe. It is worth noting that the Soviet occupation in those same areas was similarly brutal. In occupied and divided Poland, for instance, the implicit effect of the occupation policies of Germany and the Soviet Union, taken together, was to crowd those Poles not killed or deported elsewhere into the center of the country.

In regions not envisaged as lands of future German settlement, German brutality was usually the consequence of resistance activity, which in turn was likely due to certain coercive measures introduced by the occupier. Faced by a growing labor shortage, the Germans instructed the local authorities in Western Europe to draft young men for labor service in the Reich. The conscripts deserted in droves, especially in France, and this, in turn, led to combined action by the German and Vichy French authorities to hunt down the deserters. The massive hunts caused popular resentment and drove many an apolitical young man to the hitherto minuscule maquis resistance movement. The ensuing armed clashes, accompanied by the burning of villages, the taking and execution of hostages and, in general, terror exercised by both the authorities and the resisters, led to a gradual breakdown of law and order in some regions of France, developing ultimately into civil war and a struggle for national liberation.

Lawlessness reigned from the very start in occupied Poland, which the Germans considered very much a part of their *Lebensraum*. There, German terror was immediate, as was the violent response of the resistance movement. In fact, Poland was the only place in Hitler's Europe where the defending army never surrendered to the invader, and where the resistance movement began to organize even without waiting for a provocation.

The situation was somewhat similar in Yugoslavia, which was not projected as an area for German living space, but where antagonisms between Serbs and Croats, Orthodox, Catholics, and Muslims led to an immediate civil war. In that conflict, the German and Italian occupation forces became hopelessly entangled.

It ought to be noted here that whereas German political leaders often referred to the Slavs as *Untermenschen* (subhumans), their behavior toward the Slavic peoples was anything but consistent. Slovakia, Croatia, and Bulgaria, all of them Slavic-speaking countries, were treated as honorable allies. Russians, Ukrainians, Bosnian Muslims, and other Slavic speakers were readily admitted into the Waffen SS. On the other hand, most Russians were treated abominably, and the Germans unhesitatingly arrested, tortured, and shot many members of the allied Slavic nations.

But then such things could happen to anyone in Hitler's Europe, including Aryan Germans, who were the particular targets of Nazi fury in the last weeks of the war.

Collaboration was of no help to only two ethnic groups, the Poles and the Jews. Poles were allowed to cooperate with the Germans only in the so-called Generalgouvernement around Warsaw and Cracow and there only on the lowest level of administration. Overall, the Germans treated the Poles as despised slaves. Jewish collaboration was invited only insofar as it could facilitate the Final Solution. The Nazis had sentenced all European Jews to death; the question was only when and how smoothly the Nazis and their allies could execute that sentence.

A very peculiar problem was presented by countries allied to Germany, such as Italy, Finland, Slovakia, Hungary, Croatia, Romania, and Bulgaria, whose governments carefully maneuvered between drawing the maximum benefit from the German alliance and preserving at least a modicum of independence as an assurance for the future, especially in case the Third Reich would lose the war. Thus it happened that even though all the German allies participated in the war on the side of Germany, none fully committed its armed forces; that all cooperated with Germany economically, yet all also attempted to preserve some measure of economic sovereignty; and that all, except for Finland (which had hardly any Jews), assisted the Germans in the Final Solution; yet all also tried, and largely succeeded, in preserving the lives of those groups of Jews their government deemed worth saving.

Is it at all possible to speak of collaboration versus resistance in countries officially allied to Germany? Yes, if one considers that postwar retribution branded thousands of citizens in these countries as German collaborators while praising thousands of others as brave resisters. Yet those who, during the war, opposed their own pro-German government were not necesarily hostile to Germany, and those who readily obeyed their government did not necessarily sympathize with the Nazis. National Socialist groups in Hungary and Romania, for instance, were violently hostile to their own conservative regimes, even though the governments of Marshal Ion Antonescu and Admiral Miklós Horthy were closely allied to Nazi Germany. In fact, the main opponents of the collaborationist governments in those two countries were not the handful of Communists but the National Socialist Iron Guard in Romania and the National Socialist Arrow Cross in Hungary. Leaders of these parties were assassinated, imprisoned, or driven into exile by the same Romanian and Hungarian authorities who, until 1944, enjoyed the full support of Hitler.

It is worth noting here that several states that had been defeated and occupied by the German army early in the war later became virtual allies of the Third Reich. Norway had its Vidkun Quisling, and the volunteer members of the various Norwegian SS units were at least as numerous as the active members of the resistance. The government of Denmark joined the German-led anti–Comintern Pact in November 1941, and its economy was more completely at the service of Nazi Germany than the economy of, for instance, Hungary, which was an official ally of Germany. If the Vichy regime did not declare war on Great Britain, this was due mainly to Hitler's refusal to allow such a thing. In any case, during the war, French forces fought a respectable number of naval and land engagements against the Western allies—in West Africa, Syria, and elsewhere.

It should also be remembered that all of Germany's allies eventually turned against Germany, and that Romanian troops, for example, suffered nearly as many casualties fighting against Hitler as they had suffered fighting against Stalin. As for the Bulgarians, their casualties in the war against Germany in 1944 and 1945 were incomparably higher than the casualties they had suffered in their previous, mostly nominal fight against Great Britain and the United States. Bulgaria was not at war with the Soviet Union until the Soviets themselves declared war on Bulgaria, in September 1944, in order to be able to occupy the country. Bulgaria had meanwhile declared war on Germany, which led to the interesting situation whereby Bulgaria was simultaneously at war with the United States, Great Britain, the Soviet Union, and Nazi Germany.[11]

Postwar judiciary proceedings, which occupy the major part of this book, adopted an amazing number of forms. Most famous of all were the trials conducted by the International Military Tribunal at Nuremberg. Hundreds of books and thousands of articles have discussed the achievements and the shortcomings of the Tribunal. Most of the surviving important Nazi leaders were tried and executed at Nuremberg. Major principles in international law were established, such as threatening with punishment individuals and institutions engaged in the planning, preparation, initiation, and waging of a war of aggression. The definition of war crimes was extended, and a new/old crime, the massacre of innocents, was given a new name: crimes against humanity. The Tribunal ruled that such crimes would have no statute of limitation. The right of international courts to try criminal behavior on the basis of laws and principles that did not exist at the time the crime was committed was likewise established. It is true, however, that the Nuremberg Court's rejection of the age-old principles of *nullum crimen, nulla poena sine lege*, was subsequently revoked by the United Nations in whose name the Nuremberg Courts had operated.[12]

Besides disregarding the principle of no crime and no punishment without a law, the Nuremberg tribunal also chose to overlook war crimes and crimes against peace committed by the nations sitting in judgment over the Germans, particularly the crimes of the Soviet Union. It was also less than fair in its treatment of the German defense, according it far fewer opportunities than were available to the prosecution. The list of short-comings is very long indeed and perhaps for that reason the International Tribunal has had no imitators, until the recent creation of the Hague International Tribunal, to try crimes of war committed in Bosnia-Herzegovina. In fact, the jury is still out on the achievements and histori-cal significance of the Nuremberg Tribunal.[13]

Remarkably, Nuremberg was a far more important event in the history of the United States, which for all practical purposes controlled the pro-ceedings of the Tribunal, than it was in the history of France, Great Brit-ain, the Soviet Union, or even Germany. To the German people and au-thorities, the International Tribunal soon appeared as a hidden blessing: by judging the Nazi bosses, the Tribunal seemed to exculpate the other Germans. It also took the matter of retribution more or less out of Ger-man hands. Consequently, Germany barely bothered with retribution, at least until the 1970s, when it experienced a resurgence of public interest in the country's recent history and the crimes committed by Germans.

The national tribunals, often called People's Courts, came into being spontaneously in the countries officially liberated from the German yoke. In the countries formerly allied with Germany, an order for retribution was included among the clauses for surrender. Everywhere, the courts struggled with a definition of collaboration. Since no consensus existed, every national assembly, in fact nearly every court, arrived at its own definition.

Postwar Europe was dominated by the leftist political parties, which had suffered terrible defeats during the Spanish Civil War and then as a result of early German triumphs in the war, but soon experienced a pow-erful resurgence, especially after the German attack on Soviet Russia in 1941. In 1945, the Popular Fronts returned in triumph. The new govern-ments were made up nearly everywhere of Communists, Socialists, pro-gressive Catholics, bourgeois radicals, and such conservatives and mon-archists as could present impeccable anti-Nazi credentials. Opposition parties to the right of these coalitions were at first nowhere tolerated.

The new goverments and parliaments were representative of the war-time domestic resistance, along with returning anti-Nazi exiles. The post-war regimes deliberately created courts to try collaborators in which overall control was in the hands of jurists and laymen delegated by the parties of the resistance. In all this, there was barely a difference be-tween courts in countries liberated by the Western Allies and countries liberated by the Soviets. The differences arose later, as the revolutionary courts in the West were gradually divested of power, and judicial pro-ceedings passed into the hands of regular courts, which themselves had often been freshly recreated. The traditional judiciary had generally been too small and too unreliable to deal with the avalanche of postwar collaborationist trials. Many judges, if not the majority, had collaborated with the enemy, or had at least faithfully served the defunct and despised wartime and prewar regimes. But whereas the courts in Italy, France, Austria, and so forth gradually became more and more traditional in their outlook, the courts under Soviet supervision remained consistently revolutionary. In Eastern Europe, however, revolutionary behavior meant, more and more, to lose interest in fascists and wartime collaborators and to prosecute with ever greater vigor the real, potential, or imaginary enemies of the Communist regimes. These enemies were often left-wingers, even Communists.

With the exception of a few stubborn fanatics such as the fascist and anti-Semitic writer Robert Brasillach in France, and the Arrow Cross leader Ferenc Szálasi in Hungary, most defendants in the immediate postwar trials pleaded their innocence before the courts. The usual defense was that they had remained at their posts during the occupation to prevent someone more radical than themselves from taking over. Thus, the defendants intimated, the nation owed them thanks for having shouldered such an onerous assignment.

This approach achieved one of its most elaborate forms in the theory of "Shield and Sword" developed by the defenders of Marshal Pétain in France, who argued that while De Gaulle and the Free French had served as the "sword" of France during the war, Pétain and the Vichy regime had been the nation's "shield" against Nazi depredations. Even Quisling sought to make such a case in Norway, as did, Monsignor József Tiso, the former president of fascist Slovakia. However, Ferenc Szálasi appeared in the People's Court in Hungary wearing the green shirt of his movement. Unperturbed by the abuses coming his way from the judge and the prosecutor, the Arrow Cross Führer quietly explained his vision of a future in which Germany, Italy, and Hungary would share domination over a National Socialist new world.[14] Remarkably, no collaborationist trial, not even in Eastern Europe, became a show trial. Defendants had their say in court, and even though judicial irregularities were legion, no one was forced to plead guilty and none begged to be executed as had been customary during the Stalinist Great Terror and would again become customary in Eastern Europe in the late 1940s and early 1950s.

As the essays in the book also demonstrate, the number and political importance of those sentenced was extraordinarily large. In Hungary, four former prime ministers, a deputy prime minister, and scores of other cabinet members as well as several generals and high-ranking officials were executed. László Karsai points out in his essay that 300,000 Hungarians, or about 3 percent of the total population, suffered some kind of punishment. In Austria, people's courts initiated proceedings against nearly 137,000 persons, and this figure does not include the many hundred thousand civil servants, including teachers, postmen, railroadmen, and so forth, who were dismissed from their jobs. In France nearly 10,000 real or alleged collaborators were lynched during the last months of the war, or at the moment of liberation.

Many negative things have been said about the national courts, and often with good reason. Still, the fact remains that never before had the peoples of Europe attempted, on such a large scale, to deal with ordinary and political criminals in their midst. Nor had there ever been such a continent-wide soul searching. Those who were punished for good reason far outnumbered those who were punished unjustly.

It was not enough to punish; those sentenced to imprisonment had to be reeducated and reintegrated into society; at least a semblance of national unity had to be restored; the economy needed many hands for reconstruction. As time progressed, sentences became less and less rigorous. Soon there were amnesties, a process greatly hastened by the Cold War. In the East, fascists of lower class origin were often forgiven and incorporated into Communist ranks. In the West, where the left-wing coalitions had fallen apart by 1947, the tendency was to forgive everybody. Industrialists, technicians, and businessmen who had worked for the Germans were badly needed after the war, and were mostly not even indicted. By the late 1950s, hardly a collaborator and former war criminal remained in custody. It looked as if the war and its terror would soon sink into oblivion. However, this did not happen either. A new generation was growing up in Europe, prepared to question the wartime and postwar behavior of their elders. This gave rise to a new wave, not so much of new trials but of national self-examination. It turned out that many crimes that the courts had attributed to the German occupier were, in reality, committed by collaborationists or resisters.

Sarah Farmer shows that in 1953, when a number of Alsatian SS soldiers were tried and sentenced in France for the horrifying massacre their unit had committed at Oradour in central France, the president of the republic soon amnestied these French citizens in the name of national reconciliation. Forty years later, such a move would have been followed by a national outcry, and the crimes committed by Frenchmen against other Frenchmen would have been widely aired. Slowly, it also began to dawn on the public that the main victims of Nazi and collaborationist fury had been the Jews. After the war, the tendency was to list Jewish concentration camp victims among the fallen resisters. In this manner, each nation could boast a larger number of heroes, and the national guilt in the Holocaust process could be obfuscated. The trouble was that in some cases, for example, that of Hungary, nearly all the Hungarians who had died in German camps were Jews. One did not need many hands to count the non-Jewish martyrs of the resistance.

Soon the Europe-wide issue was not over the question of what to do with collaborationists or how to honor the surviving resisters but rather over the question of how to shape, and for what purpose, the nation's memory of the war years. Here, the decision is still outstanding.

Notes

1. One of the many who escaped punishment was Ante Pavelić, the brutal head of the murderous Croatian fascist state. At the end of the war, Pavelić fled from Austria with the help of Catholic church authorities. He lived for many years in Argentina and died in Madrid in 1959.

2. See Alfred M. de Zayas, *Nemesis at Potsdam: The Expulsion of the Germans from the East*, 3d ed. (Lincoln: University of Nebraska Press, 1989), and, by the same author, *A Terrible Revenge: The Ethnic Cleansing of the East European Germans, 1944–50* (New York: St Martin's Press, 1994). Zayas's rather passionate works should be supplemented with such more scholarly publications as, for instance, Wolfgang Benz, ed., *Die Vertreibung der Deutschen aus dem Osten: Ursachen, Ereignisse, Folgen* (Frankfurt: Fischer, 1995), and Albrecht Lehmann, *Im Fremden ungewollt zuhaus: Flüchtlinge und Vertriebene in Westdeutschland 1945–1990* (Munich: Beck, 1991).

3. On retribution in Hungary, see László Karsai's essay in this book. Also, Margit Szöllösi-Janze, " 'Pfeilkreuzler, Landesverräter und andere Volksfeinde,' Generalabrechnung in Ungarn," in Klaus-Dietmar Henke and Hans Woller, eds., *Politische Säuberung in Europe. Die Abrechnung mit Faschismus und Kollaboration nach dem Zweiten Weltkrieg* (Munich: Deutscher Taschenbuch Verlag, 1991), 311–57. On the Hungarian gendarmes, see Judit Molnár, *Zsidósors 1944-ben az V. (szegedi) csendőrkerületben* [The fate of Jews in the V., Szeged, gendarmerie district in 1944] (Budapest: Cserépfalvi, 1995), and László Karsai and Judit Molnár, eds., *Az Endre-Baky-Jaross per* [The trial of Endre, Baky, and Jaross] (Budapest: Cserépfalvi, 1994). On retribution in Yugoslavia, Ekkehard Volkl, "Abrechnungsfuror in Kroatien," in Henke and Woller, *Politische*, 358–94.

4. On Greece, see also Mark Mazower, *Inside Hitler's Greece: The Experience of Occupation, 1941–44* (New Haven: Yale University Press, 1993); David H. Close, *The Origins of the Greek Civil War* (London: Longman, 1995), and Gabriella Etmektsoglou, "Collaborators and Partisans on Trial: Political Justice in Postwar Greece, 1944–49," in Claudia Kuretsidis-Haider and Winfried R. Garscha, eds., *Keine "Abrechnung": NS-Verbrechen, Justiz und Gesellschaft in Europa nach 1945* (Leipzig-Vienna: Akademische Verlagsanstalt, 1998), 231–56.

5. Two of the best books on the Holocaust are, Raul Hilberg, *The Destruction of the European Jews*, 3 vols., rev. ed. (New York: Holmes and Meier, 1985), and Leni Yahil, *The Holocaust: The Fate of European Jewry* (New York–Oxford: Oxford University Press, 1990).

6. Charlotte Delbos, *Auschwitz and After*, Rosette C. Lamont, trans., Lawrence L. Langer, intro. (New Haven: Yale University Press, 1995).

7. See, Stein U. Larsen, "Die Ausschaltung der Quislinge in Norwegen," in Henke and Woller, *Politische*, 241–80.

8. On the German occupation of Denmark, see Richard Petrow, *The Bitter Years: The Invasion and Occcupation of Denmark and Norway, April 1940–May 1945* (New York: William Morrow, 1974), especially 159–229. On Danish collaboration during World War II, see István Deák, "The Incomprehensible Holocaust," and the ensuing debate over Denmark and other countries in the *New York Review of Books* (28 September, 21 December 1989; 1 February, 29 March, 27 September 1990; and 25 April 1991).

9. Michael Marrus and Robert O. Paxton, *Vichy France and the Jews* (New York: Basic Books, 1981), 241.

10. Fitzroy Maclean, *Tito* (London: McGraw-Hill, 1980), 80.

11. See Stefane Groueff, *Crown of Thorns: The Reign of King Boris III of Bulgaria, 1918–43* (Lanham, Md.: Madison Books, 1987), 386, and M. L. Miller, *Bulgaria During the Second World War* (Stanford, Calif.: Stanford University Press, 1975).

12. See "Protocol Additional to the Geneva Conventions of August 1949, and Relating to the Protection of Victims of Noninternational Armed Conflicts (Protocol II), adopted on June 8, 1977, at Geneva." Reprinted in W. Michael Reisman and Chris T. Antoniou, eds., *The Laws of War: A Comprehensive Collection of Primary Documents on International Laws Governing Armed Conflict* (New York: Vintage Books, 1994), 385–86.

13. Two of the most significant books on the Nuremberg Tribunal are Eugene Davidson, *The Trial of the Germans* (New York: Collier Books, 1966), and Telford Taylor, *The Anatomy of the Nuremberg Trials: A Personal Memoir* (New York: Knopf, 1992).

14. See Elek and László Karsai, eds., *A Szálasi per* [The trial of Szálasi] (Budapest: Reform, 1988).

JAN T. GROSS

Themes for a Social History of War Experience and Collaboration

As a preliminary to this volume's wide-ranging inquiry into the problems of war and its aftermath" in Europe, I propose that we conceive of a society's experiences of war and occupation as if they were endogenous. This may not be a particularly original insight, but it departs from routine, prima facie approach where states or societies *drawn* into war or *put* under occupation are studied primarily as entities subject to external, imposed circumstances. As a result we are more likely to find in the literature political histories of wartime regimes than social histories of countries under occupation.

And yet all social systems at all times operate within constraints that they do not set and control, or cannot anticipate.[1] This is a trivial point again, and one should be reminded that in some historical circumstances (such as war between states) these externalities might be uniquely nonnegotiable and intrusive. But then, conversely, we might also think of *internal* contingencies that are uniquely nonnegotiable and intrusive. And the impact of some such factors would be no less decisive and disruptive on the course of otherwise "normal" societal development. *Pace* assorted Marxist writings about the role of the individual in history, no serious student of the twentieth century would hesitate to list Hitler's willfulness as a major force shaping German destiny, nor that of Stalin as a crucial force shaping the destiny of Russia.

Now, if we agree that a study of war should concentrate on endogenous processes (rather than focusing on what country X has done to country Z), then we would be able to follow how societies process the enormous jolt that a war delivers to their various institutions and patterns of interaction. A social history of a society subject to war and/or occupation could make us appreciate the resulting *acceleration* of social change—circulation of elites, emancipation of entire demographic categories of the population, or technological innovation—which permits us to think about war as a revolution. In a lecture delivered at Oxford in 1929, Élie Halévy viewed this as a matter of course: "*toutes les grandes convulsions qui ont secoué le monde au cours de son histoire, et l'Europe moderne en particulier, ont été en même temps des guerres et des revolutions.*"[2]

Furthermore, as we shall see, the social history approach yields interesting and unexpected insights into periodization of the war era. It also points out antecedents and continuities where *histoire événementielle* recorded, most of all, a rupture. And it is embedded in our efforts to understand the phenomenon of political justice. For we can credibly call people to account for their actions (however improvised, contrived, or politically motivated the judicial process adopted) only if they had options, alternative choices—in a word, a social space in which their alleged misdeeds had been carried out.

I will move in this essay from east to west and, along with it, from matters of periodization to political justice. I shall begin with a sketch, laying side by side a "political" and a "social" history of wartime in Eastern Europe, hoping to demonstrate how the latter permits a new, fruitful, conceptualization of this formative epoch. And then I shall move to the theme of political justice. Ever since the Second World War in the West (and now overlaid in addition by several decades of Stalinist legacy in the East), squaring accounts between fellow citizens who viewed themselves, and each other, as victims or beneficiaries of exploitative regimes remains a persistent issue on the Continent. Fritz Stern put it well in a recent address: "Clearly, the past continues to haunt the present. In most countries the past has *again* [emphasis mine] become a battlefield of interpretations. Most nations today are engaged in some form of soul-searching, in re-examining past conduct. To confront history in this fashion is unprecedented, as have been the acknowledgments of guilt or the formal apologies tendered for past injustices. . . . The methods of investigating the past vary, the themes are often the same: the record of collaboration or resistance."[3] Naturally, political justice deals for the most part with the "record of collaboration." And it is on the issue of collaboration that I will focus my remarks in the latter part of this essay.

Social Consequences of War in East Central Europe

Before they were confined to a common lot in the Soviet bloc, the countries of East Central Europe were not particularly interested in one another. What little regional cooperation they were able to work out during the interwar period—the Little Entente—was directed against one of the countries of the region, namely, Hungary. Attempts to develop federalist solutions during World War II were also scuttled, this time by Soviet diplomacy.[4] From the perspective of the year 1950, when all countries of East Central Europe had been securely fitted into the "camp" of people's democracies with a remarkably similar framework of mono-party institutions ("geographically contiguous replica-regimes" they were called in an important study)[5], it would have been impossible to guess how much these countries' internal developments had differed throughout the decades prior to consolidation of Communist rule.

Their wartime histories were as varied as could be. Some ended up in the Axis camp, some with the Allies; some occupied, some not; some dismembered, some with their territory actually expanded. When the Ribbentrop-Molotov pact was signed in August 1939 it was met with gloom and confused disbelief all over Europe, except in Bulgaria. There, the pact was widely acclaimed and the position of the BCP significantly enhanced. Soon several hundred Bulgarian leftists who fought in the Spanish war had their citizenship restored, while Russian books, films, and newspapers were allowed into the country. A loyal Axis member, Bulgaria nevertheless managed to maintain diplomatic relations with the Soviet Union through the summer of 1944. It did not send troops to the Eastern front, or its Jewish citizens to extermination camps. It ran out of luck eventually, however, and in the autumn of 1944 managed to gain "the dubious distinction of being simultaneously at war with Great Britain, Germany, Russia, and the United States."[6] Bulgaria's neighbor, Rumania, and also Hungary, would not tolerate any overt pro-Russian activity. Politics in both countries was quite lively, with cabinets changing, coalitions being worked out, and opposition politicians speaking up. Leadership oscillated between the conservative and the radical right with the latter gaining upper hand in the last months of the war in Hungary. This, as we know, led to horrible consequences for the Jewish minority there. Rumanian Jews, though not surrendered to the Germans, suffered murderous pogroms by the Iron Guard and mass deportations to Transistria where many thousands died. Yugoslavia vacillated at first between a pro-Western and a pro-Axis orientation. It was then occupied and dismembered, and a ferocious civil war developed in which the Communist underground, intertwined within a complex tribal and national mosaic, proved victorious in the end. Over 10 percent of Yugoslavia's population died of war-related causes. This was the second highest casualty rate in World War II, surpassed only by the tragedy in Poland.[7]

Split in half in September 1939 between the USSR and Germany, Poland suffered proportionally the greatest material and population losses of all belligerents in the Second World War.[8] In a unique response to the long-lasting terrorism of the German occupation, Polish society went underground and built a complex set of institutions encompassing a framework of political parties, welfare administration, cultural outlets, numerous daily and periodical publications, a school system, a parallel economy, and a clandestine volunteer army.

Czechoslovakia, taken apart even prior to the outbreak of the war, had a segment of its territory integrated into the Reich, another one set up as a new state, and yet another given the transitory status of protectorate and placed under a quisling administration. But it was a quisling administration that deferred for a long time to the exiled president of the Republic who headed a pro-Allied government in London, while the leader of the newly created puppet state defied German orders from the time he became convinced that they were incompatible with Slovak patriotism or Christian ethics. After the summer of 1942, Father Tiso halted further deportations of Jews to exterminations camps, and only when Germany occupied Slovakia in September 1944 to suppress the Slovak national uprising did the killings resume. Still, one third of Slovak Jews survived the war.[9]

Already from these brief outlines we can see that there *were* indeed many different "national roads" to socialism.

So much for variety. But the same story can be told in a number of ways. What I sketched so far conforms to a more or less standard account of wartime experiences in East Central Europe. Yet when we put on another lens, we can focus on the social fabric of these societies rather than the political outcomes, on material life and processes rather than facades of institutions and policies. If we further consider the meaning of demographic trends rather than police actions, and that of public opinion rather than government declarations, we are likely to get a different grasp on the story. Let me direct attention first to the political economy of the war years, to the material life, where even a brief perusal of a few important themes reveals the complexity of the issues.

We know, of course, that the region's economy suffered a widespread destruction of infrastructure under the Nazi domination. But this result of the war, which we all grasp intuitively, should not prevent us from scrutinizing the economic processes that went on for the half-decade when Nazi influence was paramount. War is a powerful stimulus of economic growth. It turns out that a significant part of the area in question was not an exception to this general rule.

Perhaps the most dynamic growth was in the production of raw materials. Extraction of hard coal in Poland increased by 50 percent from 1939 to 1944, and at a similar pace production of brown coal increased in Czechoslovakia. Polish oil fields increased production by 60 percent, while in Hungary the oil industry was virtually created during those years and reached a respectable one-fourth of yearly Rumanian output by 1944. Production of natural gas doubled in Poland and in Rumania. Production of chrome tripled in Yugoslavia, while production of bauxite (the basis of the aluminum industry and a substitute for copper) doubled in Hungary where, incidentally, the production of aluminum during those years increased ninefold. Taking 1939 as the base, the combined index for electrical power production in Bulgaria, Czechoslovakia, Hungary, and Poland reached 141 by the year 1944.[10]

The years 1938–44 in Hungary, for instance, were a boom period of industrialization financed in large part by German capital. In only two years, from 1938 to 1940, the growth of manufacturing industry exceeded that achieved over the preceding two decades. In 1943, at the peak of production, industrial output was 38 percent higher than before the war. "Livestock increased by 11 percent during the war and at the time of the Russian invasion [i.e., at the end of the war] eighteen million metric quintals of cereals were housed in public stores."[11]

On a smaller scale Bohemia and Moravia registered a robust growth at the time as well (particularly in the 1941–1944 period). Even in such backward regions as Slovakia, "the regime managed to solve economic problems to the surprise even of those who were favorably inclined to the regime. . . . the situation in Slovakia is better from the point of view both of real wages and of the supply of goods,"[12] wrote a Slovak Communist functionary, Gustav Husak, in a secret report dispatched to Moscow in July 1944. Starting with a very low base in 1939, industrial production during the war increased in Slovakia more rapidly than in the protectorate. The index of total industrial production for Bulgaria shows less robust change after a significant spurt in 1939–1941 but, nevertheless, it stands at 112 for the year 1945 (with 1939 taken as a base). And among the important economic legacies of the war in Albania should be counted the considerable road networks and numerous bridges constructed by the Italians.[13]

Depending on the degree of integration, or planned future integration with the Reich,[14] the overall pattern of development in a given area (such development as there was) targeted intensification of agricultural production and favored raw-materials production to the neglect of consumer goods or industry. But even with respect to parts of Poland—that is, the most devastated country during the war—incorporation into the Reich was followed by a policy of comprehensive development. In what was called Warthegau (an area wedged between the Vistula and Oder rivers), industrial employment increased threefold—from 90,000 to 263,000 workers—between 1940 and 1943. As a general indicator of trends, let me quote finally a cautious assessment of economic historians about Bulgaria, which was least affected during the war by occupation and military activity and where "agricultural development was less favorable than that of some other countries which were more directly involved in the war."[15]

Clearly, one must recognize that there were processes under way at the time in East Central Europe that cannot be simply subsumed under some notion of "war ravages." Of course, we must take this "rosy" account with a grain of salt. I drew a deliberately one-sided picture to be polemical with standard accounts. But what moves me to do so is not simply contentiousness but also conviction that conventional narratives lose sight of a process that lasted several years and left important imprints on the affected societies.

What kinds of insights can we gain by considering the political economy of the war years? With respect to structural changes, for instance, I would point out that the economies of the region experienced growing autarky and decoupling from the international trade comprising the whole continent. Most of the industrial potential of the area was harnessed to supply the needs of the German war economy. In the territories directly under German control, such as Poland or Bohemia and Moravia, this was a simple matter resolved through administrative measures. But massive German acquisitions of French-, British-, and Belgian-held capital took place in Yugoslavia, Rumania, and Hungary as well. "In 1940, 44% of Rumanian exports went to Germany compared to 19% in 1937. In the same year 59% of Bulgarian, 49% of Hungarian, 38% of Greek, and 36% of Yugoslav exports went to Germany." German capital participation in Slovak industry increased from 4% in 1938 to 52% in 1942.[16]

Accordingly, we ought to note that the area partook during this period in a new international division of labor designed to support the imperial ambitions of the German Reich. It was an ideologically motivated division of labor, as the economic role of various territories was to a significant degree determined by Nazi racial doctrines or, should we rather say, Hitler's idiosyncrasies.[17] Furthermore, throughout the period, local economies were gradually taken over by the state. This etatization was most conspicuous in the countries under direct German occupation and when Jewish property was expropriated. But measures to this effect were executed in every country of the area.

Hence, at least five years before the Soviet Union established its domination in the region, local economies were redirected away from the West and gradually taken over by the state. And as government intervention in an economy fosters coordination and planning—indeed German planning for coal and steel production, for example, was particularly effective in stimulating Czech and Polish output—we may surmise that the conclusions of a leading authority on Balkan economic history that "the Bulgarian experience during the Second World War laid important economic groundwork for the postwar practice of central planning," could apply equally to other countries in the region.[18] They apparently do, as another author attests, regarding the case of Rumania, where "the dictatorship of King Carol II, reinforced by the demands of Nazi Germany, had built the rudiments of a central planning system which the Communists were able to exploit and were encouraged to do so by Stalin."[19]

Were we to move from the consideration of the institutional framework of the region's economies to that of individual behavior we ought to take note, for example, of the effect that expropriations and takeovers must have had on the inhabitants of East Central Europe. Such actions conspicuously demonstrated that property rights were dependent on a state's goodwill and could be destroyed with the stroke of a pen. This, of course, effectively undermined confidence and dampened the entrepreneurial spirit of indigenous would-be capitalists. Labor discipline and the work ethic collapsed (a significant drop in labor productivity was universally reported from the region) as people realized that the German war effort for which their work was being harnessed did not coincide with their own long-term interest (that Germany would lose the war was commonly believed from about mid-1942 onward) or, even worse, reduced their own prospects of survival. Second economies, with all the demoralization that they entail, prospered as never before. In an admirable book, a literary critic showed how the Poles had experienced, among other effects of the occupation, alienation of work in the purest Marxian sense of the term.[20] Work—one of the major avenues for socializing people into cooperation, providing links between the satisfaction of individual needs and the common effort, a forum for status seeking and social mobility—suddenly lost its capacity for binding the social fabric together. The product of work was appropriated by the Germans and used against the interests of the group producing it, for whom the process then became totally alienated. *In hindsight, then, we ought to note a complex process of structural changes, as well as socialization, facilitating the etatization of the economy that was to be implemented a few years later according to principles of scientific socialism.*

Likewise, the immense population losses and shifts that occurred during the war and immediate postwar years had a profound impact on the process of consolidation and character of postwar regimes. The sheer volume of death inflicted selectively upon the peoples of the area significantly altered the composition of the labor force. The destruction of East European Jewry alone created opportunities for upward social mobility for skilled workers, artisans, entrepreneurs, and professionals that would not have been made available by any postwar reform or change in the economic regime. Vacancies opened up also because nationalities not scheduled for total annihilation were killed off selectively, with elites of each nation given priority in successive waves of repression. Jews and Germans, ubiquitously present throughout East Central Europe before the war, were no longer there, or were radically reduced in numbers in the postwar era. They were urban populations par excellence. An important nucleus of the bourgeoisie, of the middle class, was removed from the region as a consequence of their disappearance.

In general, all countries of East Central Europe, except Yugoslavia, experienced a shift from being multiethnic to being nationally more homogeneous. Czechoslovakia, split three ways before the war (ethnic Germans constituted 23 percent of its citizenry), was bifurcated in 1947 between Slovaks and Czechs who together made up 90 percent of the population. National minorities added up to one third of Poland's population before the war. In the postwar period the country was an ethnic monolith, over 97 percent Polish. Rumania emerged from the war with only one numerically significant national minority, the Hungarians. Together, the two ethnic groups made up 95 percent of the population while before the war they added up to 80 percent. What did these changes mean? Simply that the legitimacy of Communist regimes was enhanced since they could take credit for providing opportunities for mobility and for satisfying nationalist aspirations?

Between the outbreak of the war and the beginning of 1943, "more than thirty million Europeans were transplanted, deported, or dispersed." And as this was a process that fed on itself, from 1943 through 1948 another twenty million were "on the move."[21] To fill the space vacated by 2.5 million expelled Sudeten Germans, 1.8 million Czechs and Slovaks were transferred into the area. In Poland four million settlers were sent to the "Western" lands. In Germany a steady westward flow of refugees drained the Soviet Zone of the most qualified manpower. In 1950 almost one-third of the population of the Bundesrepublik had not been born in the territorial area of the existing state. Edward Shils, who studied social and psychological aspects of displacement and repatriation, found that they generated "a widespread psychological regression, i.e., a collapse of adult norms and standards in speech, behavior and attitude, and a reversion to less mature patterns."[22] Certainly people who found themselves in these circumstances were much more dependent on the support of each state administration (and, therefore, were more pliable to its wishes) than they would have been had they lived in their native communities undisturbed by the high tides of history.[23] A grand theme still awaits its social and cultural historian—what was the meaning and impact of exile from East Central Europe?

Or think of the violence that people either suffered or witnessed at close range. By analogy with the well established paradigm attributing the vulnerability of European societies to fascism in the 1920s and 1930s to the generalized violence experienced in Europe during World War I,[24] we can posit that the unwelcome familiarity with the violence unleashed under World War II regimes of occupation made the methods of Communist *Machtergreifung* in the subsequent period more acceptable than they would have been otherwise. One could not hope to understand the period without the realization that the wartime experience of spiritual crisis, crisis of values, and normative disorganization profoundly affected notions of commonweal, collective good, and group interests in the societies of the region. The old operative definitions of legality, justice, legitimacy, common purpose, national interest, or *raison d'état* were put in doubt, shattered. There was more room, as a consequence, for new regulatory ideas to set up proper foundations for life in common.

Or think of the youths who leapfrogged over decades in their life cycle to become soldiers, breadwinners, or conspirators. Thus, many were forced to assume positions of responsibility for families, organizations, or causes that their elders would never have relinquished in normal times. The social revolution implemented in the postwar period allowed youth to continue occupying the center stage of society, and as such, it tapped into generational energies released by the war. And one should also mention the labor activization of women during these years. All these processes, though unwittingly, had a pronounced leveling effect on the social structure, initiating transformations that would be picked up, this time with explicit ideological justification, in the postwar years.

Even this superficial overview shows how, in the period of Nazi domination of East Central Europe, comprehensive processes of social change conducive to the etatization and leveling of the affected societies were set in motion. Apparently, the Soviet victory over the Nazis did not entail such a radical break as is customarily portrayed. Indeed, one could point to the continuities in the dynamic of social change set off by Nazi policies, and then resumed, albeit with an altogether different ideological and organizational inspiration, by Communist parties. Thus, a social history approach unveils an ongoing process, where political history suggested a most drastic rupture, and the conclusion emerges that for the adequate conceptualization of Communist takeovers in East Central Europe, we must change the periodization and begin the analysis with the outbreak of the Second World War.

On Collaboration

In response to wartime experiences, all the countries of Europe conducted trials of their own citizens after the war. These trials were as much about coming to terms with the immediate past as about setting the agenda of the newly established postwar regimes. Education of the citizenry about its past is always for the benefit of the future. But it was a hotly contested and difficult learning process. Even to deal with the responsibility of the

Germans (on the face of it, the least problematic category of perpetrators), a new jurisprudence had to be developed for the benefit of the Nuremberg Trials. And on the other end of the spectrum, when Hannah Arendt brought up the role of Jewish councils in the Nazi-engineered destruction of European Jewry, a heated debate flared up two decades after the war had ended.[25] What made collaboration such a contested issue? While other contributions to this volume carry many specific insights concerning postwar mechanisms of political justice, I wish to dwell here on the ill-defined and novel character of the phenomenon that came up before public opinion and courts of war ravaged Europe.

The term *collaboration*, in the specific connotation that preoccupies us here comes into usage in the context of the Second World War. It appeared for the first time in a statement published following the Hitler-Pétain meeting at Montoire, on 24 October 1940: "*Une collaboration a été envisagée entre nos deux pays*," said the aged Marshal in a radio appeal to his compatriots, "*J'en ai accepté le principe.*"[26] And we have it on the authority of lexicographers that such a narrow meaning (limiting the significance of the term *collaboration* to circumstances of German occupations during World War II) constitutes virtually all that the concept denotes in several European languages.[27]

The consensus in language usage on so narrowly circumscribed *signifié* is rather striking. And we may begin to question the term, as well as the practice, by departing from a commonsense observation: a sharply new and distinct concept should arise only to denote a new and distinct phenomenon. Given that armed conflicts, conquests, wars, occupations, subjugations, territorial expansions, and their accompanying circumstances are as old as recorded human history, one wonders what novelty in the phenomenon of German occupation during the Second World War calls forth the emergence of a fresh concept? I'll leave this question for the moment unanswered.

My own encounter with the problem of collaboration has occurred while studying the experiences of Polish society under German occupation. With a doctoral student's eye for neat-looking formulas, I concluded that an occupying power—in its official, institutionalized contacts with a subjugated society—will seek three kinds of "goods" necessary to rule the country: authority, expertise, and manpower. And in this tripartite division I enunciated, the term *collaboration* would best cover the harvesting of authority.[28] As I later realized, this use of the concept yielded one interesting insight: inasmuch as it denotes a set of relationships between the occupiers and the occupied *mediated by a set of officially existing institutions*, collaboration must be an occupier-driven phenomenon. And unlike many other kinds of relationships involving the vital interests of the two protagonists—say, resistance, or "second economy"—whatever takes place as collaboration must have the explicit consent of the occupier.

Naturally, designating incumbents to positions customarily endowed with political authority in occupied countries, was the business of the occupier. But if so, then whether there had been a Hacha, a Quisling, a Pavelic, a Pétain, or a Tiso was indicative primarily of a German will, not of the will of the French, the Czechs, the Croats, the Slovaks, or the Norwegians. And this meant also that pointing out the absence of collaboration—as, for example, in an often quoted phrase "certainly, Poland did not have its Quisling"—is of only limited heuristic value. It merely tells us that the Germans, locally, had not made the offer.

Thus, when we speak of collaboration we allude to the presence of a country-wide bureaucracy staffed by the indigenous population and established with the occupier's consent. But in the absence of such an organization (as in Poland, for instance), how should we conceptualize the role and function of bureaucracies with a lesser scope—urban administrations, for example? In Warsaw alone, where the administration numbered several tens of thousands employees, it was not significantly smaller than the administration of the entire protectorate of Bohemia and Moravia under Hacha. And how to approach the phenomenon of *Judenräte* set up in Nazi-established ghettos in preparation for the Final Solution? And, also, in response to the *divide et impera* strategy of totalitarian social control, how to conceptualize the role and behavior of one segment of the local population *vis-à-vis* another, set apart and targeted by the new masters for more radical measures of oppression than any other group? All these setups, and the human behavior that they entail, do not follow exclusively from calculation of individual fear or personal gain. They are also embedded in normative justifications. Thus, I would point out that a narrowly constructed concept of collaboration neglects to take into account that authority is dispersed throughout society, and that there are, therefore, several contexts in which we must seek to understand the phenomenon of harvesting authority by the occupier.

Thinking about collaboration as occupier driven implies, as one scholar put it, that we conceive the "history of collaboration by the people of an occupied country [as] a history of the occupying power as well," which seriously complicates matters. It does because German policies of occupation are very difficult to follow or lay out systematically. Indeed, one could argue that they were never set and that they evolved in ways that were unanticipated by their main architects. In April 1940 Goebbels thus spoke on this subject before a group of journalists: "If someone asks us today, what do you think of the New Europe, we have to answer that we don't know. . . . Let us first have the power, then people will see, and

we will see too what we can make of it. . . . Today we say: *Lebensraum.*
People can make of that what they want. What we want we will know
when the time is right."[29] But the "we" in whose collective mind these
ideas were supposed to sort themselves out—the Goerings, the Bor-
manns, the Himmlers, or the Goebbelses—were a vain and a quarrel-
some lot. They vied for predominance and Hitler's favor within a framework of geopolitical options that were delimited only by the führer's
visceral hatreds.

With only a slight risk of oversimplification, one could posit that beyond the elimination of the Jews and the crushing of the Bolshevik regime, there were hardly any policy options tying down the behavior of
Nazi leaders and institutions. Furthermore, were any established with
some clarity for a period of time, they were hardly ever implemented
with any consistency, due to the continual, bitter turf wars waged in the
occupied territories between the Wehrmacht, the German civilian administration, the security apparatus of the SS, and the police. And to make
matters even more complicated, with the passage of time, the relative
strength of various institutional carriers of Nazi policies, and thus of
various policy orientations, changed as well.

Collaboration—its logic, its appeal or self-justification, its social
base—emerges in each country precisely at the intersection between the
occupier's intent and the occupied's perception about the range of options at their disposal. During the Second World War the occupier's intent was never clarified and always shifting. And equally, on the side of
the other protagonist, the society of the occupied country, we cannot find
a broadly shared interpretation of the new situation arising from military defeat. If anything, a collapse of the prewar regime might release—
momentarily suppressed in the wake of national emergency—political
factionalism and embittered polemics (witness the quiltlike makeup of the
Polish underground state, for example).

The converse was also a possibility, however. For a time, the new geopolitical circumstances in continental Europe, especially in the aftermath
of the defeat of France, seemed to have adjudicated many an ideological
controversy from the interwar years. As Martin Conway put it in his
brilliant study of collaboration in Belgium, "the defeat of the 3rd Republic France and the victory of Nazi Germany appeared to demonstrate that
authoritarian states were better equipped to confront the needs of the
modern age."[30] The caving-in of Western democracies, culminating with
the blitzkrieg-delivered defeat, did not come unexpectedly, nor was it entirely unwelcome provided alternative forms of national existence could
be secured in the context of a New European Order.

And, indeed, for intellectuals dabbling in politics, this was a fertile period for exploring the idea of European unification. In France nine new

periodicals with the word *Europe* in the title were founded by mid-1941.[31] The very pinnacles of the French cultural establishment were deliberately cultivated by skilled Nazi officials. A witticism of the Francophile German Ambassador in Paris, Otto Abetz—"*il n'y a en France que trois puissances: les catholiques, le Communisme, et la N.R.F. [Nouvelle Revue Française]. Commençons par la N.R.F.*"—was apparently acted upon for, as Jean Paulhan sourly notes in his reminiscences, "*Il l'a prise.*"[32] "More than any other single event during the period 1940–1944, the exhibition of sculptures by Arno Breker at the Orangerie in 1942 was the very symbol of Occupation—and collaboration. . . . '*Tous les artistes français qui portent un nom, de Derain à Cocteau, de Sacha Guitry à Cecile Sorel, sont venus!*'."[33]

So, when thinking about collaboration, we should be mindful about social milieus sympathetic to the idea, which were quite ready to make use of opportunities created by, *faute de mieux*, the unexpected and unwelcome developments on the battlefield. Certainly, one way of interpreting the events in France was to conceive of Vichy as "a revenge [against political chaos rooted in the ideas fostered by the French Revolution] perpetrated by men who felt that they were the natural governing elite of the French state."[34] Pétain's national revolution, the *redressement national*, rang of a nostalgic aspiration to resuscitate the organic unity of the body politic lost under the double impact of the industrial revolution and Enlightenment philosophers. Stephen Spender, certainly not an apologist for right-wing sentiments, has this to say about intellectuals who fell under their spell: "the reactionaries and Fascist sympathizing writers did not give aid and comfort to Hitler and Mussolini. . . . The reactionary traditionalists stood outside Fascism while supporting it. What they believed in was civilization. They saw Fascism as a means of defending civilized standards."[35]

Simultaneously, yet another indigenous inspiration conducive to collaboration was at work in occupied European societies. Nazi élan and success naturally reverberated among the local fascist and protofascist movements, among the radicals of the right, the very opposites to the nostalgic, status-conscious reactionary enemies of the French Revolution. The *collaborateurs de sentiment*, Leon Degrelle dubbed those for whom the hour of the true revolution had struck. They were in for the *revolution des âmes*.[36]

Ideologically and socially the two groups were at opposite poles of the social spectrum. "Socially well established," so Stanley Hoffmann proceeded to characterize the *collaborateurs d'état*, "they represented the cream of the top of the civil service, of the armed forces, of the business community, of the social elites of landowners or the professions or the local notables. . . . On the other hand the collaborationists [the *collaborateurs de sentiment*, in Degrelle's terminology] were to a large extent *déclassés*—social misfits and political deviants. Not only had they not exerted political power, but they were not among the established 'social authorities' either. Their ideas had segregated them both from the republican establishment—the high commands of the parties and unions—and from the conservative social establishment."[37]

The social difference captured the generational conflict also, and could just as well be applied to any European society. In France, as Jean Paul Sartre noted, "*la défaite éxaspera le conflit des generations. Pendant quatre ans, les combattans de '14' rèprochèrent à ceux de '40' d'avoir perdu la guerre et ceux de '40', en retour, accuserent leurs ainés d'avoir perdu la paix.*"[38]

And there were, finally, those in between the extremes, aspiring neither to a new order in Europe nor to an ancien régime, not ideologues but realists desirous of accomodation within the new circumstances. For, at least through the end of 1940, German victory appeared all but unavoidable to a broad spectrum of the European public. "The cult of Pétainism," pointed out Paul Kingston, "was a cult of 'realism.'" Indeed, it was a realism with a higher calling. One that engaged its protagonists not (exclusively) on behalf of their own best interest, but for a cause—that of restraining the zeal of the occupier. "The Marshal provided *'de sa personne'* a *'bouclier'* against German excesses."[39] As Hirschfeld notes, "one of the arguments for political collaboration (put forward quite forcefully by its practitioners) has always been that things would have been worse if collaboration had not taken place."[40]

And last but not least, reactionaries, revolutionaries, and pragmatists, high-brow intellectuals, or the lumpen-bourgeoisie, with all the differences in sensibilities, social class, temperament, or beliefs that drove them to make a public stand, "collaborationists" of all kinds, could find common ground not only in their disgust with pluralist democracy but also, if not primarily, in their deep seated fear of Bolshevism. Hence the inevitable conclusion that a broad social spectrum of interested groups and a broad variety of ideas were available to engage in and to justify collaboration.[41]

Thus, what we conceive today as akin to treason—for such a connotation is attached to the term—makes reference to a vastly more complex set of behavioral options as they were perceived at the time. There is, if you will, a social history of collaboration that precedes and illuminates collaboration as a political phenomenon—and makes it intelligible. And just as its origins must be traced in the past, through time, it is specifically through the time dimension of social action that the puzzling phenomenon of collaboration can be unpacked. Here we return to the question I left unanswered earlier.

It is well known, of course, that consequences of social action are often unanticipated. But, I submit, the Nazi occupation produced a uniquely radical discrepancy between what seemed its possible and likely outcomes at the outset, and the final outcome. What made the phenomenon of *engagement* with the German occupier during World War II so unique (i.e., what turned this involvement into "collaboration") was, I think, the hiatus, the chasm between the terms of initial committment (as best they could be fathomed at the time) and the end result to which those who went along with a new order discovered themselves making a contribution. The distance between the two was unprecedented, and also that it was traveled in so brief a span of but a few years. "They," said Hannah Arendt, "who were the Nazis' first accomplices and their best aides truly did not know what they were doing nor with whom they were dealing."[42] As H. R. Kedward put it in his study: "For the French to understand that Pétain might be collaborating with his old enemy Germany necessitated an almost religious suspension of rational faculties, close to the belief that 'God moves in a mysterious way.'"[43] But four years later supporters of the Maréchal discovered that they were involved in a project that could hardly sustain the label of "*redressment national*" in the eyes of their compatriots—as over ten thousand French men and women were murdered or lynched in kangooroo courts by their fellow citizens in the aftermath of the liberation. "*D'un bout à l'autre de la guerre*," to quote Sartre's reminiscence published in its immediate aftermath, "*nous n'avons pas reconnu* [author's emphasis] *nos actes, nous n'avons pas pu revendiquer leurs conséquences.*"[44]

From Warsaw we have the testimony of Yitzhak Zuckerman, the last commander of the Jewish Combat Organization: "Our attitude about the *Judenrat* was different then. We didn't yet see it as an embodiment of treason. The *Judenrat* of 1941 was not the *Judenrat* of 1940, and that of 1942 certainly wasn't that of 1941."[45] In Eastern Europe, between the self-policing, which was the function the *Judenräte* in German-occupied Europe initially took upon themselves, and the self-destruction in which they found themselves eventually participating, there was no connection imaginable for the protagonists. We know, of course, the mechanism of incrementalism and what links each two consecutive steps down the ladder of human decency. And yet this does not illuminate the sequential logic of the whole chain, because at every step it always made more sense to stop the descent, rather then to go on. And both the prospective victims and their custodians (the former to preserve some remnants of sanity, the latter better to deceive) kept bringing this up.

The terms of involvement with the German occupiers changed rapidly as well as radically over the course of the war, and just as the goals of German occupation (or what was revealed of them) changed and instruments of their implementation got more radical, so did social constructions evolve defining the meaning of these involvements.

> If the collaborators inferred from German victory the necessity to submit to the authority of the Reich it is because they made an original and profound decision which derived from the essence of their personality: namely, to submit to the *fait accompli*, no matter what it was. This fundamental inclination, which they themselves dresssed up by calling it 'realism' is deeply rooted in ideology of our time. Collaborators are afflicted by intellectual illness which might be called historicism. . . . they confuse the necessity to submit to the factual . . . with a certain inclination to morally approve of it. . . . [T]he preeminence of the actual goes together with a vague belief in progress. . . . One does not know where one is going, but if there is change, one must be improving. . . . One accepts violence, because all great changes involved violence, and one confers to power some obscure moral virtue. And by this procedure, to conceive of his own actions, a collaborator puts himself in a far away future. This manner of judging the actual in the light of the future was a temptation for all the French, I think, resulting from defeat: it was a subtle form of escapism. By jumping a few centuries ahead to look at the present, and thus contemplating it from afar, one repositioned the present into history, changed it into a past and concealed its unbearable character.[46]

The diagnosis written in 1945 by Jean Paul Sartre derived, undoubtedly, from an inadvertent moment of introspection by one who was just considering the charms of dialectical materialism and the engagement with scientific socialism. But without drawing punches in the shadow-boxing ring of French intellectual fashions of the time, it appears certain that as prospects for German victory faded, the histrionic justification—based on anticipation of a *Pax Germanica*—lost its persuasiveness too. And on closer inspection, even the very minimalist premise—stipulating that institutions ought "to support certain German initiatives in order to prevent worse ones"—proved untenable because the ultimate intentions of the occupiers could not be found out and, consequently, there was no possibility to satisfy them more efficiently, at a lesser cost to the affected community. As Hirschfeld points out in hindsight, there is "no indication that French authorities exerted any moderating influence" on policies and outcomes inimical to their national interest that the Germans pursued.[47] Unfortunately, one need not even raise a question concerning the ability of Jewish ghetto administrations to mitigate the adverse impact of Nazi aims with respect to the Jews.

How does the concept of collaboration serve us, then, as we attempt to lay out an intelligible and heuristically rich account of the war years in Europe? In my judgment it does—and this may not be a very surprising answer—what mainstream historiographies of the war written in the past four decades had done: it puts a kind of veil over a very complex reality. It does not help to discern, for instance, that the meaning and character of involvement with the occupier must be carefully circumscribed in time, or else its terms could not be properly understood. Furthermore, by calling attention to behavior exercised by political elites (which makes the concept particularly ill suited for application to occupied Eastern Europe, where local elites were deliberately wiped out under German occupation), it dims our ability to provide an account of the multifaceted involvements between the occupiers and the occupied that proliferated in many other institutional contexts, engaging professional groups and social milieus at various points in the social hierarchy.

It may be that no single concept could encompass the rapidly and *radically* changing terms of involvement with the reality of German occupation. And I end up convinced that we need to rely primarily on middle terms—situated between collaboration and resistance—in order to make better sense of the experience of war and occupation in twentieth-century Europe.[48] We certainly did not have a well-calibrated instrument to deal retroactively with the experience. In part, this is why postwar judicial remedies deserve the label of political justice.

But there were other reasons in the works as well. The experience of war in Europe, as I tried to argue earlier, was akin to that of a revolution. In one part of the continent, the Nazi-instigated war and the Communist-driven postwar takeovers constituted one integral period. We could note this by pointing out the continuities in the transformation of social fabric, as well as the affinities in the deployed strategies of subjugation. And we also know that important protagonists viewed their post-1945 struggles as a resolution of conflicts that culminated earlier in the catastrophe of the war. One could point out as well that the legitimacy of "people's democracies" was instrumentalized via a regime-generated interpretation of the collective experience of war, just as much as by reference to Marxist ideology. "Even for the post-war generation in Yugoslavia, the War [author's emphasis] was not a futile and senseless blood-letting but on the contrary a heroic and meaningful experience that was worth more than its one million victims. The idea was hard to challenge because our whole education—lessons, textbooks, speeches, newspapers—was impregnated with it as if our history prior to 1941 barely existed."[49] Any Pole born after the war could read into this assessment by Slavenka Drakulic the details of their own experience as well. While in the USSR a glorified mythologization of what was called there the Great Patriotic War had been a most frequently invoked justification of the Soviet regime after 1945. It was certainly a cornerstone justifying Soviet imperial domination of East Central Europe in the eyes of its own citizens. The legitimacy narrative of the postwar French Fourth Republic, Gaullism, was yet another such mental construct. And thus, East and West, we find a politically constructed experience of war in the space usually reserved for revolutions, that of a foundation myth of a new regime or imperial order. Half a century later the time has come to deconstruct it.

Notes

An earlier draft of the first part of this essay was published in *East European Politics and Societies* (1989:2) as "Social Consequences of War: Preliminaries to the Study of Imposition of Communist Regimes in East Central Europe." Ideas expounded therein were used when formulating the IWM project, which resulted, among other things, in the publication of this book.

1. For individual and collective actors who might think in a fit of hubris that they fully control their destiny, one may recommend ample sociological literature on "latent functions" and "unintended consequences" of social actions.

2. "Une Interpretation de la crise mondiale, 1914–1918," in Élie Halévy, *L'Ère des tyrranies: Études sur le socialisme et la guerre* (Paris: Gallimard, 1938), 173.

3. Address delivered on 4 July 1998 at the International Bertelsmann Forum in Berlin, quoted in the *International Herald Tribune* (8 July 1998): 9.

4. See, for example, Edward Taborsky, *President Edvard Benes: Between East and West, 1938–1948* (Stanford: Hoover Institution Press, 1981), ch. 4.

5. Ken Jowitt, "Moscow 'Centre'*," *Eastern European Politics and Societies* 1:3 (1987): 311.

6. Marshall Lee Miller, *Bulgaria during the Second World War* (Stanford, Calif.: Stanford University Press, 1975), 1.

7. As István Deák pointed out in the *New York Review of Books* (5 November 1992), more recent scholarship concerning casualty figures incurred by various societies during World War II indicates that original statistics ought to be readjusted downward. This would be certainly justified with reference to Poland. But the order of magnitude, or relative rankings of casualties suffered, would not be affected.

8. One may add, parenthetically, that during the first two years of the war, prior to the mass murder of Jews by the Nazis, when German and Soviet occupations ran concurrently, the impact of the Soviet occupation—as measured by civilian deaths, deportations, and material losses—was far more injurious to the local population. For details, see my *Revolution from Abroad: The Soviet Conquest of Poland's Western Ukraine and Western Belorussia* (Princeton: Princeton University Press, 1988), especially the Epilogue.

9. See Livia Rothkirchen, "Vatican Policy and the 'Jewish Problem' in 'Independent' Slovakia (1939–1945)," in *Yad Vashem Studies*, vol. 6 (1967), 27–53.

10. M. C. Kaser and E. A. Radice, eds., *The Economic History of Eastern Europe 1919–1975*, vol. 2 (Oxford: Oxford University Press, 1986), 398–417.

11. Stephen D. Kertesz, "The Methods of Communist Conquest: Hungary 1944–1947," *World Politics* 3:1 (1950): 36.

12. Quoted by Eugen Steiner, *The Slovak Dilemma* (Cambridge: Cambridge University Press, 1973), 55.

13. Kaser and Radice, *Economic History*, 445–48.

14. And in all fairness it must be said that such plans were not firmly set concerning territories that were not immediately incorporated. For instance, the Generalgouvernement, central Polish lands, were first designated as a *Nebenland*, an "over-there" territory, somewhere on the periphery, and treated accordingly. In time Generalgouvernement was promoted to a *Zwischenland*, a more glamorous status of an area "in-between," presumably between the Reich and some other "over-there" yet further removed. And since in the *Zwischenland* German colonists were supposed eventually to reside, a more conservative attitude vis-à-vis its material resources was adopted by the occupation administration.

15. Kaser and Radice, *Economic History*, 431, 389.

16. Alan S. Milward, *War, Economy and Society 1939–45* (Berkeley and Los Angeles: University of California Press, 1979); Steiner, *The Slovak Dilemma*, 39.

17. Thus Kaser and Radice, students of the economic history of Eastern Europe, are at a loss for any other explanation as to why Germany encouraged development of an armaments industry in Hungary while remaining cool to Rumanian entreaties to be allowed to do the same, even though Antonescu was Hitler's firmest ally and fielded the second largest military force in the war with Russia. The führer, as a former subject of the old empire, Radice speculates, apparently regarded Hungarians as in some sense a master race, superior to Slavs and also to Rumanians.

18. John Lampe, paper delivered at the conference on "Effects of Communism on Social and Economic Change: Eastern Europe in Comparative Perspective," at Johns Hopkins University Bologna Center, June 1986.

19. See the review of D. Turnock's *The Romanian Economy in the Twentieth Century* (Basingstoke, Kent: Croom Helm, 1986) in *Soviet Studies* 40:1 (1988): 160.

20. Kazimierz Wyka, *Życie na niby* (Warszawa: Książka i Wiedza, 1959).

21. Eugene M. Kulischer, *Europe on the Move: War and Population Changes, 1917–47* (New York: Columbia University Press, 1948), 264. For information on population transfers in subsequent years, see Joseph B. Schechtmann, *Postwar Population Transfers in Europe, 1945–1955* (Philadelphia: University of Pennsylvania Press, 1962), vii. Relocations of ethnic groups that followed the end of World War II in Europe affected over eighteen million people.

22. Edward. A. Shils, "Social and Psychological Aspects of Displacement and Repatriation," *Journal of Social Issues* 2 (1946).

23. Communist Parties immediately seized on this opportunity. In Czechoslovakia "the Communist Party, which before the war was the only party containing both Czechs and Germans, became in 1945 a most enthusiastic supporter of the transfer scheme [of Sudeten Germans], regardless or perhaps because of its Czech-German past. The Communists profited well by this period of patriotic fervor and postwar excitement, often expressed by a thirst for revenge and for easy acquisition of other people's property. The atmosphere of violence and lawlesssness terrorized not only the Sudeten Germans but the majority of Czechs as well" (Ivo Duchacek, "The Strategy of Communist Infiltration: Czechoslovakia, 1944–

1948," *World Politics* 2:3 [1950]: 363). On the same principles underlying the politics of expulsion of Germans from Hungary, see Stephen Kertesz, "The Expulsion of the Germans from Hungary: A Study in Postwar Diplomacy," *The Review of Politics* 15:2 (1953): 179–208.

24. See, for example, George L. Mosse, *Nazism: A Historical and Comparative Analysis of National Socialism* (New Brunswick: Transaction Books New Jersey, 1978), 55.

25. I have in mind, of course, her *Eichmann in Jerusalem: A Report on the Banality of Evil*.

26. Gerhard Hirschfeld, "Collaboration in Nazi-Occupied France: Some Introductory Remarks," in G. Hirschfeld and P. Marsh, eds., *Collaboration in France: Politics and Culture during the Nazi Occupation, 1940–1944* (Oxford: Berg, 1989), 2.

27. Thus, the last prewar edition (1933) of *the Oxford English Dictionary* gives no meaning to the word *collaboration* in the sense that interests us here. *Collaboration* is generally defined there (vol. 2, p. 613 of the 1961 reprint) as "work in conjunction with another or others, esp. in a literary or artistic production, or the like." Robert's dictionary of 1953 gives the following explication for a special meaning of *collaboration* (which otherwise pertains in French to common pursuits in artistic matters): "*Mouvement des Français qui durant occupation Allemande (1940–1944) desiraient travailler au redressement de la France en cooperation avec l'Allemagne*" (p. 819). Bataglia, in his dictionary of the Italian language from 1964, as the fourth meaning of *collaboration* (vol. 3, p. 279) refers to involvement with occupation authorities, and specifically the German ones during World War II ("*per lo piu con riferimento al periodo d'occupazione tedesca durante la Seconda Guerra Mondiale*"). *Encyclopedia Brockhaus* of 1970 (vol. 10, p. 350) defines the term primarily by reference to the actions of Pétain's government in France, though in small print it also informs the reader that the word may be used more generally.

28. "Accordingly, collaborators would include those who make the occupier the beneficiary of the trust vested in them by the population that had elected them to positions of authority, or those who are ready to accept posts that are traditionally vested with authority in a given community" (Jan T. Gross, *Polish Society under German Occupation: Generalgouvernement, 1939–44* [Princeton University Press, Princeton, New Jersey, 1979], 119).

29. Gerhard Hirschfeld, *Nazi Rule and Dutch Collaboration* (Berg, 1988), 5, 32.

30. Martin Conway, *Collaboration in Belgium: Leon Degrelle and the Rexist Movement, 1940–1944* New Haven and London: (Yale University Press, 1993), 24.

31. And numerous initiatives, such as, for instance, the Groupe Collaboration headed by Alphonse de Chateaubriant came into being: "Europeanist in focus, with a strongly spiritual, indeed, anti-materialist ethos, this movement supported the moral regeneration which the National Revolution was to bring to a Europeanised France. . . . The membership of this organization may have achieved the very significant total of 100,000 by mid-1943" (Paul J. Kingston, "The Ideolo-

gists: Vichy France, 1940–1944," in G. Hirschfeld and P. Marsh eds., *Collaboration in France*, 67).

32. Gerard Loiseaux, *La littérature de la defaite et de la collaboration* (Paris: Publications de la Sorbonne, 1984), 111.

33. Sarah Wilson, "Collaboration in the Fine Arts, 1940–1944," in G. Hirschfeld and P. Marsh, *Collaboration in France*, 117, 119.

34. Stanley Hoffman, "Collaborationism in France," in *The Journal of Modern History* 40:3 (1968): 389.

35. Stephen Spender, forward to Alastair Hamilton's *The Appeal of Fascism: A Study of Intellectuals and Fascism, 1919–1945* (London: Anthony Blond, 1971), xiii.

36. Conway, *Collaboration in Belgium*, 44, 45, 61.

37. Hoffman, *Collaborationism in France*, 389.

38. Jean Paul Sartre, "Paris sous l'occupation," in *Situations III* (Paris: Gallimard, 1949), 40–41.

39. Paul J. Kingston, "The Ideologists: Vichy France, 1940–1944," in G. Hirschfeld and P. Marsh, eds., *Collaboration in France*, 50.

40. Hirschfeld, introduction to ibid., 12.

41. Radio broadcasts by Philippe Henriot, very popular at the time, "set the collaboration of Vichy firmly within the history of political struggle against Communism which half of France's electorate had in some way endorsed over the previous thirty years" (H. R. Kedward, "The Vichy of the Other Philippe," in G. Hirschfeld and P. Marsh, ibid., 37).

42. Hannah Arendt, "Organized Guilt and Universal Responsibility," in *Essays in Understanding, 1930–54* (New York: Harcourt, Brace, and Co., 1994), 126.

43. H. R. Kedward, "Vichy," 37.

44. Jean Paul Sartre, "Paris sous l'occupation," 37.

45. Yitzhak Zuckerman, *A Surplus of Memory: Chronicle of the Warsaw Ghetto Uprising* (Los Angeles: University of California Press, 1993), 320.

46. Jean Paul Sartre, "Qu'est-ce qu'un collaborateur?" in *Situations III* (Paris: Gallimard, 1949), 51–54.

47. Hirschfeld, *Collaboration in France*, 12ff.

48. A few words beginning with a small *c* can be suggested as suitable candidates—cooperation, collusion, compliance, complicity.

49. Slavenka Drakulic, *The Balkan Express: Fragments from the Other Side of the War* (New York and London: W. W. Norton and Co., 1993), 12.

Part II

THE EXPERIENCE OF WAR

A Fatal Compromise? The Debate over Collaboration and Resistance in Hungary

ON 27 JULY 1944, in a well-known pastry shop lodged in the Buda foot-hills, plainclothesmen of the Royal Hungarian Gendarmerie attempted to arrest Endre Ságvári, leader of the Young Communists. Before he was killed, Ságvári managed to wound three of the agents with his revolver. An intellectual with a doctoral degree in law, he was thirty-one years of age and hailed from a well-to-do Jewish family. Far from making him a rarity, Ságvári's origins and education typified the membership of the country's minuscule underground Communist Party (four hundred members in 1936 and around twenty at liberty in 1942). Not even his courage was extraordinary, for within Hungary's anti-Nazi movement, the Communists (and some small Zionist groups) were known to be the bravest and the most likely to fight it out with the Germans and the Hungarian authorities.[1]

Subsequently, Endre Ságvári became the most celebrated martyr of the Hungarian working-class movement: under the Communists, scores of streets, parks, and public establishments were named after him. True, his widow, herself an underground Party fighter in World War II, suffered persecution in the 1950s, but that, too, typified the lot of Hungary's "home-grown" Communists in the Stalinist period. Because Ságvári himself was conveniently dead, all the Communist leaders, from the Stalinist Mátyás Rákosi to the national Communist Imre Nagy and the opportunistic János Kádár, paid effusive homage to his memory. Only in 1989, with the end of Communism in Hungary, was there any change in this pattern; today there are precious few, if any, Ságvári streets left in the country. His bust was removed from its place near the entrance of the pastry shop where he had been killed, now an expensive garden restaurant, although attentive visitors can still find a commemorative plaque.

This little story without a happy ending sums up, it seems to me, the insoluble dilemma of World War II resistance in Hungary. It was, by any reckoning, a very small movement, consisting of a few hundred individuals from the most varied political backgrounds; their fundamental differences could barely be bridged by their common determination to oppose the Germans and the latter's Hungarian helpers. The Communists played a conspicuous role in the resistance, and after the war, the memory of their heroism was enshrined in the pantheon of the regime. Meanwhile, the memory of the non-Communist resistance was distorted, and if an individual anti-Nazi survived the war, chances were he was imprisoned or driven into exile.[2]

The attempt to create a Communist martyrology must be deemed a failure. Even when the cult of their memory was at its peak, the general public cared little for the resistance fighters, whether Communists or non-Communists. Worse still, many regarded all anti-Nazi resisters as Jewish Communists who had helped to foist Stalin and Rákosi upon Hungary. Not even the Jewish survivors were particularly enthusiastic about Ságvári and his comrades: during the war, the Communists had called for armed resistance to the conservative Hungarian government, which in the eyes of most Jews was their sole protector against German pressure and fascist extremism. Moreover, the few people who were aware of what the Communists had been doing during the war knew that the Holocaust had left the Party totally unmoved. Unlike in Poland or Bulgaria, the persecution of Jews in Hungary simply did not exist in the host of Communist flyers circulating in 1944, and not once did the Party encourage the people to give shelter to the Jews.[3] Finally, many Jews regarded the Jewish Communists as godless renegades, who were responsible for the Christian public's identification of Bolshevism with Jewry.

Yet if there is little sympathy for or public interest in the anti-Nazi struggle and its heroes, neither is there any great sympathy for or public interest in the right-wing leaders of the World War II years.

Between 1990 and 1994, a coalition of conservative and nationalist political parties governed post-Communist Hungary. During those years, the public showed growing dissatisfaction with what was felt to be the government's corrupt practices, arrogance, and inefficiency. In particular, many objected to the government's attempt to rehabilitate the interwar Hungarian regime and its feudalistic cum protofascistic political style. The controversy erupted into the open, when, in the fall of 1993, the body of Regent Admiral Miklós Horthy was brought back from exile and solemnly reburied. All observers of the Hungarian scene agree that the conservative government's drive to recreate the political and moral atmosphere of the interwar Horthy regime was one of the major reasons for its defeat and the success of the Socialists, a party led by former Communists, in the May 1994 national elections.[4] Yet among the many complaints regarding government practices in the period 1990–94, one of the least often heard was any objection to the systematic rechristening of streets named after Communist martyrs and heroes.

One of the more active propaganda campaigns of the conservative regime was led by the late General Kálmán Kéri, then the oldest member of parliament, which aimed at the moral and political rehabilitation of Hungary's participation in Germany's war against the Soviet Union. But General Kéri's plea fell on deaf ears, no doubt in part because his own earlier activities contradicted his newfangled ideals. In truth, Kéri's life and career mirrored Hungary's hopeless situation, caught in the vise between German and Soviet imperialism, and they go a long way to explain why the public cares neither for the anti-Nazi fighters of World War II, nor for Hungary's anti-Bolshevik crusade on the side of Hitler.

Kéri, who died in 1994 at the age of ninety-three, hoped to substitute, in the nation's conscience, the fallen heroes of the Hungarian anti-Bolshevik armies for the martyrs of Hungary's anti-Nazi resistance. Yet back in 1944 he himself betrayed this vaunted crusade. On October 16, after Regent Horthy had attempted to surrender to the Soviets, and while most of his fellow officers were abandoning their commander-in-chief in order to pursue the war on the side of Germany, Kéri, then chief of staff of the Hungarian First Army, went over to the Soviets.[5] Toward the end of the war he was one of the several old-army officers charged by the Soviets with creating a new democratic army to participate in the struggle against Nazi Germany. It is true that rather than being rewarded for his deed, he later spent many years in Communist Hungary's prisons and concentration camps, but this again made him no different from all other "Horthy officers" who at one point or another had sided with the Soviets. That Kéri could never see, or at least never publicly acknowledged, the contradiction between his actions in 1944 and those in the early 1990s shows that paradox is the very essence of small power politics. The indifference of the public toward the idea of rehabilitating the soldiers of World War II demonstrated that even though the image of the Communist underground has remained rather negative, society is far from being uniformly enthusiastic about the political system that these underground fighters opposed.

The real question is what effect it will have on public consciousness that today all aspects and nearly all the participants of the most tragic period in the nation's recent history have been repudiated. This is no minor issue in a society as history-conscious as the Hungarian. The public's uneasy view of the events of World War II may reflect a recognition that no matter what anyone did at that time, this small nation could not avoid its tragic fate.

Monarchists, Democrats, Bolsheviks, and Counterrevolutionaries

A brief look at Hungary's past is necessary in order to understand what collaboration and resistance were all about in World War II. A kingdom with its roots in the early Middle Ages, Hungary had lost its independence first to the Ottomans and then to the Habsburg dynasty in the sixteenth and seventeenth centuries. It regained its sovereignty, if not complete independence, in 1867, by becoming an equal partner with Austria in the so-called Dual Monarchy. The next fifty-odd years were marked by relative social peace and phenomenal progress in economic development, education, and city building as well as in liberal legislation. The latter brought equality before the law, freedom of the press, equality for all religious denominations, vigorous secularization, and the strengthening of an independent judiciary. The liberal-conservative governments of the day were unable, however, to solve three major problems. The first was that of the ethnic minorities, who together formed about one half of the total population, and whose elites were divided between those willing to embrace Hungarian patriotism in exchange for a career in the state service or the professions, and those who resisted Hungarian assimilationist efforts in the hope of eventually leading their own nationality to independence. The second was the terribly uneven distribution of landed property, which favored a few aristocratic landowners and kept millions of peasants in semiservitude or in the role of day laborers. Third was the problem of relations with the other half of the Dual Monarchy, which absorbed most of the time and energy of the increasingly nationalistic Hungarian political leaders.[6]

All these problems came to a head during World War I, when pre-1914 prosperity and optimism gave way to poverty, political radicalism, and general discontent. The defeat of the Central Powers in the Fall of 1918 came as a terrible shock to a misinformed public, yet also as a welcome relief from what was perceived to be Habsburg/Austrian oppression. The fact that in the eyes of the other peoples of the Monarchy, including the German speakers, the Hungarians were the quintessentially dominant nationality, did not in the least influence the Hungarians' perception of themselves as oppressed victims. Thus the end of the war and the outbreak of a democratic revolution in Budapest in October–November 1918 were celebrated as the beginning of an independent and more progressive Hungary that would introduce land reform and expand the hitherto very restricted suffrage. Celebration turned to despair, however, when the terrible costs of war became more visible, and when the armies of Hungary's old and new neighbors occupied much of what in prewar times had been officially known as the "Hungarian Empire" within Austria-Hungary.

The democratic regime of Count Mihály Károlyi, having proven itself incapable of defending Hungary against military attacks by Romania, Serbia, and the newly created Czechoslovakia, was replaced, on 21 March 1919, by a Soviet-style Republic of Councils. The influence of this event on later developments cannot be overestimated. The Soviet republic lasted only 133 days, but Admiral Miklós Horthy's subsequent counterrevolutionary regime drew its legitimacy for the next twenty-five years from having opposed the Hungarian Bolsheviks. During World War II, Left and Right fought it out with slogans borrowed from the 1918–19 revolutions and counterrevolution, and the post–World War II Communist regime saw itself as legitimate heir to the 1919 revolution. Mátyás Rákosi, Hungary's Stalinist dictator in the late 1940s and early 1950s, was among those who judged everything from the viewpoint of the Republic of Councils, of which he had once been a member. He and his comrades took their revenge not only on the counterrevolutionaries but also on the moderate leftists who, in Communist eyes, had betrayed the proletarian revolution in 1919.[7]

On 1 August 1919 the wildly experimental Republic of Councils was overthrown by popular opposition at home and by the Romanian army, which enjoyed the support of France. The latter hoped to create an alliance system in East Central Europe, made up of Poland, Czechoslovakia, Romania, and Yugoslavia, that would help to keep both Soviet Russia and Germany in check. Thus, both Count Károlyi's attempt to align Hungary with Wilsonian democracy and Béla Kun's attempt to ally Hungary with Lenin were ultimately crushed by France and its client states in the region. The result was Miklós Horthy's counterrevolutionary regime.

A Kingdom without a King, An Admiral without a Fleet

The interwar period in Hungary is so intimately tied to the person of the Regent, former Austro-Hungarian Vice-Admiral Miklós (Nicholas) Horthy, that it is commonly referred to as the "Horthy era." Horthy reported in his memoirs that he always asked himself, when confronted with a grave dilemma, what Emperor-King Francis Joseph would have done. His search, like that of the old emperor, was for a solution that was noble, chivalrous, and humane. Yet after World War I, he was at least partially responsible for a bloody terror in Hungary as well as for twentieth-century Europe's first anti-Semitic law; later he entered into an alliance with Hitler, and in the Spring of 1944 he washed his hands of the deportation to Auschwitz of half a million of his mostly loyal and patriotic Jewish subjects. All of these things the emperor would most likely not have done.

Horthy began his professional career, in the 1880s, by sailing on wooden naval ships. He ended his career, in October 1944, the captive of German parachuters. Just before World War I, he served as a devoted aide-de-camp to Francis Joseph and even later claimed undying loyalty to the House of Habsburg. Yet in 1921, he dispatched troops to oppose Emperor-King Charles when the latter appeared in Hungary to reclaim his throne. Horthy sincerely believed that he had devoted his entire life to the fatherland and entitled his memoirs, *Ein Leben für Ungarn* (A Life Given to Hungary),[8] yet at the end of his reign the country he served fell into ruin and chaos. The question is still being debated what Regent Horthy's personal responsibility was in this debacle. It is also an open question whether the many blatant contradictions and inconsistencies in his career were due chiefly to the troubled age in which he lived or whether they reflected his personal shortcomings.

Surprisingly, there exists no worthwhile Hungarian-language biography of the man whose name marked the history of Hungary between 1919 and 1944, and who incited such passions nearly four decades after his death in 1957. The few biographies that appeared while he was regent were sycophantic; those that appeared in the Communist era spewed bile and venom; moreover, they seem to have been written for children. A fine account at last appeared when Thomas Sakmyster, an American historian, undertook an analysis of Horthy's political career. His *Hungary's Admiral on Horseback: Miklós Horthy, 1918–1944*, published in 1994, is accurate, strongly critical when needed and yet not lacking in sympathy for Hungary and its regent. It also makes enjoyable reading.[9]

What readers of Sakmyster's book will be intrigued to discover is the intellectual mediocrity of a man who rose, without any significant outside assistance, to become Austria-Hungary's only successful naval captain during World War I and the last commander of the imperial and royal fleet. Further, by 1920 Horthy had made himself the uncontested leader of his country and subsequently firmly maintained power in a region where violent political coups were the rule. Although both his courtiers and he himself vastly overestimated his popularity, he seems to have been hated only by the political far Right and the far Left. Moreover, as has been mentioned earlier, Horthy the anti-Semite, who is often called a fascist, was seen by most Jews as their ultimate protector against fascism and Hitler. Interestingly, Horthy was not very different, in respect to intellect, from other successful conservative strongmen who dominated Europe in that period, the closest comparison being Generalissimo Francisco Franco. The Spanish leader was duller and, if possible, even less insightful than Horthy, but nevertheless won a bloody civil war, then imposed his iron will on a large and turbulent nation, and finally handed over an increasingly prosperous country to a democratically minded king and political parties. Horthy, of course, was not so lucky as to rule in isolated Spain.

Miklós Horthy was born in 1868 in the center of the Great Hungarian Plain, not a place likely to produce sailors. That he became a sailor nevertheless was because he happened to be one of seven sons; because his elder brother was killed in an accident at sea while at the naval academy; and because, in his fairly well-off gentry family, service to the state was an established tradition. Such a tradition was rather unusual inasmuch as the Horthys were Calvinists, a confessional group in Hungary generally associated with nationalist, anti-Habsburg sentiments. When a regent, Horthy often seemed somewhat out of place presiding over the many Catholic festivities of a country where two thirds of the population were Roman Catholic but where many Hungarians linked Catholicism to the alien Habsburgs. One of Horthy's brothers became a general; another was killed at the front in 1914.

The uncertainties regarding Miklós Horthy's personal contribution to his meteoric career begin with his admission to the Austro-Hungarian naval academy in 1882, as one of 42 successful candidates out of 612 applicants. He had been such a mediocre student that his parents had sent him to a private high school in Hungary that catered to less than gifted boys from good families. It is true that because the Hungarian government was most keen on achieving parity with the Austrian half in the Dual Monarchy, even in maritime service, there existed what the Americans call an affirmative action program at the military schools of the Monarchy. Thus, a Hungarian boy of noble origin enjoyed some advantages over others. Still, the Habsburg navy was tough and demanding enough not to admit a candidate without merits; nor could he have graduated four years later as one of the twenty-seven survivors of the course unless he deserved it. Like all Austro-Hungarian officers, Horthy learned German, which he thereafter spoke better than his native Hungarian, and as a naval officer he also learned to speak English, French, Italian, Croatian, as well as some Czech.

It must have been good to be a young naval lieutenant at that time; Horthy saw many ports and once even traveled around the world. He was invited to the palaces of exotic rulers, and he took part in sumptuous balls and great hunts. All this he recounts well in the most entertaining section of his reminiscences. The world was under British protection at that time, a fact that Horthy greatly appreciated and from which he drew his oft repeated conviction that the British navy would ultimately win all the wars. This did not prevent him, however, from fighting in two world wars in coalitions opposed to Great Britain. His memoirs show young Horthy a carefree but efficient and eminently reliable officer, yet what is most remarkable about this account is how similar it is to memoirs written by other members of the officers' guild. It is almost as if there had been some secret code as to how an officer should frame his memoirs.[10] Like his colleagues, Horthy is modest about his exploits, but again like his colleagues, he always emerges correct in every difficult situation. Culture for him meant an occasional visit to the opera; love meant marriage to a devoted woman from a Catholic gentry family; ideals equaled an absolute devotion to both Francis Joseph and the Hungarian "race"; and entertainment meant hunting, horseback riding, bridge, and tennis. Deck officers and crew are remembered in his memoirs as unconditionally loyal but they remain faceless and nameless; civilian existence merits barely a word, and politics consists mainly of the detestation of Serbs and socialists.

In 1909 Horthy was invited to serve as one of the four aides-de-camp to Francis Joseph, an appointment that must be attributed to both Hungarian political influence in court and his own merits. Upon the outbreak of the war he returned to service as a naval captain (colonel's rank), and during the war, due both to lucky assignments and his own daring, he accumulated many minor naval successes, a rare achievement in a fleet that was generally bottled up in port. In May 1917 he led a few ships against superior enemy forces to break an enemy blockade in the southern Adriatic; he was badly wounded in the encounter but continued to direct his ships. Ultimately he won this Battle of the Otranto, which made him the monarchy's most celebrated naval commander. Every Hungarian schoolchild later had to learn his wartime exploits by heart. In February 1918 he was made commander of the fleet over the head of several officers who were his seniors, and at the end of the war he had the humiliating task of handing over the fleet to a newly constituted National Committee of Slovenes, Croats, and Serbs as a sort of parting gift from Emperor-King Charles. By that time he also had had an unpleasant experience with mutinous sailors: incidents that increased his detestation of socialists and all other but Hungarian nationalists.

Horthy was now unemployed, attempting to take care of the family estate, and watching revolution unfold in his country. Following the creation of the Hungarian Republic of Soviets, on 21 March 1919, he joined with some old-regime politicians and young officers in plotting the overthrow of the Soviet regime. Meanwhile, the Communists were conducting a "revolutionary internationalist war" against Romanian and newly created Czechoslovak armies that were about to overrun the country. These armies were directed by French officers, a fact that did not prevent the counterrevolutionary nationalists from placing themselves under French military protection in the cities of Szeged and Arad. From there they made great efforts to undermine the Red government, whose troops were defending Hungary. Then, as well as later, when he had to choose between two evils—Bolshevism or the loss of national territory and sovereignty—Horthy chose the latter evil, believing, I would imagine, that territory and sovereignty could eventually be recovered but not the soul of a nation lost to Bolshevik ideology. At all times, Communism was for him the ultimate enemy.

Moving in and out of intrigue-ridden counterrevolutionary shadow governments, Horthy showed enough independence of mind to go his own way. After Béla Kun's Communist regime fell, on 1 August 1919, and the Romanian army occupied Budapest, Horthy left the politicians behind and transferred his minuscule "National Army" to unoccupied western Hungary. There his officers' detachments instituted a reign of "White Terror" that surpassed in brutality and scope the "Red Terror" of the Hungarian Bolsheviks. Its chief victims were Jews, members of the revolutionary committees, and poor peasants who had dared to rise against the landowners. Characteristically, Horthy both denied in his memoirs any participation in these "excesses" and excused the atrocities by arguing that soft hearts had no place in such an extreme situation. Facts show his indirect responsibility for many murders extending into 1920.

On 1 March 1920 the Hungarian parliament elected Horthy governor or regent of the Hungarian kingdom; it was left open whether the king himself would ever return to the throne but, in any case, Horthy insisted on and received nearly all the prerogatives enjoyed previously by a Habsburg ruler. This made him more than a constitutional monarch in the Western, democratic sense of the word, but much less than a dictator, which he was often accused of being. The election itself took place in the presence of armed officers who were the real power in Hungary at that time. The Entente powers immediately recognized the new regime. The same France and Great Britain that had ruthlessly undermined the democratic and ethnically tolerant Károlyi goverment, and that had sent their central European allies against the Hungarian Republic of Soviets, accepted the ultranationalist Horthy group. It is true that the latter had been the virtual allies of the Entente during the Red regime. Only that the Entente now insisted on democratic elections and a responsible government: an order that Horthy found ridiculous, and that the counterrevolutionary government did not care to abide by.

On 4 June 1920 Hungary's representatives were forced to sign the Peace Treaty of Trianon, which confirmed the territorial truncation of the country. Between October 1918 and the fall of 1919, South Slav, Romanian, and Czechoslovak armed forces had occupied two thirds of Hungary, which included 60 percent of the population. Cynically marshaling ethnic, strategic, historical, and economic arguments, depending on what best fitted their interests, these Central European regimes persuaded the Four Great in Paris to accept a fait accompli. More than three million ethnic Hungarians had become subjects of the new nation states, which were in reality heavily multinational. Austria, Poland, and Italy were also given some small chunks of Hungary.

All Hungarian political parties, including the underground Communists, protested against the dictated treaty, but the counterrevolutionary regime alone profited from it, by shifting the blame for the defeat, the revolutions, and Hungary's dismemberment onto the socialists, democrats, and liberals. The new regime's summons to a sacred struggle for a revision of the country's frontiers enabled it to impose strict discipline on the population.[11]

Because Great Britain lacked the interest and France the desire to accord justice to Hungary, the country remained diplomatically isolated until the emergence of fascist Italy and, even more, Nazi Germany, both of whom seemed interested in a program of territorial revision. This inevitably strengthened the political influence of those at home who could emotionally and ideologically identify with fascism and National Socialism.[12]

The Difficult Interwar Years

The Treaty of Trianon set the stage for a never-ending central European conflict. The Little Entente, soon to be created by Czechoslovakia, Romania, and Yugoslavia for the sole purpose of controlling the revisionist ambitions of disarmed and much smaller Hungary, subsequently overlooked the danger of German territorial revisionism. Hungary became the quintessentially have-not state ready to ally itself even with the devil himself to undo the injustices perpetrated at Trianon. In reality, the country drew some unacknowledged benefits from its dismemberment because its industrial base had remained in and around Budapest, and because it was now largely free of the ethnic problems that would lead to the breakup of Yugoslavia and Czechoslovakia, first during World War II and then after 1989.

The mainly negative ideology of the Horthy regime was born in wartime and postwar experiences: antiliberalism, because of the inability of the pre–World War I liberal regimes to solve the ethnic problem and to prepare the nation adequately for the war; anti-Semitism, because of the overwhelming participation of mostly young Jewish intellectuals in the Bolshevik regime; and conservatism, because of the great fright caused by the revolutionary slogans and egalitarian experiments of the Károlyi and Béla Kun regimes. These views were presented in a romantic nationalist, populist dressing in which the sturdy and healthy Hungarian peasant and the unspoiled countryside were extolled, while cosmopolitan and immoral Budapest, as well as the workers and the urban bourgeois, were paraded as highly suspect. All this by a regime whose main support came from the new, urban, non-Jewish middle class and intelligentsia, who clamored for active state assistance in the competition with Jewish business and professional elites.

True, the Jewish Bolsheviks who seized power in 1919 and governed the country for 133 days never admitted their Jewishness in public and were completely uninterested in Jewish issues. Still, in this small country, everybody knew who was and who was not a Jew. The result was a greatly heightened anti-Semitism in which it was immaterial that the vast majority of the Hungarian Jews had wished to have nothing to do with the Bolshevik regime. The anti-Semitism of the counterrevolutionary regime did not, however, mean any kind of anti-Jewish uniformity. Indeed, anti-Semitism ranged from the mildly economic through the political to the racist, and it is no exaggeration to say that the history of "Horthy Hungary" was marked by a political competition among anti-Semites. Even the degree of the country's alignment with Nazi Germany was largely determined, aside from the goal of territorial revisionism, by whether one aimed at a moderate or a radical solution of the Jewish question. As in so many other cases, Horthy occupied a middle position regarding the Jews, or better to say, his position swung from the middle to a moderate or a radical stance, depending on the times and on the persuasive power of those around him.

In 1921, when King Charles twice attempted to reclaim his throne, Horthy behaved most ambiguously: he assured the king of his absolute loyalty yet forced Charles into exile by claiming the threat of Entente and Little Entente military intervention. No doubt there was such a threat, but there is no proof that an invasion of Hungary would have truly ensued if Horthy had given up his post in favor of Charles. In any case, the Czechoslovak and other neighboring governments showed themselves most shortsighted in protesting the return of the Habsburgs; it is inconceivable that King Charles, or his son Otto, would have allied himself with Hitler. Domestically, the liberal and anti-anti-Semitic Charles would have been a blessing compared with Horthy and his cronies.

Irrespective of the crisis with Charles, Hungary had by then a talented new prime minister, Count István Bethlen, who in the ten years following his appointment in 1921 gradually returned the country to the liberal-conservative political practices—if not the ideology—of the pre–World War years. The regular forces disarmed the White Terrorist groups and Bethlen found an accommodation both with the Social Democratic trade unions and with Jewish-owned banking and heavy industry. As a result, Hungary was allowed to join the League of Nations, and a considerable foreign loan consolidated the failing economy as well as put an end to the inflation. Even the anti-Semitic law of 1920, which had limited the admission of Jews to the universities, was now often ignored. Politics was almost as before World War I, except that the country was much poorer, and that there now was a fascist far Right within and outside Bethlen's "Government Party."

The Hungarian parliament had been disbanded only for a short period under the Bolsheviks; it would continue in existence even during World War II. The political power of the Government Party (which went by different names) was assured by a restrictive suffrage, but other parties, too, from the socialists to the fascists, were allowed some representation in parliament. Only the Communist Party was forbidden. The press was almost entirely free and the courts were independent, although, naturally, they tended to represent the interests of the governing elite. In the Bethlen era, Horthy acted as a true constitutional monarch, allowing the prime minister to run affairs.

The Great Depression and Hitler's rise to power put an end to this relatively tranquil period: Bethlen resigned in 1931, and a year later one of Horthy's former White officers, Gyula Gömbös, became prime minister with a fascist-sounding program. Gömbös turned out to be more of a demagogue than an activist, and there was under him no drastic change either in terms of anti-Semitic legislation or the long promised distribution of large estates among the rural poor. But Gömbös brought with him a number of young right-wing radicals, especially army officers, which caused an ever widening split in the counterrevolutionary ranks. A pattern was actually set at that time wherein Hungary was governed by people who publicly claimed to represent one and the same right-wing ideology, but who in reality were divided into two distinct camps: one radical and fascistic, which we might call the New Right, and the other conservative with liberal inclinations, which we might call the Old Right. The division ran right through the Government Party, with the right-wing element in this right-wing party secretly collaborating with the openly fascist parties. On the other hand, the liberal and left-wing parties, which were diminishing in size with every election, had no choice but to support the moderates in the Government Party. Thus, in the crazy quilt of Hungarian politics, we find in one camp Social Democrats, peasant politicians, arch-conservative royalists, rich Jewish liberals, mildly anti-Semitic counterrevolutionary politicians, and such Hungarian racists for whom the German minority in Hungary and Nazi imperialism represented more of a threat than the Jews. In the other camp were pro-German counterrevolutionary politicians, most of the army officers, fascist ideologues, rabid anti-Semites, much of the non-Jewish middle class and petite bourgeoisie, and masses of poor people for whom National Socialism promised salvation from oppression by Jewish capitalists and aristocratic landowners.

Typically, the greatest hero of the anti-Nazi resistance, Endre Bajcsy-Zsilinszky, began his career as a Race Defender and ended up as a sincere advocate of democracy. Not without reason there are long quotations from Bajcsy-Zsilinszky's speeches and writings in both volumes of a recent Hungarian publication on friends and enemies of the Hungarian Jews.[13] He was hanged by the Arrow Cross regime at the end of 1944.

This oversimplified listing of party positions should be enough to demonstrate, first, that politics in Hungary was largely an affair of several very individualistic personalities and, second, that it was impossible to separate clearly Right from Left, collaboration from resistance, or fascism from antifascism. The assertions of Communist-era historiography notwithstanding, the opponents of Hungary's wartime government were not all antifascists; nor was the government simply one of fascists and fascist sympathizers.

It is difficult to say which camp was more powerful; certainly, it would be incorrect to argue that the Government Party was moving steadily to the right, toward fascism. Rather, the pendulum swung from radical to moderate and back again until the collapse of the Horthy regime on 15 October 1944. Somewhat more active than in the Bethlen era, Horthy sometimes listened to his informal council of elders, made up mostly of aristocrats and led by Count Bethlen, who invariably counseled moderation in foreign policy as well as in anti-Jewish legislation and social reform; or he listened to army officers and the like who urged Horthy to make himself a dictator, to steer an outright fascist course, and to go to war on the side of Germany. A succession of prime ministers appointed by Horthy after the death of Gömbös in 1936 started out with a moderate program but ended up by being more radical and more pro-German than Horthy would have liked them to be. The main reason for this was that these politicians had been invested with an impossible task: to fight Bolshevism in every one of its manifestations; to rely on Germany for political, military, and economic help; and to reduce the Jewish presence in the economy and society, yet also to keep the domestic fascists at bay and to preserve Hungarian independence vis-à-vis Nazi Germany. The cabinets themselves were divided between such staunch anti-Nazis as for instance the near-permanent Minister of Interior Ferenc Keresztes-Fischer, who in 1944 landed in a Nazi concentration camp, and such Nazi agents as the near-permanent Minister of Finance Lajos Reményi-Schneller, who after the war ended up on the gallows. Horthy would not dare dismiss Reményi-Schneller for fear of angering the Germans, yet he would not dismiss Keresztes-Fischer, whom he trusted, which angered the Germans.

In the secret parliamentary elections of 1939 (only the second secret elections in Hungarian history), the combined total of "leftist" votes amounted to but a fraction of the votes cast for the Arrow Cross and other National Socialist parties. Despite these gains on the far right, the Government Party won the elections without great difficulty. It is more than likely that after the elections, many of the defeated leftist groups and grouplets would have disapppeared from the scene had the conservatives in the Government Party not supported their continued existence as a counterweight to the fascists inside and outside the ruling party. Especially after the Battle of Stalingrad, the government of Prime Minister Miklós Kállay used the newspapers and spokesmen of the Left to spread anti-Nazi propaganda and to indicate to the Western Powers that Hungary was preparing to desert Germany. However, this did not prevent the conservative government from persecuting the Communists, whom it wanted to see rejected by the more moderate "left-wing" opposition groups.

The Even More Difficult War Years

Beginning in 1938 Hungary was on the road to recovering parts of the old Hungarian kingdom, always with German help and always at the price of more closely adhering to German policy goals. Meanwhile also, the economy passed from the deepest depression to something approaching prosperity, thanks mainly to the German rearmament program, which provided Hungarian factories with full employment, and agricultural producers with great profits. True, Hungary could pride itself on some small acts of defiance toward Germany, such as its unwillingness in 1938 to participate in a planned German military campaign against Czechoslovakia (Chamberlain and Daladier made the campaign unnecessary at Munich), or its not allowing German troop trains to travel through Hungary to attack Poland in 1939, or its receiving Polish refugees with open arms and letting Polish soldiers pass through Hungary on the way to France. Yet the fundamental reality of Hungary becoming a German ally could no longer be changed, or perhaps it could never have been changed. The choice was, after all, between occupation or alliance.

Riding on a white horse in his Habsburg naval uniform, Horthy entered first southern Slovakia, then northern Transylvania, and finally north central Yugoslavia, all of which had once belonged to Hungary. These were his finest hours, and for them he was most grateful to Hitler. Moreover, he greatly admired the Wehrmacht and the German conservative allies of Hitler. But because Horthy also feared and loathed the Arrow Cross mob in Hungary, he alternately enthused over and cautiously defied the Führer when the two met periodically during the war.

In June 1941 Hungary took the fateful step of entering the war against the Soviet Union. Horthy claimed later that he had been tricked into this by his prime minister, but in reality the war represented the fulfillment of his old dream: a crusade against Bolshevism for which he had argued in an amateurishly worded circular addressed to twenty-three heads of state.[14] He was naive enough to expect that he could achieve the destruction of Bolshevism without heavy loss of Hungarian life, without his country becoming a German satellite, and without Great Britain and the United States resenting his alliance with Hitler. On the other hand, it is not easy to see how Hungary could have avoided entering the war in view of the political ideology of its elite and the fact that Hungary's neighbors and bitter rivals—Slovakia, Romania, and Croatia—had also joined in the war. The aim was not to gain Soviet territory but to preserve and perhaps to enlarge territories that Hungary had recovered from its neighbors since 1938.

Hungary entered the war in June 1941, not because the Germans demanded it, but so as to win favors. A year later, it was the badly pressed German High Command that insisted on the dispatch of an entire Hungarian army to the Russian front. In the winter of 1942–43, this Second Army was annihilated at the River Don. Horthy managed to withdraw the remaining Hungarian soldiers from the first front lines, and thereafter Hungary engaged in a neutralist course aiming at leaving the war. Under the anti-Nazi prime minister Miklós Kállay, Hungary attempted to reach a secret agreement with the Western Allies; in expectation of this event, restrictions on Jews and leftists were greatly relaxed in Hungary. All this took place with the approval of Horthy, who however would not think of abandoning the German allies without at least a warning. The unrealistic Hungarian plan was to defend Hungary against the Bolsheviks while awaiting the arrival of the Anglo-American forces. However, the Western Allies were not interested in a separate peace, and in any case they were not even near the country. On the other hand, Hitler was being kept informed of Hungarian moves by traitors and spies in the highest government agencies.

On 19 March 1944 the German army and SS marched into Hungary. There was no resistance, for Horthy had been summoned to Germany and was made to stay there on the night of the invasion. In any case, the government never thought of armed resistance, if for no other reason than because it still needed German help against the Red Army. Prime Minister Kállay went into hiding; other conservatives and liberals were arrested by the Gestapo. Horthy now appointed an unconditionally pro-German cabinet of officers and civil servants who proceeded to mobilize the nation for the war and undertook a radical solution of the Jewish question. With only a minimum of German assistance, the Hungarian authorities collected nearly half a million Jews from the countryside and sent them to Auschwitz. The brutality of this procedure defies imagination, especially in view of the fact that it was done by institutions that a few decades earlier had been models of legal procedure. The utter callousness and greed manifested by so many may have been the result of twenty-five years of counterrevolutionary methods and propaganda.

Horthy wrote in his memoirs that he had been powerless to stop the deportations that were undertaken by Adolf Eichmann and co., and not by the Hungarians, and that he knew nothing of the real goal of the transfer of the Jews. He might have been right, at least initially, about his powerlessness, but as for the rest, he was lying. He had been informed about Auschwitz very early in the game but preferred to ignore it; perhaps because he felt no compassion for the Jews of the countryside, whom he considered unassimilated and of little value. Not so with the Budapest Jews! When their turn came, in June–July 1944, he took military measures to oppose the gendarmes who—he feared—were also planning a coup d'etat against him. Worldwide protests against the deportations as well as vehement objections by such conservatives as Count Bethlen, who was by then in hiding from the Germans, also helped Horthy in his decision, as did, incidentally, the temporary weakening of the German resolve to proceed with the deportations. Ultimately, about 40 percent of the Hungarian Jews survived.

It is often asked why Horthy did not resign in the spring of 1944 to show his opposition to such horrors. His answer was that if he had done so, even the Budapest Jews and the many thousand Jewish men who had been drafted in the Hungarian army as forced laborers, would also have been deported to Auschwitz. Further, power would have fallen in the lap of the Arrow Cross, the radical fascist party. This is most probably true, but we must add that Horthy really cared little for others beyond those whom he considered "good" Jews, the decorated war veterans and the capitalists, some of whom came close to being his personal friends.

Early in September 1944, following the sudden turnaround of Romania, the Red Army arrived in northern Transylvania, and in the same month its advanced units entered Trianon Hungary. Earlier, Horthy dismissed his pro-Nazi cabinet and appointed one that he hoped he could trust to negotiate secretly with the Soviets. But he did not dare dismiss some of the German agents in the cabinet. Now, at last, Horthy and his advisers were ready to face reality and surrender to the Soviets, but because they still tried to set some conditions, negotiations proceeded slowly. Also, hardly anyone around the regent could be trusted: at the end, secret radio contacts with the Hungarian delegates in Moscow had to be handled by Horthy's only surviving son, Miklós Jr., and by the widow of his elder son István.[15] The Germans were, of course, privy to these plans. They prepared a coup d'etat and as a first step, on October 15, they kidnapped Miklós Horthy Jr. The same day, the regent announced his intention to surrender but because the army high command did not follow his instructions, the surrender attempt failed immediately.

Instead of a surrender, German SS and parachuters arrested Horthy, causing him to sign a piece of paper that made the Arrow Cross leader Ferenc Szálasi his successor.[16] Horthy thus chose his son over the country, which showed again that he was no statesman. Yet he demonstrated no greater weakness and hesitation at that moment than his ministers or the few military leaders who remained loyal to him. In contrast, the other side knew exactly what it wanted: the Germans wished to gain time before the Red Army would arrive at Vienna; the Arrow Cross aimed at enjoying the pleasures of power, if only for a few weeks, and the army officers wished to continue fighting, or at least hoped to avoid Soviet captivity by wihdrawing with the Germans. It is often asked why Horthy was not as successful as King Michael of Romania in turning his country against the Germans. The answer is that the Romanian army command could be trusted by the king but not the Hungarian officers by Horthy. The secret of this situation lies, among others things, in Horthy being, after all, a parvenu, and in the Hungarian officers being much more categorically pro-Nazi than the Romanian officers.

In all these events, the small Hungarian resistance movement played no role. Horthy had previously established contacts with the resistance leaders, but because his own intentions were vague and the resistance movement itself weak and divided, the contacts amounted to nothing. On October 15, the resistance movement did not lift a finger against the Nazi coup d'etat.

The Horthy regime had failed: it did not protect the country against German and Soviet imperialism; it was unable to preserve its territorial reacquisitions (in fact, Hungary lost some additonal territory after World War II); it gave up half a million of its most industrious citizens to the German murder factory; it did not save the country from devastation and ruin; it did not even succeed in protecting the privileged social classes in whose interests the counterrevolution had been made. It is unlikely, however, that any other regime would have done better; some others in Hitler's Europe did definitely worse. It should be understood that the extent of material and human losses suffered by European states during the war, and their postwar treatment, depended on luck, geography, and great power politics. At no time was their postwar fate a function of wartime merits and demerits; witness the relative luck of National Socialist Austria, collaborationist France, and fascist Slovakia, but also the catastrophic experiences of anti-Nazi Poland.

Miklós Horthy himself was neither better nor worse than most other military men who emerged as political leaders in the interwar years. He was neither a fascist nor a liberal; he was not a monster, but he was not a humanitarian either. He was no democrat but never tried to be a dictator. He claimed to have been a lifelong anti-Semite; still, under his reign and despite the deportations, more Jews survived the Nazi terror, in sheer numbers, than in any other country within Hitler's Europe, except perhaps Romania. He was no more unintelligent than Marshal Pétain or Generalissimo Franco, and he was certainly less cruel than General Antonescu of Romania. Like so many other statesmen of the period, Miklós Horthy might merit a little sympathy, but he does not deserve admiration.

What followed was a half a year of agony while the Arrow Cross government persecuted the remaining Jews as well as tried to terrorize the more and more reluctant population into getting itself killed at the front. The latter was mostly a short streetcar distance away from the center of Budapest. The arrival of the undisciplined and occasionally murderously brutal and rapacious Red Army meant liberation for the Jews and the political prisoners but it became a much resented occupation for the rest of the population. All this no longer affected Horthy who was an honored prisoner of the Germans. Liberated by the Americans in the spring of 1945, he was alternately treated by the latter as an illustrious statesman and as a suspected war criminal. While in various American camps and prisons, Horthy learned to make his bed and to scrub his cantine. Tito's Yugoslavia demanded Horthy's extradition for massacres committed by local commanders of the Hungarian army in northern Yugoslavia. For these Horthy was not responsible. Fortunately for him the Hungarian government evinced no interest in having him returned to Budapest, and Stalin actually showed some sympathy for the admiral, with whom he would have been perfectly prepared to cooperate. The first antifascist government, appointed in December 1944 by the Red Army, actually included three Horthy generals, among them the prime minister. Because the Americans would not think of extraditing Horthy to Communist Yugoslavia, he was set free. He then settled in Estoril, Portugal, where he and his wife survived thanks mostly to the generosity of some Jewish friends. The admiral died a few months after the 1956 revolution in Hungary.

Jewish Assimilation: Success and Dilemma in Hungarian Politics

No other country in Europe had been as hospitable to Jewish immigration and assimilation, and no country had won more enthusiastic support from its Jews than the Hungarian kingdom. One might say that there had existed, since the revolutions of 1848–49, a silent agreement between the ruling gentry and the enlightened, educated, and patriotic segment of the Jews for a division of labor in modernizing Hungary. The Jews would contribute the investment capital, supplied by some great Western banking houses, and their own business acumen, dynamism, and diligence. Meanwhile, the non-Jewish political elite would provide the legislative and administrative assistance necessary for economic expansion.[17]

The resulting success of Jews was truly dazzling: although they constituted only 5 percent of the pre–World War I population, Jews created, owned, and managed almost all of Hungarian heavy industry and mining, and nearly every one of the great banks. They were hardly less successful in commerce, small entrepreneurship, crafts, the free professions, and all aspects of culture and the arts. By the beginning of the twentieth century they had also made significant inroads into state service, the judiciary, the officer corps, and large landownership. Assimilation for the Jewish elite increasingly took the form of intermarriage and conversion. Hungarian Jews were, as a whole, very patriotic; they supported both Emperor-King Francis Joseph and the governing conservative-liberal parties in Hungary, and they would not even think of creating a separate Jewish political organization. However, a small minority among them, mostly the sons of assimilated and successful bourgeois, chose the road of political radicalism, and it was this group that provided the revolutions of 1918–19, especially the Communist revolution, with much of their leadership. The reasons for this are complex. Suffice it to say here that these young Jewish intellectuals did not become radicalized because they felt rejected by the nation as Jews. On the contrary, they saw themselves as the vanguard of the nation; they had severed all contact with the Jewish community, and they determinedly ignored their Jewish origin.[18]

Post–World War I Hungary was not only poor but inundated by refugees from the newly lost territories. Many of these refugees were civil servants and professionals who now engaged in a desperate competition with the Jews for even the lowliest positions in commerce or the professions. This, combined with the desire to find scapegoats for the lost war, the country's dismemberment, and the frightening experience with the revolutionary Republic of Soviets, led to an explosion of middle-class anti-Semitism.

Jews As a Decisive Factor in Hungary's Relations with Nazi Germany

Jewish memory tends to divide the interwar era into three distinct periods: (1) the White Terror, marked by violence against socialists and poor peasants, and quite particularly against Jews; (2) consolidation under Prime Minister István Bethlen (1921–31), which brought a return to the legality and some of the liberal-conservative practices of the prewar era; and (3) the penetration of Nazi ideology into Hungary, followed by anti-

Semitic legislation, alliance with Germany, the Holocaust, and finally the reign of terror of the Arrow Cross government.

In reality, the lines separating the three periods were far from clear. For instance, the Bethlen era in the 1920s guaranteed economic domination by the mostly Jewish financial and industrial elite, but for Jewry in general, the era of the patriotic Gentile-Jewish symbiosis was over. Even the most moderate counterrevolutionary expressed the hope that Jews would gradually cede their positions to the growing and increasingly frustrated "Christian" middle class, and that most Jews would eventually emigrate. The 1930s, on the other hand, while they brought the fascist-style politics of Prime Minister Gyula Gömbös (1932–36), also led to a silent political alliance between the Jewish elite and conservative politicians for the containment of Nazism. Finally, the anti-Jewish laws of 1938 and 1939 can be, and have been seen by both Jews and non-Jews, either as a first step toward the complete expropriation of the Jews or as effective measures to safeguard the lives and even the modest livelihood of Jews in an increasingly Nazified Europe.

The German alliance and immense domestic pressure brought a series of anti-Semitic measures. The three laws bearing on the issue that were adopted between 1938 and 1941 can be seen either as absolute abominations or as maneuvers aimed at taking the wind out of the sails of the Germans and the domestic fascists. The truth is that while these laws visited considerable economic hardship on a number of middle-class Jews, and even led to the death of thousands in the Jewish labor formations sent to the front by the army, their destructive effect cannot be compared with the persecution that descended on the Jews in other parts of Europe. In March 1944, at a time when most of the over three million Polish Jews were dead, 95 percent of the Hungarian Jews and thousands of Jewish refugees from abroad were alive, and the Jewish factory owners and bankers in Budapest derived immense profits from the manufacture of arms for the German and Hungarian armies. In fact, whenever Hitler pushed Horthy to take drastic measures against the Hungarian Jews, the latter replied that this would bring the collapse of the Hungarian war industry.

No one likes to discuss this subject today, but it must be said here that the immediate interest of the Jews, namely survival, was not necessarily identical with the interest of the Allies, which was to defeat Germany, or with the interest of such satellite regimes as that of Hungary, for whom some resistance to German demands might conceivably have brought better treatment after the war. It is wrong to say, as some Hungarian conservative politicians are arguing today, that Hungary collaborated with the Germans mainly so as to save Jewish lives, but it is also wrong to say, as the Allies did during the war or as left-wing critics of the Horthy regime have been asserting ever since, that Hungary should have resisted the Germans outright. How was such a resistance to be achieved when arms for resisting the Germans could only have been had from Germany; when most of the army officers were Nazi sympathizers; and when the population generally expected its economic betterment from Germany? It is easy to counter, of course, that the army should have been purged and the populace reeducated, but such a statement ignores the consequences of the Peace Treaty at Trianon, the nature of Hungarian interwar politics, and the hostility of Hungary's fascist neighbors. Moreover, Horthy was correct in saying that had there been military resistance the Jewish community would have been annihilated—as it was in Poland or in the Netherlands. And while it is true that anti-Semitic legislation in Hungary prepared the way for the wholesale robbery of Jewish property in 1944 as well as for the deportation, by brutal Hungarian gendarmes, of nearly half a million Jews before the eyes of an indifferent public, it is also true that in such countries as for instance France, where there had been no anti-Semitic laws before the German occupation, thousands of Jews were also deported by brutal French gendarmes before the eyes of an indifferent public. Meanwhile, in fascist Italy, where Mussolini had introduced some anti-Semitic measures as early as 1938, the public rather sucessfully resisted the efforts of the German occupiers and their Italian henchmmen to deport the Jews to Auschwitz.

It is not easy to generalize about people of such varied convictions and interests as the heads and members of Hungary's wartime governments, or even about Regent Horthy, who personally could never decide whether he was a former Austro-Hungarian admiral steeped in a tradition of religious tolerance and admiration for all things British, or a White terrorist, who hated the bourgeois, the liberals, and the Jews, and admired Nazi Germany. A nonracist anti-Semite, Horthy had some close Jewish friends among the Budapest financial aristocracy, yet he at least tolerated, if not outright ordered, the pogroms of 1919, and and he was personally responsible for the anti-Semitic sloganeering of the counterrevolutionary movement.

It is also true, however, that both Horthy and his governments endeavored to satisfy German demands primarily through economic collaboration; that, in foreign policy, they tried to preserve a modicum of freedom; and that until Hungary's occupation by the German army on 19 March 1944, they stubbornly resisted all German demands for the extermination of the Jews.

In April 1943, at a meeting at Klessheim, Hitler demanded that Hungary finally solve the Jewish question. According to a German report on the meeting, Horthy's reply to Hitler's comment on the matter was, "What, then, should [I] do with the Jews after they have essentially been denied almost every opportunity to earn a living. Why, [I] couldn't kill them." Goebbels wrote in his diary on 8 May 1943: "The Jewish question is solved least satisfactorily by the Hungarians. The Hungarian state is permeated by Jews, and the Fuhrer did not succeed during his talk with Horthy to convince the latter of the necessity of more stringent measures. . . . He [Horthy] gave a number of humanitarian counterarguments which of course do not apply at all to this situation."[19]

How to Resist, Whom to Resist?

The lineup on the issues of collaboration and resistance was as complicated as everything else in the politics of the country. Before the German invasion of 19 March 1944, there were barely any German soldiers in the country. Therefore, violent resistance could only be directed at the Hungarian government. Such activity was engaged in only by the two revolutionary groups: the Communists and the extreme Right. But while the Communists, being insignificant in number, achieved nothing with their calls for sabotage and armed struggle against the "feudal/capitalist/ fascist" domestic oppressors, the Arrow Cross succeeded in mobilizing a large number of people, and it engaged in occasional violence. As the elections of 1939 had shown, the Arrow Cross was very popular among the miners and heavy industrial workers, and it was quite successful in organizing violent strikes around that time. Those ended only after the Germans pointed out to the Arrow Cross leaders that the strike of the fascist hard-coal miners, for instance, although officially directed against the conservative and "Jewish infested" Hungarian government, in reality mainly harmed the German war effort. All in all, both far Left and far Right were effectively controlled, until March 1944, by Minister of Interior Ferenc Keresztes-Fischer and the police, who delighted in locking up Communists and Arrow Cross agitators in the same prison cells. Also, during the war working-class discontent reached its nadir because of Horthy's territorial reacquisitions and the economic boom.

Full economic and military collaboration with the Third Reich was advocated primarily by the General Staff, the right wing of the Government Party, and paradoxically, but not illogically, a part of the Jewish establishment. The anti-Jewish legislation had not affected the owners of big business; only as a precautionary measure did they transfer a part of their shares to non-Jewish relatives and friends. All through the war, Jewish-owned industrial enterprises produced airplanes, guns, and machinery for the German armed forces, a fact that Horthy himself invoked when turning down German demands for the deportation of Jews.[20]

Beginning in 1942, when it became clear that Germany would not easily win the war, and that actually, it was very likely to lose it, Horthy and the newly appointed Prime Minister Miklós Kállay began to make plans for leaving the German alliance. This, as has been mentioned earlier, was no easy matter. The Allies were still hundreds of miles away, and surrender was likely to provoke not only a German invasion but also an invasion by pro-Nazi Romania, Slovakia, and Croatia. Furthermore, it was clear that the army and much of the public would revolt against such a decision; that all the regained territories would again be lost; that a surrender would bring the Bolsheviks into the country and that, as a consequence, the old order would collapse, along with the rest of Hungary, into ruins. On the other hand, not to find a way out of the war threatened an even worse outcome. So rather than choosing either total war on the side of Germany or surrender to an absentee enemy, Kállay's conservative government attempted to buy time for itself. Unfortunately, its emissaries were not taken seriously by the Western Allies, while their secret missions were betrayed to the Germans. Finally, after the Russian front had come too close, in the spring of 1944, and after Hitler had begun to find the presence of nearly a million Jews in Hungary intolerable, he ordered the military occupation of that country. Only Endre Bajcsy-Zsilinszky met the invaders with armed opposition: he fired his pistol at the Gestapo men who came to arrest him and was wounded during the encounter.

Because the German occupation of Hungary was followed by the Holocaust of Hungarian Jewry, the mobilization of the non-Jewish population for total war, the Soviet invasion of the country, and Hungary's destruction, Hungarians have been asking themselves ever since what could have been done to avoid it. During the first thirty years after the war, the unanimous judgment of both Communist and democratic authors was that Kállay should have turned against the Germans and ordered armed resistance, at least on the day of the German invasion. Yet such a move was scarcely possible in a country whose pro-German elements, especially within the military, wielded enormous influence and power. A more sophisticated view is that of Randolph L. Braham, the foremost historian of the Hungarian Jewish Holocaust, who wrote: "Ironically, it appears in retrospect that had Hungary continued to remain a militarily passive but politically vocal ally of the Third Reich instead of provocatively engaging in essentially fruitless, if not merely alibi-establishing, diplomatic maneuvers, the Jews of Hungary might possibly have survived the war relatively unscathed."[21]

Unfortunately, it is highly unlikely that had the Kállay government collaborated more vocally or even more assiduously, the Hungarian Jews would have escaped unscathed. The Final Solution was too important for the Germans to let so many Jews stay alive and even thrive in Central Europe. Still, Braham's statement makes clear that in 1944 at least, Jews and non-Jews did not have the same immediate interests, and the meaning and consequences of resistance and collaboration cannot be given a uniform interpretation. For the Jews, every day gained improved their chances of ultimate survival; therefore, it was not in their interest for the government to provoke German aggression by making Hungary practically neutral in 1943, and later by actually trying to withdraw from the war. But it was very much in the interest of Hungary as a whole to show, no matter how symbolically, that it was not a German satellite.

Three Great Crises

The Catastrophe on the Don

World War II thrust Hungary into a series of tragic situations that decisively influenced the country's history and left an indelible mark on its collective remembrance of the period. In the winter of 1942–43, the Red Army broke through the thinly held lines of the Second Hungarian Army on the Don River (the only Hungarian army at the front), inflicting casualties on the great majority of the 200,000 soldiers and 60,000 Jewish forced laborers in that formation.[22] In the postwar era, Communist politicians and historians described the Second Army as a fascist horde taking part in a criminal assault on the Soviet people, but they exempted the ordinary soldiers from the condemnation by characterizing them as victims. (To be precise, only dead soldiers qualified for the status of victim. Most of the survivors as well as the widows and orphans of the fallen were treated abominably in the Communist era.)

These writers claimed that the officers had deserted their men, and that the tens of thousands who fell into Soviet captivity were well treated and trained to become the builders of a better, progressive Hungary. However, already during the Communist period, under the more relaxed rule of János Kádár, a new view was allowed to surface. It still blamed the Horthy regime for participating in the criminal war but asserted that the government had deliberately sacrificed the Second Army in order to be allowed to keep the rest of its forces at home. Furthermore, it was noted, rather than being bandits and cowards, the ordinary soldiers and officers fought bravely on the Soviet front. Some officers allegedly even led their men into armed clashes with their German allies, who cruelly mistreated the Hungarians during the great retreat from the Don. In this way, the entire Second Army, from its generals on down, came to be seen as the sacrificial victim of a cunning government at home, clearly a break with the orthodox view of history as class war. More important, from that time on, the nation was allowed to mourn its dead.

The foremost advocate of this new view was the writer István Nemeskürty, whose *Requiem egy hadseregért* (Requiem for an Army) created a sensation when it appeared in 1972.[23] Half a million copies of the book were sold in a country of ten million inhabitants. Nemeskürty also asserted that the Horthy regime had deliberately staffed the Second Army with left-wing elements. This claim has since been proven wrong; in any case, the small band of left-wingers in Hungary at that time could not have made up a regiment, much less an entire army.

Since 1990 attempts have been made, as we have seen, to rehabilitate not only the Second Army but the entire wartime regime and the anti-Bolshevik campaign. The public's dilemma remains, however: Should they praise an army for its misguided bravery or those soldiers who ran away from a senseless war? Should they condemn Regent Horthy and Prime Minister Kállay for having abandoned an entire army to its fate, or laud them for refusing to sacrifice even more soldiers at the front and for wanting to strengthen the army at home for an eventual conflict with Germany?

The Failure of Resistance

Hungarians failed to resist the Germans either on 19 March 1944, when the latter occupied the country, or on 15 October of the same year, when Horthy's attempted surrender led the German SS to force his resignation and bring the Arrow Cross to power. Both Communist and democratic historians and politicians have blamed Horthy and his advisers for the failures, accusing them of cowardice and ineptitude. We are told that the regime should have established closer contacts with the resistance; that it should have armed the workers and Jewish forced laborers; and that in general, it "should have allied itself with the masses." For their part, Hungarian fascist émigrés have celebrated the events of 15 October as a clear manifestation of the nation's desire to continue the struggle against Bolshevism.

The truth seems to be that the masses were unmobilizable one way or the other, but that those with any power—the army, the civil service, and perhaps even the factory workers—preferred Germany to Bolshevik Russia. Unlike Jews and leftists, ordinary nonpolitical Hungarians had little to fear from the Germans and much to fear from the Red Army, although, of course, it would have been in Hungary's ultimate interest to help force the German army to evacuate Hungary and thus hasten the end of a devastating war.

The Holocaust and National Conscience

The most harrowing moral issue for Hungarians is the Holocaust. After the Germans occupied the country in March 1944, Horthy obediently appointed a pro-Nazi government, mostly from the right wing of the Government Party, and himself withdrew from the conducting of affairs. Upon receiving notes of protest from the all over the world about what was being done to the Jews, he finally emerged from seclusion and re-asserted his authority in July, forbidding any further deportations. By then it was too late for the Jews outside the capital, about 430,000 of whom had been deported to Auschwitz, but it was not too late for the 160,000-odd Jews in Budapest or the 100,000 to 150,000 employed by the military in forced-labor battalions.

Who helped and who resisted the deportations?[24] Adolf Eichmann, who had come to Hungary in March, commanded a team of less than two hundred SS men and secretaries; therefore, the deportation was chiefly the work of the new Hungarian government under General Döme Sztójay as well as of the provincial and municipal authorities, the cruel and greedy gendarmes, and to a certain extent, the Jewish Councils. This means that thousands of Hungarians played an active role in the deportations; conversely, there is no evidence of anyone forcibly resisting the deportations. Some county prefects and mayors resigned rather than doing the job, others were dismissed, but all were easily replaced, usually by their deputies. Most Catholic bishops and other church leaders protested in letters to the government, but only one or two went so far as to criticize openly a regime whose vast majority consisted of professing Christians. A few bishops took the risk of protesting to the Gestapo or of intervening for individuals, but only one or two tried to enter the ghetto in order to bring solace even to the "Christian" Jews there. Nor, as has been stated before, did the resistance movement undertake any action. On the other hand, many convents, monasteries, Catholic social organizations, individual priests, and thousands of civilians offered shelter to Jews who had not been deported, especially toward the end, when the Russians were near and public opinion had begun to turn against the Arrow Cross bandits.[25]

After 1945 the Communist regime attempted to dissipate the moral burden of the Holocaust largely by ignoring it and by blaming the Hitlerite fascists and Hungarian ruling circles for the persecution and death of "Communists, progressive patriots, and other victims of fascism." In Communist parlance, the nearly half a million Jewish dead had become merely "the other victims."

A breakthrough came in the 1970s with the appearance of a few novels and historical studies that dared to present the Jews as the primary victims of fascism. Then, at last, the responsibility of the general public began to be debated, if rather cautiously, and statistical data on the extent of the disaster began to appear. But even in this period, the otherwise innovative and courageous historian György Ránki did not feel free to devote more than about five pages to the Holocaust in his 1,400-page *History of Hungary, 1918–45.*[26]

Both Ránki and others took it for granted that the survivors would remain Hungarians; none raised the question of whether the Holocaust had effectively undone the one-and-a-half-century-old tacit alliance between the Hungarian liberal gentry and the modernistic segment of the Jews. Today, however, nothing stands in the way of free debate, and it rages on, with some young Jews concluding, from the Holocaust and postwar manifestations of anti-Semitism, that the only solution for Jews remaining in Hungary is to claim ethnic minority status. The great majority of Jews, however, still believe in assimilation and prove it by marrying non-Jews and making themselves virtually indistinguishable from other Hungarians. Moreover, public opinion surveys show that the great majority of non-Jews are willing to live with and even marry Jews. In other words, the Hungarian Jewish community, variously estimated at between 15,000 and 100,000, is likely to disappear into the Hungarian nation.

On the non-Jewish side, rational opinions about the Holocaust range all the way from the sincerest contrition to claims that the deportations were the work of the Germans and only a few Hungarian traitors. The latter view was generally the position of a center-right governmental coalition in the early 1990s. On the extreme right, of course, there are those who deny the whole thing. Although the latter position is patently absurd, it is true that numerically more Jews survived in Hungary than in any other country, except perhaps Romania, of what was once Hitler's Europe, and a number of these survivors have played a most conspicuous role in the politics, ecomomy, and culture of post–World War II Hungary.

On 19 March 1944 there were some 825,000 persons in Hungary who, according to the country's 1941 Nuremberg-type law, were considered racially Jewish. This figure included nearly 100,000 persons who had converted to Christianity or whose parents had already done so. It also included Jewish refugees from Austria, Slovakia, Croatia, Romania, and Poland, whom the Hungarian government had harbored until that time.[27]

Clearly, not all the Jews were deported to Auschwitz, not even all those from outside Budapest, for about 150,000 men between the ages of eighteen and forty-eight had been called up for labor service within the army from all over the country, and ultimately a large proportion of these survived the war. It was one of the many paradoxes of the period that the

Nazi-infested army, which was guilty of the cruel death of thousands of Jewish forced laborers on the Eastern front in 1942–43, deliberately or inadvertantly saved the lives of Jewish males in 1944 by calling them up for service even while their families were being packed into cattle cars.[28]

A further dilemma for judging the period is precisely how to evaluate the army's conscription of Jews, including thousands of medical doctors and other professionals, as slave laborers. On the face of it, nothing could seem more objectionable, and it has been so treated by the historians of the Holocaust. But what exactly was the army to do? It would have been as unthinkable for it not to call up young Jewish males while non-Jews were being drafted for service at the front as it was for it to send Jews to fight shoulder to shoulder with the Nazis.[29] In fact, the Germans often objected to the spectacle of Hungarian Jews at the front, for even if the labor service men were not in uniform, they wore Hungarian military caps and marched in military formation. This, at a time when Polish and other Eastern Jews had long been gassed. The trouble was that many, although by far not all, military commanders horribly mistreated the Jewish forced laborers. At the end, and this is crucial, forced labor proved to be a life-saving device for many thousands.

Whether or not Jews should have resisted the deportations, and whether or not the Jewish Councils were guilty of collaboration with the authorities have been the subject of international debate since World War II. Hungarian historians of the Holocaust, especially Randolph Braham, are very critical of the Hungarian Jewish Council, which, according to them, failed to warn the Jews in the countryside of their impending doom. Rather, it called on them to obey orders.[30] This subject, too, would require another essay. The fact that the Hungarian government protected the Jews until 19 March 1944, and then again between August and October, meant that the Germans and Hungarian Nazis had very little time to proceed with the Final Solution, the shortest time available for this undertaking anywhere in Axis Europe. Hence the 40 percent survival rate. The Jewish leadership gambled on Hungarian protection, and, as was the case in many other countries, the gamble neither paid off completely nor failed completely. As for wartime Hungary's leaders, some well deserved their execution after the war; others amply merited the gratitude of the Jewish community; still others, among them Regent Horthy, deserved to be both commended and imprisoned.

There is no denying that Jewish willingness to do absolutely anything to avoid the Final Solution effectively assisted the German war effort and thus prolonged the war. How important Jewish-owned industry was for the German military is proven by the fact that following the occupation of Hungary, the SS negotiated a secret deal, in April–May 1944, with a consortium of Hungarian Jewish bankers and industrialists. According to the terms of that agreement, the closely related Baron Weiss, Baron Kornfeld, Mauthner, Chorin, and other Jewish aristocratic families ceded their combined properties to Himmler's SS in exchange for a considerable sum in U.S. dollars and German marks and a plane flight for their families to neutral Portugal. The SS scrupulously respected the agreement even to the point of forging Hungarian passports as well as Portuguese visas and transporting the families to safety in chartered Lufthansa passenger planes. As a result, almost all of Hungarian heavy industry and its armaments industry in particular, including a large factory producing Messerschmidt fighter planes, passed into the hands of the SS, if only for a few months. All this took place behind the back of the Hungarian government.[31]

Epilogue and Conclusion

After the failure of Horthy's attempt to surrender on 15 October 1944, and after the Red Army had shown itself unstoppable, neither Hungary as a whole nor the Jews in particular had anything to gain from collaboration with the Germans, economic or otherwise. Nor was there any point in obeying the puppet Arrow Cross government led by that exalted fool, Ferenc Szálasi. At last, both Jews and non-Jews had the same interest in getting rid of the Germans and the Arrow Cross as soon as possible and in preparing for the reconstruction of the country under Soviet occupation. Now, there was some genuine resistance activity by army officers, intellectuals, Zionists, and a few Soviet-backed partisan groups. Their accomplishments were minimal and their casualty rate very high, but under the circumstances this was the only decent thing anyone could have done. The general population continued to be passive, but there were fewer people willing to offer active support to the SS and the murderous Arrow Cross militia. The latter, incidentally, was made up mostly of teenagers and hoodlums.

In Budapest, the war lasted until 13 February 1945, when the last German soldiers were killed or captured after a long siege. By then, the majority of Hungarian soldiers had surrendered or simply gone home, although a few hundred thousand of them withdrew with the Germans and were finally captured by the Western Allies in Germany. Since the Germans never surrendered and the siege of Budapest lasted nearly two months, the city was in ruins, as was much of the rest of the country.

Because of the many frontier changes during and after the war, and the collapse, in 1944–45, of all governmental institutions, no one knows how many Hungarian citizens perished during the war or even who exactly should be counted as a Hungarian citizen. The same incertitude applies to statistical data on Jewish casualties. Some surviving deportees were not reported in the statistics because they had emigrated directly from Germany; thousands had been in hiding during the months of persecution and never reported their survival to the authorities; thousands of others figured simultaneously as casualty and/or survivor statistics in postwar Hungary, Romania, Czechoslovakia, or the Soviet Union. Several hundred thousand non-Jewish Hungarians also perished in the war, a very large part of them in Soviet POW camps.

The arrival of the Red Army brought liberation to the political prisoners and the Jews. The others could at best feel relieved that the active fighting was over. Yet no one could really feel free, for aside from a great deal of looting and raping, the Red Army immediately made itself feared by its practice of arresting and dragging away thousands of civilians, women as well as men. Since the Red Army soldiers showed little interest in distinguishing one Hungarian from another, underground Communists and Jewish survivors of the Nazi concentration camps were almost as likely as the rest to fall victim. The civilian deportees were taken to Russia, together with the captured Hungarian soldiers and Jewish forced laborers, where the majority of them died.

Within a few years of the war's end, it became immaterial whether one had been a leftist, a centrist, or a rightist under the old regime. The Communists recruited thousands of so-called Little Fascists into their party; at the same time, they persecuted liberals, Social Democrats, and, especially after 1949, even fellow Communists. All this makes the Hungarian historical memory of this era resemble a confusing and terrifying nightmare. Did the Jewish forced laborer turned Communist political police officer have the right to torture Arrow Cross criminals? Whose fate was more to be bemoaned, that of the Jew gassed at Auschwitz, or that of the peasant draftee who died of starvation in a Soviet POW camp? Who were the nation's worst enemies, the fascists or the Stalinists?

No one is sure of the use of historical memory, aside from providing historians, journalists, writers, and filmmakers with a livelihood. In Hungary, at least, one of the things history teaches Hungarians is that it is a terrible mistake to be a small country in Central Europe. Not only can it make the nation a helpless tool in the hands of others, but it can also bring out the worst in members of that small nation. The other lesson these events teach us, however, is that once a regime abandons the path of decency and legality, it cannot expect the population to rally behind the flag of decency and legality when there is a national emergency. The counterrevolutionary regime of Admiral Horthy had taught the population to discriminate against some of its fellow citizens and to take for granted the redistribution of property on the basis of denominational membership and race. It had also taught the population to accept gifts of land from another power in exchange for at least a partial surrender of national sovereignty. The ensuing moral corruption and public indifference devastated the social elite and the nation as a whole in 1944 and thereafter. Even though Hungary was too small and too exposed to avoid the bloodshed and destruction of World War II, conditions could have been improved, especially for the persecuted, had the population shown more compassion and courage than it actually did.

World War II was a shameful episode in the history of the nation: small wonder that even today the public does not know how to live with its memory.

Notes

1. Not surprisingly, there exist only propagandistic biographies of Endre Ságvári, written for children or for adults being treated as children. See, for instance, Ottó Hámori, *Endri: Történetek Ságvári Endre életéből* (Endri. Tales from the Life of E. S.) (Budapest, 1957). The police record regarding the attempt to arrest Ságvári is reproduced in a documentary collection: János Harsányi, ed., *A magyar szabadságharcosok a fasizmus ellen* (The Hungarian Freedom Fighters against Fascism) (Budapest, 1966), 310–11.

On the Hungarian Communist movement, see especially Bennett Kovrig, *Communism in Hungary: From Kun to Kádár* (Stanford, Calif., 1979); Miklós Molnár, *From Béla Kun to János Kádár: Seventy Years of Hungarian Communism*, Arnold J. Pomerans, trans. (New York, 1990); and Charles Gati, *Hungary and the Soviet Bloc* (Durham, N.C., 1986).

2. General literature on the Hungarian anti-Nazi resistance is not much better than literature on Endre Ságvári. The best known such work, Gyula Kállai, *A magyar függetlenségi mozgalom* (The Hungarian Independence Movement) (Budapest, 1978), has as its main merit that having been published in 1979, it is a shade less biased than works written in Stalinist times.

A member of the Communist resistance during World War II, Kállai was jailed under Mátyás Rákosi's Stalinist regime in the early 1950s and rose to political prominence again in the 1960s under his fellow "home-grown Communist," János Kádár.

3. On this, see the articles of Peter Gosztonyi in *Menora-Egyenlőség* (Toronto, Ont.) (June 1974, and 30 June 1979), and Randolph L. Braham, *The Politics of Genocide: The Holocaust in Hungary*, rev. ed. (New York, 1994), 1127–28.

4. On the conservative-nationalist government of the years 1990–1994, and its defeat at the May 1994 elections, see István Deák, "Post-Post-Communist Hungary," the *New York Review of Books* (11 August 1994).

5. On the events of 15 October 1944, see Ágnes Rozsnyói, *A Szálasi-puccs* (The Coup d'Etat of Szálasi) (Budapest, 1977); Elek Karsai, ed., *Szálasi naplója*

(The Diary of Szálasi) (Budapest, 1978); Károly Vigh, *Ugrás a sötétbe* (Leap into the Dark) (Budapest, 1985); and Géza Lakatos, *Ahogy én láttam* (As I Saw It) (Budapest, 1992).

6. Of the many brief histories of Hungary in a Western language, here are some of the more recent and more successful: C. A. Macartney, *Hungary: A Short History* (Chicago, 1962); Péter Hanák, ed., *One Thousand Years: A Concise History of Hungary* (Budapest, 1988), and Peter F. Sugar, ed., *A History of Hungary* (Bloomington and Indianapolis, 1990). The latter, intended as a collegiate textbook, is a collaborative work in which experts expand on the historical periods discussed in this essay.

The two most important recent histories of modern Hungary in English are Jörg K. Hoensch, *A History of Modern Hungary, 1867–1986*, Kim Traynor, trans. (London and New York, 1988), and Andrew C. Janos, *The Politics of Backwardness in Hungary, 1825–1945* (Princeton, 1982). See also, István Deák, "The Historiography of Hungary," *The American Historical Review* 97: 4 (October 1992): 1041–63.

7. Some of the more important works on the revolutions of 1918–1919 are Tibor Hajdu, *The Hungarian Soviet Republic* (Budapest, 1979); Peter Pastor, *Hungary between Wilson and Lenin: The Hungarian Revolutions of 1918–1919 and the Big Three* East European Monographs, 20 (Boulder, Colo., 1976); Peter Pastor, ed., *Revolutions and Interventions in Hungary and Its Neighboring States, 1918–1919*, East European Monographs, 240 (Boulder, Colo., 1988); Rudolf Tökés, *Béla Kun and the Hungarian Soviet Republic* (New York and Washington, 1967); and Iván Völgyes, ed., *Hungary in Revolution, 1918–19: Nine Essays* (Lincoln, Nebr., 1971).

8. Nicholas Horthy, *Ein Leben für Ungarn* (Bonn, 1953). The English translation, uninspiringly entitled, *Miklós Horthy, Memoirs*, appeared in New York in 1957.

9. Thomas Sakmyster, *Hungary's Admiral on Horseback: Miklós Horthy, 1918–44*, East European Monographs, 396 (Boulder, Colo., 1994).

10. On the subject of officers' memoirs, see István Deák, *Beyond Nationalism: A Social and Political History of the Habsburg Officer Corps, 1848–1918* (New York-Oxford, 1990), 213–24.

11. On the Treaty of Trianon in June 1920, see Francis Deak, *Hungary at the Paris Peace Conference* (New York, 1942); Béla K. Király, Peter Pastor, and Ivan Sanders, eds., *Essays on World War I: Total War and Peacemaking, a Case Study on Trianon* (New York, 1982); and Mária Ormos, *From Padua to the Trianon, 1918–20* (New York, 1990).

12. Here is a sampling of the rather rich literature, in a Western language, on Hungary in the interwar period: István Deák, "The Historical Foundations: The Development of Hungary from 1918 until 1945," in Klaus-Detlev Grothusen, ed., *Ungarn*, "Südosteuropa-Handbuch," 5 (Göttingen, 1987) 36–66; Mario D. Fenyö, *Hitler, Horthy, and Hungary: German-Hungarian Relations, 1941–44* (New Haven-London, 1972); Gyula Juhász, *Hungarian Foreign Policy, 1919–45* (Budapest, 1979); Stephen Kertesz, *Diplomacy in a Whirlpool: Hungary between Nazi Germany and Soviet Russia* (Notre Dame, 1953); Kovrig, *Communism in Hungary*; C. A. Macartney, *Hungary and Her Successors: The Treaty of Trianon*

and Its Consequences, 1919–37 (New York, 1937), and *A History of Hungary, 1929–45*, 2 vols. (New York, 1956–57); and Zsuzsa L. Nagy, *The Liberal Opposition in Hungary, 1919–45* (Budapest, 1983).

13. László Karsai, ed., *Kirekesztők* (Excluders) (Budapest, 1992); and *Befogadók* (Welcomers) (Budapest, 1993), the first volume being a compendium of anti-Semitic and the second of philo-Semitic statements.

14. In his circular, dated October 1932, Horthy charged the Bolsheviks with the sinking of the Titanic in 1912 as well as with having arranged railroad accidents and the disappearance of statesmen. In another letter, addressed to Czechoslovak president Thomas G. Masaryk, he challenged the latter to a duel, or if Masaryk was too old and sick, then he, Horthy, would be willing to fight Foreign Minister Edvard Beneš under the most severe conditions, without bothering to ask whether Beneš was qualified to give satisfaction in a chivalrous encounter and leaving the choice of weapons to his despised opponent. It seems that better council prevailed, and neither of these letters was actually mailed. On all this, see Miklós Szinai and László Szücs, eds., *The Confidential Papers of Admiral Horthy* (Budapest, 1965), 54–58, and 79–80.

15. Back in February 1942, Horthy had his son István elected by parliament as vice-regent. It remains unclear whether this was done, as the far Right and the far Left claimed, in order to create a Horthy dynasty, or whether the main purpose was to prevent a fascist takeover following the death of the regent. The fact is that István Horthy was a liberal and a friend of the Jews, and he hated the Nazis. His accidental death at the front as a combat pilot, in August 1942, was a tragedy for Hungary.

16. On the brief Arrow Cross rule between 16 October 1944 and, in western Hungary, late in March 1945, see Margit Szöllősi-Janze, *Die Pfeilkreuzlerbewegung in Ungarn: Historischer Kontext, Entwicklung, und Herrschaft* (Munich, 1989). Also, Karsai, *Szálasi naplója*, and Éva Teleki, *Nyilas uralom Magyarországon* (Arrow Cross Rule in Hungary) (Budapest, 1974). The best documentary collection on the subject is that of Elek Karsai and László Karsai, eds., *A Szálasi per* (The Trial of Szálasi) (Budapest, 1988). See also, Karsai, *Szálasi naplója*.

17. On the history of the Hungarian Jews, see especially Braham, *The Politics of Genocide*, and by the same author, as editor, *Hungarian-Jewish Studies*, 3 vols. (New York, 1966–73), as well as William O. McCagg Jr., *Jewish Nobles and Geniuses in Modern Hungary*, East European Monographs, 3 (Boulder, Colo., 1972; 2d ed., New York, 1986); Péter Hanák, ed., *Zsidókérdés, asszimiláció, antiszemitizmus* (The Jewish Question, Assimilation, Anti-Semitism) (Budapest, 1984); and István Bibó, *Zur Judenfrage am Beispiel Ungarns nach 1944*, Béla Rásky, trans. (Frankfurt/Main, 1990) The original of this volume appeared in Hungarian, in 1948, as *Zsidókérdés Magyarországon 1944 után*. A sociologist and political writer, István Bibó (1911–79) opposed both the Nazis and the Communists. Following the Soviet armed intervention against the revolutionary Imre Nagy government on 4 November 1956, he alone of all the members of the cabinet remained at his post until finally ousted by János Kádár's Soviet-supported counterrevolutionary regime. Subsequently, he spent six years in jail, which fatally undermined his health. Bibó is seen today as the best and most judicious

analyst of Hungarian society and politics in the interwar and immediate post–World War II periods.

Elek Karsai, ed., *Vádirat a nácizmus ellen* (Bill of Indictment against Nazism), 3 vols. (Budapest, 1958–67), is an important documentary collection on the persecution of Jews in Hungary.

18. On the role of Jews in the Hungarian Republic of Soviets, see Charles Gati, *Hungary and the Soviet Bloc* (Durham, N.C., 1986), 100–107.

19. The Horthy statement is cited in, among others, Lani Yahil, *The Holocaust: The Fate of European Jewry* (New York, 1992), 499. The Goebbels diary entry is in Louis P. Lochner, ed., *The Goebbels Diaries, 1942–43* (Garden City, N.J, 1948), 357.

20. The most important German document regarding Horthy's unbending position regarding the Jews of Hungary at Klessheim in April 1943 is reproduced in Randolph L. Braham, ed., *The Destruction of Hungarian Jewry: A Documentary Account*, 2 vols., (New York, 1963), 1965–66. For a historical account of what happened at Klessheim, see Fenyö, *Hitler, Horthy, and Hungary*, 124–30.

21. Braham, *The Politics of Genocide*, 233–34.

22. Let me note here that statistical data on such things as the number of Second Army soldiers and forced laborers, or the casualties they suffered, or the number of Hungarian Jews gassed at Auschwitz, or the total number of wartime Jewish dead, are not much better than guesses. There exists no reliable information on these subjects.

On Hungary's military participation in World War II see, among others, Ferenc Adonyi, *A magyar katona a második világháborúban, 1941–45* (The Hungarian Soldier in World War II (Klagenfurt, 1954); Jenő Czebe and Tibor Pethő, *Hungary in World War II: A Military History of the Years of War* (Budapest, 1946); and Peter Gosztonyi, *Der Kampf um Budapest, 1944–45* (Munich, 1964).

23. Budapest, 1972.

24. The best study of the Hungarian Holocaust is Braham, *Genocide in Hungary*. See also, R. L. Braham and Béla Vágó, eds., *The Holocaust in Hungary: Forty Years Later* (New York, 1985) and the documentary collection edited by Braham, *The Destruction of Hungarian Jewry*. See also, István Deák, "Could the Hungarian Jews Have Survived?" in Michael R. Marrus, ed., *The Nazi Holocaust*, 4 vols. (Westport/London, 1989), 4:504–23; and László Karsai and Judit Molnár, eds., *Az Endre-Baky-Jaross per* (The Endre, Baky, Jaross Trial) (Budapest, 1994). The three men tried in 1945–46 by the People's Court in Budapest were the chief Hungarian officials charged with deporting Jews in May–July 1944.

25. On this, see Jenő Lévai, *L'Église ne s'est pas tue: Le dossier hongrois 1940–45*. Intro. and trans. by L. Bolgár and T. Schreiber (Paris, 1966).

26. György Ránki, ed., *Magyarország története, 1918–19, 1919–45* (History of Hungary, 1918–19, 1919–45), "Magyarország története tíz kötetben," 8 (Budapest, 1976).

27. Note, however, that between fourteen thousand and sixteen thousand Jews whose citizenship was in doubt were expelled from Hungary to Galicia in 1941 where they were massacred by the SS.

28. On Jewish forced labor in the Hungarian army, see Randolph L. Braham,

The Hungarian Labor Service System, 1939–45, East European Monographs, 31 (Boulder, Colo., 1977). Also, the documentary collection by Elek Karsai, ed., *"Fegyvertelenül álltak az aknamezőkön": Dokumentumok a munkaszolgálat történetéhez Magyarországon* ("Weaponless They Stood on the Minefields": Documents on the History of Labor Service in Hungary) (Budapest, 1962).

29. It is true, however, that because Finland did not discriminate against its Jews, at least three hundred members of that tiny community (two thousand in total) fought during World War II, in Finnish uniform, alongside the German army. See Hannu Rautkallio, "Finland," in Israel Gutman, ed., *Encyclopedia of the Holocaust*, 4 vols. (New York, 1990), 493.

30. See Braham, *The Politics of Genocide*, chapter 14.

31. On this so-called Manfréd Weiss Affair, see Braham, *Politics of Genocide*, 514–24; György Ránki, *1944 március 19* (19 March 1944) (Budapest, 1978): 225–30; and Elek Karsai and Miklós Szinai, "A Weiss Manfréd vagyon német kézbe kerülésének története" (The History of the German Acquisition of the Manfréd Weiss Fortune), *Századok* (Budapest), 95, 4–5 (1961), 680–719.

JAN T. GROSS

A Tangled Web:
Confronting Stereotypes Concerning
Relations between Poles, Germans,
Jews, and Communists

THE YEARS of the Second World War were among the most consequential in all of Polish history. As a result of war the country suffered a demographic catastrophe without precedent. It lost its minorities—Jews in the Holocaust, and Ukrainians and Germans following border shifts and population movements after the war. A third of its urban residents were missing at the conclusion of the war, either killed or exiled abroad. Poland's elites were wiped out. Fifty-five percent of its lawyers were no more, along with 40 percent of its medical doctors, one third of its university professors and Roman Catholic clergy.[1] The scale of material devastation matched that of population loss. Then the postwar generation was raised on war movies, war-themes-obsessed literature, and official propaganda studded with (West) German/Nazi/fascist villains and Soviet/Russian/communist heroes. Needless to say, everyone had their share of wartime family stories either to tell or to listen to.

For all the impact it made and the coverage it received, as long as the communists held the reigns of power in Poland, the Second World War was a deeply politicized subject. And despite a multitude of excellent monographs on a wide range of topics, historiography of the war could not grapple with fundamental subjects—such as the regime of Soviet occupation from 1939 till 1941 in the eastern half of the country, for example, or the makeup and politics of the underground state loyal to the government-in-exile in London, or even the Warsaw Uprising staged by the Home Army (AK) in August and September 1944, when 250,000 civilian casualties were suffered in the city while the Red Army, poised across the Vistula river dividing Warsaw, offered no support to embattled city residents and refused landing rights to Allied planes bringing supplies to the insurgents. Émigré historiography tried to fill the gaps, and over the years scholars established in Western academia wrote important studies on Polish subjects as well. But a free circulation of ideas was impeded, as was, of course, a free circulation of scholars, who would be frequently denied passports, or visas, and access to indispensable sources. As a result, the 1939–1948 decade is a vast open field for historical research, with new fascinating archival collections newly accessible in Poland, Russia, and the Ukraine. Important synthetic studies are yet to be written on the period.

In what follows I will take one thread—the history of Polish-Jewish relations in this fateful decade—in order to confront the stereotyped thinking prevailing on this subject in Polish historiography. Of all the wartime topics involving staggering human suffering and loss of life (Warsaw Uprising, deportations, Katyń, the Home Army—to use a few code words) that were hotly contested among official historiography, émigré authors, and writers who increasingly published in the uncensored samizdat during the 1970s and 1980s, this one has not stimulated in the émigré literature or among the uncensored publications a single piece of writing that could not have appeared in the then government-owned publishing houses in Poland. There was, apparently, a consensus of sorts that the matter had been sorted out and did not need to be revisited. And when in 1987 an eminent literary scholar, Jan Błoński, published a thoughtful essay entitled "The Poor Poles Look at the Ghetto" (in a reference to Czesław Miłosz's poem "The Poor Christians Look at the Ghetto"), the public reaction was loud and clear. The venerable Catholic weekly *Tygodnik Powszechny*, which put it in print, was overwhelmed with letters of protest from its readers and was compelled to publish "A Reply to Jan Błoński," authored by a distinguished attorney, who in the past defended several oppositionists in political trials and had been sentenced himself to death by a Stalinist court in the 1950s.[2] On this occasion he felt compelled to defend the "good name" of his compatriots who were collectively slandered, he believed, by Błoński's suggestion that Poles shared responsibility for the genocide of Jews. "[P]articipation and shared responsibility," wrote Błoński, "are not the same thing. One can share the responsibility for the crime without taking part in it. Our responsibility is for holding back, for insufficient effort to resist."[3] Clearly, the issue could not be revisited without stirring up powerful emotions. And so, it has been left in limbo for most of the time, with predictable consequences. When a random sample of a thousand Poles was asked in 1993, "Do you think that during the war the Jewish nation suffered as much as the Polish nation, or more, or less?" 6 percent of the respondents answered that the Polish nation suffered more, 32 percent that both nations suffered about the same, 12 percent that they could not compare, and 3 percent that they could not tell.[4] Thus, apparently, fifty years after the war, over half of the Polish society does not know that Polish Jews were wiped out during the Holocaust.

Polish-Jewish Relations under the German Occupation

A noted public intellectual, historian of literature, and essayist, Jan Józef
Lipski, had written and spoken on the subject of Polish-Jewish relations
on many occasions. Indeed one of his essays, entitled "Two Fatherlands,
Two Patriotisms—Remarks about Xenophobia and Self-centeredness of
the Poles," has been recognized as a masterpiece that boldly confronted
various deceptively simplistic and one-sided patriotic stereotypes.[5] In a
concise statement delivered in April 1983, at the fortieth Warsaw Ghetto
Uprising anniversary celebration, after acknowledging that the Polish
underground offered but token, symbolic military assistance to the fighting Jews, Lipski goes on as follows:

> The conscience of the Polish nation would be sick and mortally wounded if we
> did not ask ourselves another question: even if not with weapons in hand did
> we at least do as much as was possible to help and save the Jews? Paying
> homage to the ghetto fighters, as well as to its defenseless inhabitants who had
> been killed, we also have the right and duty to pay homage to those Poles who
> lost their lives while helping the Jews. There were many Poles who had died a
> heroic death for their contribution to this most dangerous—aspect of the Polish
> war. For daring to get involved, they are most deserving of admiration. Ex-
> traordinary courage was required at the time in Poland to join in this struggle.
> Can everyone of millions of ordinary people be expected to behave as a hero?
>
> And yet, there are times, and causes, that demand heroism. We, who remem-
> ber, let us ask ourselves if there was not too much indifference—even though
> mixed up with fear, but indifference nonetheless? Did we all do as much as was
> possible, or less, or nothing at all in those times when dying people and our
> own moral norms called for doing more than was possible? Yet Poles are often
> wronged when, in the world, too far reaching generalizations are drawn con-
> cerning the collaboration of some Poles in the tracking down of the Jews, or
> blackmailing them. Criminal and amoral social margins exist in every commu-
> nity, and among their victims at the time in Poland were not only Jews but also
> general Grot Rowecki [commander of the underground Home Army, AK] and
> thousands of other soldiers of the anti-Nazi conspiracy. We should reject irre-
> sponsible generalizations in this matter, just as we should reject generalizations
> that wrong other nations. Anti-Polonism is not morally any better than anti-
> Semitism or anti-Ukrainianism."[6]

What strikes in Lipski's statement—composed of one question and
two almost equal in length paragraphs—is his search for balance, for
equivalencies. In the first paragraph, he examines, roughly speaking, attitudes. He tells us that while there may have been too much indifference
among the Poles vis-à-vis the plight of the Jews, the Poles also demon-

strated extraordinary heroism in assisting the Jews. In the second paragraph, he examines, roughly speaking, behavior. Some Poles—a criminal
margin—undoubtedly victimized Jews, but these Poles also victimized
other Poles. Furthermore, Lipski points to the extraordinary quality of
the Polish victims of denunciations. Thus, a further impression of equiva-
lence is conveyed as, on the one hand, we have the overwhelming number of Jewish dead but on the other, a smaller no doubt, yet exclusive,
self-selected group of freedom fighters—a general and thousands of soldiers. Then, in the final point, we are taken beyond the wartime period
to find out that the Jews have actually victimized the Poles as well. For
those "irresponsible generalizations" that one may come upon "in the
world" are spread by Jews—Lipski says so explicitly in his speech at Warsaw University in 1981 for example—and, as we learn from the last coda
of this paragraph "anti-Polonism is not morally any better than anti-
Semitism."

As to the question opening the quote—*the important question* that we
must answer in order to confront the subject matter of Polish-Jewish relations during the war—it is left suspended in midair. Lipski identifies the
issue—did Poles offer as much assistance and help to the Jews as was
possible?—but he does not answer his own question. Neither does he
volunteer to prescribe a norm: there are times, he argues, that mandate
heroism, and yet, he says, we cannot expect ordinary people to behave
heroically; nor does he provide us with an unambiguous description of
what had actually happened: Poles, according to him, were too passive,
and extraordinarily heroic at the same time.

In spite of the limitations of Lipski's argument, it is appealing that in
his statements he does not close off the issue. There is a certain hesitation,
and thus an opening of sorts, in his texts as when he says, for example,
that "the evaluation of how Poles behaved vis-à-vis the Jews during
World War II cannot be, unfortunately, 'simple and unambiguous.'"[7] And
he can be quite daring when he states, for example, that "a significant
part of [Polish] society was neutral, oblivious, to the extermination of the
Jews." "Have we never heard during the occupation," he asks, "the sentence 'after the war monuments will be built for Hitler'"—presumably to
celebrate Hitler's "solution" of the Jewish problem.[8] But, admirable as
they are in their sincerity, these observations do not serve as starting
points of inquiry: what did it mean to be "oblivious" to the spectacle of
the Holocaust in wartime Poland? How large was the "significant part"
quoted in his assessment? How did anti-Semitism manifest itself during
the occupation? Lipski perpetuates the irrelevant (in the light of the question he had himself posed) framework of the discussion where the socially
marginal phenomenon of extortionism from Jews (*szmalcownictwo*)[9] is
contrasted with the socially marginal phenomenon of heroism (i.e., active

assistance to the hiding Jews), while the investigation concerning attitudes and behavior of the missing in-between—that is, the vast majority of the Polish society—is left undone.

The standard commentary on Polish attitudes toward the Jews includes one very powerful argument that deserves closer scrutiny. It establishes, with compelling force, that Poles did on Jews' behalf as much as could have been expected. Continues Lipski:

> I know people who were caught by the Germans while wielding weapons and who survived concentration camps. But I don't know anybody who survived after being caught when hiding a Jew. There is more to it: a soldier in the Home Army knew that in case of arrest he would be tortured, his wife might be arrested, that he would probably be executed; but he could hope that his children would survive. Those who were hiding Jews could not even hope for this.[10]

The punishment for helping Jews during the German occupation in Poland was death. Entire families were executed if Jews were found hiding in their houses or apartments. Such is the truth about those times. Is it, therefore, surprising that Poles generally obeyed the German injunction? The answer to this question would be relatively easy—no, it is not surprising—but for the fact that there were other kinds of activities prohibited by the Nazis under penalty of death that the Poles massively engaged in. Simply: if we adopt a certain framework for the explanation of people's behavior it must be consistently applicable across the whole range of comparable choices in a given situation. And while we need not match every episode of one kind of behavior with another (which should also be covered by the purported explanation), a wide discrepancy in frequencies would indicate that we did not identify a correct underlying mechanism.

And thus, while helping out the Jews was probably the most difficult and daring of wartime pursuits—because it was so irrevocably sanctioned with death, and because one's family was inevitably endangered as well—one could argue that the "cost" difference between joining an anti-Nazi conspiracy and helping out the Jews was frequently marginal. The comparison is spelled out in the just quoted passage: for a conspirator there is death following torture, arrest of a wife or a husband, and as he or she would be interrogated as well, most likely there is a torture session in store for the spouse, maybe even death or a concentration camp. The child would survive, though orphaned and traumatized. For helping out a Jew the whole family died, though without being tortured.

Once again—while remembering that we are merely weighing merits of an argument, not real motivations of people who actually had to make these horrifying choices—one could point out that while undeniably, for individuals with a large family, there was a difference between the projected costs of the two courses of action, for childless couples it would have been rather subtle; and for single men and women, especially those who did not live with their parents, it would have been altogether negligible. And is it indeed the case that these Poles, unburdened as yet by family obligations and already independent, presumably mostly young, engaged in anti-Nazi conspiracy with a zeal commensurate to their efforts on behalf of the Jews?

Besides, let us not forget that collective responsibility was widely used by the Germans in their efforts to stamp out conspiratorial activity and, more generally, in order to enforce compliance with numerous regulations. Poland, as stated earlier, suffered proportionally the largest casualties of all the belligerents. In addition to three million Polish Jews, over two million other citizens died of war-related causes. Many thousands were shot in public executions throughout occupied Poland in reprisal for various forms of resistance. How many among them fell for hiding the Jews? It turns out, that "[o]ne cannot precisely determine the number of Poles who lost their lives in the defence of Jews. Sz. Datner in his book *The Forest of the Righteous (Las Sprawideliwych)* enumerates over *one hundred* [emphasis mine] documented cases; information about executions is also provided by W. Bartoszewski, and Z. Lewinówna as well as S. Wroński and M. Zwolakowa."[11] Even assuming that each known case stands for a family (i.e., three or four people who were put to death) the volume of casualties suffered by the Poles as a result of involvement in anti-German conspiracies would be, roughly speaking, a hundredfold greater! Why is it then that so many people pursued conspiratorial activity in Poland and so few were involved in actively helping out the Jews? Why is it that in the memory of witnesses who lived through the war, bringing assistance to Jews appears, in retrospect, as far more risky and daunting than joining the underground network? Clearly, some other factor must have been at play as well for we may not explain the difference solely by reference to the perceived threat of German sanctions.[12]

To my mind the stereotypical diagnosis of Polish-Jewish relations during the war is misleading both in terms of the general image it conveys as well as in terms of the particulars it advocates. Here is the general picture that I read into this position: in the midst of a situation that was utterly unprecedented—namely, a whole nation being put to death by a group of human beings who systematically, deliberately, and over a long period of time applied themselves to this task—in the midst of this scandal of inhuman proportions there exists yet another group of people that keeps its sanity and, on the whole, maintains a balanced judgment. It is on the whole reasonable. It fears sanctions that ought to be feared. Common sense is invoked to explicate the behavior of Polish society when confronted with the extermination of the Jews. The uniqueness of the situation is removed and a straightforward cost-benefit analysis is introduced, plus an observation about the normal distribution of moral character in a population (a "social margin" of heroes who helped the Jews, and a "social margin" of scum who blackmailed them). Thus, there are innocuous causes explaining Poles' behavior vis-à-vis the Jews during the Second World War, a behavior that was also, on the whole, innocuous and easily understandable.

Thankfully the poet rings alarm bells. "Next to the atrocious facts" of the Holocaust, says Czesław Miłosz in his Norton lectures, "the very idea of literature seems indecent."[13] How does the idea of cost-benefit calculation fare in comparison, or of the explanation that there is scum in every society, or the indignation at having a "good name" slandered by "irresponsible generalizations"? None of these purported explanations can help one understand, or can even describe what has happened; none gives a sense of why the surviving Jews are so profoundly and irrevocably scandalized by the Poles' behavior; none brings a better grasp of why public opinion in Poland is so aggressive, or rather defensive, about the subject of wartime Polish-Jewish relations.[14]

In what follows I will suggest a reverse to the mechanism of causation stipulated by the cost-benefit analysis. I will do so by introducing into our discussion the neglected dimension of the attitudes concerning Jews that prevailed in Polish society at the time of the German occupation. And I will argue that it is *because* the Poles were not ready to assist the Jews and by and large refrained from doing so that the death punishment for harboring Jews was meted out by the Germans systematically and without reprieve and the task of helping the Jews was so difficult.

Wartime Anti-Semitism among the Poles

Without beating about the bush let us state clearly that during the Second World War, during the German occupation of Poland, more or less all milieus of Polish society did not sympathize with the Jews. Solid evidence in support of this claim can be retrieved from underground publications. Over two thousand underground periodicals appeared during the occupation, and their editors enjoyed unlimited freedom to print what their wisdom, party line, or personal taste dictated.[15] All political parties and factions, all social groups had their publications, and one could gauge from these writings the state of public opinion on a particular subject. It turns out that with the exception of the communist press and central publications of the Home Army, the underground periodicals were not sympathetic to the Jews. They did not condone Nazi atrocities, though some appreciated the usefulness of the end result, but they all admitted the existence of "a Jewish problem" in Poland, and the need to find for it some solution after the war—such as emigration, for example. Here, for example, is a characteristc passage produced somewhere in the middle of the Polish political spectrum, not by the radical right or even the national-ist press—published in the periodical *Poland* (*Polska*) originating in a milieu of *Sanacja* sympathizers.[16] In the 17 December 1942 issue of the magazine, one may read the following article about prostitution, entitled "The Ways of the *Volksdeutsche*":

> Hitlerite periodicals and propaganda publications constantly speak of Jews as criminals against humanity, they put out many well-deserved accusations against them, they condemn the Jews ruthlessly for depravation and demoral-ization of the young generation as pornographers and pimps. . . . And yet an interesting phenomenon ought to be registered. Jews have been locked behind walls in Polish cities or bestially murdered. One would think then, that this scourge and immoral occupation would disappear from our cities, just as Ger-mans had assured us. But this horrible and debasing occupation was taken over very eagerly in our cities from the Jews by the *Volksdeutsche* . . . who are not different from the Jews at all; they only emulate their ways. It is inconceivable for a decent Pole to have anything to do with these practices. Let us make sure that this horrible activity remains the exclusive domain of the chosen nations— the *Volksdeutsche* and the Jews. It is their privilege.

Much of the published writing referred to such incidentals, only tan-gentially related to the primary focus of German policies vis-à-vis the Jews during the war. And perhaps because of the gratuitousness of com-ments about the Jews in such contexts, the prejudice comes out in a sharp relief. But there was, of course, a much more direct and frightening mate-rial presented on the right of the political spectrum. Here, for example, is an excerpt from an article published in the milieu of the Socio-Political Committee *Pobudka* (The Wake-Up Call). It was carried by the periodi-cal *Words of Truth*, published on 30 October 1943:

> Who are the jews [small letter in original], whom they were for us, and whom they still may become—all should know this. Jews spread among us like pesti-lence, and Poland was a jewish breeding ground. One fourth of the 14 million jews of the whole world lived and fattened themselves on our Polish misery. Did they feel any gratitude because of this? No! In every war jews were on the side of our enemies, or in the best case—on the side of the stronger. The Polish nation suffered loss after loss, while jews took advantage of every war and every national uprising to enrich themselves and enlarge their influence. . . . Germans did not kill all the jews . . . about 2,275,000 jews were murdered, there are about 550,000 in the ghettos, in camps, and in hiding, and about 525,000 emigrated mostly to the Soviet land. This million of mostly young jews

will come out of hiding, from ghettos, from the forests, and will return with the Soviet army when it approaches our borders. Jews will emerge in the critical moment, wreaking vengeance on us and trying to deprive us of the fruit of victory thanks to their influence in the West and possibilities in the East. But we grew wiser in the last quarter-century and we know that a jew is our enemy. . . . If jews would remain neutral we're ready to forgive them a lot and to support their emigration to depopulated territories of southern Russia, or anywhere else. During the peace conference we must insist on recognizing jews as citizens of a nonexistent state, so that they cease to be Polish citizens. The jewish problem in Poland must come to an end.

One may always argue that a few excerpts of journal articles constitute but impressionistic evidence and that they do not prove a general point.[17] But there is persuasive corroborating evidence illustrating the breadth of anti-Semitism among the Polish public, beyond what had been written in the underground press. A number of individuals whose specific task during the war was, among other things, to report on prevailing attitudes among the Poles had their opinions recorded, and we may consult them today. I am referring to people whose responsibility was to be informed, to state objective truth as best they could, and who were certainly not prejudiced against their countrymen, or bent on portraying them as anti-Semites despite evidence to the contrary. Here is what political emissaries, as well as heads of the civilian and military underground in Poland, conveyed in their reports dispatched to the government in exile in London throughout the duration of German occupation.

Jan Karski, who gave such a forceful interview in Claude Lanzmann's *Shoah*, arrived for the first time in Angers (where the Polish government in exile had its official residence at the time) as an emissary from the occupied homeland in the winter of 1940. Later, at the conclusion of his second mission, he would be the first credible witness to personally inform members of allied governments about the Nazi extermination of Jews in Poland. He didn't have such horrible news to report on his first trip but what he had to say was enough for the Polish government in exile to falsify his report, so that allied governments or public opinion in the West would not be informed about the extent of anti-Jewish sentiments in Polish society. "One can feel all over that the [Jews] hoped Poles would recognize that both nations are injustly exploited by the same enemy, and that the Poles' attitude toward them would reflect this awareness. But such an understanding is lacking among the broader masses of the Polish society. Their attitude toward Jews is ruthless, often without pity. A large part avails itself of the prerogatives [vis-à-vis the Jews] that they have in the new situation. They use these prerogatives repeatedly, often even abuse them. To some extent this brings the Poles closer to the Germans. . . . The anti-Semitism of a broad strata of the Polish society did not diminish at all." The Nazis, noted Karski in conclusion, were able to make of the Jewish question "something akin to a narrow bridge upon which the Germans and a large portion of Polish society are finding agreement."[18]

As this was not yet the period of systematic killings of the Jews by the Nazis, what the "large portion of Polish society" apparently agreed to was not murder. Rather, it was the isolation of the Jewish people as well as the economic squeeze to which they were subjected. The government delegate, the head of the civilian underground structure in occupied Poland, was more specific in an autumn 1941 report dispatched to London: "German policies toward the Jewish minority stimulate two kinds of responses. The inhuman terror to which the Jews are subjected is universally condemned and evokes a lot of pity. But the social and particularly the economic isolation are generally approved. A certain fear, especially in merchant circles, goes with it—namely that the Jews might eventually return to their dominant position in the economy."[19] Frankly, there was no dominant position in the economy that the Jews could return to because they had never occupied one. But a Jewish owner could return to his street-corner store, which a Polish plenipotentiary had taken over as a result of German-introduced measures. And this, naturally, was sufficient cause for resentment. On 25 September 1941—three months after the beginning of the Soviet-Nazi war and after the first wave of mass killings of Jews—the commander of the Home Army, Grot-Rowecki, sent the following telegram to London:

> I report that all statements and policies of the government and the National Council concerning the Jews in Poland create the worst possible impression in the country and facilitate propaganda directed against the government. This was the reaction to the "day of the Jewry" (*Dzien Żydowstwa*), to Szwarcbard's speech, to the nomination of Lieberman, as well as to greetings conveyed on the occasion of the Jewish New Year [in a radio broadcast]. Please accept it as a fact that the overwhelming majority of the country is anti-Semitic. Even socialists are not an exception in this respect. The only differences concern how to deal with the Jews. Almost nobody advocates the adoption of German methods. Even secret organizations remaining under the influence of the prewar activists in the Democratic Club or the Socialist Party adopt the postulate of emigration as a solution of the Jewish problem. This became as much of a truism as, for instance, the necessity to eliminate Germans. . . . Anti-Semitism is widespread now.[20]

Nor would these attitudes change under the impact of the Holocaust. If we move three years forward, to the eve of the Warsaw uprising, when the overwhelming majority of the Polish Jews had been killed, we find the political emissary Celt coming back from his mission to Poland with the following message: "The government delegate asked me to inform you that according to him 'the government exaggerates in its love for Jews.' The delegate understands that such moves may be necessary for the sake of foreign policy, but he advises prudence and restraint. Both under General Sikorski and now the government is too forthcoming in its philo-Semitism, because the country does not like Jews."[21] The government delegate and the commander of the Home Army, to whom information filtered from all over the occupied territory, were in the best position to generalize about the state of mind of the Poles during these years.

Now that we have heard about prevailing attitudes among the Poles from the horses' mouths, it might be possible to consider hypotheses about what had actually happened between Poles and Jews, and why it happened. Take any Polish book on the subject, preferably one with a happy ending, written by or about Jewish survivors who lived through the war assisted by the Poles. One realizes immediately from such a reading that the hiding Jews, as well as the Poles who were helping them, were vulnerable to denunciation. German functionaries, Gestapo agents, or extortionists who blackmailed Jews (the so-called *szmalcownik*), as the literature on the subject tells us, were few and far between in occupied Poland, and therefore the likelihood of a chance encounter with any of them was negligible for a hiding Jew. Why was it so difficult and dangerous, then, to hide a Jew? Reading Bartoszewski and Lewin's volume, *Righteous among Nations*—compiled to show the record of assistance extended to Jews—makes one realize that the precariousness of a Jew's existence among the Poles was due to a generalized, diffuse hostility toward the Jews. Historical record shows, I think, beyond reasonable doubt that a constant danger for a Jew hiding on the Aryan side, *and for the Pole helping him to do so*, came from a casual passerby, a house superintendent, a neighbor, a child playing in the courtyard who might, and frequently did, reveal a Jew's presence outside the ghetto—as in this brief episode from the life of a ten-year-old Jewish boy: "No sooner had I stood by the river when some boys came along, somehow noticed that I was a Jew, and in order to thoroughly convince themselves that I was, three of the rascals jumped me. They pulled down my trousers and started shouting at the top of their voices: 'Jew, Jew, Jew.' Then they grabbed me, twisted my arms behind my back and started deliberating whether to drown me or to hand me over to the German police. I took advantage of a moment when one of them loosened his hold of me, kicked him, and ran away."

There weren't any socially marginal people involved in this encounter, or scum, just children.[22] It was a matter of course that Jews should be identified when found outside of their designated area of residence. In a moving volume of little vignettes about his wartime childhood, Michał Głowiński—nowadays one of the foremost literary scholars in Poland—describes a quarter of an hour spent in a tiny Warsaw café. He was in transit at the time between safe houses. His aunt, who thanks to good "Aryan" looks could move around freely, was making the arrangements. She took the boy along on this day and brought him to a little café. She sat him at a least visible corner table, bought him a pastry, and left to make a few telephone calls after promising to return in a little while (of which she also duly informed the proprietor).

At the beginning I thought that everything is calm, that I am sitting quietly as a mouse, eating pastry, nothing is happening and what the women are talking about (there were no men around) does not concern me. But after a while . . . it was impossible to doubt that all the attention was focused on me. Women—either customers, or employees—surrounded the proprietor and were whispering something. They were also looking at me very intensely. . . . I also heard fragments of the conversation that clearly, I couldn't doubt this, were about me. . . . I heard: "Jew-boy [*Żydek*], certainly a Jew-boy . . . she perhaps not, but he a Jew-boy . . . she dropped him on us."[23] Women were deliberating what to do with me. . . . I tried not to think how this will end. . . . I couldn't doubt that my situation was getting worse by the minute. Women were no longer satisfied to observe me from a distance, they were no longer satisfied with figuring my ethnicity from a distance, they wanted to make sure, perhaps as a final justification for a decision that they might have already taken. After all, I heard one of them say: "We must call the police." Agitated and visibly curious ladies came closer, approached the table where I was sitting. Interrogation began. . . . They tried to ask questions very politely, sometimes sweetly, but I was not deceived by this manner; one needn't be very perceptive to feel that it merely covered hostility and aggression. They spoke to me as one addresses a child, and at the same time a suspect, a criminal in fact. . . . I heard not only questions addressed to me but also their commentaries and opinions, which they uttered on the side. . . . The most frequent was the dangerous word "Jew-boy," but I could also hear the most horrible sentence again: "We must call the police. . . ."

If I knew anything about mythology then, I would have thought that I found myself in the power of Furies, of Erynias, who wanted to claw me into pieces. But would this be a fitting comparison? These ladies, after all, were not obsessed by a hatred that they couldn't control, they did not thirst for vengeance, for they had nothing to avenge on me. These were normal, simple, in their own way decent and honest women, who worked hard and toiled from dawn to dusk to take care of their families in the difficult circumstances of the occupation. I can't preclude that they were good mothers and wives, probably God-fearing, and endowed with a whole plethora of virtues. They just found

themselves in a situation that they considered difficult and potentially threatening, and they wanted to deal with it. But they did not think what the cost of the
solution might entail. Perhaps it exceeded their imagination, but they had to
know what would have happened if they "called the police." Perhaps, this was
beyond the scope of the moral reflection they were capable of. . . . When Maria
saw my table encircled by the women, she immediately realized what was going
on. She took me by the hand and we immediately walked out. I survived.[24]

Let us simply take note that hiding Jews, as well as those who were
helping the Jews during the war in Poland, had to be on the lookout not
only for extortionists and Gestapo agents; they had to be wary of ordinary folks, casual passersby, and their own neighbors.

Consider, by way of contrast, the difference surrounding the climate of
secrecy required for underground work. The folklore of the occupation
includes innumerable stories about the incompetence of the underground,
how people were sent to a wrong address, mumbled some absurd pass-
word only to be patiently directed to an altogether different house or
apartment by a neighbor who wasn't involved in this particular conspiracy but knew where the action was nonetheless, *and covered up for it.*
One would be hard put to ask to identify such stories *à propos* the hiding
of Jews. As if, in a manner of speaking, except for Gestapo agents and
rare ideologically motivated supporters of Nazism, everybody in Poland
was involved in an anti-German conspiracy.[25] One could say the exact
opposite about helping the Jews—except for those who were actively involved, everybody, it seems, was against it.[26] Of course some would
more actively and some less actively demonstrate their opposition, just as
some would display more active and some less active involvement in the
underground. While in casual conversations with acquaintances or even
strangers, people would openly discuss their black market transactions
(to mention another activity prohibited by the Nazis under penalty of
death), and the young in particular would cue (by dressing in a certain
way for instance), hint, exaggerate, or even falsely ascribe to themselves
connections and credits earned in the underground, yet one would look in
vain for a memoir or a piece of literature in which some protagonist
boasts in casual company that he or she is hiding Jews. Not only would
this be dangerous (as we know, Poles lived dangerously in those days and
were proud of it) but, worse, it would be awkward, for it would most
likely not meet with social approval.

What differentiated conspiratorial work from helping out the Jews in
Poland during the Second World War was not, primarily, the relative
severity of sanctions if one were caught but that, by contrast with involvement in the anti-Nazi conspiracy, there were relatively few people involved in assisting the Jews and that they were not supported in these

efforts by the surrounding milieu.[27] Jews, by and large, were perceived as an alien element and they were either ignored or else the prevailing attitude toward them was hostile.

It is precisely *because* those assisting the Jews were few and *because* they were engulfed in a social vacuum that it was much more difficult and dangerous to help the Jews than to engage in the anti-German underground, not the other way around. This follows from a simple and well-established sociological principle according to which the enforcement of any norm of behavior depends on the degree of the group's acceptance of the validity of the norm. Had the German-stipulated norm, "Do not help the Jews," been as unacceptable to the Poles as the norm, "Do not engage in patriotic activity," or "Do not engage in market transactions," it would have been enforced more or less as successfully as the other two. If every other Pole "had his Jew," so to speak, just as he had his black market contacts or conspiratorial connections, it would have been much easier to hide among the Poles, and the Germans could not have killed everybody they caught helping out a Jew, just as they didn't kill every conspirator they apprehended. The Nazis did not want the Poles to kill the Jews, or even to help kill the Jews; they only wanted the Poles not to interfere with the Jews' isolation—and to this injunction the Poles by and large consented. The deviant behavior of a few, who were censored for helping the Jews by their own community, was sanctioned severely and very effectively policed.

Let me rephrase the argument one more time: We know three things about the subject of our inquiry—about the Polish attitudes toward the Jews during the war, we know that there was widespread anti-Semitism; about Polish behavior, we know that relatively few people were involved in helping out the Jews; and about the German-created context, we know that the death penalty was meted out for helping Jews hide. The cost-benefit explanation entirely ignores attitudes, that is, the issue of anti-Semitism, and explains Polish behavior solely by the German-created context. What I have suggested as an alternative explanation links attitudes, behavior, and the situational context.

Holocaust in Szczebrzeszyn

But for a proper grasp of the issue it is imperative to move beyond generalities and immerse ourselves briefly in the wartime life of provincial Poland. Dr. Zygmunt Klukowski, director of the county hospital in Szczebrzeszyn, was an amateur historian and an ardent local patriot of *zamojszczyzna*.[28] Moved by a sense of duty and civic responsibility, he

enjoyed the respect of his fellow citizens. Klukowski noted his daily actions and moods, wrote regularly about hospital business and the condition of his patients. But he also collected information from other people
and reported the content of innumerable conversations as well as personal observations as he went about town. Since he was competent, cour-
teous, reliable, and he provided indispensable services, he knew pretty
much everybody, and people confided in him. On the pages of his diary he
is a formidable informant regarding local affairs.

Szczebrzeszyn experienced more than the usual share of turmoil in
these troubled times. Germans came there first, then relinquished the area
to Soviet occupation for about two weeks and returned in early October.
In later phase of war *zamojszczyzna* suffered German colonization experiments with the accompanying terror and breakdown of "public order."
Klukowski captures the rapid collapse of norms of civility under the
impact of war. "Shops were looted in town yesterday," he writes on
18 September 1939. "Both Jewish and Polish shops were looted. But since
Jewish shops are much more numerous, one heard that Jews were being
robbed. It happens like this. A few soldiers come in first, take something
for themselves, and then they proceed to throw the merchandise into the
street. There, crowds of Christian (!) [author's emphasis] population are
already waiting, both city people and country folk. They grab whatever
they can and quickly take it home. Then others rush into the store and
jointly with soldiers rob and destroy everything. If a shop is closed soldiers break the doors open and it gets robbed even faster." Five days later
he notes that robberies continued, and since shops had already been
emptied, looters were breaking into people's apartments.[29]

Already in this early period of the occupation Jews were beaten up and
harassed by the German authorities. Klukowski also records episodes
when the Polish population applauded or joined in such brutalities. He
further draws attention to symptoms of the breaking down of solidarity
within the Polish community. He deplores voluntary sign-ups for work in
Germany, female fraternization with German soldiers, and the plague of
denunciations. "As a consequence of denunciations gendarmes all the
time take away from various people some hidden items. And they don't
have to look for them. They come into a house and say up front that in
such and such a place, such and such an item is to be found."[30] Cooperation with the German authorities is so routine by the summer of 1940 that
we are barely surprised when reading about a manhunt for hiding Jews,
of whom only fifty, instead of the requested three hundred, showed up for
scheduled departure to a nearby labor camp: "Alongside the police and
two militiamen quite a few volunteers from among town inhabitants took
part in it, including the mayor Borucki."[31]

Yet, through early 1942, Polish and Jewish populations of Szczebrze-szyn were subjected to a commensurate level of terror by the occupiers. There were more restrictions placed on the Jews, they were more casually beaten up in the streets and humiliated, they were stripped of their posses-sions (though many managed to give some for safekeeping to their Polish neighbors), but the dangers to which they were exposed were not of a different order of magnitude. "Everybody is anxious that the Germans might come to fetch him at any moment. I am so well prepared that I always keep a packed suitcase ready," writes Klukowski.[32] In Szczebrze-szyn periods of heightened terror alternated with days, sometimes weeks, of relative calm. Then, about March 1942, terror against the Jews inten-sified abruptly.

Trainloads of Jews from abroad passed through the railroad station. Jewish residents of various little towns in the vicinity were being resettled. Bełżec appeared to be their destination. Horrifying stories about resettle-ment from Lublin reached Szczebrzeszyn. By early April people already knew that full trainloads arrived daily at Bełżec and then left empty. On April 11 most Jews from Zamość were taken away and the news of un-speakable horrors committed on this occasion paralyzed the little town. The arrival of the gendarmes was expected at any time. "Most Jews keep out of sight; they either left town or hide. Some were frantically carry-ing things away and attending to some urgent business. All the scum ["*szumowiny*"] are milling around, a lot of [peasants with] wagons came from the countryside and stood waiting the entire day for the moment when they could start looting. News keeps reaching us from all directions about the scandalous behavior of segments of the Polish population who rob emptied Jewish apartments. I am sure our little town will be no differ-ent. . . . Everybody in town is very tense. Many people would like this to end one way or the other because panic among the Jews spreads around and affects all the inhabitants."[33]

And then for a few days the tension let up. There were no more passing trains to Bełżec. Until May 8, when at "about three o'clock in the after-noon all hell broke loose in town. A few armed Gestapo men arrived from Zamość. First they requested that one hundred Jews show up for work within an hour, and then, assisted by local gendarmes, they took to their bloody work. Shots were ringing continuously. People were shot at as if they were ducks; they killed also in apartments, anybody—women, chil-dren, men without discrimination. It is impossible to estimate the number of dead and wounded. There must have been over a hundred."[34] The hospital and Klukowski were forbidden to tend to the wounded Jews. He was shaken by this injunction, but afraid to break it, especially after two Gestapo agents came over looking for Jews they were told were there.

Klukowski noted at this time a general breakdown of "law and order" in the surrounding countryside. "Guerillas are all over. They take from peasants primarily food. It's impossible to tell who is who—there are Polish guerrillas among them, Soviet guerrillas, German deserters, regular bandits, what not."[35] Germans seemed unable to stop this descent into chaos. They frequently resorted to measures of collective responsibility, killing scores of randomly picked peasants for allegedly abetting bandits. And yet the Jews had nowhere to go, they could not find shelter in the midst of this deepening disorder. "On the next morning—after the murderous eighth of May . . . behavior of a certain part of the Polish population left a lot to be desired. People were laughing, joking, many strolled to the Jewish quarter looking around for an opportunity to grab something from deserted houses."[36]

A new wave of mass killings of the Jews took place in the area—in Krasnobród, again in Zamość, and in Tomaszów. In early July some 1,500 Jews of Józefów got killed on the spot.[37] On August 8, all Jews of Szczebrzeszyn were ordered to assemble in the square, near the *Judenrat*, with a few belongings, in order to be taken to work in the Ukraine. Nobody showed up voluntarily. From midday on local gendarmes, gestapo, Sonderdienst soldiers, as well as Polish policemen, *Judenrat* members, and Jewish policemen went around taking Jews out from their apartments and hiding places. Terrorized Jews brought to the assembly point, remained there in complete silence. "Quite a few Poles, especially boys, eagerly help in the search."[38] When finally led out of town late in the evening, some Jews tried to run away. Shooting started in all directions. Poles in the streets panicked. The column of Jews was driven with blows and shots to the station. Some one thousand Jews from Biłgoraj and vicinity were taken out to the train station in Zwierzyniec on this day as well.

After this *Aktion* only "productive" Jews were allowed to remain in town. Every day a few Jews were shot, but people no longer paid any attention. And so it went for a couple of weeks. The final roundup began on October 21. Nine hundred Jews were led out of town in the afternoon. Some four to five hundred had been killed right away. "Nobody ever dreamed that things like that are possible. I am completely overwhelmed, I cannot find a place for myself, I cannot do anything."[39] The bloody spectacle continued for several days. Jews were being hunted down, killed on the spot, or brought to the cemetery in groups for execution. On October 26, "I saw near the hospital, in the compound of well-known rope makers named Dym, fifty Jews were found and taken out. We counted as they were led to the police station. A crowd of spectators stood around and watched. Some volunteered assistance: they ripped through walls and roofs searching for Jews, and then beat them with truncheons. . . . From opened-up Jewish apartments people grab everything they can lay their

hands on. Shamelessly they carry loads of poor Jewish belongings or merchandise from little shops. . . . All of this together makes an unbelievable
spectacle, hard to describe. Something equally terrifying, horrible, was
never seen or heard about by anybody anywhere."[40]

And the same spectacle gets repeated all over the area. Under the November 4 entry Klukowski notes a three-day-long *Aktion* in Biłgoraj and
Tarnogród. Afterward the road from Biłgoraj to Zwierzyniec where
Jews were loaded on the trains was covered with corpses. Those who had
scattered throughout the countryside were hunted down by everybody.
"Peasants afraid of reprisals catch Jews in hamlets and bring them to
town or sometimes kill them on the spot. In general some terrible demoralization has taken hold of people with respect to Jews. A psychosis took
hold of them and they emulate the Germans in that they don't see a
human being in Jews, only some pernicious animal, that has to be destroyed by all means, like dogs sick with rabies, or rats."[41]

Klukowski leaves an unusually comprehensive account. He makes no
apologies for anything that he had witnessed or done (as when he refused,
following a German prohibition, to treat wounded Jews, for example, or
accepted for his hospital a "donation" of linen and household goods
from the gendarmes after an *Aktion*).[42] But he does not tell us, in substance, anything we didn't know about the mechanism of destruction.
What is it, then, that makes his memoirs so significant? We owe Klukowski the realization of a simple fact that easily escapes attention despite
voluminous readings about the period—namely, *that Poles have witnessed the Holocaust*. And this, to my mind, is the most remarkable significance of the document he left behind. His testimony *proves that this
entire process had taken place in full view of the surrounding population*.
The most revealing information in Klukowski's memoir is two numbers
he quotes from a conversation with Szczebrzeszyn's mayor: that 934 Jews
were deported on the first day of the *Aktion* and that about 2,300 were
killed in town over the next two weeks.[43]

These proportions may vary from town to town and from ghetto to
ghetto. I would guess that from the largest agglomerations a greater proportion of the Jewish population was deported rather than murdered on
the spot. But in countless small towns where from a few hundred to a few
thousand Jews were confined to their quarters, by no means walled in and
out of sight of the Gentile population, a significant proportion, if not the
majority, were killed right there. Holocaust, in other words, was not confined to the pitch dark interiors of gas chambers and covered vans. It took
place in full daylight and was witnessed by millions of Poles who, as we
have seen, by and large did little to impede it, to slow it down, or to
interfere with it. In Polish historiography the significance of these circumstances has not been evaluated and is only barely recognized. Or else the

firmly held conviction that there are two separate histories (and ipso facto historiographies) of the war, one Polish and one Jewish, and that they overlap only marginally when there is talk of extortionists and of heroes (these proverbial "social margins" of wartime historiography), would have to be cast off. In light of the evidence and analysis here presented, I submit that the Holocaust of Polish Jews is a central feature of Polish history of the Second World War, and that it cannot be excised for some special treatment.

Jews under Soviet Rule, 1939–41

That Jews welcomed the Soviet occupation of southeastern Poland in 1939 and willingly collaborated with the Communist administration set up in these territories was well known in Polish society already during the war. And this view was never subsequently challenged by historians. It thus stands out as an example of either extraordinarily self-reflective lucidity in a society under occupation, or of an uncritical dullness on the part of historians who simply incorporated into their interpretations what was believed at the time.

The stereotype of Jewish behavior under the Soviet occupation is made up of two components. First, Jews are reported to have enthusiastically welcomed occupation of southeastern Poland by the Red Army, and second, Jews are known to have developed particularly good relationships with the Soviets as evidenced by their collaboration in the local administration and the apparatus of coercion. One ought to note, in the first place, that the initial welcome of the Red Army should have made Jewish behavior, and perhaps its motivation, indistinguishable from that of other "minorities" (the Ukrainians, for example, who were a majority population in this area) and thus at least removed the odium of some special rapport with the Soviets. But, more generally, a proper evaluation of the initial response to the confusing and new circumstances requires that we reconstruct what people knew *at the time* about unfolding events, or else we won't understand their motivation or behavior. Furthermore, as the historical record will show, Jewish behavior and rapport with the Soviets *changed over time* and must be differentiated by social category. In fact, upon close scrutiny, one could contend that Jews have suffered more than other ethnic groups as a result of sovietization of southeastern Poland, and that Jews manifested their hostility toward the Soviet regime uniquely and overtly.[44]

In 1939 neither the Polish government nor the military were envisioning or preparing to fight a war with the Soviet Union. Indeed, Poland was never officially at war with the USSR, and while the country had been at war with Germany since 1 September 1939 on the western front, what eastern Poland experienced late in the month was not nearly as clear-cut and unambiguous. When informed on September 17 about the Red Army's invasion of Poland, the supreme commander, just before crossing into Romania where he was interned, issued orders not to oppose the Soviets (which didn't matter since communication between scattered Polish detachments was already broken). Local Polish authorities and officers as often as not gave orders or instructions to greet and welcome entering Soviet units. It was not clear to many whether the Soviets came as allies or as enemies. And one could easily succumb to wishful thinking in assessing their intentions, for they employed clever deception—to wit, the Red Army detachment that marched with its regimental band into the border town of Ostróg to the tune of the "First Brigade," the signal piece of Piłsudski's Legions.[45] To compound the confusion, it is not clear that the Red Army soldiers knew the specific purpose of their mission as they passed by, waved, and otherwise communicated their amicable intentions.

The friendly reception of Red Army detachments in villages, hamlets, and towns all over Western Ukraine and Western Belorussia is a well-established fact. All over the Ukrainian countryside groups of peasants hoisted flags in the blue and yellow Ukrainian national colors in joyful celebration of the long-awaited collapse of the Polish state. Occasionally a mixed crowd with church banners greeted Red Army units singing, "in the confusing elation, Communist songs mixed with religious hymns."[46] Colors, songs, and inscriptions during these welcoming episodes were a mixed bag, just as the people who were lining the roads were mixed up. Where did Jews fit into this situation? They were part of the general confusion.

Crowds lining up along the roads and greeting the Red Army soldiers were reported to have been composed predominantly of "minority" youth.[47] Not surprisingly, for one should hardly expect local youth, in some godforsaken backwater, to quietly sit at home when an army goes by their little hamlet and does not kill or rob anybody! In many instances—when the Germans were evacuating an area they had conquered, but which the Soviets had to occupy according to the Ribbentrop-Molotov agreement—welcoming ceremonies were organized on explicit instructions, and people were forced to attend.[48] We have no clear evidence to judge the size of the welcoming groups. We read repeatedly that the majority of local residents were fearful and suspicious of the Red Army and, invariably, that it was young people one could see cheering in the streets. Undoubtedly only a small fraction of the local population showed up on these occasions. But what Poles and Ukrainians reported, often with biting irony, the Jews did not deny: "Jews greeted the Soviet army with joy. The youth was spending days and evenings with the soldiers." "Jews received incoming Russians enthusiastically, they [the Russians] also trusted them [the Jews]." "The first days of the Bolsheviks' presence were very nice. People went out into the streets, kept looking over tanks, children walked after soldiers."[49]

What could have been the motivation of young Jews milling in these crowds? Undoubtedly there were Communist sympathizers among them. There were some young Zionists in the streets as well. But left-wing and secular ideologies captured only a few hearts and minds locally and were not representative of the spiritual or mental outlook predominant among the shtetl Jews. But even a few enthusiasts could make a spectacle of themselves that their neighbors would have remembered forever: "I have to say that if someone ever experienced total happiness, it was [for us] the day when the Red Army came. I imagine that Jews awaiting a Messiah will feel that way the day when that Messiah finally comes. It is hard to describe this feeling—this anticipation and this great happiness. Finally our wait was over, they came to Lwów. First tanks came—and we wondered how to express ourselves, what to do: throw flowers? Sing?"[50]

We may sympathize, in hindsight, with the cold shower that such young idealists would soon receive in ever greater doses upon confrontation with the reality of everyday life in Stalin's Russia.[51] But the vast majority of local residents responded to the Soviet presence, one way or another, on opportunistic grounds. They were motivated less by preconceived ideological notions than by immediate experiences and expectations. The Jews, for instance, had a very clear awareness as to what might have happened had the Soviets not arrived.

It took a good many days before the Red Army, moving along a sparsely developed road and transportation network, would show the flag in outlying areas. But it was there that the bulk of the population of this backward half of a relatively underdeveloped European country lived at the time. Wherever ethnic strife filled the power vacuum created in the interim period, the local minority (whatever that minority happened to be in a given place) might suffer brutal persecution at the hands of its neighbors. Many residents of these backwaters—including Polish military settlers or landowners, who were the most exposed—expressed relief at their first sight of the Soviet military, or fled into the neighboring towns where the Soviets had already established their presence.[52] In the absence of landowners, Jews provided a second best target of *jacquerie*, and as peasant crowds converged on the towns of Western Ukraine and Western Belorussia, they had innumerable shtetls to choose from. Apparently, as always in the Jewish Diaspora, only a central authority could protect it from the surrounding population.

To justify its invasion of Poland, the Soviet government announced that it was compelled to enter Polish territory in order to protect the interests of national minorities, specifically those of the Ukrainians and the Belorussians. This pretense at national liberation was of course but a fig leaf used to cover Soviet imperial ambitions. Yet initial Soviet policies (replacement of the Polish state administration with locally recruited volunteers, for instance) as well as a variety of steps taken to follow up on the promise of national liberation (immediate promotion of local languages into the public sphere, for example) created a general atmosphere of ethnic emancipation. People belonging to ethnic minorities—and one should be mindful that these so-called minorities were a significant majority in the Soviet occupied territories—lost the humiliating sense of being second-class citizens. "You wanted Poland without Jews, so now you have Jews without Poland," was an expression one woman recalled from the period, turning around a Polish nationalistic slogan from before the war.[53] Furthermore, for the entire Jewish community, this initial sense of emancipation came not solely in the context of discriminatory policies of the prewar Polish administration, but also in the context of the brutalities Jewish communities were suffering at the time from the invading Germans.

This is important to remember: Jews had been brutalized by invading Germans beginning in September 1939, and the awareness of this harsh treatment had spread to Jews in southeastern Poland by the time of the Soviet invasion.[54] Even more to the point, however, Jews had actually experienced treatment at German hands in a sizable chunk of the territories eventually occupied by the Red Army, because the Wehrmacht, as mentioned earlier, had come there first. During the following months a steady trickle of horrors would feed into the Jewish community via refugee stories.

Hundreds of thousands, perhaps millions, had been displaced by the war in September 1939, but the Jewish experience was again unique in its severity, especially in the vicinity of the shifting border separating the German and the Soviet zones of occupation. Entire Jewish communities— men, women, and children—were uprooted by the Germans and driven eastward over the river into the Soviet zone where, as often as not, they were denied entry. They would then linger for days in a no-man's land— abused, pillaged, raped, shot at until they bought their way in, or got in by stealth or good luck. Let the story recounted at the time by twenty-two-year-old Rosa Hirsz stand in lieu of many:

> I spent a long time in the so-called neutral zone. Germans robbed me thrice. They even took a packet of needles, they took my coat and linen, they said they needed linen for their wives and children. There were instances when Germans

took clothes away from Jewesses and gave them to Polish women. I saw how Germans took all clothing from some Jews and tore it to pieces, just to harm the Jews. Young Germans were the worst. With older ones one could manage somehow and cross the border for a few pennies. I finally managed to bribe a patrol and with some other young Jews I found myself on the other side. As soon as we moved in a little, Germans alerted the Bolsheviks and from both directions shots were fired at us. We hid in a ditch. Three in our group, including one young woman, were killed on the spot. Others miraculously survived. We spent two days in the ditch near the Soviet border without food or drink. As soon as we raised our heads shots would be fired. We could not stand it any longer and risking our lives we crawled on all fours toward the Soviet border, without food or drink. A Soviet patrol caught us. They were quite friendly. They gave us something to eat and to drink and then "assisted us" to get over to the German side. We were ready to commit suicide. We were totally exhausted mentally and physically. We were dead tired and could not see how to extricate ourselves from our predicament. A German patrol beat us with rifle butts. They thought we were trying to get in from the Soviet side. In our presence, unashamed that a lot of people were watching, Germans raped two young Polish women and then savagely beat them. We spent another ten days in the neutral zone. We witnessed horrible mistreatment of people. We saw the arrival of a group of Jewish artists with Turkov and Ida Kamińska. They were well dressed and must have thought they would be left in peace when they identified themselves as actors. Germans ordered Ida Kamińska to strip naked. They took her precious coat, all of her underwear, and her dress, and when she stood completely naked a young German officer ordered her to act. My heart was breaking when I looked at this wild scene. I admired her comportment. With a faint smile she gave away everything, her face was pale, but she did not want to show the Germans that she was afraid. The same happened to the whole group of actors who showed up on the border. Completely naked they were allowed into the border zone. We were lucky that the Gestapo enforced the principle of racial purity in the border zone. Some German military were quite eager for Jewish girls whom they wanted to make happy and in exchange smuggle across the border, but they were afraid of the Gestapo. Finally we managed to get over to the Soviet side. It was at the end of the month, during a pitch-dark night, when we got to Białystok bypassing Soviet patrols. Even though I had no place to stay and I was constantly hungry, the feeling of freedom and the return of my human dignity after weeks spent with the Germans gave me strength to bear all the discomforts. Most important was that one could freely walk the streets; Soviet bands were playing cheerful marches. Nobody was pulling Jewish beards off in the streets, and one didn't see pale, trembling people.[55]

Since the very beginning of World War II Jews were extremely vulnerable. They sensed and experienced this vulnerability and responded accordingly. They were particularly endangered by the absence of a central authority and by the German presence. Soviet occupation of southeastern Poland held both in abeyance. The sense of relief that was initially detectable in the Jewish community (and I have to caution that we have no evidence to judge how widespread it was, as there were vivid memories in the older generation of mayhem in these areas, which followed the October revolution and continued during the 1920 Polish-Bolshevik war) at the prospect of Soviet administration must therefore be properly put in context, since the only viable alternative to the Soviet occupation at the time was the establishment of the German administration, not the continuation of Polish statehood.

Local Jews and the Soviet Administrative Apparatus

Now that we have contextualized the initial Jewish response to the Soviet occupation of southeastern Poland, we can proceed to evaluate the claim of massive Jewish participation in the Soviet administration. We have very good evidence with which to do so, and it indicates, unambiguously, that Jews were not involved, except sporadically, in the Soviet-sponsored apparatus of administration in the villages (i.e., where the vast majority of the local population lived at the time).

After Hitler invaded Russia in the summer of 1941, the USSR finally joined the Allies in their war against Germany. It also recognized the Polish government in exile and signed an agreement to release Polish citizens sent to camps and forced settlement in the Russian interior in 1939–41. The Soviets also allowed the formation of a Polish army in the territory of the USSR. This army was then evacuated to Persia in 1942 and fought gallantly along the Allied troops all the way to Germany. Some 130,000 people were evacuated from Russia at the time—soldiers and their families. At the request of the Historical Bureau of the Army all the evacuees were queried about their experiences under the Soviet occupation. Several questionnaires were distributed, and some twenty thousand answer sheets collected at the time—sometimes running into dozens of pages of wide-ranging narratives—are preserved in the Hoover Institution Archives. We thus have testimonies from all over the occupied area, and from people of every profession (duly marked on each questionnaire) that permit us to reconstruct numerous details of life under the Soviet regime. Among other things, we know scores of names of members of village committees and personnel of rural militias that served all over the area—*and Jews are only infrequently mentioned among them.*[56] We also know that higher echelons of local Soviet administration—on county (*raion*), *voivodeship* (*oblast*), or city level—were staffed by functionaries brought in from the east and while there were Jews among them, of course, they were not any more numerous than in the administrative apparatus in the Soviet interior.

What about the shared memory of Jews lending helping hands to the Soviet invader, then? Clearly, there is a discrepancy between broadly generalizing statements provided by witnesses who speak about the ubiquitous presence of Jews among Soviet functionaries, and detailed depositions left by the very same witnesses stating the names of those who were involved, without mentioning Jews. I think that the explanation lies in the enormous expansion of the state sector under the Soviet rule, eventually encompassing all of the economy. The state was the only employer in the area and hiring was conducted without discriminating against the Jews or the Ukrainians. Members of the "minorities" could get jobs—as teachers, foremen, engineers, accountants, civil servants—that they could not have had under the Polish administration. Consequently, there *were* Jews in the Soviet administrative apparatus, in the economic bureaucracy, or in the local militia, and there is no reason to think that they would have been less rude or abusive than any other such Soviet functionary. But that they were remembered so vividly and with such scorn does not tell us that Jews were massively involved in collaboration, but rather of how unseemly, how jarring, how offensive it was to see a Jew in *any* position of authority—as an engineer, a foreman, an accountant, a civil servant, a teacher, or a militiaman. That is why this remembrance was so deeply engraved. And it was also an easy memory to carry about during these exceedingly confusing times, because it simplified matters and comfortably rested on the paradigm of Polish public opinion that associated communism and Jews (*żydokomuna*). I conclude, therefore, that claims concerning Jewish collaborationism draw on impressionistic evidence, and neglect an inherently complex and confusing reality of the Soviet occupation. But when they are used rhetorically as a *pars pro toto* allegedly to capture the meaning of the entire Jewish experience under the Soviet occupation, they are simply wrong and can be refuted by solid evidence.

In the first place, one reads in the testimonies of numerous Polish witnesses that all the national minorities—Ukrainians, Jews, and Belorussians—soon learned their lesson and but a few months into the Soviet occupation grew nostalgic for Poland. Standing alone this would be important evidence difficult to reconcile with the image of sustained Jewish collaborationism. But even more significantly, this change of mood was promptly followed by overt action in the face of two policies then carried out by the Soviet authorities. Here we touch upon the second misunderstanding about mutual relationships between Jews and the Soviet authorities. The conventional narrative of those years glosses over what in effect was Jewish resistance and Soviet repression of the Jews.

Repressions of the Jews

In the early Spring of 1940 the signing up of all residents for Soviet citizenship (a so-called passportization) was initiated as well as registration for population transfers to Germany in accordance with one of the stipulations of the Soviet-German pact. In the only well-documented manifestation of their mass behavior under the Soviet occupation, the Jews refused to take up Soviet identity cards and signed up in droves for repatriation into what was by then *Generalgouvernement*, a part of Poland occupied by the Germans. "Never in my life have I seen such a determined resistance as when Soviet authorities wanted to force the Jews to accept Soviet citizenship," recalls a witness to these events. "Their resistance defies description."[57] And we need not even draw on archival material to document the Jews' eagerness to get away from Soviet rule. Nikita Khrushchev, then first secretary of the Ukrainian Communist Party, toured Lwów in the company of the head of the Ukrainian NKVD, the infamous Ivan Serov, and wrote in his memoirs: "There are long lines standing outside of the place where people register for permission to return to Polish territory. When I took a closer look, I was shocked to see that most of the people in line were members of the Jewish population. They were bribing the Gestapo agents to let them leave as soon as possible to return to their original homes."[58]

Whatever judgment we might be able to pronounce about this behavior with the benefit of hindsight (presumably, that it was collective insanity—an opinion that some witnesses were lucid enough to articulate on the spot),[59] this was undeniably a collective manifestation of defiance and an open, public rejection of the Soviet regime.[60] And it was treated as such. In the arsenal of Soviet repressive measures one of the most ferocious was forced deportation. It aimed at removal of an entire category of the population (presumably inimical to the Soviet regime) into some remote part of the Soviet interior, taking all who had been targeted—including children, the sickly, or the elderly—without exception. One of the four big deportations carried out by the Soviet authorities from southeastern Poland, the June 1940 deportation, was made up of refugees from the German-occupied part of the country. It was predominantly made up of those very Jews who had queued up for repatriation to the *Generalgouvernment*.

Jews were sent into forced settlement during other deportations as well. Statistics compiled in 1944 by the Polish Ministry of Foreign Affairs on the basis of 120,000 personal files from the Polish Red Cross records in Teheran show that among Polish citizens who found themselves in the Soviet interior (for the most part forcibly deported in 1940–41),

52 percent were ethnic Poles, 30 percent were Jewish, and 18 percent were Ukrainian and Belorussian.[61] Thus, the ratio of Jews in this group was roughly three times their ratio in the total population of Soviet-occupied southeastern Poland. By that measure alone the Jews were more heavily repressed than the Poles, whose ratio among the deportees was less than double their ratio in the total population of these territories. Whatever the imprecision of statistics compiled in wartime, we may safely dismiss a view stipulating that the Jews were beneficiaries of the Soviet rule and enjoyed some special rapport with the Soviet authorities.

As perverse irony of the Jewish fate would have it, victims of deportations turned out to be the lucky ones. And it is not the death rate (some 25–30 percent) but the survival rate among them that stands out in comparison to the all-out extermination of the Jewish population that managed to stay put in the Western Ukraine and Western Belorussia. Given what the Nazis had done, it would have been best for the Jews if they all had been deported into the Soviet interior prior to the outbreak of the Russo-German war. But if the Soviets had indeed implemented such a policy, it would not have been for love of the Jews.

One final note on deported Jews: once the Polish Jews found themselves in the USSR, they could not get out. Out of some 130,000 prewar Polish citizens who had been evacuated from the USSR by the Polish authorities, Jews numbered about 8,000. They made up about 30 percent of the deportees and about 6 percent of the evacuees.[62] So much for the preferential treatment.

The third dimension of Jewish experience under the Soviet rule that needs to be mentioned has less to do with mental states, real or imputed sympathies, and police measures, but is grounded instead in the tedious reality of everyday life. Thus, a brief commentary on socioeconomic aspects of sovietization and how it affected the Jews is in order.

Soviet authorities instituted a new economic regime in the occupied territories, and property rights were effectively suspended there. Short of collectivizing agriculture (though peasantry was put under gradually more oppressive tax burdens and property use restrictions), they abolished private property. Jews were the ethnic group most affected by these measures. Not because they owned so much, but because so many Jews owned so little. Sociologically speaking, Jews were an impoverished stratum of self-employed craftsmen and tradesmen. Consequently abolishment of private property touched them strongly, for they had no reserves of accumulated possessions to draw on, and were additionally burdened by the claims for material assistance from vast numbers of destitute Jewish refugees. Despite previously unavailable employment opportunities that opened up for Jews in industry or administration, as a group they suffered material calamity under the Soviet regime.

Sovietization, naturally, affected more than the material aspects of community life. It also radically undermined what we would call today civil society. Indeed, community institutions folded up soon after the Soviet authorities established themselves in southeastern Poland. Pinchuk quotes numerous memorial books as well as Yad Vashem sources to illustrate this process. In the words of an eyewitness from Łuck: "[C]ommunity and social life of the local Jewish organizations stopped entirely. With the entry of the Red Army nobody dared to call a meeting of an organization or institution. All community or national contacts from that day on went underground."[63] In reality the situation varied significantly from one place to another since so much depended on local authorities, but the dissolution of all institutions supporting Jewish community life became universal. As a witness from Lwów stated in his deposition: "In the end the Jewish community in Lwów ceased to exist and transformed itself into a shelter for the homeless. In the final instance only the funeral *artiel* [cooperative] remained, and was put in charge of the cemetery."[64]

As Soviet authorities promoted all-out secularization, synagogues—all places of worship, irrespective of denomination—were closed up or placed under an enormous tax burden, which the already impoverished population could not long sustain. Jewish religious life was additionally affected by a ban on official use of Hebrew. Books in Hebrew were purged from public libraries, and the well-developed school systems with instruction in Hebrew—Horeb and Beth Jakov schools—were closed.[65] Yiddish, language of the toiling masses, was promoted instead, but only up to a point.[66] Only the Yiddish-language theater prospered and fared better than before the war.[67]

The dissolution of the kehillah undercut the very material ability of a host of religious, educational, and social welfare organizations to function. Political parties dissolved or were banned, their leaders and prominent members arrested, and Bundists and Zionists were hunted down with particular diligence. To quote a witness of these events from Pińsk: "Systematically and mercilessly all activists were removed from among the Jewish masses. All those who might or could have expressed opposition to the reeducation of the population were eliminated."[68] In a memorandum on the "State of European Jewry at the Beginning of World War II," sent from the relative and only temporary security of Lithuanian-administered Wilno, Moshe Sneh informed Nachum Goldman that "the spiritual elite of Polish Jewry" has now found refuge in Lithuania. "To Lithuania fled those Jews who were threatened equally by Nazi and Soviet occupation, that is, Jewish intelligentsia of Zionist and Socialist persuasion, Zionist and Bundist leaders, authors, journalists, teachers, scientists, Hasidic and non-Hasidic rabbis, whole yeshivot, and a large section of the Jewish plutocracy."[69] The Jewish population—just as the

Ukrainian, Polish, or Belorussian—was both deprived of the institutional infrastructure underpinning its community life—and systematically "decapitated" as a broad spectrum of the Jewish elite was removed through arrests, deportations, or forced exile abroad.

My sense is that the social context of Jewish life in this territory over preceding decades had rendered the Jewish community particularly vulnerable to such deprivations. During the interwar years Jews could not count on favorable treatment by the Polish-dominated state and local administration, and they were simultaneously under hostile pressure from the majority ethnic group residing in a given area. Thus, they were alien to all powers and therefore thrown upon themselves and their own self-reliance. Hence, the destruction of their communities' infrastructure must have been truly incapacitating.

But in the experience of the Jewish community a confusing paradox was associated with the process of sovietization. In short order, following the Soviet annexation of this area, Jewish community life as well as a dense network of cultural and political institutions were destroyed, secularization was imposed on the Jews, and leading citizens were arrested. Why would any Jews have any illusions about what the Soviet regime had in store for them, then? They did, I believe, because the Soviet approach to "nationality problems" was unusual. According to the traditional pattern of discrimination, familiar to national minorities, as long as such groups kept to themselves they were tolerated. Only when the processes of social change led segments of the minority population out of self-imposed isolation, or when they actively sought assimilation, would the dominant nationality be provoked to show anger, contempt, and frequently violence. The opposite was true under the Soviet regime: here Jewish insularity, willful Jewish separation from the rest of society, was not tolerated. Jews could acquire Soviet citizenship with all the rights and entitlements that went with the honor, but they could not sustain their community life anymore. Once again they could not be simultaneously Jews and citizens of the state that had jurisdiction over them. This reversal of the pattern of discrimination was disorienting, and initially scores of people grew to appreciate the "nationality policy" of the new regime.

Finally, especially for younger Jews, there was also another experience of emancipation. Because of its self-imposed insularity and hostile surrounding social environment, Jewish community life was all encompassing. And those for whom institutions, practices, and customs of traditional Jewish life felt oppressive and those who wanted out because they could not fit, or fell out, or had hopes, dreams, and aspirations that could not be fulfilled within the boundaries that the community drew around itself—all those, primarily young, socially marginal, unusually open minded, gifted, or sensitive—welcomed the change. They sensed that the new regime offered an easy way out of the confining limitations of the Jewish community. Not exclusively by the so-called opportunities afforded Soviet citizens but also, perhaps primarily, because under the impact of sovietization the social control mechanisms of the Jewish community were so swiftly and utterly destroyed. It was, in other words, the perspective of emancipation *from* Jewishness as much as emancipation of the Jews that drew youngsters into the streets to cheer the Red Army and later to work on behalf of the Soviet occupiers. That these images of emancipation were mostly in the eye of the beholder matters little, for people are motivated primarily by their own representation of reality.

Given the socioeconomic circumstances of the Jewish population—that refugees made up such a significant fraction of the total; that Jews were predominantly self-employed, and hence belonged to the propertied, capitalist class; that the language of Jewish religious identity and practice, Hebrew, was cast off by the Soviets who for the sake of emancipation of the common man and secularization promoted Yiddish instead—for all these reasons, even though not deliberately discriminated against as an ethnic group, the Jewish community suffered probably the heaviest adverse impact of sovietization. I am hesitant to engage in comparisons of collective sufferings by entire communities (hence the word "probably" in the preceding sentence) because each was undermined differently by different aspects of Soviet policies. Jews, for instance, were relatively unaffected by the wiping out of the Polish state institutions and administrative apparatus because they did not partake in them. Here, Poles were the primary victims, just as Ukrainians or Belorussians would have been, had forcible collectivization been implemented. But, undeniably, as individual property owners or as persons who came from a foreign country and had close relatives living abroad, Jews were singularly ill suited to be welcomed into the fold of Soviet society. Hence the sorry fate of the Jewish population that did not suffer necessarily *qua* its Jewishness, but rather *qua* the ways in which it was politically and socioeconomically unacceptable.

As we revise stereotypes about our own history—and congratulate ourselves for being able to do so—it may be prudent to remember that ideas we hold about the past or present are a potent force capable of mobilizing people to action. And whether we imagine the surrounding world in accordance with the "material of facts," or in some other way—stereotyped, prejudiced, and unrelated to facts—the consequences of our deeds that may follow are, in each case, just as real. A report was sent to the government in exile on 8 December 1939 describing as follows the mood and condition of the Polish population under the Soviet occupation: "Jews are so horribly persecuting Poles and everything that is connected to Polishness under the Soviet partition . . . that at the first opportunity all the Poles here, from the elderly to the women and children, will take such a horrible revenge on the Jews, as no anti-Semite has ever imagined possible."[70] As a description, we know, these words were flawed, but they were, unfortunately, accurate as a prediction. When Hitler invaded Russia in the summer of 1941 the *Einsatzgruppen*, special SS detachments entrusted with the task of killing the Jews, had little trouble enticing the local population (Poles, we must be reminded were locally in the minority) to stage bloody pogroms all over the area.[71] As a prelude to the systematic German killing of them all, the Jews were brutalized by their neighbors to avenge miseries inflicted on the local people by the Soviet authorities—as if the Stalinist regime favored the Jews, and did not count them among its victims.

Postwar Polish-Jewish Relations

Mental constructs, including stereotypes, have a great staying power. They linger long after the people, events, or circumstances that inspired and brought them to life have left the stage of history and are no longer with us. And so, even though most Polish Jews had been killed during the Second World War, the stereotype about the special affinity between Jews and communism, the "Judeo-commune" syndrome, survived the war. If anything, it got reinforced by a widespread consensus among the Poles that during the opening year and a half of the war, when Hitler and Stalin were de facto allies dividing the spoils and each occupied about half of Poland, Jews openly sided with the Soviets and assisted in the subjugation of southeastern Poland. And then, when the Soviet-sponsored "Lublin" government of "national liberation" got established in the closing months of the war, including a number of Polish communists of Jewish extraction who spent the war years in Russia, the stereotype was further perpetuated.[72] In popular sentiment a nefarious role was attributed to Jews—they were portrayed as particularly zealous collaborators of the security police serving the new regime.

Let me state immediately that I do not consider counting Jews in the communist apparatus of repression as a very fruitful undertaking. For one, highlighting an inordinately high number of Jewish-born members therein does not lend itself to a simple interpretation.[73] Communists of Jewish extraction, just as people of other nationalities in various countries where communist regimes were installed, worked in the security apparatus qua communists and not qua Jews—or Poles, or Georgians—and they were not forcing on the reluctant population some "Jewish, Polish, or Georgian interests," but rather the "interests of the people."

By now it is very well known to students of totalitarianism that communists had an instrumental attitude to all values and institutions, and that they also exploited ethnic prejudices to gain and establish themselves in power. Hence, it seems to me, to the question of why Jewish communists worked in the security apparatus of their respective countries, the most sensible, perhaps the only, answer is simply, "and why not." But, in view of the persistent stereotype, it behooves us to ask whether indeed the dominant postwar Jewish experience in Poland was that of partaking in the imposition of scientific socialism on reluctant fellow citizens and attendant persecution of ethnic Poles. And, if I may anticipate the following pages, I will answer this question in the negative. Rather, I am prepared to argue, the dominant Jewish experience in post–World War II Poland was that of fear.

The Central Special Commission

In the closing months of the war, as Poland's territory was successively liberated from German occupation, the remnants of Polish Jewry who miraculously survived the war were coming out of hiding and returning from the concentration or labor camps where they had been held until then. In view of the utter destruction of their communities, their own exhaustion, and the resulting massive need for all kinds of assistance, survivors promptly established an organization called the Central Committee of Jews in Poland. It was an umbrella organization put together by representatives of all prewar Jewish political parties, with territorial branches wherever a significant number of Jews tried to settle.[74] The Committee attempted as best it could to address the various needs of the Jewish population. I want to call attention to one of its less known initiatives.

Admittedly the Special Commission established by the Central Committee of Jews in Poland was an ephemeral institution. It existed only for a period of eight months, from July 1946 to March 1947. In addition to a short life span its name was also rather enigmatic. Thus, we should not be surprised that two boxes containing its files attracted little attention from scholars perusing archives of the Jewish Historical Institute in Warsaw. And yet its records tell a fascinating story. Here is a fragment of the Commission's final report dated 30 May 1947:

> The main task of the Central Special Commission (CKS) was to organize the adequate protection and defense of Jewish institutions and thereby assist the authorities in their defense of the lives of the Jewish population in the country, to prevent panic, and to facilitate the peaceful constructive efforts of the Jewish society trying to rebuild its existence. The first measure of the CKS was to

establish close contacts with Security Services of Democratic Poland [capital
letters in original]. These services approved of our efforts and offered us comprehensive assistance. . . .

Contacts between Special Commissions (KS) and the Ministry of Public Security (MBP), Citizens' Militia (MO), and the Voluntary Workers' Citizens'
Militia (ORMO) were established all over the country, and collaboration
proved fruitful. . . . During their existence the KSs made over *2,000 interventions with the Authorities* [emphasis in original] in the country. . . . The work
of our information network was comprehensive. We had our people in factories, in open markets, at schools, at universities, etc. Our people were going
to church services."[75]

Thus, under the enigmatic label of "Special Commission," we find a
Jewish organization that in defense of Jewish interests collaborated with
the secret police. In this manner the stereotype pointing to close association between Jews and security police in postwar Poland finds a concrete
embodiment. What did this collaboration entail and how did it come
about?

The Special Commission was established in the aftermath of the 4 July
1946 Kielce pogrom, which caused panic among Jews residing in Poland
at the time and prompted their massive flight from the country.[76] Jews
had been leaving Poland for some months before, but after Kielce the
wave of departures swelled. Still, tens of thousands of people, exhausted
by the horrors of their wartime experiences, could not leave their country
on a moment's notice. And many were not even contemplating a departure. So, as one consequence of the tragic events in Kielce, the Jewish
community decided to establish a self-defense organization. During a discussion held at the Presidium of the Central Committee of Polish Jews
about the situation faced by the Jewish community in Poland, the idea of
reactivating the Jewish Combat Organization ("ŻOB," as the wartime
Jewish underground was called) was broached. And when finally the
Central Special Commission was established, in a symbolic gesture Itzhak
Zuckerman, "Antek," the last ŻOB commander, was designated its
chairman. It was not accidental that when news of the Kielce pogrom
reached the Committee the very same evening Zuckerman, accompanied
by Marek Edelman, set out for Kielce to bring the remaining Jews into
safety.[77]

The Jewish community interpreted the Kielce pogrom as a sign of
pending ultimate danger. We have no precise statistics enumerating all
the Jews murdered in Poland after the war. In any case such numbers
would be difficult to interpret. After all this was a time when a civil war
of sorts, as well as postwar banditry, were rampant. Tens of thousands
of people lost their lives due to violence in this period. Dr. Lucjan Dobroszycki, who studied this epoch and always paid meticulous attention

to numerical evidence, counted some 1,500 Jewish victims. Given the general level of disorder at the time, and the fact that many victims were not killed qua Jews but as targets of political violence or armed robbery, only a fraction of these deaths can be attributed to anti-Semitism. Still, one must be careful about the circumstances of each episode for, as it turns out, even victims of robberies could be deliberately targeted because of their ethnicity. Especially dangerous for the Jews in this respect were the railroads.[78] In addition to such assaults we encounter aggression specifically directed against Jews on the occasion of pogroms, when crowds of assailants act motivated by a belief that Jews committed a ritual murder of a Christian child, and when Jews returned to their prewar domiciles. Regarding the latter, murderous threats or actions were an effort to preempt returnees' claims on property that in the meantime had been taken over by the local population.

Still, no more than a few dozen people were killed by mob violence. And since many, perhaps most, could not return to their places of origin (incorporated into the Soviet Union after the war) the numbers of returnees killed in their domiciles were also limited. Hence, it was perhaps not murders of Jews qua Jews that evoked such a panicked reaction among the Jewish population, but the atmosphere of widespread anti-Semitism they encountered after the war ended. For even though anti-Semitism was nothing new in their interaction with Polish society, after the experience of the German occupation it acquired a new meaning: in view of the just experienced Holocaust no one could be oblivious to the realization that anti-Semitism could open up the gates to an ultimate catastrophe. Let us ascertain, therefore, how widespread were anti-Jewish sentiments in Poland fifty years ago.

Postwar Anti-Semitism

State administration acts rather slowly, as we know, and it does not send circulars in response to individual complaints. Thus, it is fair to assume that the Ministry of Public Administration must have received a good number of interventions before circulating a memorandum entitled "In the Matter of Attitude toward Citizens of Jewish Nationality" to all the voivodes (i.e., chief administrators of the largest territorial units, voivodeships), district plenipotentiaries, and presidents of Warsaw and Łódź. Dated 5 June 1945 the memorandum was issued barely one month after the capitulation of Nazi Germany:

> The Ministry of Public Administration has been appraised that voivodeship and county authorities, as well as offices of general administration, do not always apply the necessary objectivism when dealing with individuals of Jewish

nationality. In the unjustifiably negative attitude of the said authorities and offices when handling such cases, and especially when making it difficult for Jewish returnees to take apartments that are due to them, a highly undemocratic anti-Semitic tendency rather clearly comes to the surface. The Ministry of Public Administration calls attention to this undesirable phenomenon and emphasizes that all loyal citizens of the Polish Republic, irrespective of nationality and religious denomination, should be treated the same, and that they ought to be helped within the boundaries of existing law. Therefore the Ministry of Public Administration implores you to make sure that the authorities and offices within your jurisdiction abide by the recommendations of this memorandum.[79]

In the archives of the Voivodeship Office in Cracow one can find several complaints not unlike those that must have come to the attention of the authors of the memorandum. They were frequently passed on to the authorities through the intermediary of Jewish committees.[80] A thorough study of this matter would require a search for evidence in over a dozen voivodeship archival collections. But already a few examples from the Cracow office can give us a sense for what was at issue. Thus, at the begining of July 1945 in Chrzanów

a registration clerk at the Citizens' Militia office requested that citizen Schnitzer Gusta, who returned from a camp, prove her identity by bringing a witness who would testify as to her identity and that she lived in Chrzanów before the war. When citizen Schnitzer Gusta presented to the clerk at said office as her witness the chairman of the County Jewish Committee in Chrzanów, citizen Bachner Lesser, the clerk stated in the presence of the witness that he had no confidence in the presented witness and that he would only trust a witness of non-Jewish extraction and that he would register the citizen [Schnitzer] only when she presented such a witness.[81]

Admittedly this is a trivial matter, but for this very reason also meaningful. For we cannot even justify the awkward, offensive, language of the militia clerk by the administration's attempt to stem the tide of Jewish claims and revindications. At the time, so soon after the liberation, in the entire Chrzanów county there were altogether 105 Jews.[82]

Jewish committees all over Poland complained about the anti-Semitic attitudes of Citizens' Militia personnel. But, interestingly enough, the attitude of the Security Offices (*Urzędy Bezpieczeństwa*), the most politicized organs of the administration, also often made the Jews uneasy. In the documents of Cracow's Special Commission we find a memorandum on a theatrical "revue" put on by the sports club "Force" in, of all places, Oświęcim (Auschwitz) on 24 and 25 January 1947. "The themes and content of this show were to make fun of the Jews in various sketches and songs. We want to stress that the main part in these anti-Jewish gimmicks was played by the commander of the Security Police in Oświęcim."[83] The following is another demonstration of poor judgment and lack of sensibility again in Chrzanów, where the town office at some point began sending daily request for laborers to the Jewish Committee demanding on July 5, for example, that "twelve persons of female sex be designated for washing dirty linen of Red Army soldiers." And it mattered less, in the eyes of the Jewish Committee that filed the complaint that the town office did not honor its promise to pay the honororarium, than the very fact of its issuing the request in a form "emulating methods of the occupiers, which makes the Jewish Committee responsible if the labor contingent does not appear in designated time and place. Such requests are issued only to the Jewish population with the intermediary of the Committee. In this manner the town office in Chrzanów perpetuates traditions established by the occupiers who communicated with the Jewish population with the help of 'Judenrat.'"[84]

Of course the state administration at the time of reconstruction had other more pressing issues than pestering the Jews. And the central administration—as demonstrated, for example, by the previously quoted memorandum of the Ministry of Public Administration—was sensitive to issues of racial discrimination. But ordinary citizens dealt mostly with officials at the local level, and here very often they encountered hostile treatment. Even though they could complain and get higher levels of state bureaucracy to intervene on their behalf, such repeated difficulties added up to make a shocking impact.

Jews encountered hostility not only in governmental offices but also in their places of employment. In a detailed study of how the working class was brought into the fold of the new regime immediately after the war, Padraic Kenney describes many strikes that took place between 1945 and 1947 in the industrial city of Łódź. Some of these confrontations were over the perceived favoring of the Jews—as, for example, a strike in the old Biederman mill in June 1945 that lasted for two and a half days over only one demand: "[W]e don't want a Jew director."[85] Interestingly, "[i]n 1945 anti-Semitic incidents or statements . . . were not yet expressing . . . hatred of the communists; attacks on Jews in 1945 at no time referred to the PPR" (acronym of the Polish Workers' Party, as the communist party was known at the time). The association between Jews and communism was firmed up in the workers' minds apparently only after the Kielce pogrom. In the immediate aftermath, between July 8 and 11, workers meetings were called in factories all over Poland to pass resolutions condemning the pogrom. In several Łódź factories, according to reports of the activists involved, the workers' response was lukewarm, and only a few signed prepared petitions. But the daily newspaper in Łódź, as part of an official propaganda campaign, published headlines about workers in several factories (which were duly named) allegedly signing the resolution and requesting the death penalty for those guilty of the pogrom. And then

> [s]trikes broke out at nearly a dozen factories. . . . Warned a Central Committee report: "The situation in Łódź is serious, as evidenced by the mood among strikers, the strikes' swift leaps from factory to factory, and the aggression of striking women in all factories; they clawed and screamed ferociously. . . . Striking workers use such anti-Semitic arguments as "A pregnant Jew gets sixty thousand zlotys, and what do I have?" [or] . . . "Why don't Jews work in factory shops? Poland is ruled by Jews." Łódź Jews described a "pogrom atmosphere" in the city; there were rumors, for example, that Jews in the Bałuty district (a large worker district and a location of the Jewish ghetto during the war) had murdered a Polish child. While the strikes themselves were easily broken up once the workers had made their demand (usually that a retraction be printed in the newspaper) the hostility lingered long after. The sentencing of the pogrom leaders sparked more protests.[85]

From provincial towns one heard in these years numerous stories about physical assaults, windows broken in Jewish houses, offensive graffiti, or verbal threats. "It is an undeniable fact," wrote Jan Kowalczyk, the Cracow Voivodeship Commissar for Productivization of the Jewish Population, to the Presidium of the District Commission of the Labor Unions "that the living conditions of the Jewish population in county towns are extremely difficult. Because of the terror of reactionary elements [a phrase often encountered in the official language of the time whenever social phenomena disapproved by the administration took place] the Jewish population runs away from those locations in order to save their lives and concentrates in larger towns."[86] Indeed, county and voivodeship Jewish committees urged the Jewish population to move to larger towns where the committees tried to provide support in finding adequate living accomodations and employment. But even in larger towns Jews were not safe.

> On Friday evenings after dark, according to Jewish religious custom, the shabbat service takes place. The services are held in one synagogue at 27 Miodowa Street, which also has an entrance from 8 Warszauer Street. After the service begins a crowd of hoodlums and teenagers assembles and, primarily from the direction of Warszauer no. 8, attacks the synagogue, throws stones, and with special bottles ruins the roof and breaks the windows. And so it goes every Friday, each time from a different side. These acts of public violence are accompanied by frightening screams, verbal abuse, laughter, and often attempts to enter the synagogue. Because these attacks take place every Friday and twice the rabbi was hit with a stone when he was praying at the altar, so not being able anymore to take this in stride, we call this to your attention,

citizen voivode, as well as to the attention of the Public Security Office [UB] with a request for an immediate regulation, which would permit the Jewish population to finally worship in peace."[87]

One could try to pass over these episodes because in the old Jewish section of Cracow, Kazimierz, a sort of demimonde and lumpen proletariat resided for many decades after the war. But this was far from an isolated case. In fact Jewish orphanages, old people's homes, summer camps, or buildings housing Jewish returnees were frequently targets of similar attacks. And indeed, three weeks after this complaint was sent to the voivode's office, on 11 August 1945, a pogrom took place in Cracow, this time in other parts of the city as well. One of the badly beaten victims reported later on attitudes of various witnesses to these dramatic events— soldiers, militiamen, railroad workers, health service personnel, in other words, people whose opinions could not be dismissed as confined to socially marginal elements.

> I was carried to the second precinct of the militia where they called for an ambulance. There were five more people over there, including a badly wounded Polish woman. In the ambulance I heard the comments of the escorting soldier and the nurse who spoke about us as Jewish scum whom they have to save, and that they shouldn't be doing this because we murdered children, that all of us should be shot. We were taken to the hospital of St. Lazarus at Kopernika Street. I was first taken to the operating room. After the operation a soldier appeared who said that he will take everybody to jail after the operation. He beat up one of the wounded Jews waiting for an operation. He held us under a cocked gun and did not allow us to take a drink of water. A moment later two railroadmen appeared and one said, "[I]t's a scandal that a Pole does not have the civil courage to hit a defenseless person," and he hit a wounded Jew. One of the hospital inmates hit me with a crutch. Women, including nurses, stood behind the doors threatening us that they were only waiting for the operation to be over in order to rip us apart.[88]

From today's perspective we would not consider as an extenuating circumstance the fact that the invalid using his crutch as a weapon, the nurse, soldier, or railwaymen were all speaking and acting blinded by a passion, firmly convinced that Jews murdered Christian children in order to use their blood for matzoh.[89]

This medieval prejudice brought people into the streets in postwar Poland on many occasions and in many different towns—in Cracow, in Kielce, in Bytom, in Białystok, in Szczecin, in Bielawa, in Otwock, and in Legnica. And the whole matter was treated on occasion, one is tempted to say, with a disarming simplicity: on 19 October 1946 a few tipsy fellows were looking for a child in a building where Jewish returnees lived in Cracow, at Stradom Street no. 10. A small crowd began to assemble in the street, and when the guards of the building proceeded to disperse it, "the head of milita patrol [which in the meantime had been called by alarmed residents] told one of our guards that 'if your child got lost, citizen, you would also be searching around' [*"gdyby obywatelowi zginęło dziecko, to obywatel też by szukał"*]."[90] That simple. This may allow us to better understand what was on the mind of Cracow's voivode when he wrote his June 1945 situational report: "There were no serious anti-Jewish demonstrations of any kind in the Cracow voivodeship last month. Despite this, however, there are no indications that attitudes toward Jews in society have changed. They are still of such a kind that a smallest incident is sufficient to generate the most outrageous rumors, and to provoke a serious outburst."[91]

So much for attitudes of the general public. And what were the views on this matter of the local elites, one might want to know. Luckily, we may shed some light on this issue as well, thanks to the record of a meeting held on 19 August 1945 in the cinema "Raj" ("Heaven") in Bochnia. This is where delegates of the Peasant Party assembled for a county meeting, about one thousand people in all according to an anonymous rapporteur who submitted this account to the Voivodeship Office. The gathering by invitation only (*"za zaproszeniami imiennymi"*) brought together local activists, the elite of Stanisław Mikołajczyk's opposition Peasant Party.

> In turn the third speaker took the rostrum (his name unknown), and by analogy to a thesis from Kiernik's speech that Poland must be a monoethnic state [the matter prieviously discussed concerned expulsion of the German population from newly incorporated territories], put out a resolution that Jews should also be expelled from Poland, and he also remarked that Hitler ought to be thanked for destroying the Jews (tumultuous ovation and applause). Citizen Ryncarz Władysław, who was presiding at the time, immediately reacted to this speech by cutting it short and condemning what was said."[92]

In line with a tradition of Jewish humor, one could comment on this episode by pointing out that it contained both good news and bad news for the Jews.

These were the circumstances, the overall context in which the Central Special Commission (CKS) was established. After the Kielce pogrom it became clear that entire Jewish communities—and not only isolated individuals in secluded villages, in the privacy of their apartments, or when traveling by night trains—were imperiled with loss of life. During the month of July, after the decision to establish the CKS was made in Warsaw, special commissions were set up by voivodeship Jewish committees and then by their local branches. All political parties collaborating on the Jewish committees participated in this endeavor. Lists were drawn of all the apartment buildings housing refugees, all the old people's homes,

Jewish party headquarters, orphanages, and other Jewish institutions that needed protection, and they were put under guard. About half of the personnel worked pro bono. The remainder were paid from the budget of the Central Special Commission. Over three million zlotys (a substantial sum at the time) were paid out each month in salaries for security guards. Some 2,500 people were issued weapons.

Special commissions in principle were subordinate to the ORMO (the Voluntary Workers' Citizens' Militia), but in practice functioned under the authority of Jewish committees and the Central Special Commission in Warsaw. Their principal tasks in the field were twofold: to put up armed guards at designated locations, and to establish a system of communication that would alert the nearest outpost of the militia, or the security service of impending danger. Telephones were installed wherever possible or procedures established for maintaining contact by sending out messengers. Plans of all the protected buildings were drawn, together with a sketch of neighboring streets including the closest outpost of Security Services (UB) or the militia. One can find these sketches today in the CKŻP documents deposited at the Jewish Historical Museum.

One should not, however, exaggerate the professionalism of the special commissions personnel or procedures. The armed organs of the Jewish committees were far from an awesome sight. "In reality these were doormen, caretakers, and other workers used for various menial tasks. . . . Heads of various Jewish institutions and departments claimed the right to use these guards since it was not clear who was in charge of them, the committee or the special commission. . . . Their condition was pitiful. They were dirty, unshaven, unkempt, altogether pretty disgusting to look at."[93] But at least someone with a weapon was patrolling the premises.

Fortunately, they had only rare opportunities to use their weapons. The final report of the CKS notes two such episodes, in Rabka and in Białystok, without mentioning details. The list of 108 employees of special commissions presented for a special award after the commissions were abolished on 1 April 1947 includes the names of two individuals who had lost their lives in the line of duty—in Ząbkowice and in Łódź.

As to denunciations filed by special commission members and employees, for the most part they were about circumstances or developments that could endanger Jews or buildings in their custody. But this mandate could be interpreted broadly. Thus, for instance, after a meeting to elect a workers' council in a knitting factory in Nowa Ruda, a denunciation was sent to the local security service office about a speaker (a member of the Communist Party, as was duly noted) who requested that no Jews be allowed on the council after a candidacy of a Jewish female worker was put up from the floor. The chairman of the meeting, we read in the denunciation filed by the Jewish committee in Nowa Ruda, assured the assembled, who cheered him wildly, that he would certainly see to that.[94]

There are other instances of denunciations with dire consequences. The final report of the Central Special Commission, which I already quoted, includes a sentence: "On the basis of our information the Authorities [emphasis in original] have liquidated four gangs of NSZ [National Armed Forces, a nationalist underground organization] and WIN [Freedom and Independence, an illegal underground continuation of the wartime Home Army] in Wrocław and Szczecin." What human tragedies are covered by these few words we could tell perhaps if we had access to the archives of the Ministry of Public Security, for the CKŻP documents contain no further details. One can only hope that the designation of "four gangs" was a self-congratulatory report padding, as was another "success" described in glowing terms in the final report—"Special Commission in Włocławek discovered a center of propaganda and agitation that was distributing anti-Semitic literature. The center was liquidated." A memo preserved in the archives gives us a closer insight into what had actually happened:

> To the county UBP [Security Office] in Włocławek, Włocławek 1 February 1947. In the middle of December 1946 or thereabout, when I was in a certain establishment in a company, I found out that in the town library in Włocławek there are books with antidemocratic content. We decided to clarify this matter by sending as members of this library members of our committee, citizens ŁEPEK ICEK and ŁEPEK HELCZE [capitals in original]. Our members, after looking through the catalog, spotted a book with especially anti-Jewish content, entitled *Jewish Danger*, which we enclose with the above. We want to add that our members also noticed that in the aforementioned library there are also books with anti-Soviet content."[95]

Unfortunately, in those days books could be denounced by semiliterates, with dire consequences, and as a result of the Łepek siblings' report the town library was closed in Włocławek and its librarian arrested. Energetic activists from Włocławek pleaded with the CKS that it assign the task of cleansing public libraries and reading rooms to special commissions all over Poland. Thankfully, there are no traces in the archives that their advice was heeded. This, in a nutshell, is the balance sheet summarizing the activities of the only Jewish institution in postwar Poland that in defense of Jewish interests collaborated with the secret police.

Concluding Remarks

The history of the Special Commission established by the Central Committee of Polish Jews is but a small episode in the long history of Polish-Jewish relations. But it is an episode situated in the focal point of an extraordinary phenomenon: massive emigration of the Jews from Poland after the Second World War. And, after all, an exodus from their fatherland by a quarter million people (this is, more or less, how many Jews left Poland by the end of 1948) not compelled to do so by government order or by administrative pressure is a real challenge and intellectual puzzle that has been taken up neither by Polish historiography nor by public interest journalism.[96] The Jews left behind everything—their dead ancestors, their belongings, and a material culture accumulated over centuries. Barely alive, literally, they left for a devastated Europe, not knowing where they would end up. And what they knew makes the whole matter even more of a mystery—for they went, in the first place, into camps for displaced persons situated in Germany! Was this another wave of emigration in search of better material living conditions? And if not, if it was a flight of a whole people from the threat of persecution, how do we come to terms with this, how is this to be written into a narrative of postwar Polish history? In a frequently quoted phrase Theodor Adorno declared the impossibility of writing poetry after Auschwitz. By this measure we are faced with an intellectual problem of staggering dimensions— how was anti-Semitism possible in Poland after the war?

War spawns heroic narratives and offers rich myth-producing material. Certainly for the self-awareness of the Polish nation in the twentieth century it has been of primary significance. It had all the elements that have ever served to forge Polish national identity: treacherous neighbors, unreliable allies, territorial partition, staggering human loss among the elites, deportations, even a national uprising staged against overwhelming odds. But through this rich material—a formidable national calamity transcended by exemplary heroism—there runs a fault line, an unspeakable "heart of darkness." It was too dangerous to help the Jews any more than they had been helped by their fellow Polish citizens—in other words, "we were scared" by the threat of German sanctions—runs the most spirited defense of Polish attitudes toward the Jews during the war. Certainly not the stuff from which legends are made. The Polish population took advantage of the opportunities created by the Germans to exploit the Jews and thus shares responsibility for the Holocaust, write critics of the Poles' behavior whose voices are barely audible in Poland. Either way, the myth-producing quality of the war period is shattered. And, as a result, the whole experience gets compartmentalized in the collective memory of the nation, and in the works of historians as well.

The history of Polish Jews during the war became a specialized subject, for the most part neglected. Fifty years after the war even monographs about the principal ghettos—the Warsaw ghetto, the Łódź ghetto, or the Białystok ghetto—remain to be written. Holocaust studies have not made it into the curricula of Polish universities.[97] But can one tell about the war and occupation in Poland without the mass murder of Polish Jews being a central part of the story? It is, after all, a chapter of Polish history as much as an epilogue in the history of the Jews in Europe. Indeed, one may ask—given the place increasingly occupied by the Holocaust in critical self-reflection about "Western civilization"—are there many other episodes of Polish history endowed with equally universal significance?

The spiritual legacy of Polish Romanticism contains two powerful ideas: a conviction about righteousness and the exemplary destiny of the oppressed, and a belief in the universality of freedom. The national poet Adam Mickiewicz wrote: "*Ibi patria, ubi male*: whenever in Europe liberty is suppressed and fought for, there is the battle of your country."[98] "For your freedom and ours" has been the traditional watchword of Polish patriots, derived from a belief in the brotherhood of victims. Both ideas—that the persecuted weak are right until proven otherwise, and that liberty of mankind is indivisible—were embedded in the poetic interpretation of Poland's fate worked out throughout the nineteenth century in an unprecedented accumulation of creative genius, by Adam Mickiewicz, Juliusz Słowacki, Zygmunt Krasiński, and Cyprian Kamil Norwid, while the country was partitioned by more powerful neighbors and when its patriots also fought continuously against the oppression of other peoples. This fate, according to the Romantic mythos, preordained Poland to an exemplary destiny: to become, as Polish messianism would have it, "the Christ of Nations." And suddenly, during the Second World War— also a paradigmatic time, stigmatized by a calamity of partition and loss of national independence, the sacrifice of its best sons on the altar of patriotism, and the bloody defeat of a national uprising—Poles failed to recognize a fellow victim, not in some faraway land but in the neighbor living right across the street. Have they not, by this failure, betrayed their own destiny? Whatever the answer, a yet to be written definitive history of the German occupation of Poland would have to discuss how a combination of anti-Semitic prejudice among the Poles and deliberate, skillful Nazi policies leading to dehumanization of ghetto residents, resulted in excluding the Jews, in Polish eyes and practice, from the brotherhood of victims.[99]

Notes

1. See Antoni Symonowicz, "Nazi Campaign against Polish Culture," in Roman Nurowski, ed., *1939–1945 War Losses in Poland* (Poznań: Wydawnictwo Zachodnie, 1960), 83.

2. Błoński's article was published in *Tygodnik Powszechny* on 11 January

1987, and Władysław Siła Nowicki's reply on 22 February 1987. Both texts, together with several other articles published in the follow-up of Błoński's essay, as well as a discussion on these matters held at a conference in Jerusalem one year later are published in English in a volume, *"My Brother's Keeper?" Recent Polish Debates on the Holocaust*, Antony Polonsky, ed. (London: Routledge, 1990). In the roundtable discussion in Jerusalem, Błoński specified his argument: "To put it most generally, Polish responsibility is, in my opinion, centered on indifference, indifference at the time of the Holocaust. Naturally not the indifference of everyone. There were those who were not indifferent and we pay tribute to them. The result of this indifference was that Jews died with a feeling of solitude, with a feeling of having been abandoned. This indifference was explicit, one could somehow feel it when one was a child" (Ethical Problems of the Holocaust in Poland. Discussion held at the International Conference on the History and Culture of Polish Jewry in Jerusalem on Monday 1 February 1988, Błoński, *My Brother's Keeper*, 188).

For an analysis of letters to the editor of *Tygodnik Powszechny*, which the publication of Błoński's article engendered, see an unpublished MA thesis at the Institute of Sociology of Warsaw University in 1992 by Ewa Koźmińska—*Polsko-żydowskie rozrachunki wojenne. Wyzwania Holokaustu: Analiza listów do redakcji "Tygodnika Powszechnego" w odpowiedzi na dyskusję, Błoński-Siła Nowicki.*

3. Błoński, *My Brother's Keeper*, 46.

4. Ewa Koźmińska-Frejlak and Ireneusz Krzemiński, "Stosunek społeczeństwa polskiego do Zagłady Żydów," in *Czy Polacy są antysemitami? Wyniki badania sondażowego*, Ireneusz Krzemiński ed. (Warszawa: Oficyna Naukowa, 1996), 98.

5. Jan Józef Lipski's monograph entitled *Workers' Defence Committee*, published by the University of California Press in 1985, offers a wonderful portrait of Lipski's intellectual and political biography, as well as an aperçu of the entire milieu of the progressive Polish intelligentsia. My point is to take under scrutiny the views of a most enlightened individual from a libertarian, courageous, and unprejudiced milieu. If one can demonstrate that even the most open-minded approach to the issue addressed to a Polish audience does not confront what has actually happened we could be reasonably sure that the rest of the spectrum of views on this issues will be even less satisfying.

In addition to the article "Two Fatherlands, Two Patriotisms," Lipski addressed the issue of Polish-Jewish relations during the war in two speeches originally delivered at important anniversary celebrations. In March 1981 at Warsaw University, where a symposium was organized in connection with the thirteenth anniversary of the so-called March (1968) Events, Lipski read a long paper entitled "The Jewish Problem"; two years later he spoke at the fortieth anniversary of the Warsaw Ghetto uprising. All three texts, plus a few other essays on contemporary Polish politics, came out together (1985) in a book distributed by an independent publishing house, *Myśl*, entitled *Dwie ojczyzny i inne szkice*. The substance of all three of Lipski's statements on Polish-Jewish relations during the war is the same. Indeed, he uses occasionally identical phrasing. All quotes are from the 1985 *Myśl* edition. The English-language edition of his "Two Fatherlands, Two Patriotisms" can be found in *Between East and West: Writings from "Kultura,"* Robert Kostrzewa, ed. (New York: Hill and Wang), 52–71. All translations are mine.

6. Lipski, *Dwie ojczyzny*, 1985, 113–14.
7. Ibid., 34.
8. Ibid., 37.
9. Blackmailing hiding Jews and delivering them into Germans hands for a reward. The word itself comes from slang usage of the word *szmalec* (literally: lard) where it means "money," as in loot or dough.
10. Ibid., 36.
11. Dr. Ruta Sakowska, is an esteemed researcher of the Jewish Historical Institute in Warsaw now entrusted with the critical edition of the Ringelblum Archives. I am quoting from her doctoral dissertation originally published in 1953 and revised and republished in 1993—*Ludzie z dzielnicy zamkniętej* (Warszawa: Państwowe Wydawnictwo Naukowe), 239.
12. Lest I be suspected of flippancy and of underestimating the ferocity of German policies: in a myriad of individual, concrete situations many things had not been done in occupied Poland *because* of the fear of anticipated German repressions. And it makes perfect sense to say "we feared the Germans and therefore . . ." some delivery of underground newspapers did not take place there and then; a certain piglet had not been slain for black-market sale (all livestock was branded and had to be accounted for to the Germans); a Jewish acquaintance was told to go away and denied overnight shelter on a certain occasion. But the formula "we feared the Germans and therefore . . ." is not a sufficient explanation for general social phenomena characteristic of this period—or else, there would be neither the underground state, nor the black market, nor the Warsaw uprising, nor, in all likelihood, independent Poland at the conclusion of the war, since all the people would have died of starvation over the years on physiologically inadequate official food rations. Something else besides the fear of German sanctions motivated people to act one way or another—nothing mysterious indeed—namely their attitudes, norms, and the values they had been socialized to.

On another note, there is interesting evidence pointing out that the rescuers themselves did not perceive the risks involved as inordinately high. Nechama Tec interviewed several Poles who assisted Jews during the war for her book *When Light Pierced Darkness: Christian Rescue of Jews in Nazi-Occupied Poland* (New York/Oxford: Oxford University Press, 1986). In their opinion the risk of falling victim to random Nazi violence was so high that it almost equalized the presumed "calculable" risk of repression for actually breaking the German-imposed rules. "There was no guarantee whatsoever that one would survive, regardless of whether one followed the German directives or not" (Tomasz Jurski). "I felt threatened with and without the Jews. I could have been caught by the Germans during a raid for no reason at all" (Stefa Krakowska). Paradoxically, this may have induced people to violate German inductions: "if one could be punished for anything at all, or nothing, then one might as well do something worthwhile" (Stach Kamiński). "In fact," as yet another rescuer, Roman Sadowski, perceptively observed, "[m]aybe those who were engaged in some kind of anti-Nazi activity were less likely to be caught because they were more cautious, more aware. We were prepared and trained" (171). For a general argument along these lines with reference to involvement in the underground, see my *Polish Society under German Occupation—Generalgouvernement, 1939–44* (Princeton, Princeton University Press, 1979), esp. chs. 10 and 11.

13. Czesław Miłosz, *The Witness of Poetry* (Cambridge, Mass.: Harvard University Press, 1983), 84.

14. Readers are reminded of the public reaction provoked by Jan Błoński's January 1987 article.

15. For a general catalog of the Polish underground press, giving runs and duration of various publications, see Lucjan Dobroszycki, *Centralny katalog polskiej prasy konspiracyjnej, 1939–1945* (Warszawa: Wydawnictwo MON, 1962).

16. The term *Sanacja* refers to the ruling (post-1926 coup), regime in Poland. It is derived from the Latin root *sanus*, by reference to bringing "health," cleaning-up, to the political life of the country. For an excellent discussion of interwar Polish politics, see Antony Polonsky's *Politics in Independent Poland, 1921–1939* (Oxford, England: Clarendon Press, 1972).

17. A researcher at the Jewish Historical Institute (ŻIH) in Warsaw, Paweł Szapiro, spent a considerable amount of time culling *every* reference to "matters Jewish" in the wartime underground press. Thus a full record on this subject can be obtained. He also published a book, *Wojna niemiecko-żydowska: Polska prasa konspiracyjna 1943–1944 o powstaniu w getcie Warszawy* (London: Aneks, 1989), containing texts of all the articles published in the underground press about the April 1943 uprising in the Warsaw Ghetto. It is a sobering illustration of the point I have just made.

18. The manuscript of Karski's report can be found in the Hoover Institution archives (Stanisław Mikołajczyk Collection, box 12) with handwritten lines scribbled across the cover page: "Attention!! Pages 6+9+10+11 have double pages." Indeed, doubled pages paginated as 6a, 9a, 10a, and 11a are very carefully prepared. They begin and end exactly in the same place (once including a hyphenated word), for easy substitution. Karski was instructed, as he told me when I queried him about the document, to draft a sanitized version, omitting his description of the anti-Semitism prevailing in the Polish society, by a close confidant of then Prime Minister General Władysław Sikorski, Professor Stanisław Kot. Polish *raison d'etat* vis-à-vis the Allies required that the matter be covered up, he was told. For both versions of the document in their entirety, see *Mówią Wieki*, November 1992, 2–9.

19. See my *Polish Society under German Occupation: The Generalgouvernement, 1939–44* (Princeton: Princeton University Press, 1979), 184–86, for references to archival sources containing relevant documents.

20. See note 18.

21. See note 18.

22. It is some relief to know that the Polish boys got a thrashing at home when their parents learned about the episode from a woman the Jewish child told about it, and who knew his father. Władysław Bartoszewski and Zofia Lewin (eds.), *Righteous among Nations: How Poles Helped the Jews, 1939–45* (London,

Earlscourt Publications, 1969), 411–12. As Michał Głowiński sadly commented in retrospect on his own childhood encounter when he was threatened with denunciation by three fellow boys from the orphanage where his family placed him—"In the cruelty of children the cruelty of the epoch is concentrated and reflected. It mirrors swineries perpetrated in the grown-up world" (Michał Głowiński, *Czarne Sezony*) [Warszawa: OPEN, 1998], 116).

23. The standard word used in parlance of the common people in Poland when refering to Jews is "Żydek," instead of "Żyd." It is a diminutive with a derogatory connotation, not exactly a "kike" perhaps, though close. Hence I translate it as "Jew-boy." It would be used in reference to a grownup as well as a child. There are many much more directly pejorative terms to choose from as well. One would use "Żydek" as a matter of course, without a particularly vicious or ridiculing intent.

24. Michał Głowiński, *Czarne Sezony* 93–96.

25. This, in any case, was the conclusion of a Dr. Schöngarth, commander of the SD in the *Generalgouvernement* who spoke as follows during one of the conferences on security problems with the governor general in 1941: "We must consider as members of the resistance movement not only those who actually belong to the organization. *Sicherheitspolizei* considers all the Poles as members of a resistance movement in the broader sense of the term" (Hans Frank, *Okupacja i ruch oporu w dzienniku Hansa Franka*, vol. 1, L. Dobroszycki et al., eds. (Warszawa: Książka i Wiedza), 366.

26. In Hochberg-Mariańska's introduction to a 1947 book of personal testimonies by Jewish children who survived the war, we read that several Poles who had helped Jews during the war requested anonymity for fear of hostile reactions in their own communities if their wartime deeds became known (Maria Hochberg-Mariańska's introduction to *Dzieci Oskarżają* [Kraków]: Centralna Żydowska Komisja Historyczna w Polsce, 1947). See also Nechama Tec's memoir *Dry Tears: The Story of a Lost Childhood* (New York: Oxford University Press, 1984). It is a fascinating theme—why those whom later we will honor as Righteous Among Nations were afraid of their neighbors should those neighbors find out that they had helped the Jews during the war. I have a hypothesis that somewhat anticipates what will be argued in this essay. In the first place, I believe, they feared becoming victims of robbery (see, in this respect, Shraga Feivel Bielawski, *The Last Jew from Węgrów* [New York: Praeger, 1991], 92, 147). In popular imagination, Jews were associated with money, and people were persuaded that those who sheltered Jews during the war must have enriched themselves as a result. But they also had another reason. Their wartime behavior broke the socially approved norm and demonstrated that they were different from anybody else and, therefore, a danger to the community. They were a threat to others because, potentially, they could bear witness. They could tell what happened to local Jews because they were not—neither by their deeds nor by their reluctance to act—bonded into a community of silence over this matter, a community of silence that shrouded the issue in many a place. As an illustration of this point I recommend a stunning documentary by a young filmmaker Paweł Łoziński entitled *Miejsce urodzenia* (The Birthplace), or a book by Henryk Grynberg, the film's protagonist, under the same title. Łoziński follows Grynberg as he returns

to a little village where he was hiding with his family as a child during the war. He comes on a quest to hopefully find the details of his father's death. One spring day in 1944, his father left the hiding place in the forest on a regular errand to get food for the family and never came back. To make a long story short, in the last sequence Grynberg's father's skeleton is dug out, together with a glass bottle the man always carried with him to bring milk to his children. All was known in the village—who killed him, why (over a cow he left for safekeeping and, as the end of the war was approaching, was likely to reclaim soon), and where he was buried—and was fearfully kept under wraps for forty years, and only reluctantly revealed at Grynberg's prodding.

In an identical circumstance, in which wartime murder of local Jews by their neighbors is a well-kept secret known to all in the community fifty years after the war, see Aharon Appelfeld's moving reminiscence from a 1996 return trip to his native village published in the *The New Yorker* (23 November 1998), as "Buried Homeland," especially p. 54.

27. See, for example, Tec's *When Light Pierced Darkness*, especially pages 58, 59, and chapter 10.

28. Zygmunt Klukowski, *Dziennik z lat okupacji zamojszczyzny* (Lublin: Ludowa Spółdzielnia Wydawnicza, 1958).

29. Ibid., entry of 23.9.1939.

30. Ibid., entry of 25.4.1940; see also pp. 113, 149, 183.

31. Ibid., entry of 12.8.1940.

32. Ibid., entry of 10.3.1941.

33. Ibid., entry of 13.4.1942.

34. Ibid., entry of 8.5.1942.

35. Ibid., entry of 17.5.1942.

36. Ibid., entry of 9.5.1942.

37. Ibid., entry of 24.5.1942 and 17.7.1942. In a bizarre coincidence members of the 101 Reserve Police Batallion would be tried after the war for these killings in Józefów, and Christopher Browning would use the trial records to write his pathbreaking *Ordinary Men: Reserve Police Battalion 101 and the Final Solution in Poland* (New York: Harper and Collins, 1992).

38. Klukowski, *Dziennik*, entry of 8.8.1942.

39. Ibid., entry of 21.10.1942.

40. Ibid., entry of 26.10.1942.

41. Ibid., entry of 26.11.1942.

42. Ibid., entry of 29.10.1942.

43. Ibid., entry of 4.11.1942. Similar conclusions can be drawn from numerical account of the activities of the Reserve Police Battalion 101 investigated by Browning: between July 1942 and November 1943 it killed in its area of operation a "minimum" of 38,000 Jews and it deported to Treblinka, between August 1942 and May 1943, the total of 45,200 Jews (Browning, *Ordinary Men*, 191, 192).

44. Before the war Jews made up somewhere around 9 percent of the total population in the territories later occupied by the Red Army. They were scattered, amounting to no more than 5.2 percent in the Wilno voivodeship and reaching the high of 12 percent in the Białystok viovodeship. Being settled predominantly

in urban areas, however, they were a more visible minority than these numbers suggest. If one adds to these figures some 250,000 to 350,000 war refugees who flocked into this territory from Western and Central Poland, one ends up with about 1.5 million Jews living there in 1939–41, about 11 percent of the total population. The number of Jews in some of the largest cities such as Lwów, Białystok, or Wilno, for example, is reported to have doubled within a month or two following the outbreak of the war. For various estimates, see Shimon Redlich, "The Jews in the Soviet Annexed Territories 1939–41," in *Soviet Jewish Affairs* 1 (1971) 81; Bernard Weinryb, "Polish Jews under Soviet Rule," in *The Jews in the Soviet Satellites*, Peter Meyeer, Bernard Weinryb, Eugene Dushinsky, and Nicolas Sylvain, eds. (Syracuse: Syracuse University Press, 1953), 331; Szyja Bronsztajn, *Ludność żydowska w Polsce w okresie międzywojennym: Studium statystyczne* (Warszawa: Ossolineum, 1963), 114; Dov Levin, *The Lesser of Two Evils: Eastern European Jewry under Soviet Rule, 1939–41* (Philadelphia and Jerusalem: Jewish Publication Society, 1995), 18.

45. Even among high officers of the Polish Army and functionaries of the administation—i.e., among those who were presumably best positioned to know what was going on—confusion was widespread. In Tarnopol county, prefect Majkowski urged the town population through loudspeakers to give a friendly welcome to the entering Soviet army. Posters signed by the mayor of Stanisławów and appealing for a calm, friendly, reception were put up throughout the city on the morning of 18 September. In Równe the county prefect came out personally with a retinue of local officials to great the spearhead of the Soviet column. He thanked the Red Army profusely for bringing help to Poles locked in combat with the German invaders. In Kopyczyńce a city official spoke from the town hall balcony: "Gentlemen, Poles, soldiers, we will beat the Germans now that the Bolsheviks are going to help us," while Red Army commanders embraced Polish officers. Soviet columns marched through Tarnopol and Łuck side by side with detachments of the Polish army, each giving way to the other at intersections (Hoover Institution [HI], Polish Government Collection [PGC], individual testimonies nos. 4102, 7568, 10015, 10204, 3435, 7557; Anders Collection [AC], 4307).

46. HI, PGC, Nieśwież, 13.

47. See, for example, the following county reports from the HI, PGC, białostocki, p. 3; białystok, p. 3, 4; sokolski, p. 9; mołodeczno, p. 5, 9; postawy, p. 5; dzisna, p. 4; brasław, p. 3; prużana, p. 2; nadworna, p. 17; łuck, p. 5; lida, p. 2, 3; szczuczyn, p. 1; nowogródzki, p. 10, 11; horochów, 2; sambor, p. 6; kowel, p. 7.

48. HI, Poland. Ambasada USSR Collection, Box 46, Stanisława Kwiatkowska; Box 47, Alicja Sierańska; PGC, 3194, 4060, 7508; nieśwież, p. 13; postawy, p. 5; wilejka, p. 5; sokolski, p. 9; kołomyja, p. 22; kostopol, p. 5.

49. Yad Vashem [YV], 03/2309, 03/1791; PGC, drohobycz, p. 2; PGC, Box 131, Palestinian protocol no. 187.

50. Interview with Celina Konińska, who at the time was a member of the Communist Youth Organization (Tel Aviv, summer 1980).

51. To continue Konińska's account: "First contact with the Russians, I mean with the Soviet soldiers, struck us as something strange and unpleasant. We thought that every soldier was a communist and therefore it was also obvious to

us that each must be happy. So their comportment, their behavior, struck us as queer. First of all their looking after things, after material objects—watches, clothing—with so much interest and so much rapacity. We waited for them to ask about life under capitalism and to tell us what it was like in Russia. But all they wanted was to buy a watch (we met those who wanted to buy, not those who just took it). I noticed that they were preoccupied with worldly goods, and we were waiting for ideals." Or take the case of this left-wing Zionist, who also must have sensed that something was amiss when he asked a newly met Soviet officer about the prospects of emigration to Palestine and heard in reply that the Soviet authorities would gladly create Palestine for Jews, but . . . "right here . . . One of them, himself a Jew, said to us, 'You want to go to Palestine? Fine, l'shana habaah b'Yerushalayim—next year we shall be all in Jerusalem. The Soviets will be there too'" ([Hashomer Hatzair] *Youth Amidst the Ruins: A Chronicle of Jewish Youth in the War* [New York: Scopus, 1941], 88, 90).

52. When "anarchy" began in Drohiczyn county, "everybody hoped that some pacification detachment would come—it didn't matter whether ours or foreign—and restore order." Józef Użar-Śliwiński, a Polish military settler who wrote these words, fled to Drohiczyn where "the Soviet authorities and the military had already arrived." Only after three weeks did he dare return to his village (HI, Poland. Ambasada USSR Collection, Box 47). A forester from Dolina county recalls that he "had to leave the house and all posessions and hide with the whole family in the forest until the Soviets came" (HI, Poland. Ambasada USSR Collection, Box 47; see also PGC, 2432, 8764; AC, 1078). For a more general discussion of the anarchy and civil war in this area, see my *Revolution from Abroad: The Soviet Conquest of Poland's Western Ukraine and Western Belorussia* (Princeton: Princeton University Press, 1988), 35–45.

53. HI, Poland. Ambasada USSR Collection, Box 48, Barbara Lejowa.

54. For some preliminary statistics, see Szymon Datner's "Zbrodnie Wehrmachtu w Polsce w czasie kampanii wrześniowej," in S. Bronsztajn, ed., *Ludność żydowska w Polsce*, 269.

55. HI, PGC, Box 131, Palestinian protocol no. 85; see also Palestinian protocols nos. 120, 124, 182, 188; AC, 10559, 15526.

56. For ample evidence indicating the absence of Jewish functionaries, see chapter 2 of my *Revolution from Abroad* where I quote lists of names of local functionaries on the basis of testimonies preserved in the Hoover Institution Archives. One may also consult recently opened Soviet archives for confirmation. See, for example, *Okupacja sowiecka (1939–41) w świetle tajnych dokumentów: Obywatele polscy na kresach północno-wschodnich II Rzeczypospolitej pod okupacją sowiecką w latach 1939–1941*, Tomasz Strzembosz, Krzysztof Jasiewicz, and Marek Wierzbicki, eds. (Warszawa: Instytut Studiów Politycznych, PAN, 1996). In a contemporaneous Soviet document on the establishment of temporary authorities and peasant committees in Western Belorussia, the following individuals are listed as operating within the jurisdiction of the War Council of the Belorussian Front: "Brykov, Babayev, Otvalko, Kotovitch, Kushtel Joseph Antonovich, Bogdanovitch Vladimir Benediktovich, Puzyrevski Mikhal Adamovitch, Tomko Leon Igantevitch, Kirilenko Iosif Antonovitch, Leisha Vasili Dominikovitch, Gasiul Boris Martinovitch, Lukianov Matviey Grigorevitch, Bielski Joseph

Antonovitch, Yefimov Nikifor Ilitch, Sherstnev Pavel Grigorevitch, Yurkevitch Andrei Andreievitch, Zilberman Moysey Borysovitch, Gaukshtel Nikolai Frantzevitch, Boronov Dimitri, Pazurevski, Gradkovski Kazimir Adamovitch, Titovich Aleksander Antonovitch, Parfenov Yevstigenij Fedorovitch, Pitiukevich Wilhelm Walerianovitch, Lysenok Nikifor Andreyevitch, Rafalovitch Aleksander Mikhailovitch, Sharanovich Motel Leibovitch, Leonard Mikhailovitch Dubickij." Among the twenty-eight persons listed above, perhaps three or four, judging by their names, might be Jewish (*Okupacja Sowiecka*, document no. 1, 49–55). For further evidence see also document no. 49, 194–97; document no. 50, 198–99; document no. 52, 205; document no. 53, 207.

57. HI, AC, 12128. See also HI, AC, 10560, 12332, 12333, 12334; PGC, Box 131, Palestinian protocol no. 186.

58. *Khrushchev Remembers*, Strobe Talbott, ed. (Boston: Little Brown, 1970), 141.

59. Chaim Hades (*sic*!) from Brześć wrote the following: "I stood long hours in line and I finally got the authorization card for departure, which was considered at the time a pot of luck. A German officer turned to a crowd of standing Jews and asked: 'Jews, where are you going? Don't you realize that we will kill you?'" (HI, PGC, Box 131, Palestinian protocol no. 148).

60. Dov Levin, in his important recent study, puts it as follows: "Over time, however, the sense of relief dissipated and the Soviet regime wore out its welcome. Passive resistance increased, and some Jews actively opposed the arrangements imposed by the new regime. They refused to work on the Sabbath, adhered strictly to religious customs, crossed the borders between the annexed areas, maintained contacts with foreign countries (even transferring information), and criticised the regime (behind a smokescreen of jokes and other devices). This unwillingness to acquiesce was especially prevalent in groups and organizations that previously had been known for nonconformism. Some of these now merged into new underground frameworks in order to continue inculcating their ideologies and values. . . . Zionist groups did not reject the fact of the annexation of their areas of residence. Even so, their positions and behavior in response to Soviet anti-Zionism constituted acts of organized resistance, however passive most of them were. . . . In due course, the very term underground became a specific synonym for clandestine Zionist activity of various kinds by Jews in the annexed territories" (*The Lesser of Two Evils*, 235–36).

61. HI, PGC, Box 588, "Obliczenie ludności polskiej deportowanej do ZSSR w latach od 1939 do 1941." For a more recent estimate of the national composition of the deportees, excluding labor camp inmates, see Grzegorz Hryciuk, "Zasady i tryb deportacji: Liczebność i rozmieszczenie zesłańców," in *Życie codzienne polskich zesłańców w ZSRR w latach 1940–46*, Stanisław Ciesielski, ed. (Wrocław: Wydawnictwa Uniwersytetu Wrocławskiego, 1997), 31. According to Hryciuk's data about 23 percent of the deportees were Jewish, while 63 percent were of Polish nationality.

62. Shimon Redlich, "Jews in General Anders' Army in the Soviet Union 1941–42," *Soviet Jewish Affairs* 2 (1971): 97. Klemens Nussbaum, following Anders, quotes an even smaller number of four thousand evacuated Jews ("Jews in the Polish Army in the USSR, 1943–44," *Soviet Jewish Affairs* 3 [1972]: 95).

63. YV, SH, 191–2131, quoted after Ben-Cion Pinchuk, *Polish Shtetl under Soviet Rule* (in manuscript), 56.

64. HI, AC, 14528.

65. Dov Levin, *The Lesser of Two Evils*, 141–42; 29–30.

66. On the eve of the 1940–41 school year, in the summer of 1940, there were 1,003 Ukrainian-language schools, 314 Polish-language schools, 7 Russian-language schools, and 20 Yiddish-language schools in the Lwów district (*Czerwony Sztandar*, 20 August 1940). About 10–12 percent of the population in the area was Jewish, the rest more or less equally divided between Poles and Ukrainians. These numbers do not reflect the influx of refugees, predominantly Jewish, who dramatically swelled the population of Lwów and other towns in the district. By January 1941 the total number of Yiddish-language schools in the Lwów district had been further reduced to fourteen (*Czerwony Sztandar*, 5 January 1941). Naturally, the Yiddish-language Bund-sponsored school system, TSISHO, as well as the Zionist-sponsored Tarbut, were both closed.

67. Dov Levin, *The Lesser of Two Evils*, 143–46.

68. Pinchuk, *Polish Shtetl*, 68.

69. Ibid., 68.

70. The dispatch was authored by the son of General Januszajtis and may be found in the archives of the *Studium Polski Podziemne*j in London (3.1.2.1).

71. In the first two thousand individual statements collected from survivors of the Holocaust immediately after the war by the Jewish Historical Commission and now deposited, over seven thousand of them, in the Jewish Historical Museum in Warsaw (Relacje indywidualne, collection no. 301), one may find details about such pogroms in Bolechów, Borysław, Borczów, Brzeżany, Buczacz, Czortków, Drohobycz, Dubna, Gródek Jagielloński, Jaworów, Jedwabne, Kołomyja, Korycin, Krzemieniec, Lwów, Radziłów, Sambor, Sasów, Schodnica, Sokal, Stryj, Szumsk, Tarnopol, Tłuste, Trembowla, Tuczyn, Wizna, Woronów, Zaborów, and Złoczów. A concise article with summary data on this subject was presented by Dr. Andrzej Żbikowski at a conference on the *Holocaust in the Soviet Union* held at Yeshiva University in New York in October 1991 and entitled "Local Pogroms in the Occupied East Poland Territories, June–July 1941."

72. Lublin is the name of the city where, since 1 August 1944, the Committee for National Liberation (PKWN) established in Moscow on July 20 took seat, as a temporary executive authority for liberated Polish territories. It published a "Manifesto" on July 22 (known as the "July Manifesto") denouncing the London government in exile and declaring itself as the only legal authority in Poland during the period of liberation.

73. Let me also point out that the numbers at stake in our case—a few dozen names altogether—are trivial given the total Polish population of around 27 million at the time.

74. For a recent study of the Central Committee of Polish Jews and its politics, see David Engel, *East European Politics and Societies*, vol. 10, 1996.

75. Żydowski Instytut Historyczny (ŻIH), Centralny Komitet Żydów w Polsce (CKŻP), Komisja Specjalna (KS), box no. 3–7, "Sprawozdanie z działalności CKS przy CKŻP," pages 1, 3, 4. CKS files are deposited in two boxes numbered "1–2" and "3–7."

76. The pogrom, which lasted for almost an entire day and involved the participation of hundreds of Kielce inhabitants, resulted in the murder of forty-two Jews. It began with the made-up accusation of a young boy who, at the instigation of his father, declared that he was held captive for a few days in the basement of a house where Jewish returnees lived in Kielce (the house, incidentally, did not have a basement). A squad of Citizens' Militia was then dispatched to search the house and investigate the matter, and the pogrom started. Both militia and uniformed soldiers were involved in the killings. There was certainly massive incompetence on the part of security forces and the way they responded to unfolding events, maybe even foul play. The main preoccupation among Polish historians and journalists addressing the subject (such as there was, for the matter was considered taboo) was mostly about whether this was a deliberate provocation by the security police. The best study of the Kielce pogrom can be found in Bożena Szaynok's *Pogrom Żydów w Kielcach 4, 7 1946r.* (Warsaw: Wydawnictwo Bellona, 1991).

77. The episode is described in Yitzhak Zuckerman's *A Surplus of Memory: Chronicle of the Warsaw Ghetto Uprising* (Berkeley: University of California Press, 1993), ch. 15. Zuckerman does not mention Edelman in this context, but Marek Edelman, the Deputy Commander of ŻOB during the Warsaw Ghetto uprising, recollects that they both went to Kielce (personal communication).

78.

On the third of October [1946] at seven in the evening I boarded a train from Warsaw to Cracow. I was accompanied by my husband, Henryk Liberfreund, and Amalia Schenker. We rode in a compartment with a couple more passengers, including a nun. A candle was burning. We traveled peacefully until we reached Kamińsk station near Radomsko. In the meantime the candle burned out and passengers were sleeping in darkness. During the train stop in Kamińsk a man in civilian clothes, wearing a cap with an eagle sign and toting a submachine gun, entered the compartment. He checked the passengers one by one with a flashlight. When he reached my sleeping husband, he pulled the coat covering him and said "I got you, kike, *heraus, heraus, aussteigen.*" My husband drew back, unwilling to get off the train, and the man pulled him by the arm but could not budge him. Then he whistled and immediately another man appeared, whom I did not see very well, accompanied by the train conductor. I started screaming terribly, and then the first assailant pushed and pulled me using the words "*heraus, aussteigen.*" I pulled myself away; in the meantime the train took off, and the assailant pushed my husband off the train and jumped after him. I continued to scream and I don't know what happened afterward. I wish to add that nobody's documents were checked, not even my husband's. Other passengers and the conductor did not pay much attention to the whole episode; quite the opposite, they laughed and behaved rather improperly. One man sitting next to my husband was accosted by the assailant with the words "you Jew." But he stated that he could show documents that he was not a Jew, and he was left alone.

The following, unusually detailed description—for the most part murders on the railroad leave little trace in the archives—is supplemented by an unsigned memorandum entitled "Information," dated three days after the event:

On the Cracow-Warsaw line, trains go through Kamińsk about fifteen minutes after Radomsko. Railroad line cuts through this village situated in a wood, with houses built along the track. Inhabitants of these houses before the war, during the war, and now, for the most part live off the passing trains. This applied especially to coal transports that passed thereby. Almost all the people in the vicinity made a living from coal pushed off these trains, especially at night. In two of these houses, one right next to the station and the other a one-story house farther down, there lives a bunch whose central figure is a woman of dubious reputation. . . . They party at night and drink and from time to time they stake a passing train in expectation of some spoils. Jewish passengers are now victimized by these bands, for they can be easily scared with a gun, taken off a train, robbed of cash and possessions in a forest, where all of this is taking place, and then they can be made to disappear, and thus one gains an easy living for oneself and one's companions. This area should be carefully watched and put under observation.

Whether anything noteworthy was observed I cannot tell, but the circumstances of Liberfreund's disappearance were not found out (ŻIH, CKŻP, CKS, box 1–2, pages 156–58).

79. The phrasing of this document is somewhat oblique and awkward in Polish as well, State Archive in Cracow (SAC), Urząd Wojewódzki (UW) 2, File 1073.

80. I.e., local agendas of the Central Committee of Polish Jews established in several localities with sizeable Jewish populations.

81. SAC, UW 2, File 1073, memo from the County Jewish Committee in Chrzanów to the Sociopolitical Department of the Cracow Voivodeship dated 11 July 1945.

82. SAC, UW 2, File 1071, Card 183, "Stan liczebny poszczególnych narodowości w chwili obecnej."

83. ŻIH, CKŻP, CKS, box 1–2, "Komisja Specjalna w Krakowie, Oświęcim, 27.1.1947. On 20 October 1945 deputy commander of the Soviet counterintelligence agency SMERSH, Nikolai Selivanovsky, who in 1945–46 was serving as advisor to the Polish Ministry of Public Security, sent to Lavrentii Beria in Moscow a lengthy "Report on the Situation of the Jewish Population in Poland." The document can currently be found in the "special files" (osobye papki) of Molotov and Stalin in the State Archives of the Russian Federation (GARF), fond 9401, opis 2, delo 104, pp. 81–89. He described in it, among other things, an episode illlustrating anti-Semitic attitudes of employees of the Ministry of Public Security. "In the Ministry of Public Security," writes Selivanovsky in his report, "there is a box for suggestions to improve the work of this authority. In the box there were found two anonymous letters with the following contents: "Why does democratic Poland exist only for the Jews? Why do only they have power there and everything is for them? Why do they all have high positions, why are they the kierowniki, the bosses? Why can they use their diamonds and gold to gain the ranks of colonels, lieutenant colonels, majors, in short all kinds of officers, rather than we rank and file'" and more in a similar vein. Excerpts from this and other NKVD reports from Poland contained in Stalin's "special files" were recently published in Poland as Teczka Specjalna J. W. Stalina. Raporty NKWD z Polski 1944–46,

Tatiana Cariewskaja and others, eds. (Warszawa: Rytm, 1998). Selivanovsky's report also offers a telling example of anti-Semitism among the personnel of the Citizens Militia—forty militiament were arrested for participation in the anti-Jewish pogrom in Cracow in August 1945. I am grateful to Natalia Aleksiun for sharing with me the entire text of the October 20 report.

84. APK, UW 2, file 1073. As I read only Cracow voivodeship archives all my examples are from that area. But I want to stress again that the hostility of local authorities was a general phenomenon. In a recent article Ewa Koźminska-Frejlak quotes yet another reprimand sent out from the Ministry of Public Administration—in that case to the Kielce voivodeship authorities: "In Jędrzejów the county head (starosta) Feliks turns down all cases presented by Jews. The same situation prevails in Chęciny and Chmielnik. The city Council in Ostrowiec called representatives of the Jewish committee and requested that all Jews be sent to work in a mine." See Ewa Koźminiska-Frejlak, "Polska jako ojczyna Żydów—żydowskie strategi zadomowienia się w powojennej Polsce (1944–49)," in Kultura i Społeczeństwo, vol. 43, 1 (1999): 131.

85. Padraic Kenney, Rebuilding Poland: Workers and Communists, 1945–50 (Ithaca: Cornell University Press, 1997), 111, 114, 115.

86. APK, KWZ, file 14, p. 87.

87. APK, UW 2, file 173, Pismo Żydowskiego Zrzeszenia Religijnego w Krakowie do Obywatela Wojewody Krakowskiego, 25, 7, 1945.

88. ZIH, individual statements, collection no. 301, doc. no. 1582, Hania Zajdman.

89. See a very moving recollection by Michal Głowiński, entitled "It Is I Who Killed Jesus Christ," in which he describes an anti-Semite priest who taught religion and hatred against Jews in his primary school immediately after the war, and a beating he suffered as a result from a fellow student (Głowiński, Czarne sezony 144–55).

90. ŻIH, CKŻP, CKS, box 1–2, folder 1, p. 114, notatka do MBP dated 6.11.1946.

91. APK, UW 2, file 905, p. 26.

92. APK, UW 2, file 914, "Sprawozdanie z powiatu bocheńskiego," dated 21.8.1945.

93. ŻIH, CKŻP, box 3–7, p. 107, "Sprawozdanie KS przy WKS w Warszawie."

94. ŻIH, CKŻP, CKS, box 1–2, p. 282, Komitet Żydowski w Nowej Rudzie do Urzędu Bezpieczeństwa w Nowej Rudzie, Doniesienie; 8.12.1946.

95. ŻIH, CKŻP, box 1–2, p. 317. See also Andrzej Friszke, "Żydzi w szkolnych podręcznikach," Więź, vol. 42, 1 (1999): 23–36.

96. Natalia Aleksiun-Mądrzak recently published a multipart article on the subject in the Biuletyn ŻIH.

97. On the scandalous treatment, or rather neglect, of this subject in primary- and high-school history textbooks, read the special issue of the quarterly Biuletyn Żydowskiego Instytutu Historycznego (no. 3–4, 1997) devoted to the analysis of coverage of "Jewish Subjects in School Textbooks." Thirty-nine different textbooks approved by the Ministry of Education and published between 1994 and 1997 are reviewed in this issue.

98. Lewis Namier, *1848: The Revolution of the Intellectuals* (New York: Doubleday and Co., 1964), 58.

99. I wish to end on a positive note, however, in recognition of a number of great authors in Poland who always spoke on this subject with audacity and wisdom—Jerzy Andrzejewski, Jan Błoński, Czesław Miłosz, Zofia Nałkowska, Stanisław Ossowski, or Kazimierz Wyka—and a new generation of scholars who in recent years have taken on the subject with critical and open minds: Natalia Aleksiun-Mądrzak, Alina Cała, Barbara Engelking-Boni, Ewa Koźmińska, Paweł Szapiro, Bożena Szaynok, or Andrzej Żbikowski. We are on the verge, I believe, of a major reassessment of the epoch by Polish historiography, and a new sensitivity and awareness concerning all matters Jewish among the Polish public.

Part III

TRIALS AND POLITICAL EXPEDIENCY

MARTIN CONWAY

Justice in Postwar Belgium:
Popular Passions and Political Realities

JUSTICE IS of interest to historians principally because it is inescapably imperfect. If judicial procedures were conducted according to the absolute standards of the divine Day of Judgment that so haunted the medieval Christian imagination, casting down the wicked into hell and raising the virtuous to heaven, the role of the historian would be no more than to act as the accomplice of the Celestial Recorder. In fact, it is of course precisely because the definition and execution of justice is inextricably intertwined with, and molded by, wider social and political forces that historians of different eras have long found in the records of judicial proceedings a privileged window into the mentalities, structures, and internal tensions of diverse societies. The vast, sometimes chaotic or overly bureaucratic but also often impressively rigorous systems of justice that were established in most European states after the Second World War to judge those accused of collaboration and other crimes committed during the war years form no exception to this rule. Acting according to improvised procedures, severely constrained by a lack of resources and pressurized by the requirements of political authorities and the demands of popular expectations, the judicial authorities charged with the investigation of murky events could only hope to dispense a rough and approximate justice. The bitter legacies of the war years and the volatile amalgam of fears, hopes, and material sufferings that suffused the liberation of Europe all too rarely provided an environment conducive to the dispassionate dispensation of justice.[1]

The improvised and imperfect nature of postwar justice should not be used—as has become increasingly fashionable in recent years—to discredit the entire project of the prosecution of crimes committed during the war years. Amid the inevitable examples of miscarriages of justice and of inconsistencies in the judgments and sentences passed, it is important to bear in mind that the prosecutions also represented an attempt to pursue those responsible for manifold forms of suffering and to do so in a manner that reasserted principles of justice and liberty. Postwar justice in western Europe was imperfect but its purpose was not unworthy, and not all of the judgments and sentences were incorrect.

It is, however, less the content of the trials themselves than the ways in which the prosecutions were determined by the political and social circumstances of their time that constitute their historical importance. As a number of studies have demonstrated,[2] the shape and character of the various purges and prosecutions provide an excellent means of analyzing the dynamics of European societies in the immediate postwar years. The devising and implementation of the structures of justice constituted a highly politicized arena in which mass pressures and elite concerns were focused with a rare intensity. The drafting of legislation, the calculation of the criteria of guilt and innocence, and the nature of the sentences passed all aroused considerable public controversy and frequently occupied a dominant position both in political debate and private conversations. In effect, the prosecutions became one of the central means by which European societies debated not only their past failings but also their future character.

The importance of the postwar prosecutions as a contested space in which wider social and political conflicts were made manifest is well demonstrated by the example of Belgium. In some respects, the prosecution of those accused of collaboration proceeded more smoothly in Belgium than in a number of other European states. During the German occupation of 1940–44, the government-in-exile in London had issued decrees that revised the legal code in order to facilitate the subsequent prosecution of those who had chosen to serve the German cause as well as ensuring that all such prosecutions would be conducted by the Belgian military (rather than civilian) judicial authorities. The rapid liberation of Belgium in the first days of September 1944 avoided any vacuum of power and there were far fewer acts of spontaneous vengeance against those accused of collaboration than occurred during the much more protracted liberation of France. Aided by the firm support of the Allied military authorities and by the fortuitous absence in detention in Germany of King Leopold III, the Belgian authorities returning from London were able to reestablish their authority and to put in place the structures of military justice. Detention camps were established for those accused of crimes during the occupation, and a substantial bureaucracy of legal and police personnel was employed to prepare and conduct the trials. By 1946, 134 chambers of the *Conseils de Guerre* were in operation throughout the country. Dossiers were opened on 405,067 individuals accused of collaboration, and 57,254 were prosecuted. Of these, 2,940 were sentenced to death (of whom 242 were executed); 2,340 were sentenced to life imprisonment. By 1947 the majority of the trials had been completed and the bureaucracy gradually dismantled. In the early 1950s a large number of those sentenced to terms of imprisonment were released from jail prematurely. Unlike in many other countries, however, no amnesty was declared for wartime crimes and some former collaborators remain deprived of their civil rights.[3]

The postwar prosecutions were facilitated by the fact that it was in some respects easier in Belgium than in a number of other countries to define the frontier between what constituted acceptable and unacceptable behavior during the German occupation.[4] The German invasion of neutral Belgium on 10 May 1940 and the capitulation by King Leopold III as commander in chief of the Belgian armed forces on 28 May initially fostered an overwhelming desire for some form of accommodation with the apparently victorious Third Reich. Leopold III remained in the country and experienced a rather genteel imprisonment in the Palace of Laeken outside Brussels. In common with much of the political and social elite, he sought to develop some form of relationship with the German authorities, even traveling to Berchtesgaden in November 1940 for an inconclusive meeting with Hitler. This rapprochement proved, however, to be short-lived. As it became apparent in the winter of 1940–41 that the war had not in fact ended, the Wehrmacht authorities who governed occupied Belgium preferred to lend their support to emphatically collaborationist groups. Thus, in Francophone Belgium, they backed the Rexist movement led by Léon Degrelle, which, since its emergence as a dissident Catholic movement in 1936, had evolved rapidly toward a quasi-fascist stance. In Dutch-speaking Flanders the German authorities supported that strand of Flemish nationalism, represented primarily by the *Vlaams Nationaal Verbond* (VNV), that already during the occupation of the First World War had looked on the Germans as ethnic and ideological allies in their struggle for independence from the Francophone-led Belgian state.

Initially, neither the Rexists nor the Flemish Nationalists were negligible political groups but their progressively more emphatic espousal of the Nazi cause created a gulf between them and the large majority of the Belgian population, both French and Dutch speaking. The (illegal) appointment of collaborationists to prominent positions in the central and local bureaucracy, the ranting tone of much of the pro-German press, and, above all, the creation in 1941 of small Flemish and Francophone military units that fought alongside the German armies on the Eastern Front were all developments that offended the patriotic and increasingly pro-Allied sensibilities of the population. Collaborationists rapidly became a self-defining minority whose loyalties, political actions, and social behavior separated them from the majority. Against them stood a plethora of Resistance groupings and also the Belgian government in London. During the military campaign of May 1940, a profound political division had developed between the king and the government of national union headed by the Catholic prime minister Hubert Pierlot. While Leopold III remained in occupied Belgium, the government fled initially to France, hoping to continue the military struggle against the Germans. The French collapse in June 1940 initially caused the ministers to lose heart and to seek to return to Belgium. When this, however, proved not possible, Pierlot and three other senior ministers traveled to London, where in October 1940 they established a government-in-exile formally committed to the Allied cause.

This process of political polarization did not exclude the existence of a considerable gray zone of actions that constituted neither resistance nor collaboration. The king's stance of remaining in Belgium, refusing to support the German cause or the government in London, was symbolic of the *attentiste* attitude of much of the political, social, and economic elite, especially during the early war years. The form of indirect rule imposed on Belgium by the German authorities provided manifold opportunities for these notables to act as intermediaries between the population and the German occupiers. The state bureaucracy, the forces of law and order, and the principal industrialists all pursued a policy of *le moindre mal* by working with the Germans with the stated aim of alleviating suffering and protecting the national interest. Where exactly such accommodation shaded into collaboration lay at the heart of many of the principal postwar trials. Nevertheless, the difficulties of defining collaboration perhaps seem more evident to historians than to the Belgians who lived through the war years. After the liberation, few found it difficult to define who was a collaborator. The polarization of the latter war years, the existence of a legal government-in-exile, and the voluntarist extremism of the pro-German minority all helped to create a sense of a clear dividing line between the guilty collaborators and the innocent patriotic majority.

Despite such apparent clarity, the process of postwar prosecution aroused considerable controversy and public debate. This was especially so in the immediate postliberation period. Between September 1944 and the autumn of 1945, no issue—with the possible exception of the closely related controversy surrounding the wartime actions of Leopold III—aroused such sustained public passion. Parliament, the press, and, more especially, the informal arenas of debate, such as the street, workplace, and private correspondence, all bore witness to this intense and at times almost hysterical concern with the punishment of those "mauvais belges" whose actions were felt to be at the root of the sufferings and deprivations of the war years.

The passions aroused by the repression were in part the consequence of a number of conjunctural or "accidental" factors, notably the unexpected continuation of the war, the unpopularity of the postliberation government led by Hubert Pierlot, and the intense material suffering during the winter of 1944–45. But the issue of justice also straddled what can be seen in retrospect to have been two of the central fault lines of postwar Belgian politics. The first of these was the division between those committed to the reconstruction of a modified version of the prewar status quo and those diverse forces that since the 1930s had sought to replace the parliamentary state inherited from the nineteenth century by some form of new political and social order. For the former, the postwar repression was essentially an opportunity to crush those dissidents of the extreme right (the Flemish Nationalists and the predominantly Francophone Rexists) who had chosen to side with the Nazi occupying forces. For the latter, however, the purges always encompassed a much wider agenda. The repression of wartime crimes could not, they argued, be limited to actions of explicit collaboration; it must also embrace the administrative and social elite who had chosen to accommodate themselves to the apparent German hegemony in 1940 as well as those industrialists who, whatever their personal sentiments, had worked either directly or indirectly for the German war economy. For groups such as the left-wing resistance coalition, the *Front de l'Indépendance-Onafhankelijkheidsfront* (FI), the repression therefore became a means of calling into question the established political order and the social hierarchies upon which it was based. The war, they argued, had revealed "la carence des fausses élites" and must lead to a radical restructuring of the Belgian political community.[5]

The second fault line traversed by the issue of postwar justice was that between the mass of the population and the political elite. As contemporary observers frequently remarked, the demands for action against collaborators emanated above all from the people.[6] Though there clearly were differences of degree and emphasis, all of the evidence that we possess (notably the secret reports based on postal censorship) emphatically states that at least until the summer of 1945 a large majority of the population supported vigorous action against former collaborators. Various groupings, such as the Communists and the FI, sought at different times to exploit this sentiment, but they did not invent it. Indeed, it would seem that popular demands for severe action always exceeded the positions adopted by all of the major political forces. This divergence between the insistent popular calls for vengeance and the more pragmatic and limited view of repression that had become dominant in elite circles by the spring of 1945 highlighted the wider division that existed in postwar Belgium between the mass of the population and a small and relatively closed political and social elite. Far from undermining the position of this elite, the German occupation had in many respects strengthened it. The system of indirect rule in German-occupied Belgium had reinforced the power of privileged Belgian intermediaries such as the civil servants and local notables while the experience of exile in London created a division between many of the postwar political leaders and the mass of their compatriots who had experienced the reality of occupation.

The purpose of this contribution is to examine some of the ways in which the issue of justice impacted upon the political evolution of Belgium between the liberation and the end of 1945 and, conversely, the ways in which the nature, extent, and structure of the postwar purges were determined by this broader political context. This is not to claim that the repression was no more than a product of these wider forces. On the contrary, one of the most distinctive features of the process of justice in postwar Belgium was the relative autonomy maintained by the military justice authorities from political influences.[7] This independence was in part a reflection of the widespread public respect for the judicial process. The failings of the government were incessantly criticized, as on occasions were those lawyers who, it was felt, committed themselves too energetically to the defense of their collaborationist clients. But the courts themselves remained largely above criticism. Their actions commanded respect, and, after the oppression of the German occupation, their formal and ponderous procedures possessed an evident emotional importance as a symbol of the reestablishment of the principles of impartial justice.

This autonomy was also, however, a product of the relations of power between the judicial and political authorities. Amid the plethora of competing and overlapping responsibilities of Belgian and Allied authorities during the liberation and its aftermath, the military justice authorities succeeded in establishing a position of considerable independence. This success owed much to the controversial and authoritarian figure of Walter Ganshof van der Meersch. As chief military prosecutor (*Auditeur Général*) and *Haut Commissaire à la Sécurité de l'État*, a title that granted him wide authority over matters relating to the internal security of the country, Ganshof van der Meersch behaved at times as an almost proconsular figure. He dominated the implementation of the repression legislation that he had helped to draft in London and energetically repulsed all attempts to circumscribe the independence of the structures of military justice.[8]

Relations between the government and Ganshof van der Meersch were never without tensions but they deteriorated during the spring of 1945 as the new government headed by Achille Van Acker sought to impose its own priorities on the process of repression. The success of these efforts at imposing governmental control were, however, only limited. Thus, though a decree-law was issued by the Van Acker government in May 1945 defining the criteria that should be deemed to constitute economic collaboration, the interpretation of this law remained the domain of Ganshof van der Meersch and his staff. The frustration felt by Van Acker was revealed in August 1945 when in an improvised speech to parliament the prime minister accused the military judges of taking upon themselves the right to interpret the laws and of prolonging the process of repression in order to continue enjoying the privileges of their offices. Outraged by these remarks, the principal prosecutors and judges collectively threatened to resign, obliging the minister of justice to use the occasion of a speech to the Senate to withdraw the force of Van Acker's comments and pay fulsome tribute to the dedication and courage of the military judges.[9]

The relationship between the judicial and political spheres was therefore always complex. The respect accorded to the judicial process and the institutional independence enjoyed by the military justice authorities limited the opportunities for direct political intervention. At the same time, however, the postwar repression could not remain immune from the influence of wider political and social forces. This was particularly true at the moment of liberation in September 1944. The euphoria of release from German oppression, so long anticipated but also unexpected in its suddenness, provoked a wave of actions against those believed rightly or wrongly to have served the German cause. This "fureur populaire" followed patterns that in some respects recalled the traditions of a bygone era. There were a number of lynchings and incidents of torture, as well as ritual humiliations such as the shaving of women's heads that expressed the almost carnivalesque character of the moment.[10]

In other respects, however, these actions displayed a popular concern with the reassertion of the principles of law after the arbitrariness of the occupation. Whatever the excesses of some *exaltés* and the injustices perpetrated against innocent victims of misidentification or of malicious rumor, the street theater of September 1944 was focused primarily on the legal rituals of the arrest and incarceration of collaborators. As the minister of justice in 1945, Charles du Bus de Warnaffe subsequently remarked, fears in some bourgeois circles that the liberation would serve as the pretext for a St. Bartholomew's Day massacre proved to be mistaken.[11] Rather than supplanting the police and the judiciary, the resistance groups and crowds sought to participate in that legal process by apprehending collaborators and transferring them into the hands of the sometimes embarrassed authorities.

The events of September 1944 expressed therefore not merely the transient intoxication of liberation but also a deeply held belief in the necessity of a "justice sévère et expéditive."[12] Far from subsiding, this conviction hardened during the subsequent weeks. The prosecution of all of those responsible not merely for wartime crimes but also more generally for the sufferings of the war years remained throughout the autumn of 1944 a central and at times obsessive concern of a large majority of the population.[13] This strength of feeling was reflected in the continuation of local improvised acts of justice but it was above all to the government that the people looked for decisive action and against whom their ire came to be directed when their expectations were not fulfilled. As early as mid-September complaints were being voiced at the premature release of some collaborators and at the failure to arrest others, but it was during the subsequent month that such criticisms became widespread.[14] The profound unpopularity that enveloped the government led by Hubert Pierlot during the autumn of 1944 had many origins. Shortages of foodstuffs and of fuel, as well as the government's awkward attempts to enforce the demobilization of the resistance movements, were no doubt sufficient to lose much of its credibility. If there was, however, one factor above all others that turned the population against the government and led eventually to its resignation in February 1945, it was its failure to meet popular expectations regarding the repression.

These criticisms were in some respects unjust. By the end of October, the structures of military justice were already in place. The internment camps had been largely brought under central control, and the conditions in them were gradually improved. Though some detainees against whom there was no real evidence were gradually released, the prosecution of others went ahead rapidly.[15] Amid the manifold disruptions caused by the continuation of the war, these measures were no small achievement. But they in no way served to satisfy public opinion. There was, as a British Foreign Office report commented in December, "extreme bitterness" in all sections of the population at the failure of the Pierlot government to respond to the popular expectation of harsh action against all categories of war criminals.[16] In particular, the suspicion rapidly developed that while the miserable mercenaries of the Nazi cause, the "lampistes" as they were often called, were being punished harshly, the major figures—those who possessed the greatest influence or financial means—remained at liberty.[17] As a Brussels patriotic group commented in March 1945, the process of justice had become "une vaste comédie." There appeared to be no logic or purpose to the decisions of the authorities, and the minister of justice, Verbaest, seemed overwhelmed by the enormity of the task.[18]

Not surprisingly, the political opponents of the Pierlot government sought to exploit public dissatisfaction at the perceived failings of the repression. The prosecution of major industrialists was one of the principal demands voiced by the *Front de l'Indépendance* in its conflict with the government over the disarmament of resistance units in November 1944, and both the FI and the Communists returned repeatedly to this theme over the subsequent months. Conscious no doubt of the popular appeal of such demands, they posed as the advocates of a wide-ranging purge at all levels of Belgian society, emotively contrasting the actions of the gov-

ernment in firing on the FI demonstrators in Brussels on 25 November
while releasing alleged collaborators from detention.[19]

Despite such attempts at political manipulation, it is clear that the demands for a more vigorous repression transcended conventional partisan
divisions. Subsequently, some on the political right portrayed the six
months or so after the liberation as a time of a quasi "terreur blanche"
when a small minority of politically motivated resistance militants had
pursued their partisan policies of vengeance. Yet, though the arbitrary
actions of some resistance groups do appear to have aroused considerable
disquiet, there is little evidence that demands for the severe punishment of
war criminals were confined to a small minority. The people did not want
mob rule by ill-disciplined resistance units but support for a rapid and
severe purge remained overwhelming and insistent. Political figures were
well aware of public feelings on the issue[20] but the clearest evidence of
public opinion emerges from the weekly reports on postal censorship
compiled by the Ministry of National Defense. Exploiting their powers in
time of war, the authorities secretly opened and inspected all mail sent
abroad (as well as to the Congo) and to Allied and Belgian soldiers. Many
thousands of letters were examined each week and the detailed reports
provide a privileged insight into the preoccupations and attitudes of the
Belgian population.

An incomplete collection of these reports has recently become available
to historians in the papers of the prime minister Achille Van Acker and
they provide striking illustration of the public obsession with vengeance
against compatriots who had served the interests of the enemy. Though
the reports for the final months of 1944 are absent, those compiled during
the spring of 1945 reported a swelling chorus of bitter denunciations of
the failings of the repression. The authorities were denounced for acting
too slowly, for the inequality in their treatment of different categories of
defendants but, above all, for failing to punish those convicted of wartime
crimes sufficiently severely. Though some correspondents justified the
need for a "répression totale et rapide" in terms of justice or the need to
protect the country against a resurgence of the extreme right, the dominant logic was the simple one of punishment and of revenge. The censors
reported a "désir unanime de mesures fermes et énergiques" (6 April
1945), a "désir unanime de châtiment" (14 April 1945) and the "désir
ardent du public, de voir un châtiment exemplaire aux traîtres et pro-
allemands, quel qu'ils soient" (20 April 1945).[21]

Clearly, such evidence should not be accepted at face value. The reports available date from the spring of 1945 at a time when the imminent
collapse of the Third Reich fixed public attention on the horrors of the
Nazi regime and thereby on those who were perceived to have served its

interests. Many correspondents may, moreover, have exaggerated their feelings in private letters to distant friends and family, expressing their bitterness with a misleading enthusiasm and hyperbole. It is possible too that the military censors may have chosen to overemphasize the strength of public feeling on an issue with which they were in sympathy. Nevertheless, even allowing for such qualifications, it seems impossible to question seriously the evidence that emerges from these reports of a Belgian public preoccupied with the need for the energetic prosecution of wartime crimes.

This reality in turn raises the question as to why so many Belgians felt so strongly about this issue. In the difficult months of late 1944 and in 1945, there was no lack of other problems—the intense material shortages, the conflict between the resistance and the government, or the status of Leopold III, for instance—vying for public attention. And yet the issue of the repression seems, at least until the summer of 1945, to have remained at the forefront of public preoccupations. Certainly, this concern was not universal. Within the haute bourgeoisie there was not surprisingly always a concern that the "psychose de l'incivisme" could expand all too easily into an attack on other social targets.[22] It is possible also to distinguish between the virulent concern with repression evident in many of the tightly knit industrial communities of central Wallonia and Flanders with the less intense climate of the rural areas of northern Flanders and of Namur and the Luxembourg. Such distinctions are, however, always perilous. Rural repression was frequently as much a reality as was its urban equivalent, and sweeping generalizations, such as that the postwar purges were imposed on Flanders by the Belgian state, are little more than retrospective constructions.[23] The demands for justice may not have been universal but they were emphatically national and popular in character.

The bitterness that the issue of the repression aroused among the population had complex origins, but, as in many other areas of western Europe, its principal emotive force seems to have lain in the way in which it combined local desires for revenge with broader social and political themes. Postwar hostility toward those who had served the enemy was always intensely local in character. If political campaigns for a sterner repression policy stressed the threat that former collaborators allegedly posed to the future of the nation, the focus of popular feelings was always much more local. It was the physical presence of those accused of collaboration, denunciation or profiteering that was at the origin of numerous neighborhood disputes. Actions against collaborators frequently took on the character of archaic affirmations of community identity: lists were posted of individuals "invited" to leave communes; demonstrators paraded their victims around the streets or exposed them to public ridicule in the town square; houses of accused collaborators were sacked and their possessions distributed among local victims of the war.[24]

This rough justice reflected in part the localism that has long been a distinctive element of Belgian political culture. But it was also the more immediate consequence of the sufferings of the German occupation. The war had narrowed horizons. Local loyalties to family and neighborhood had taken precedence over wider concerns. The difficulties of travel and dependence on unofficial networks of local support had in effect confined much of the population within their communities. Never before had the institutions of local government—above all the *Maişon Communale*—acquired such a centrality in people's lives. It was the commune that distributed rationing stamps and acted as the essential intermediary between the population and the German authorities. The bitterness of local attitudes toward collaborators was, thus, in many respects the product of the stored-up resentments of the years of occupation. The sufferings, frustrations, and simple physical promiscuity of those years had left a volatile legacy that found expression in the denunciations and spontaneous acts of revenge that multiplied after the liberation. Communities vented their vengeance on those individuals accused of having exacerbated the sufferings of their neighbors either by having served the interests of the enemy or by having profited financially from the material sufferings.

This pursuit of wartime collaborators in some respects reflected no more than the primitive logic of revenge. Just as many Belgians had taken pleasure in the assassination of collaborators during the occupation or relished the material sufferings of the Germans in 1945, so they demanded the investigation and, above all, harsh punishment of those guilty men (and, more rarely, women) perceived to have been responsible for their own wartime sufferings. These accusations were often vague or misplaced and displayed exaggerated notions of the consequences of the actions of local collaborators. It was easier and also more satisfying to blame hardships on particular individuals than on the inevitable dislocations caused by the war or the actions of faceless German officials. As in all such local settlings of accounts, reputation and rumor were more important than evidence and accusations focused all too easily on the most exposed or vulnerable members of the community.

At the same time, however, the popular bitterness against collaborators also served as a metaphor for the expression of wider social and political concerns. Denunciations of economic profiteers, for example, frequently took the form of virulent urban attacks on a rural population believed to have enriched themselves during the occupation by selling food at black-market prices to their urban compatriots.[25] More generally, the pattern of popular accusations reflected the social tensions exacerbated during the occupation between the working classes and a prosperous elite of industrialists and property owners. The working class had been exposed most directly to the dangers and hardships of the war and had experienced a marked decline in its living standards.[26] Conversely, prosperous members of the bourgeoisie, cushioned by their influence and financial wealth, had been protected from many of the deprivations of war or in some cases had benefited from them. Not surprisingly, therefore, in the industrial regions of both Wallonia and Flanders, postwar demands for justice were strongly influenced by this social tension. Industrialists were denounced not merely because they were alleged to have contributed to the German war effort but also because to many workers it seemed that they had profited from the war to enrich themselves at the expense of their employees.[27]

Political aspirations were also inextricably intertwined with the demands for justice. As all observers recognized, there was a widespread hope that the war would lead to a more just social and political order.[28] This understandable optimism that the sufferings of the occupation would not prove to have been in vain transcended conventional political divisions. It found expression in the widespread support for enhanced systems of social security as well as in the numerous programmes of social and political reform. The desire for justice jutted awkwardly into this climate of reform. Especially in the minds of many politicians and administrators, the vindictive and negative spirit of prosecution of past crimes appeared to be the antithesis of a forward-looking programme of reconstruction. For much of the population, however, the pressure for the comprehensive prosecution of war criminals appeared to be an essential element of the process of postwar change. A metaphorical language of cleanliness and of sweeping away those responsible for the failures of the past frequently accompanied the popular rhetoric of the postwar purges. Only through an "assainissement total" could the basis be created for a new society and nation. Purges were therefore not just acts of revenge; they were also, however imperfectly, statements of a wider commitment to justice and freedom.[29]

The role of the postwar purges both as an expression of local community dynamics and as a means of articulating a wider social and political agenda helps to explain why the issue of justice possessed such emotional importance for many Belgians in the months following the liberation. It also explains, however, why it did not fit easily into the conventional divisions of Belgian political life. Certainly, as has already been seen, the *Front de l'Indépendance* sought to recuperate the issue of justice and use it to its own ends. In April 1945 the FI attempted to make itself the mouthpiece for popular dissatisfaction by proposing more rigorous measures for the prosecution of economic and political collaborators.[30] These efforts were never, however, successful. The image of the FI was too tarnished after its confrontation with the government in November 1944 to appeal to a broad cross section of the population and, although the FI long continued to advocate a wide-ranging purge of wartime collaborators, this failed to prevent its decline into a movement of marginal political importance.[31] The Communists made similar efforts to exploit the issue. Even after their return to the government in February 1945, they continued to use the failings of the policy of repression to attack the Catholic minister of justice, du Bus de Warnaffe, as one element of its more general goal of transforming the government of national unity into a more progressive "Popular Front" government.[32]

The powerful Socialist Party too sought to turn the issue of justice to its own advantage. The publication in February 1945 of an outspoken pastoral letter by the primate of Belgium, Cardinal Van Roey, criticizing the excesses of the postliberation repression enabled the Socialists to pose as the vigilant defenders of repression against the supposedly indulgent stance of their coalition partners, the Catholic Party.[33] This was a theme that appealed to the anticlerical prejudices of many Socialists and one that gained in strength after the political crisis provoked by the king's release from German detention in May and the eventual departure of the Catholic Party ministers from the government in August 1945. The logic of the Socialist Party's new position at the head of a predominantly secular coalition government, as well as the prospect of the first postwar parliamentary elections in February 1946, led Socialist leaders such as the party's president Max Buset to portray the policy of repression as part of the wider struggle between the forces of liberal democracy and those of a Leopoldist and clerical neofascism.[34]

These opportunist efforts to incorporate popular pressures into Catholic-Socialist political rivalries were never fully successful. Whatever the tendency of some on the Catholic right to view the entire postwar purges as a Communist plot, the newly reconstituted Catholic Party, the CVP-PSC, remained committed to the legal process of repression of wartime crimes.[35] Moreover, the real division was increasingly not that between the Socialist-led government and its Catholic opponents but the gulf that emerged between the vast majority of the political elite and much of the population. While many Belgians continued to demand a harsh and wide-ranging repression of wartime crimes, elite attitudes evolved rapidly during the spring and summer of 1945 toward a much more pragmatic definition of the repression. In particular, there was an increasing awareness among the political elite of the damage that lengthy and controversial prosecutions could inflict on the recovery of the country. During 1945, both in parliamentary debates and in contributions to the press, there was a new sobriety in the comments of many politicians. Unambivalent crimes, they argued, must be punished but the investigation of past actions must not be allowed to prejudice the political, economic, and moral reconstruction of the country.[36]

This new attitude was typified by the Socialist prime minister, Achille Van Acker. When he replaced Pierlot in February 1945, he promised to strike "vite et fort" against those guilty of wartime crimes. Often repeated in his subsequent public speeches, such declarations were, as Van Acker no doubt intended, widely seen as providing reassurance of his commitment to the policy of repression. From the outset, however, his efforts were principally directed toward ensuring that the prosecutions were completed as rapidly as possible. As he declared to the Senate on forming his second government in August: "La préoccupation principale doit être d'en finir [i.e. the repression] aussi vite que possible, de ne pas laisser s'envenimer la plaie."[37] To this end, those interned without charge were released, a new accelerated procedure was instituted for minor crimes, and a revised version of Article 115 of the legal code was decreed in May 1945 specifying the forms of wartime economic activity that were deemed punishable. This clarification of the criteria governing economic collaboration was in many respects no more than an overdue rationalization. A vast number of dossiers had been opened on those suspected of having collaborated economically with the Germans, and some definition of which actions should lead to prosecution was clearly essential. The terms in which the new text were formulated clearly indicated, however, that it was also intended to ensure that prosecutions were limited to those economic adventurers who had worked wholeheartedly for the Nazi cause. Those who had sought to resist German commands were to be exempted from punishment, and the investigation of economic collaboration, the decree stated, should not be permitted to prejudice "la reprise de l'activité industrielle et agricole du pays."[38]

The subordination of the pursuit of justice to the wider economic and moral interests of the nation evident in the actions of Van Acker was a stance shared by all of the principal political forces (with the partial exception of the Communists) from the middle of 1945 onward. This did not signify an abandonment of the repression of wartime crimes or still less the pardoning of those responsible for them. On the contrary, the trials of almost all of the major political collaborationist figures occurred during the latter months of 1945 or 1946 and culminated in harsh sentences. But there was a newfound belief, as Van Acker declared in a speech at Namur on 19 December 1945, that the repression was "une plaie qui ne peut durer des années. On ne reconstruit pas sur la haine."[39] The consensual policy of the political elite was therefore to confine the process of repression to the prosecution of clear acts of treason such as serving in the armies of the Reich, espousing its ideological goals, or assisting its police. Conversely, they sought to prevent it from becoming an obsessive witch-hunt of all wartime *faiblesses* or a means of calling into question the actions of those—notably the senior civil servants and industrialists—whose willingness to adapt to the German presence had formed the basis of the administration of Belgium during the occupation.

This policy was to some extent the product of specific pressures. Privately, influential industrialists such as the Baron De Launoit lobbied hard for the judicial investigation of their wartime activities to be brought to an end, and the employers' organization, the *Comité Central Industriel*, protested at the atmosphere of suspicion that surrounded many businessmen. To have maintained economic production during the war was, they argued, a patriotic act that had provided employment for their workers and saved the country from starvation.[40] More generally, however, this pragmatic approach to the issue of postwar justice was the consequence of the overriding priority accorded in 1945 and 1946 to the economic and political reconstruction of the country. In economic policy, this led governments to favor increases in industrial production to the exclusion of any other measure—such as wage increases for coal miners, the nationalization of key industries, or the investigation of the wartime actions of the industrialist elite—which might prejudice this goal.[41] Similarly, in the political sphere, the dominant objective was the restoration of the unitary Belgian state and the parliamentary liberal order enshrined in the Constitution of 1831. This goal encompassed certain reformist measures, such as the introduction of universal social security and eventually women's suffrage, but excluded other reforms—notably the regional devolution of power or a radical democratization of central and local government—that might have called into question the political order. In this wider context, the postwar repression became essentially a tool of political and economic reconstruction rather than a means of challenging the status quo.[42]

This limited and instrumentalist definition of the repression was at odds with the more violent and, in some respects, radical vision of much of the population. The people did not all want radical political or economic change but they did demand the energetic prosecution of those responsible for the sufferings of the war years and their exemplary punishment. The conflict between these contrasting definitions of the process of postwar justice came most dramatically to the fore during the popular disturbances that followed the end of the war in May 1945. These appear to have started at Ronse (Renaix) in West Flanders on the night of 23–24 April, when local resistance members stuck up posters demanding that ten reputedly collaborationist families should leave the town. Similar actions were reported a few days later in towns on the Belgian coast, notably at Knokke and Blankenberge.[43] It was, however, the announcement of the capitulation of the Reich on 8 May that gave a national momentum to these crowd actions. Amid the spontaneous celebrations that ensued, crowds in many areas of the country seized the opportunity to sack houses of collaborators, to parade those accused of wartime misdeeds around the streets or to force them to leave town. Further incidents occurred over the subsequent weekend of 12–13 May and throughout the following week, most notably in the west of the country. The most troubled areas were the provinces of West and East Flanders and the Hainaut where the generalization of attacks on collaborators led the provincial representative of the security authorities to send an alarmist report to his superiors on 16 May describing a "carence grave de l'autorité constituée."[44] In fact, passions seem to have subsequently calmed down before a second and more politically directed wave of protest actions and demonstrations erupted primarily in Brussels and Francophone Belgium at the end of May.[45]

As in September 1944, the form of these popular disturbances was an amalgam of traditional crowd actions and more contemporary attitudes. In some cases, the exuberance of celebration (and alcohol) played a major role, but in others the sacking of houses was carried out in a much more methodical and ritualized manner.[46] Many collaborators were assaulted and in some relatively isolated cases these actions had fatal consequences. At Oostende on 13 May a former employee of the Gestapo was thrown into the harbor and drowned while at Lessines; on 29 May a former Rexist was lynched on the railway station platform when he was discovered returning incognito from Germany. More frequently, however, the violence was largely symbolic, and collaborators (and their families) were merely exposed to the humiliation and insults of their fellow citizens.[47] Above all, there was a strong localist flavor to the disturbances. Collaborators were paraded around the streets, dragged to the town square, and obliged to pay obeisance to the war memorial, or taken to the frontiers of the commune and expelled. Such actions obeyed an improvised logic of community justice, and, rather than explicitly rejecting the superior authority of the law, the demonstrators saw themselves as remedying its failings by punishing those collaborators who had been released or by apprehending those who had succeeded in returning clandestinely to Belgium after the final collapse of the Reich.[48]

The immediate stimulus for the disturbances lay in the highly charged events of early May. The May Day parades and the German surrender as well as the controversy surrounding the possible return of Leopold III and the strikes that broke out in many industrial regions in May all served to create what Ganshof van der Meersch described on 12 May as "une vive et dangereuse effervescence."[49] Above all, however, popular emotions were heightened by the liberation of the principal Nazi death camps in April and the subsequent return to Belgium of emaciated former detainees. The revelation of the horrors of the camps provoked a wave of indignation that found its outlet in attacks on those who had assisted, however indirectly, the Nazi authorities. Local incidents frequently broke out in the wake of the return of prisoners from Germany or, as for example in the case of the disturbances at Ath, after a funeral service for those political prisoners who had died in Germany.[50]

In part, therefore, the May disturbances were not so much specifically an attack on former collaborators as a response to wider events. But they also had their origins in popular bitterness at the perceived slowness and leniency of the repression. Anger at the return to communities of former collaborators released from preventive detention had been mounting over the previous weeks, and the immediate reaction of the government to the disturbances was to order the redetention of all those collaborators whose liberty might provoke "un légitime scandale."[51] More generally, the crowd actions reflected the popular concern to achieve the comprehensive investigation and punishment of those who had served the Nazi cause. As the commander of the *Gendarmerie* in Mons reported to his superior on 16 May, the demonstrations in his area were an expression of popular exasperation at the fact that no collaborator had yet been executed in the city as well as the failure to prosecute "les industriels, commerçants ou fermiers accusés par la rumeur publique de collaboration économique ou de profits illicites pendant l'occupation." The only way of calming popular anger, he concluded, was to reintern all former detainees, extend the investigations of economic collaboration, and execute a number of prominent collaborators.[52]

Though the first demonstrations appear to have been purely local initiatives, many of the subsequent ones did benefit from a degree of external organization. The FI resistance movement played a part in instigating some actions, and, after initially reacting cautiously, the Communist Party changed its stance at its central committee meeting on 14 May and encouraged its membership to take the lead in organizing demonstrations as well as channeling them into attacks on the policies of du Bus de Warnaffe, the Catholic minister of justice. The consequence was the second wave of protest meetings and actions, which occurred in the last days of May and early June.[53] Despite these efforts at orchestration, the demonstrations initially enjoyed considerable public support. Mainstream newspapers such as *Le Soir* expressed their comprehension for the actions of the protesters and it was only once they became more widespread and more politicised that fears of "straatanarchie" began to temper public attitudes. Even so, the postal censors reported a "satisfaction générale" with the actions in letters sent during the first week of June.[54]

It would be wrong to exaggerate the importance of the events of May. Some regions, such as Liège, were hardly affected and the disturbances

were in many respects the transient product of an exceptional combination of circumstances. They posed little danger to the established political
order, and compared with other events that occurred at the same time,
notably the major wave of strikes that swept Wallonia during May and
the controversy surrounding Leopold III's wish to return to the country,
they had a limited political impact. The disturbances did, however, en-
capsulate the tension between the popular desire for a repression based
on revenge and punishment and the elite attitude that it should be subordinated to the greater good of national reconstruction. The crowd actions
were a last and, in some respects, desperate attempt to reclaim a popular
definition of postwar justice from the elite, but their consequence was
merely to accelerate the transformation of the purges into a judicial process carefully segregated from popular pressures.

The spectacle of what the Socialist newspaper *Le Peuple* termed "la
vindicte populaire"[55] reinforced the conviction of the government and of
the military justice authorities that the repression must be expedited as
rapidly as possible. At a press conference on 6 June the minister of justice,
du Bus de Warnaffe, sought to blame the demonstrations on "exciteurs
poursuivant un but politique" and insisted that the decisions of the courts
must remain indifferent to the appeals of the street.[56] This determination
to ensure that the prosecutions were removed from the dangerous realm
of public passions was assisted by the divisive political legacy of the disturbances. The belated decision of the Communists and their FI allies to
espouse the cause of the demonstrators brought the issue of the repression
much more directly into the sphere of political controversy. During the
subsequent summer the Communists campaigned energetically for a
more wide-ranging repression, organizing a large number of public meetings at which the issue of justice was closely linked to demands for the
abdication of Leopold III.[57] Conversely, the public disorder during May
and the subsequent Communist-directed campaign gave an unprecedented impetus to Catholic misgivings about the process of repression. In
June Du Bus de Warnaffe warned Belgians against imitating the "totalitarian" methods of foreign powers, and denunciations of a "justice à sens
unique" perpetrated by "de lakeien van Moscou" were frequently voiced
in Catholic and Leopoldist circles.[58]

The incorporation of the issue of the repression into partisan disputes
between Left and Right blunted its political impact. Rather than a focus
around which public passions could mobilize, it became part of wider
political disputes and as a consequence it lost both its autonomy and
much of its emotional force. There was no recurrence of the May Demonstrations, and, despite the rhetoric voiced on the political extremes, the
Van Acker government proceeded steadily with its limited but rigorous
policy of repression. The trials of leading Flemish Nationalists and Rex-

ists helped to assuage popular demands for justice and the repression became a primarily bureaucratic and judicial process. At the heart of this change was a marked evolution in public opinion. As the reports of both the *Sûreté* and the postal censors indicated, bitterness at the shortcomings of the repression remained strong throughout the summer of 1945. But, after a further brief rise in passions in early September at the time of the first anniversary of the liberation, the issue rapidly died away and during the autumn it ceased to be cited by the censors as a theme in correspondence.[59] Though its legacy was long evident in bitter local disputes and isolated violent attacks on former collaborators, the repression had in effect ceased by the end of 1945 to exercise a major influence over public or private debate. It had become a concern not of the present or the future but of the past.

In retrospect, the history of the postwar repression in Belgium—as in much of western Europe—can be seen to have been inseparable from the wider process of political normalization and economic and social reconstruction. The form and, more especially, the scope of the prosecutions was the product of a complex relationship between three overlapping dynamics: the rituals and procedures of the judicial process, the popular pressure for investigation and punishment, and the dictates of the national interest as perceived by the governing elite. These three forces occasionally worked in unison but they more frequently came into conflict with one another. Thus, if the first factor remained relatively constant throughout 1944 and 1945, it was the second that provided much of the initial energy behind the purges but the third that from the spring of 1945 defined the focus and the limits of the repression.

The ascendancy of this pragmatic governing mentality and the marginalization of popular demands for a more wide-ranging purge make it all too tempting to see the process of repression in terms of a radical potential that was gradually superseded by predominantly conservative goals. Rather than serving as a cathartic exploration of how Belgian society had responded to the challenge of German occupation, the postwar trials focused on specific crimes that were individual or ideological in nature. The extreme Right—or at least its collaborationist Flemish Nationalist and Rexist variants—was forcibly disbanded. Economic profiteers and the agents of the German police were punished for their criminal opportunism. So too were those who out of ideological enthusiasm or material necessity had betrayed their country to serve in German military and paramilitary units.

The investigation and prosecution of these crimes was a substantial achievement but it did not call into question the structures of the Belgian social and political order. Indeed, to a large extent the repression contributed to a stabilization of the prewar world. The dissolution of Rex and of the Flemish Nationalist *Vlaams Nationaal Verbond* (VNV) rid the parliamentary parties of their most irritating and threatening prewar opponents. In social terms, few of those prosecuted were powerful figures while—as became obvious during their trials[60]—many of the modest servants of the German cause came from the least favored sections of society. Conversely, none of the prewar political elite and very few major industrialists, local notables, or civil servants (other than German nominees) were held to account for their wartime actions. Far from expelling the prewar elite from their positions of authority, the repression became one of the central means whereby that elite recovered its leadership role from their collaborationist usurpers.[61]

To contrast this conservative reality with popular demands for a more wide-ranging purge is in many ways misleading. The postliberation desire for revenge was insistent and occasionally violent but it was not necessarily radical. The focus of the people's anger was more personal than political, and demands for the exemplary punishment of those responsible for wartime sufferings did not imply a commitment to major social or political changes. In one important respect, however, the popular mood after the liberation did challenge the norms of the political system. The calls for a thorough investigation of wartime behavior were based on the belief that those who had held positions of responsibility at both a national and local level during the war should be held to account for their actions. This in turn reflected the wider change that had taken place in popular attitudes. The events of the war years had cracked open the pervasive culture of deference within Belgian society and had created expectations of a new relationship between governors and governed. The pressures for a postwar investigation of wartime actions were one expression of this less deferential mentality and help to explain the cynical disillusionment that surrounded the process of repression once it had been deflected by the elite into the prosecution of explicit acts of collaboration. In this way, the postwar purges represented not merely a successful process of conservative reconstruction but also an abortive attempt to redefine the nature of citizenship within the Belgian political community.

Notes

1. See, for example, the contribution of Mark Mazower to this volume.
2. E.g., P. Novick, *The Resistance versus Vichy: The Purge of Collaborators in Liberated France* (London: Chatto and Windus, 1968); P. Romijn, *Snel, streng en rechtvardig* (Houten: De Haan, 1989).

3. See L. Huyse and S. Dhondt, *Onverwerkt verleden: Collaboratie en repressie in België, 1942–52* (Leuven: Kritak, 1991). This important work has also been published in a French edition as *La répression des collaborations, 1942–52* (Brussels: CRISP, 1993). See also L. Huyse's contribution to this volume and J. Gilissen, "Étude statistique sur la répression de l'incivisme," *Revue de droit pénal et de criminologie* 31 (1952):513–628.

4. On the wider history of Belgium during the war years, see E. Verhoeyen, *La Belgique occupée* (Brussels: De Boeck-Wesmael, 1994); J. Stengers, *Léopold III et le gouvernement: les deux politiques belges de 1940* (Paris and Gembloux: Duculot, 1980); M. Conway, *Collaboration in Belgium: Léon Degrelle and the Rexist Movement 1940–44* (New Haven and London: Yale University Press, 1993).

5. E.g., *Où en est l'épuration?* (Brussels: FI, 1944); F. Demany, *Histoire de la résistance belge et du front de l'indépendance* (Brussels: FI, 1944).

6. E.g., A. Wauters, "Note sur la situation en Belgique au 15 septembre 1944," 7, Centre de recherches et d'études historiques de la seconde guerre mondiale, Brussels (henceforth CREHSGM), PW 1/87; "Que veut le peuple belge?" *Indépendance* (7–8 April 1945).

7. F. Dumon, "La Répression de la collaboration avec l'ennemi (1944–1952)," *Revue Générale* 1 (1996): 57–65.

8. E.g., W. Ganshof van der Meersch, *Réflexions sur la répression des crimes contre la sûreté extérieure de l'état belge* (Brussels, 1946); *Journal des Tribunaux*, 26 March 1994; K. Hoflack and L. Huyse, "De afrekening met de vrienden van de vijand," in L. Huyse and K. Hoflack, eds., *De democratie heruitgevonden* (Leuven: Van Halewyck, 1995), 27–44.

9. *Annales Parlementaires* Chambre des Représentants (8 August 1945), 657, and Sénat (10 August 1945), 563, and (29 August 1945), 648; "Procès-verbal de la réunion . . . " (16 August 1945), and Huwart to Ganshof van der Meersch (17 August 1945), Rijksarchief Brugge (henceforth RAB), Archief Achille Van Acker (henceforth AAVA), file 594. I am grateful to Michel Nuyttens of the Rijksarchief Brugge for granting me access to the Van Acker papers.

10. "Le Parti Communiste . . . ," *Le Drapeau Rouge* (25 September 1944); du Bus de Warnaffe to Van Acker (30 April 1945), RAB AAVA, File 403; Reports of Captain J-L Merckx (September 1944), Archives Générales du Royaume, Brussels, Archives Van Zeeland, File 0864. I am grateful to Vicomte Van Zeeland for permission to consult his father's papers.

11. *Annales Parlementaires* Chambre des Représentants (27 April 1945), 360.

12. "Une proclamation des partis . . . ," *Le Peuple* (5 September 1944).

13. CASUM Report 12th Army Group U.S. Army (21 September 1944), CREHSGM, AW 3; "La Trahison et la Justice," *L'Aurore* (29 September 1944); "Le Programme du gouvernement," *La Libre Belgique* (4 October 1944).

14. E.g., Compte-rendu of Conseil Général of Parti Socialiste Belge (17 September 1944), Institut Emile Vandervelde, Brussels (henceforth IEV); Roch to Van Acker (2 October 1944), RAB AAVA, File 483; "Een waarschuwend woord," *Het Belfort* (21 October 1944).

15. Comité ministériel restreint (16 October 1944), and "La Réorganisation administrative . . . (3 November 1944), RAB AAVA, Files 442 and 473.

16. Belgium and Luxembourg (19 December 1944), Public Records Office, London, Foreign Office 123/581; "Nécessité d'un nouveau gouvernement," *L'Aurore* (25 November 1944).

17. J. Rens, "Impressions de mon voyage . . . ," 11, CREHSGM, PR 5/387; "Aux suivants de ces Messieurs," *Le Monde du Travail* (17 November 1944); "The British in Belgium," *The New Statesman and Nation* (2 December 1944).

18. Pro Patria to Van Acker (11 March 1945), RAB AAVA, file 416; "Le Mois politique," *La Revue Nouvelle* (1 February 1945); "D'une Semaine . . . ," *Le Soir* (14 February 1945); "La Répression," *L'Appréciation* (24 February 1945).

19. *Où en est*; "Le Pays ne veut pas . . . ," *Le Drapeau Rouge* (28–29 November 1944); "La Justice sur la pente," *Front* (4 March 1945).

20. E.g., *Annales Parlementaires* Chambre des Représentants (15 February 1945), 180.

21. Contrôle des Communications Rapport Général (6, 14, 20, and 28 April 1945), RAB AAVA, file 574. The reports are in French but are based on analysis of letters written in all languages.

22. *Annales Parlementaires* Sénat (29 August 1945), 633; Baronne Albert Houtart "Cahiers," CREHSGM, PH 11.

23. See the remarks of E. Witte, "Tussen restauratie en vernieuwing," in E. Witte, J. Burgelman, and P. Stouthuysen, eds., *Tussen restauratie en vernieuwing* (Brussels: VUB, 1990), 33.

24. E.g., "Personnel de maîtrise" (10 October 1944); Lt. De Poerck to Auditeur Général (11 May 1945), and M. Gossart "Incidents du 14 mai . . . ," RAB AAVA, Files 483 and 641B; "La justice populaire . . . ," *Indépendance* (12–13 May 1945).

25. E.g. "Les fermiers sont-ils des affameurs?" *Indépendance* (13 April 1945).

26. The National Bank estimated that in January 1945 retail prices were 88 percent higher than in 1938 but that wages had risen on average by only 40 percent: "Note résumée . . . " (9 October 1946), RAB AAVA, File 588.

27. "Analysis of Coal Strike and Labor Situation" (7 February 1945); "Entretien avec le Lieutenant Brancart" (15 May 1945); and Administration de la Sûreté de l'Etat Bulletin Journalier (11 September 1945), RAB AAVA, Files 645, 641B, and 639.

28. E.g., Rens, "Impressions," 15.

29. "Nécessité d'un nouveau gouvernement," *L'Aurore* (25 November 1944); Demany, *Histoire*; "Compte-rendu du meeting . . . " (26 September 1945), CREHSGM, PL 7/50.

30. "De Zuivering na zes maanden ondervinding," *Het Belfort* (25 March 1945); "Le FI et l'épuration," *Indépendance* (13 April 1945).

31. Rapport moral 2e Congrès National FI (10–12 May 1946), CREHSGM, PR 20/7; Administration de la Sûreté de l'Etat Rapport Mensuel (June 1946), RAB AAVA, File 639.

32. *Annales Parlementaires* Chambre des Représentants (21 March 1945), 294–95; "La Justice ne peut rester . . . ," *Le Drapeau Rouge* (30 April 1945).

33. Cardinal Van Roey, *Directives religieuses pour l'heure présente* (Brussels, 1945), 9; "Le Conseil national du PSB . . . ," "Au Cours d'un meeting . . . ," and

"Les Inciviques ont des complices . . . ," *Le Peuple* (19 February, 30 May, and 9 June 1945).

34. M. Buset Radio speech (February 1946), IEV, Papiers Max Buset; Huyse and Dhondt, *Répression*, 292–94.

35. *Annales Parlementaires* Sénat (25 September 1945), 678–79; Administration de la Sûreté de l'Etat Bulletin Journalier (12 October 1945), RAB AAVA, File 639; "Une importante réunion . . . ," *Vers l'Avenir* (24 October 1945).

36. *Annales Parlementaires* Chambre des Représentants (14 February 1945), 159–65; "Le problème de l'épuration," *Forces nouvelles* (3 March 1945); "Repressie na seven maanden," *De Nieuwe Standaard* (16 May 1945); "Bilan sommaire . . . ," *Vers l'Avenir* (29 December 1945).

37. *Annales Parlementaires* Chambre des Représentants *(*14 February 1945), 154–55; and Sénat (10 August 1945), 563; Van Acker Radio speech (11 March 1945), RAB AAVA, File 428; "Achille Van Acker . . . ," *Le Peuple* (3 May 1945).

38. *Moniteur Belge* (28–29 May 1945), 3406–09; Van Acker to De Launoit (28 December 1945), RAB AAVA, File 423.

39. "Discours prononcé à Namur . . . " (19 December 1945), RAB AAVA, File 428.

40. "Note pour le gouvernement" (23 January 1945), De Launoit to Van Acker (7 August and 22 November 1945); and "Appel au gouvernement" (October 1945), RAB AAVA, Files 543, 416, 423, and 596.

41. Conférence du Charbon (26 February 1945), Van Acker radio speech (19 May 1945); A. De Smaele speech (26 September 1945); and C. Huysmans Radio speech (23 August 1946), RAB AAVA, Files 649, 427, 542, and 602.

42. M. Conway, "The Liberation of Belgium, 1944–45," in G. Bennett, ed., *The End of the War in Europe 1945* (London: HMSO, 1996), 117–38; Huyse and Hoflack, eds., *De democratie.*

43. Administration de la Sûreté de l'Etat Rapport Mensuel April–May 1945, and Ministère de Défense Nationale Rapport de Sécurité (May 1945), RAB AAVA, Files 639 and 641B.

44. Rapport du Capitaine Drapier (16 May 1945), RAB AAVA, file 641B; *Annales Parlementaires* Sénat (17 May 1945), 378–82.

45. "Des Manifestations . . . ," *Le Peuple* (25 May 1945); "Dans tout le pays . . . ," *Le Drapeau Rouge* (8 June 1945); Ganshof van der Meersch to Ministre de Défense Nationale (11 June 1945); and Administration de la Sûreté de l'Etat Bulletin Mensuel (June 1945), RAB AAVA, Files 673 and 639.

46. Lt. De Poerck to Auditeur Général (11 May 1945), RAB AAVA, File 641B; "La justice populaire . . . ," *Indépendance* (12–13 May 1945).

47. Commissaire Delcort to Commissaire en Chef (14 May 1945), RAB AAVA, File 641B; "L'Epuration," *Le Soir* (16 May 1945); "Un incivique pendu . . . ," *Le Peuple* (1 June 1945).

48. "Devant la carence de l'épuration," and "Gosselies," *Indépendance* (3 and 15 May 1945); *Vlaamsch Weekblad* cited in RAB AAVA, File 632.

49. Ganshof van der Meersch to Minister of Justice (12 May 1945), RAB AAVA, File 641B.

50. "Le Crime qui doit être payé," *L'Aurore* (28 April 1945); "Gosselies,"

Indépendance (9 May 1945); Gendarmerie of Mons to Commandant de Corps (16 May 1945); and Administration de la Sûreté de l'Etat Rapport Mensuel (April–May 1945), RAB AAVA, Files 641B and 639.

51. "L'Epuration," *Le Soir* (16 May 1945); "Le Problème de l'épuration," *Le Peuple* (18 May 1945).

52. Gendarmerie of Mons to Commandant de Corps (16 May 1945), RAB AAVA, File 641B.

53. R. Dispy "Les Tâches immédiates du Parti," *Guide du Militant du Parti Communiste de Belgique* (May 1945), 4; "Les Promesses de M. Van Glabbeke . . . " and "Pour en finir avec les traîtres," *Le Drapeau Rouge* (14 and 24 May 1945); Rapport sur la situation politique et l'activité du FI Comité National du FI (29 July 1945), 8, CREHSGM, PR 20/7.

54. "Pour une justice rapide," and "L'Ordre doit régner," *Le Soir* (2 May and 9 June 1945); Lt. De Poerck to Auditeur Général (11 May 1945), *Vlaamsch Weekblad* and Contrôle des Communications Rapport Général (1–7 June 1945), RAB AAVA, Files 641B, 632, and 639.

55. "La Répression," *Le Peuple* (31 May 1945).

56. "M. du Bus de Warnaffe . . . ," *Le Soir* (7 June 1945); "Prévention et Répression des Grèves—Maintien de l'ordre" (25 May 1945), RAB AAVA, File 583.

57. FI Liège to Van Acker (6 June 1945), and Administration de la Sûreté de l'Etat Bulletin Journalier (11 October 1945), RAB AAVA, Files 673 and 639; "Op den Vooravond van den Grooten Kuisch," *Het Belfort* (10 June 1945); "Compterendu du meeting . . . " (26 September 1945), CREHSGM, PL 7/50.

58. "Mauvais souvenirs d'occupation" (13 June 1945), and Administration de la Sûreté de l'Etat Rapport Mensuel (August 1945), RAB AAVA, Files 598 and 640; "Nieuwe politieke Zeden," *De Nieuwe Standaard* (29 May 1945).

59. Rapport hebdomadaire des Postes Territoriaux de la S.E. (25 August–1 September and 1–8 September 1945), and Contrôle des Communications Rapport Général sur le courrier hebdomadaire (31 August, 23 September and 9 November 1945), RAB AAVA, Files 639 and 640.

60. E.g., "Conseil de Guerre de Tournai (A)," *Le Courrier de l'Escaut* (21 December 1944); "Conseil de Guerre," *La Meuse* (15–16 April 1945).

61. See B. De Wever and P. Gunst, "Van Kamerleden en burgemeesters," in Huyse and Hoflack, eds., *De democratie*, 69–89.

The Criminal Justice System As a Political Actor in Regime Transitions: The Case of Belgium, 1944–50

SOCIETIES THAT are struck by an acute political crisis of vast magnitude are like surfacing icebergs abruptly showing their full size and complexity. Basic aspects of their functioning that are otherwise hard to observe appear with great clarity. Key moments of such nature fall into two categories. The first group can be labeled "middle-range crises," such as the witch-hunt in the early 1950s in the United States, May 1968 and its immediate aftermath in France, and the violent campaigns of the ETA in Spain and of the IRA in Northern Ireland and Britain. War and revolution belong to the category of "full regime crises." They force societies to cope with traumatic transitions: the end of and, eventually, the restoration of national integrity, the fall and rise of regimes. For the last six decades Europe has witnessed several examples of transitions of the latter kind: the breakdown and restoration of democratic states in the thirties and the forties and, more recently in Southern and Eastern Europe, the termination of authoritarian systems and the process of the construction or reconstruction of a democratic regime.

Such critical episodes in the life of a society create large opportunities for the social scientist: they produce lablike conditions for studying the relations between various societal sectors, such as the political order, the legal system, and the economy. The problem we want to deal with here is that of the role of the legal system, especially the criminal justice system, in transitional periods.[1] The focus will be on one particular case: the redemocratization of Belgium (1944–50) after the defeat of the Germans and their Belgian collaborators.

Courts and the Return to Democracy

In an essay on regime transitions, A. Stepan differentiates several paths to redemocratization.[2] In three of these, warfare and foreign occupation play a vital part in the process of restoration: the return to democracy takes place after the downfall of an external conqueror. There exist

differences between the countries that walk this path. They are linked to
the answer to four crucial questions: (1) did the population perceive the
leaders of the original regime as culpable for the conquest; (2) did the
previous leaders collaborate with the occupier; (3) did a resistance movement unconnected to the defeated democratic leadership become a competing center of national identification and authority; and (4) did the occupation bring enduring changes in the social, economic, and political
structures of the country. Stepan writes: "The more the answer is in the
negative for all questions, the more likely it is that the outcome after re-
conquest will be the restoration of the previous democratic system, with
full legal continuities between the old and new democratic regimes."[3] According to Stepan, the obvious European cases that fit this particular road
to redemocratization are the Netherlands, Belgium, Norway, and Denmark. For reasons that fall outside the main argument of this chapter, I
disagree with this author's interpretation of the conditions that guided
Belgium's return to democracy. But he is right in stating that the ultimate
outcome was "restoration with full legal continuities between the old and
new democratic regimes." How was this stability achieved and what was
the role of the judiciary in general, those manning the criminal justice
system in particular?

Courts and the Quest for Political Stability

A major trend in comparative politics defines stability as the "long-term
ability to make decisions and secure adherence to them without the use of
naked force."[4] Stability thus has two components: an instrumental one,
effectiveness (the ability "to satisfy the basic functions of government as
defined by the expectations of most members of a society,"[5] mainly by
producing public order and by making the economy grow) and an evalu-
ative one, *legitimacy* (the capacity to secure loyalty and keep the conviction alive that the political institutions are trustworthy).

The judicial system has a key role in the establishment of legitimacy. It
does so partially by granting to, particularly through decisions of a supreme court, the acts of the new authorities the stamp of legality. The fate
of the Weimar republic is a forceful illustration of what happens if the
judiciary refuses to confer legality on a new regime. But another task of
great importance is given to the criminal justice system: the trial and punishment of those who collaborated with the occupying force so as to strip
them of all remaining legitimacy. In addition, prosecution of these people
is seen as "necessary to assert the supremacy of democratic values and
norms and to encourage the public to believe in them."[6] This latter assignment is the major focus of this chapter.

But criminal courts also have a task to fulfill in the area of effectiveness. Judges will be confronted with firm demands from the newly installed elites to severely sanction disruption of the public order. There will be equally strong suggestions to be cautious when dealing with economic collaborators of the old regime. A far-reaching purge of managerial manpower can be counterproductive as it endangers the badly needed economic reconstruction of the country.

Dilemmas

Young democracies affirm that they highly value the rule of law and human rights. But posttransition justice involves a number of decisions that may trespass upon these legal principles.

Justice after transition has to take place within a temporal frame. "This frame," Offe writes, "consists of the answers to two questions. First, from when on are acts that occurred in the past liable to corrective action?" In other words, do we accept ex post facto criminal legislation? It is the *nullum crimen sine lege, nulla poena sine lege* principle which is at stake here.[7] The second question, according to Offe, is "up to which future point in time is legal action to be taken?"[8] This involves the problem of eventually lifting or upholding the existing statute of limitation. One potential source of retroactive justice is the posttransitional conflict between legal systems, between the legal legacy of the past and the laws and regulations of the new or reconstructed democracy. A major discussion in France, during and just after the war, was precisely on the legality of the Vichy regime and of the acts of those who, believing Vichy to be the legal and legitimate government of France, obeyed its laws.[9] The clash between two legal systems is not the only possible source of retroactive justice. Novick, after comparing the retroactivity question in postwar Belgium, France, Holland, Denmark, and Norway, concludes: "All of the Western European countries found their existing treason legislation inadequate to deal with the unanticipated phenomenon of lengthy occupation and widespread collaboration. All had to repair this lack by one form or another of retroactive legislation."[10] In each of these five countries legislative, administrative, and judicial tricks were used to camouflage the reality of retroactive justice.

Posttransition justice tends to be emergency justice. In the first months after the transition, the survival of the successor regime depends on fast action against pro-authoritarian officials and their following. Such operation is seen as a necessary protection against sabotage from within. Moreover, without judicial action against the old elites, other forms of social and political disturbance may be triggered, with a risk of vigilante justice. The climate, however, is then seldom well suited for a scrupulous sorting out of all the gradations in the responsibility for the abuses of the past. Finally, mildness with regard to economic collaborators can create inequality before the law and, consequently, generate in the populace cynism and distrust toward the political system.

Dealing with the past may force the successor elites to violate the codes of the *Rechtsstaat*. Judges, on the other hand, are the guardians of the constitution and the custodians of human rights. This may become a cause of great concern for the leaders of the new regime and a source of bitter antagonism between them and the judiciary. A crucial challenge thus for the judiciary is to reconcile ethical imperatives, the needs for legitimacy, and the political demands for effectiveness.

The Purge of the Belgian Quislings

The Belgian cabinet could not expect any sympathy, respect, or authority from the electorate on returning from exile. Its indecision in the months of May and June 1940 remained fresh in people's memories, and it was also reproached for having kept itself out of harm's way. This lack of legitimacy tarred the entire political class for months. There were thus many reasons to organize the elimination of the collaborators as efficiently as possible. The legitimacy of the reinstated leadership partly depended on the speed and the thoroughness with which the unpatriotic governors of occupied Belgium and their following were expelled from the political and public forums.[11] But the returning elite also knew that its authority and legitimacy were challenged by a new and unquestioned power, the resistance movements. It had to avoid every political move that could push the resisters in the direction of revolutionary action.[12] Any suggestion of weakness in the government's handling of the collaborators would certainly have been a provocation in the eyes of the resistance movements.

Figures

A striking feature in the policy of Belgium was the outspoken desire, especially evident in the months before and after the liberation, to expel the collaborators from the society. A much heard expression was that "there was no place left for those who had betrayed their country." A second trait lies in the tendency—especially in the early stages of the operation— to judge the population under absolute standards of good and bad. Sensi-

TABLE 1
Penalized collaborators per 100,000 inhabitants

	Belgium	France	Netherlands
Total number of punished persons	963	309	1216
Of which			
Were executed	3	2	0.4
Received prison sentences cum disqualification[a]	582	90	553
Received only civic disqualification	265	119	602
Received other sanctions	113	98	61
Population size in millions (1945)	8.3	42	9.3

[a] Judgments by default not included.

Sources: Belgium: J. Gilissen, "Etude sur la répression de l'incivisme," in *Revue de Droit Pénal et de Criminologie* (1950–51), 513–628; France: H. Rousso, "L'épuration en France: Une histoire inachevée," in *Vingtième Siècle* 33 (March 1992), 78–105; Holland: A. D. Belinfante, *In plaats van Bijltjesdag* (Assen: Van Gorcum, 1978).

tivity to the many shades of gray between "black" and "white" was very low indeed. The result of those policy choices was that the purge initially affected extremely large numbers of citizens and that severe sanctions hit them.

The number of unpatriotic citizens who suffered punishment in one or another form (by the authorities) was about 80,000. (All figures are approximate.) Those who received prison sentences numbered 48,000. However light the sentence, imprisonment was almost always accompanied by other sanctions: a fine, confiscation of personal goods, police supervision after the end of the prison term, the obligation to reside in a specific town. Damages had to be paid to the state, out of the marital goods or from the heirs, if necessary. There was also introduced some form of "national indignity," which implied a series of civic disqualifications and a prohibition on some kinds of professional activity. This sanction was in most cases an extension of a prison sentence. It was, however, also used independently as a "milder" punishment for the small fish. As such it was applied to 22,000 collaborators. In addition, special measures were taken to purge the national and local public administrations.

Figures about Belgium are easier to interpret if they are put into a comparative perspective, as is done in table 1. A comparison of their respective purges, taking the size of their populations into account, shows that Belgium and the Netherlands dealt in a more severe way with their disloyal citizens than France did. These global figures hide, however, an important contrast. Prison sentences in the Netherlands were more restricted in time than in Belgium. Differences also appear in the area of civic disqualification. The total number of those who received this punishment (in combination with a prison sentence or as the only sanction) is approximately 70,000 in Belgium (or 847 per 100,000 inhabitants), 107,000 in the Netherlands (or 1,155 per 100,000), and 90,000 in France (or 209 per 100,000). At first sight Belgium and the Netherlands again belong to the same category, disqualifying four times more collaborators than France. But the impact of the sanction was different. In Belgium deprivation was in most cases lifelong and its scope was extremely large, including the right to take up public functions and jobs in the legal media and teaching professions. In the Dutch case this sanction was almost always limited in time (ten years) and restricted to the loss of active and passive voting rights. The overall conclusion is that collaborators in Belgium were less better off than those who lived in the two neighboring countries.

Political Strategies

The trial and punishment of *military collaborators* and *informers* was executed without much public or political debate. But the search for legitimacy made the restored elite very sensitive to what would happen to the *political collaborators* of the German conqueror. These men and women were responsible for the expulsion of the old leadership and for the establishment of an authoritarian regime. The problem was that the prewar penal law did not cover the many forms of political action that only in the context of the total warfare of World War II took a collaborationist dimension. Simple extension of the scope of penal law was not self-evident, since part of the political behavior in question could be seen as falling under the constitutional right of freedom of opinion, speech, or association. How could a person who, before the war, became a member of a party that participated in the Belgian parliamentary game but joined forces with the German occupier be punished if he stayed a member after May 1940? Was a man whose only political activity had been subscribing to a collaborationist journal culpable for a crime? With the country still occupied, the Belgian government-in-exile defined membership in pro-German movements and similar forms of political action as ordinary crimes.[13] The result was that tens of thousands of Belgians were punished for what was strictly political behavior.

Legitimacy is only one of two dimensions of stability. Effectiveness is the other one. According to the mainstream of political science publications, effectiveness is the capacity of a regime to satisfy the basic functions of government, particularly by making the economy grow.[14] Economic reconstruction was a huge task in a country in which the industrial infrastructure was crippled by four years of German looting and several months of bombing by the Allied forces. Providing food, clothing, and coal to the population was for more than a year an almost impossible mission for the political leadership. Of crucial importance was the unconditional cooperation of the economic, financial, and industrial elite. It was precisely at this point that the purge of the collaborators risked becoming counter-productive. More than 110,000 complaints had been received on the basis (solely or partially) of article 115 of the penal code that made economic collaboration punishable. Nearly 60,000 of these files referred to blue collar workers who volunteered to work in Germany. They were not at the heart of the problem. The other suspects were commercial and industrial people. The opening of a file was a serious handicap for most of the involved commercial and industrial businesses: it meant seizure of the books and sometimes required sequestration of goods and assets. All this could considerably mortgage the search for economic recovery. In May 1945, after nine months of hesitation, the government edited an interpretative law in which article 115 of the penal code underwent a substantial reduction of its scope. The prosecutor had to prove now that the wartime behavior of a businessman or of a plant manager was explicitly aimed at helping the German war machine. Completely in tune with Belgium's preference for delicately balanced compromises, the government also ruled to dismiss all charges against the 60,000 blue collar workers. This double surgical operation caused in fact the decriminalization of much of the formerly punishable economic behavior: only 2 percent of all files resulted in a court case (against 43 percent for military collaborators, 33 percent for political collaborators, and 18 percent for police informers).[15]

The Role of the Belgian Courts

Manipulation of the criminal process for political purposes, here the granting of legitimacy to a restored elite, was a risky enterprise after Belgium's return to democracy. The transition was a victory over a regime that had violated almost all codes of the *Rechtstaat*, including the sacred principle of separation of powers. How might the restored elites not respect these codes? The consecutive governments therefore chose not to try to impose their will on the criminal justice system that traditionally is charged with adjudication, that is, the civil courts. Instead they turned to the existing military courts and made them competent for the trial of collaborators. This strategy opened several doors for political intervention, while keeping such intervention formally within the realms of legality. One opportunity was linked with the appointment of military personnel as judges: three of the five judges in every military court were army officers. It was to be expected that these nonprofessional judges would be easier targets for external pressure.

Vulnerable Prosecutors

Political use of the judicial process was also facilitated by what happened in the prosecutor's office. The Belgian military procedure involves the merger, in the hands of the prosecutor, of competencies that in the civil procedure are spread over several judicial roles: to start an inquiry, to make an arrest and extend or terminate it, to write a search warrant and execute it, to proceed against or discharge a suspect, to require a penalty. One former prime minister has, in Parliament, spoken of these prosecutors as "armés d'une puissance comparable à celle d'un roi-nègre."[16] Unlike judges, prosecutors are members of a strict hierarchical organization in which guidelines move from top to bottom. Some of these guidelines may come from the head of the Department of Justice, a political figure. In sum, prosecutors in military courts had unusually large competencies and were more vulnerable to political pressure. But there is more. The manpower of the military prosecuting offices had to be increased tenfold. That was the only way to deal efficiently with the 405,000 files of Belgians suspected of unpatriotic behavior (7 percent of the adult population). At first, it was thought that the civil justice system would serve as a sufficient source for appointments. But this turned out to be a vast miscalculation as can be seen in table 2. The share of practicing prosecutors and professional judges in the consecutive waves of appointments sank from 29 percent in September 1944 to 1 percent in the spring of 1945. The minister of justice then redirected his efforts and solicited members of the bar. Their share in the recruitment figures rose quickly to a maximum of 89 percent in the second trimester of 1945. But in no time, as table 3 tells us, the reserve of experienced advocates was exhausted and very young lawyers had to be recruited as prosecutors.

This was an important development. Fidelity to legality and the rule of law, if it is imbued in the minds of members of the judiciary, is a strong safeguard against political and partisan use of the judicial process. It is not clear where and how such fidelity originates. Abel and Lewis, dealing with this problem, write: "How much of this behavior can be attributed to the office —which is supposed to embody legality— and how much to the background or training of its occupant?"[17] But it looks

TABLE 2

Professional origin of newly recruited military prosecutors[a]

Professional origin of all mil. prosecutors	Period of recruitment					
	Sept 1944	Oct–Dec 1944	Jan–March 1945	April–June 1945	After June 1945	Total
Civil judge or prosecutor	29%	8%	4%	1%	—	10%
Lawyer at the bar	57%	80%	85%	89%	82%	78%
Other	14%	12%	11%	10%	18%	12%
Total	100% (n=126)	100% (n=169)	100% (n=132)	100% (n=91)	100% (n=33)	100% (n=551)

[a] Based on the decrees of appointment as published in the *Belgisch Staatsblad* (Official Gazette).

TABLE 3

Seniority of lawyers at the bar recruited as military prosecutors[a]

Seniority of recruited lawyers	Period of recruitment					
	Sept 1944	Oct–Dec 1944	Jan–March 1945	April–June 1945	After June 1945	Total
At least 8 years of practice	37%	20%	15%	21%	4%	19%
4–7 years of practice	29%	25%	15%	38%	37%	27%
Less than 4 years of practice	34%	55%	70%	41%	59%	54%
Total	100% (n=72)	100% (n=135)	100% (n=112)	100% (n=81)	100% (n=27)	100% (n=427)

[a] Based on the decrees of appointment as published in the *Belgisch Staatsblad* (Official Gazette).

plausible to hypothesize that men who just left law school were badly equipped to offer resistance against political intrusion in their activities as prosecutors.

Time Pressure As a Source of Inequality

Immediately after the liberation of large parts of Belgium, in September 1944, the government declared that the purge had to be as swift as possible. Pressure on the military judges and prosecutors resulted in verdicts that were ill advised. At that time—the country was still at war—

TABLE 4
Sentence to be demanded for various forms of military collaboration according
to the prosecutor-general

	Circular nr. 946 of 16 October 1944	Circular nr. 1478 of 29 November 1945
Waffen-SS	death penalty	15–20-year prison sentence
Flemish/Walloon Legion	death penalty	5-year prison sentence
Feldgendarmerie	death penalty	15–20-year prison sentence
Gestapo (SIPO)	death penalty	15–20-year prison sentence
SS-Flanders	death penalty	1–5-year prison sentence

information on the real significance of various forms of collaboration was
scarce. Consequently, issuing prosecutorial guidelines was a troublesome
business. In one of his first circulars the prosecutor-general asked the
local prosecutors to demand the death penalty in most of the cases of
military collaboration. But once the war had ended and the flow and
quality of information grew, the Office of the Prosecutor-General had to
amend the guidelines. Table 4 shows the considerable differences that
occurred in one year. In the meantime thousands of collaborators had
been punished on the basis of the first circular. Grave inequality before
the law was the result.

An Ambiguous Attitude toward Economic Collaboration

It has been mentioned earlier in this chapter that the government edited a
law, in May 1945, that de facto decriminalized most of the cases of economic collaboration. The reaction of the top of the judiciary toward this
decision was ambiguous. There was, on the one hand, firm protest
against what was blamed as an intolerable intrusion of the government
into the criminal justice system. But a close analysis of the exchange of
letters between the prosecutor-general and the local prosecutors reveals
that his policy did in fact not divert from the government's. On May 13
1945, two weeks before the interpretative law was published, the prosecutor-general sent out a circular letter in which he wrote that the "prosecutors who are charged with the investigation of economic collaboration
must consider the effects a judicial operation could have on the economic
activity of the country, at a moment that national recovery requires an
extraordinary effort" (my translation from Dutch). The prudence with
which the chief prosecutor approached the wartime behavior of the industrial elite is to be seen as a sort of autocensorship in view of the common good.

The Ambivalence of the Criminal Justice System

It is in the differential treatment of political collaboration on the one side and of economic collaboration on the other that the political use of the criminal justice system is most visible. How exceptional is such a situation?

In sociolegal studies of criminal law and criminal justice, strong arguments have been developed to support the proposition that in Western Europe, the judicial reaction toward criminal behavior is ambivalent : property crimes (theft, burglary, larceny, robbery) and crimes of violence (various types of assault, theft) have generally been prosecuted more rigidly than violations of certain other rules, especially rules in the area of economic regulation. Infringements of the second type (tax evasion and fraudulent foreign exchange transactions, price control violation, fraud in customs duties, but also violation of the building code, water pollution, etc.) are treated with rather different judicial and administrative procedures, which in many cases aim at decriminalization of the charges.[18] The specific handling of these latter crimes is linked with some of their characteristics: the victim is diffuse and abstract ("the economy," "the state"); the legal grounds, on which prosecution is based, are challenged or are at least not deeply anchored in the legal consciousness of the justiciables;[19] these offenses are, proportionally, more to be found in the higher strata of the population. The last attribute has a central place in the argument: the differential treatment of white collar crime is theoretically linked with the legislators', judges', and administrators' resentment against a traditional criminal prosecution of holders of key positions in the social and economic order. A highly publicized trial and conviction of such persons and the imposition of imprisonment are considered by some groups in society to do more damage to the social order than the crime itself. That is precisely what happened in the case of economic collaborators.[20]

But how can we reconcile this theory with the fate of the political collaborators? Political assistance to an occupying power has, as an offense, many of the characteristics that we attributed to economic collaboration. The victim, "the integrity of the state," was diffuse. The legal grounds for prosecution and the procedural techniques that were used were challenged by the defendants and their lawyers. Their argument was that in the Belgian legal tradition, political crimes, if need be, have to be judged by a grand jury. Lastly, the offenders often belonged to the intellectual and administrative elite: teachers, journalists, writers, civil servants. But political collaboration was prosecuted without the cautiousness that usually accompanies the handling of infringements with these three attributes. This problem suggests the need for an amendment to the "ambivalence theory": the autocensorship that legislators, prosecutors, and judges apply only operates when applicable to men and women who belong to a totally unquestioned elite. In the eyes of the traditional elites, the Belgian leaders and members of the Germanophile movements had already been before the war, because of their extreme rightwing ideas, a danger to democracy. Accordingly, there was no need for prudence and generosity.[21]

Political or Partisan Justice?

All political trials, writes Christenson, differ from ordinary trials because they address simultaneously a legal and a political agenda. But they are not equal in their ranging of that dual agenda. Partisan trials "proceed according to a fully political agenda with only a façade of legality (although the legalism might be turgid)." The issue in all these trials is the same: "expediency in the use of power." A second category includes those that operate under the rule of law: "They are fair trials despite their political agenda."[22]

In terms of formal legality the trials of Belgian collaborators fall into the second category. Every procedure was covered by law. But the real conditions, as described earlier in this article, in which the criminal justice system worked made the dominance of the political agenda a constant possibility. Reality sometimes deviated from what the formal codes predicted. Force majeure and intense time pressure have been invoked to justify dubious procedural techniques. Belgium also espoused the principle of collective guilt through the disqualification of people because of their membership in collaborationist movements. Offe notes that in such cases the defendants "are not —or only marginally— given a legal chance to invoke excuses that might exonerate them individually." Even if they are given this chance, they will be forced to collect evidence to prove their innocence, so that the burden of proof is reversed.[23] Another problem is that such purge operations tend to become highly politicized. There is one vigorous illustration of this latent reality. Two thirds of those who were accused of political collaboration did not appear before the courts, but were registered on a very special list. Registration, which was planned as a sort of summary proceedings, implied the loss of a series of political and civil rights. It was the military prosecutor, and he alone, who decided in the first instance which persons were sent to the courts and which put instead on the list. Tens of thousands of Belgians were registered. However, not the size of the group but the timing of the campaign is important. Almost 60 percent of all registrations were made between December 1945 and 15 February 1946, that is in two months time. Finishing the remaining part of the operation took the prosecutors more than two years. The extreme speed with which the registration started is no coincidence. Seventeen February 1946 was the date of the first afterwar elections. In this electoral campaign the parties of the left fought a bitter battle with the Catholic Party, then in opposition. It was thought that most of the political collaborators were Catholics. Preventing them from becoming a candidate or from voting could give the Catholic Party a serious drawback. The government, which was based on a coalition of left parties, put pressure on the prosecutors to deprive as many political collaborators as possible of their eligibility and of their right to vote. Once the elections were over, the tempo of the operation slowed down considerably.

Contextual Factors

The Belgian case suggests that the line between partisan justice and political justice under the rule of law is very thin indeed. But in judging transitional justice and its partial degradation into partisan justice one has to take into account the factors that constitute attenuating circumstances.

Many analysts argue that of the factors affecting the direction of postauthoritarian justice, the determining one is the balance of power between the forces of the past and the successor elites at the time of the transition. Huntington has set forth a typology of power relations at the time the transition toward democracy starts.[24] First is the violent overthrow or the collapsing of the repressive regime. There is then a clear victory of the new forces over the old order. This is the way redemocratization occurred in Belgium. Democracy can arrive, second, at the initiative of reformers inside the forces of the past: "those in power in the authoritarian regime take the lead and play the decisive role in ending that regime and changing it into a democratic system."[25] Some of the postcommunist countries belong to a third category: democratization resulted from joint action by, and the negotiated settlement between, governing and opposition groups. The widest scope for partisan punishment arises in the case of an overthrow. Almost no political limits exist. The result is that in the words of Jose Zalaquett, "complete victors hand out a tremendous amount of punishment, but not necessarily justice."[26]

A second factor is the international context at the time of the transition. Political justice in Belgium came at a moment when supranational codes with respect to human rights and the rule of law were either weak or absent. This has considerably changed since then. The Council of Europe published its Convention for the Protection of Human Rights and

Fundamental Freedoms in 1950. Later came the International Convention on Civil and Political Rights and the Helsinki Accords. Surveillance and monitoring bodies, ranging from the International Commission of Jurists to the International Helsinki Committee have become operational. This supranational legal framework has been and still is of great importance in decisions dealing with the past in postcommunist Eastern and Central Europe. A strong motive for not neglecting the signals coming from abroad was the possibility that violations of law codes might compromise these countries' membership in the Council of Europe. Supranational legal norms on human rights, and the rule of law and institutions implementing such laws, were absent when in postwar Belgium the collaborators were judged. Serious procedural irregularities occurred. Today, many men and women view the trials of the second half of the 1940s as a contravention of the most fundamental principles of the Rechtsstaat. They want to keep the memory alive as a warning against new legal transgressions.

Notes

© Luc Huyse. A shorter version of this chapter was published in N. Kritz, ed., *Transitional Justice: How Emerging Democracies Reckon with Former Regimes*, vol. 2 (Washington, D.C.: United States Institute of Peace Press, 1995), 141–51.

1. Political science publications on regime change have for a long time disregarded the problem of transitional justice. That is true for, among others, such well-known work as J. Linz, A. Stepan, eds., *The Breakdown of Democratic Regimes* (Baltimore, Md.: Johns Hopkins University Press, 1978). G. O'Donnell, P. Schmitter, L. Whitehead, eds., *Transitions from Authoritarian Rule: Southern Europe* (Baltimore, Md.: Johns Hopkins University Press, 1982) has a few, but quite insightful, pages on settling accounts with the past. An exception is S. Huntington, *The Third Wave: Democratization in the Late Twentieth Century* (Norman: University of Oklahoma Press, 1991). There is a vast sociolegal literature on the interlocking of politics and courts, but it seldom deals with the role of the judicial system in regime transitions. A few exceptions: O. Kirchheimer, *Political Justice: The Use of Legal Procedure for Political Ends* (Princeton, N.J.: Princeton University Press, 1961); H. Hannover, E. Hannover, *Politische Justiz 1918–1933* (Frankfurt: Fischer, 1966); H. Koch, *In the Name of the Volk: Political Justice in Hitler's Germany* (London: Tauris, 1989). A new and fast growing body of literature is interdisciplinary in nature. Useful compilations are: N. Kritz, ed., *Transitional Justice: How Emerging Democracies Reckon with Former Regimes*, three vols. (Washington, D.C.: United States Institute of Peace Press, 1995); "Law and Lustration: Righting the Wrongs of the Past," special issue of *Law and Social Inquiry* 20:1 (1995); "Accountability for International Crimes," special issue of *Law and Contemporary Problems* 59:4 (1996); A. James McAdams, ed., *Transi-*

tional Justice and the Rule of Law in New Democracies (Notre Dame: University of Notre Dame Press, 1997). Case studies can be found in K. Asmal et al., *Reconciliation through Truth: A Reckoning of Apartheid's Criminal Governance* (Cape Town: David Philip Publishers, 1996), and J. Borneman, *Settling Accounts: Violence, Justice, and Accountability in Postsocialist Europe* (Princeton, N.J.: Princeton University Press, 1997).

2. A. Stepan, "Paths toward Redemocratization: Theoretical and Comparative Considerations," in G. O'Donnell, P. Schmitter, L. Whitehead, eds., *Transitions*, 64–84.

3. Ibid., 66.

4. The definition is S. M. Lipset's, taken from his chapter "Political Sociology" in N. Smelser, *Sociology: An Introduction* (New York: Wiley, 1967), 442.

5. S. M. Lipset, "Political Sociology," in R. K. Merton, ed., *Sociology Today* (New York: Harper and Row, 1959), 108.

6. Huntington, *Third Wave*, 213.

7. This principle of legality means that no conduct may be held punishable unless it is precisely described in a penal law and no penal sanction may be imposed except in pursuance of a law that describes it prior to the commission of the offense. See also article 7(1) of the European Convention of Human Rights: "No one shall be held guilty of any criminal offense on account of any act or omission which did not constitute a criminal offense under national or international law at the time when it was committed. Nor shall a heavier penalty be imposed than the one that was applicable at the time the criminal offense was committed."

8. C. Offe, "Coming to Terms with Past Injustices," 33 *Archives Européennes de Sociologie*, at 197.

9. P. Novick, in his book on the purge of collaborators in liberated France, devotes a whole chapter to the *nullum crimen sine lege* problem (P. Novick, *The Resistance versus Vichy: The Purge of Collaborators in Liberated France*, New York: Columbia University Press, 1968, 140–56).

10. Novick, *Resistance versus Vichy*, 209.

11. A complicating factor was that a large part of the collaborating population belonged to political movements of the extreme Right that had won between 15 percent and 20 percent of the parliamentary seats in the prewar elections of 1936 and 1939. These movements had thus been for a longer time redoubtable competitors for power. See: W. Brustein, "The Political Geography of Belgian Fascism: The Case of Rexism," *American Sociological Review* 53 (1988): 69–80.

12. See G. Warner, "La Crise politique belge de novembre 1944: un coup d'état manqué?" ("The Political Crisis of November 1944 in Belgium: An Aborted Coup?" *Courrier Hebdomadaire du Crisp* 798 (1978): 2–26.

13. The Supreme Court ruled shortly after the liberation of the country that all the legislative measures taken by the Belgian government-in-exile had full legality, including the law that in December 1942 had changed the scope of criminal legislation on collaboration. The argument was that the government had not created new rules but had only interpreted an existing body of penal arrangements.

14. "In the modern world, such effectiveness means primarily constant economic development" (S. M. Lipset, *Political Man: The Social Bases of Politics*

[New York: Doubleday, 1963], 70), and from the same author: "In new states or postrevolutionary regimes . . . effectiveness means one thing: economic development" ("Political Sociology," in N. Smelser, *Sociology*, 445).

15. The source is J. Gilissen, "Etude sur la répression de l'incivisme," *Revue de Droit Pénal et de Criminologie* (1950–1951): 513–628.

16. "armed with an authority that resembled the omnipotence of an African king" (J. Pholien, Senate, 9 April 1946).

17. Abel and Lewis write: "There is some evidence that professional identity strenghtens the 'independence' of the judiciary and its willingness to defy or at least obstruct grossly illegal acts by the more political branches" (R. Abel, P. Lewis, eds., *Lawyers in Society, Vol. 3, Comparative Theories* [Berkeley: University of California Press, 1989], 482).

18. The key reference here is E. H. Sutherland, *White Collar Crime* (New York: Holt, Rinehart and Winston, 1949).

19. See the publications of the Knowledge and Opinion about Law Research Group, esp. A. Podgorecki et al., *Knowledge and Opinion about Law* (London: Martin Robertson, 1974).

20. Studies of the Dutch, French, and Norwegian treatment of economic collaboration came to a similar conclusion. See A. Belinfante, *In plaats van Bijltjesdag: de geschiedenis van de bijzondere rechtspleging na de tweede wereldoorlog (The Trials of Dutch Collaborators)* (Assen: Van Gorcum, 1978); H. Rousso, *Le Syndrome de Vichy* (Paris: Seuil, 1987); D. Tamm, *Retsopgoret efter besaettelsen (The Trials after the Occupation)*, 2 vols., (Kopenhagen: Jurist- og Okonomforbundets Verlag, 1984).

21. The French and Dutch situation was different. In both these countries political collaboration was performed by persons who in the prewar period either belonged to the traditional elite groups, or did not constitute a real political threat. As a consequence political collaborators were spared or were granted a general pardon shortly after the war. See Belinfante, *In plaats van*; Rousso, *Le Syndrome*.

22. Ron Christenson, *Political Trials: Gordian Knots in the Law* (New Brunswick, N.J.: Transaction Books, c. 1986), 10–11.

23. C. Offe, "Coming to Terms with Past Injustices," *Archives Européennes de Sociologie* 33 (1992): 195.

24. Huntington, *Third Wave*, 114.

25. Huntington, *Third Wave*, 124.

26. J. Zalaquett, cited in A. Boraine, J. Levy, R. Scheffer, eds., *Dealing with the Past: Truth and Reconciliation in South Africa* (Cape Town: IDASA, 1994), 103.

"Restoration of Confidence": The Purge of Local Government in the Netherlands As a Problem of Postwar Reconstruction

IN APRIL OF 1945 German troops retreated from Winschoten, a small provincial town in the northern part of the Netherlands.[1] Even before Allied liberators arrived, the local people gathered at the town hall to celebrate. They dragged the Nazi-appointed mayor from his office and threw him into a nearby canal. They then hurled into the water the mayor's portraits of Adolf Hitler and the Dutch Nazi Party leader Anton Mussert. When the unfortunate civil servant managed to clamber up the bank, soaking wet, he was promptly arrested by resistance fighters and imprisoned to await trial. This rather unceremonious transfer of power demonstrated on the spot that the enemy had been defeated. Throughout the Netherlands, the emotional outbursts that accompanied this process underline the immense relief of the population at large at the liberation of Nazi oppression. In particular, this sentiment is indicative of the close link between local government and the people and shows how much pressure the German occupation had placed on the relationship between citizens and their local government.

This chapter is intended as a case study of the phenomenon of political purges in the aftermath of World War II. The purge of the mayors and the denazification of local government in the Netherlands are presented here to show which problems faced the postwar process of political purge within a recovering liberal democracy. In doing so, I will touch upon some more general aspects: uneasiness about the idea of political purge in general and debate about whether the purges should or should not be used to reinvigorate the system of government. The central topic will be the purge of the mayors, because these officials took a central position and simultaneously their experience is illustrative of what happened to all Dutch civil servants.[2] During the German occupation they virtually became part of the National-Socialist system of government in the occupied Netherlands; this gave them extremely difficult policy decisions and burdensome political responsibilities. At the same time, their assignment implied the need to provide, by means of their position, a last stronghold for what under Nazi rule could remain of the traditionally very pluralistic civil society in the Netherlands. The postwar purge involved a sometimes controversial attempt to Evaluate each mayor's stance toward the Nazis, and his decisions. The general objective of this evaluation was to "restore confidence" in the government apparatus. I will describe how that confidence could get lost during the occupation, what legal measures the Dutch government-in-exile took to prepare for the purge, and how the purge was carried out. I intend to show how the objective to "restore confidence" was both obvious and subject to political manipulation.

Before coming to this point, the historical background needs some clarification. The German occupation and Nazi dictatorship still are considered a crucial and formative experience in the recent history of the Netherlands, in 1940 a small nation of about nine million in northwestern Europe. During the first decades of the twentieth century, the Dutch experienced a period of comparative stability in political and social life.[3] The country managed to remain neutral during World War I, although it certainly did not remain unaffected by the transformations that the Great War effectuated in the fields of domestic and international politics, economics, and culture. In political life, liberal parliamentary democracy was established in the immediate aftermath of the war, when men and women gained universal suffrage by means of proportional representation. This facilitated the development of an elaborate variation of civil society that has been characterized as "pillarization" (in Dutch: *verzuiling*) along vertical denominational and ideological lines. Roman Catholics, Protestants, Liberals, Socialists, and various religious and political dissenters all formed their own organizations that usually contribute to civil society: political parties, trade unions, mass media, educational systems, consumer cooperations, sports clubs, and the like. Each of these was linked to specific churches or political convictions. These so-called pillars enabled the ruling elite to work together at the top levels at the same time as the rank and file would live and work more or less in segregated ways.

In the interbellum, the international position of the Netherlands was the prolongation of the policy of neutrality that had kept the country out of World War I. The Dutch took pride in their position as a colonial power in the East and West Indies. Neutrality was the expression of a continued and eventually desperate search for political independence and security from agression. At the same time, the concept of neutralism was politically disseminated as an ethical stand par excellence, positioning the Netherlands as a moral beacon among bellicose nations. These three influences—domestic political immobilism, incapacity to deal with the world economic crisis, and impotent aloofness in international relations—have contributed to the traditional point of view in historiography that the Netherlands remained badly defended and morally unprepared for war and dictatorship and therefore in 1940 helplessly succumbed to German agression.[4] This image is in need of reconsideration, because in many respects Dutch society developed responses to the challenges of the interbellum years that would only be fully deployed in the period of reconstruction and renewal after 1945. Anyway, between the wars the negative experience prevailed and was responsible for a sense of crisis in the sociopolitical system. An obvious solution was offered by different Fascist and National Socialist movements that gained some influence without altogether endangering the existing political order as such. At the same time, the acceptance of political democracy within the dominant political movements remained frail and superficial and debate about a reform of government and public institutions along more authoritarian lines was always in the air during the 1930s. To put it briefly: in the interwar years political democracy was not completed in practice nor uncontested as a principle.

In May 1940, German armies invaded the Netherlands, Belgium, and France in a swift move to establish their domination in Western Europe. After five days of war, the Dutch army had to surrender, while Queen Wilhelmina and her government escaped to exile in London for the duration of the war. After a short period of military rule, the Netherlands was placed under the authority of a civil German government. On 29 May 1940 a *Reichskommissar*, Dr. Arthur Seyss-Inquart was appointed as the supreme authority in the Netherlands. Directly representing Adolf Hitler, he led a government of supervision, a so-called *Aufsichtsverwaltung*, in the Netherlands. The Dutch bureaucracy had been instructed by its own government in official guidelines issued in 1937 to carry on their tasks in the interest of the population. Under the new regime, Dutch civil servants were supervised by German authorities. The occupier set itself the long-term goal of integrating the Netherlands into Hitler's Third Reich. For the time being, however, it was not decided in Berlin how this was to be achieved; in general the occupied Netherlands had to be prepared for integration through a policy of nazification. Such remained the situation for the greatest part of the occupation, which was to last until the fall of 1944 (for the southern provinces) and until the spring of 1945 (for the other parts of the country).

Initially, the German authorities hoped to find substantial groups among the Dutch prepared to accept National Socialism and collaboration. During the summer of 1940, Dutch elites indicated a willingness to reach some political understanding with the occupant in line with the prevailing attentist tendencies elswhere in Western Europe, like France, Belgium, Norway, and Denmark. Within a year, the occupiers realized that such accommodation was not identical with unconditional selfnazification, and consequently, Seyss-Inquart and his associates changed their policy and turned toward the Dutch Nazis to focus their effort for political revolution. The Germans chose to employ the Dutch Nazi Party, the NSB (*Nationaal-Socialistische Beweging*, or National Socialist Movement), to recruit Dutch executors in their effort to reorganize Dutch society along National-Socialist lines. At the same time, they did not transfer much political power to the party's leadership. This especially frustrated NSB leader Anton A. Mussert, who never got the chance to head an indigenous Nazi government like Pierre Laval in France or Vidkun Quisling in Norway.

At this point, it must be stressed that the Nazi revolution in the Netherlands had largely taken the character of a "revolution from abroad."[5] On the one hand, it should not be overlooked or denied that Dutch Nazis were an endogeneous force of some importance during the mid-1930s, or that they contributed in many respects to the German afforts to nazify the occupied Netherlands. On the other hand, it remains undisputed that they would never have managed to take over (or share) political power had a German invasion not occurred. Moreover, the German authorities themselves wanted to be in control, pointing the way in which the Netherlands ought to be integrated into the political structure of the Third Reich. They did not allow for an independent Dutch way to National Socialism and only wanted to employ Dutch Nazis as supporters and executors of their own policy. At the same time, the machinations of diverse factions that represented the power structure of Hitler's empire utilized parts of the Nazi Party, the pro-SS tendency or leading members of the civil service, to serve their own goals.

In the course of the occupation, contradictions between the German regime and its Dutch political partners on the one hand and an emerging resistance movement on the other gradually escalated. One important factor in that process was the changing prospect of the war, in which the outcome of the Battle of Stalingrad (early 1943) was a crucial turning point for the Dutch as well, as it fed hopes that the Germans after all would be on the losing side. A second contribution was the growing hardship, as a result of war and oppression, represented especially by the conscription of Dutch workers for forced labor in Germany. A third source of inspiration for resistance was ideologically rooted. The National Socialist endeavour to break up Dutch civil society with its characteristically pluralistic institutional life was met by sometimes rather succesful tactical moves from specific interests. Despite repression and persecution, for instance, denominational school boards managed to keep a certain degree of independence. Sometimes the spirit of resistance led to abandonment, as when the independent trade unions were abandoned by their member at the moment that the Nazis announced the takeover of these organizations and the merger into one Nazi-dominated substitute. While it needs to be said that resistance was never general and that in many places compliance with Nazi initiatives was a common phenomenon, it remains true that people from all parts of society proved willing to take enormous risks to resist the occupant, convinced as they were that the familiar sociopolitical order was worth taking these risks for. When in 1944 total war was declared by the Germans, and the Allies were on their long way to liberating Western Europe, oppression and persecution evolved into an outright terror that cost thousands of lives during the last winter of hardship: the so-called Hunger Winter of 1945–46.

Loss of Confidence: "Like a Mayor in Wartime"

In the summer of 1940, the occupier began the process of nazifying the administration. The internal government was led by Dr. Friedrich Wimmer, the *Generalkommissar für Verwaltung und Justiz*, who was authorized to issue mandatory regulations to Dutch civil servants. In the three biggest cities, Amsterdam, Rotterdam, and The Hague, as well as in the eleven provinces, the Reich commissioner appointed *Beauftragten* as supervisors over the Dutch mayors and provincial governors. I would like to draw a distinction between two types of nazification, which were applied simultaneously: nazification of personnel and of policy. Nazification of personnel was the replacement of civil servants and sitting administrators with Dutch National Socialists, most of whom were members of Anton Mussert's Nazi Party, the NSB. Nazification of policy was the implementation of National Socialist measures on orders from the Germans. Both related very strongly to the position of the mayor, as the key figure in Dutch local government. Contrary to many other democratic countries, in the Netherlands the mayor is not elected by the people. While the elected city council is recognized as the supreme authority on the local level, mayors play a dual role. As chair of the city council and as the municipal executive of mayor and aldermen, they personify the city government. But the mayor is appointed by the crown and is responsible for monitoring compliance with provincial and state regulations. When city councils pass resolutions that conflict with provincial or national interests, the mayor is required to report them to the higher authorities for reversal.

It goes without saying that for this administrative system to function the mayor must have the confidence both of the city council and the population, and of the central authority he or she represents, namely the provincial governor and the minister of the interior. For the most part, this system has functioned reasonably well since 1851. However, the German occupation of the Netherlands between May 1940 and May 1945 was a dramatic disruption. The occupiers wanted to force a radical breach with the administrative tradition that had been in place in the Netherlands since early modern times. This tradition is characterized by a balance between local, regional, and national authorities and by power sharing among the various representatives of the local elite and the collegiate administration. In this way, the administration was (and still in many ways is) elaborately interwoven with all sections of civil society: political organizations, school boards, organizations for social work and welfare, and cultural institutions. Under German rule, local government was transformed, first into an object and then into an instrument of a policy intended to nazify the Netherlands.

In general, war and occupation put unprecedented pressure on the local government as well as on the society of which it is a part. This goes for practical problems, such as evacuation, billeting, rationing, and war damage. An equally big source of problems was, of course, the broad range of controversial political decisions faced by local administrators. What stance should they take toward the German authorities in the Netherlands? After Queen Wilhelmina and her ministers fled to London on 13 May 1940, the mayors were left with the burden of being a beacon for the people. Their actions were supposed to compensate for the absence of the legal government. When the war left a city damaged, many administrators responded by immediately initiating restoration projects, both to combat lethargy and to show the occupation force what the Dutch were really worth. In 1940 the local government showed that it had a great capacity to solve problems on its own. But this independence was a double-edged sword. The mayors were expected to base their conduct on a set of secret government instructions from 1937, which were founded on the 1907 Convention of the Hague regulating international occupation law.

These instructions said that in the event of an enemy occupation, civil servants had to stay at their posts in the interest of the population. They were permitted to resign only if their remaining in office was more beneficial to the occupier than to the citizens, or, if remaining in office would lead to disloyalty toward their fellow citizens or the nation. However, it remained unclear what they should do if the Germans violated occupation law. This forced the civil servants to choose the lesser of two evils. During the occupation, most administrators, including mayors, decided to stay in office as long as possible, believing that this was in the interest of the people. The highest-ranking civil servants assumed that direct German rule would be more radical and cruel, a less desirable option. The instructions of 1937 had instructed civil servants to act as a shield between the occupier and the people. The secretary-general of the Ministry of the Interior, Dr. K. J. Frederiks, tried to guide the mayors in their difficult choices between the lesser of two evils. But as the German occupation policy became more radical and the administrators became a tool toward this end, the policy of the lesser of two evils lost favor with the public. To this very day, when Dutch people feel the need to make too many concessions to stay in a certain position, they may say that they feel "like a mayor in wartime."

One of the first victims of nazification of personnel was the mayor of The Hague, S. de Monchy, who was sacked on 1 July 1940. The firing was punishment for allowing a nationalist demonstration in his city. In August 1940 Seyss-Inquart issued a decree that regulated the way in which German authorities would make decisions about the dismissal and nomination of mayors, alderman, and high-ranking officials within the local government structure. Implementing this policy, the German authorities first turned to the bigger, strategically important cities and fired all mayors whom they considered unsympathetic to the Nazis.[6] After the strike in February 1941, the occupier sacked the entire city councils of Amsterdam, Zaandam, and Hilversum and replaced them with pro-Nazi commissioners. Smaller towns were soon to follow. On 10 May 1940 the Netherlands had more than 1,000 municipalities and 925 mayors.[7] By January 1943, 130 NSB mayors had already been appointed, and they governed 39 percent of the population. By October 1943 there were 248 NSB mayors (governing 45 percent of the population), and by July 1944 there were 275 (governing just over half of the population). In early September 1944, 327 of the 925 Dutch mayors from 1940 had been replaced by Dutch Nazis.[8] In August 1941, the Nazis introduced the National-Socialist "leader principle" in the Dutch administrative system. This was essentially the fulfillment of the nazification of policy.[9] This measure abolished municipal councils and dismantled the system of collegiate administration. The mayor became the sole leader of the municipal administration, no longer responsible to any one in the local community, and responsible to the supervising authorities, especially the Germans, more than ever.

This put an end to the system of functional decentralization that had characterized the Dutch administrative model; from this time on, the apparatus became an instrument of German' occupation policies. Frederiks, responsible for local government in the Ministry of the Interior, wanted most of all to hold together the administrative apparatus, so he focused on combating the nazification of personnel. He hoped his own leadership would help the mayors and councils navigate the dangerous waters of the occupation. He felt that an infiltration by NSB members would erode the bonds of professionalism and personal loyalty that held his corps of mayors together, and would eventually destroy his authority over that group.[10] Moreover, before the war, the NSB had been relatively new on the political scene, and its powerful position during the war was entirely due to its alignment with the German Nazi party. Members of the NSB were known as political usurpers and social outcasts. Most people believed that these misfits were totally incapable of running a community. It was therefore a source of great annoyance, and amusement, when in 1942 the NSB set up a crash course for future mayors because there were too few qualified candidates in their ranks. Frederiks's policy did slow down the nazification of personnel. But it could not put off this process indefinitely, because the Germans were resolved to appoint as many sympathizers and joiners as they could to key posts.

At the same time, the occupiers were rapidly implementing the nazification of policy. This created a great deal of uneasiness. One of the priorities of the German authorities was the introduction and execution of anti-Jewish measures. The process that eventually would lead to the mass murder of a large majority of Jews in the Netherlands (107,000 of the 140,000 Dutch and foreign Jews who lived in the country at the eve of the occupation) formally started in October 1940, when civil servants, administrators, and elected representatives were ordered by the German authorities to register at town hall whether they were of Jewish ancestry or not. Later that month, all Jews were excluded from such positions. From January 1941, the whole Dutch population was registered by name and address, and Jews were registered separately. This was done, again on German orders, by means of the municipal registry offices. The process of registration was soon replaced by segregation, spoliation, and eventually deportation, all under the authority of the special Jewish branch of the German police. The German authorities employed the assistance of local authorities to enforce anti-Jewish measures and to hand out orders to report for deportation. Frederiks and his allies were powerless to devise a strategy to withstand the process.[11]

As a matter of fact, this is true for the whole process of nazification of policy, partly due to the fact that there was no authoritative interpretation of occupation law upon which to base a policy. The government instructions from 1937 stated that measures taken by an occupation force should be tested against the 1907 Convention of The Hague. In 1941, however, the Dutch Supreme Court declared itself—quite controversially—incompetent to test specific occupation measures against the Convention. This left the civil servants to test the German measures that they themselves were charged with implementing. All civil servants were now isolated, more or less on their own, and left with the task of making decisions based on their own conscience. This is why, after the leader principle was implemented, several mayors resigned; in their eyes the measure had created an unacceptable context for making decisions. Frederiks did not support this move. He felt that there was still room to act in the interest of the nation and tried to unite as many patriotic mayors as possible behind his policy. Frederiks regularly resisted German measures through formal protest or by threatening to resign. Whenever the Germans persisted, he tried to get the occupier to take formal responsibility for its measures. This occurred everywhere within the Dutch bureaucracy: civil servants who considered themselves good patriots were constantly withdrawing, both mentally and formally, from policy areas in which they felt that the occupier was infringing on their own authority and on Dutch constitutional law. As long as the German authorities were willing to take formal responsibility, these civil servants accepted the situation. They hoped to have a positive effect in policy areas where they still had some influence. Along the same lines, the occupier and the civil service colluded to persecute Jews between 1941 and 1943. Disgust with this policy was expressed in symbolic protests and later in actual resistance as well. But these acts created no more than an occasional obstacle to the deportation policy.

The nazification of personnel was implemented at such a moderate pace that the relations between German and Dutch authorities were strained but not broken.[12] Local administrators had too little power to stop the nazification of policy, which became clear in 1943, when the Germans radicalized their occupation policy. They then started the mandatory drafting of Dutch men for forced labor in Germany. And from December 1943, the Germans began commandeering local citizens for the construction of fortifications. These measures were expressly forbidden by occupation law and by the government instructions from 1937. Now no one could continue to claim that staying in office was serving a higher purpose. Frederiks advised the mayors concerned not to cooperate with the new measures and even to go into hiding, if needed, to avoid reprisals. A resistance movement emerged that accused the civil servants still in office of collaboration. One resistance newspaper even called the civil servants "our own, homemade whips."[13] The government-in-exile also began criticizing its civil servants and condemned their bureaucratic collaboration in radio broadcasts from London. It was telling that Frederiks complained, in 1944, that in the end he was fighting a war on four fronts: against the occupiers, the NSB, the government in London, and the resistance movement. He, too, admitted that the escalation in the final year of the war greatly undermined his authority and that nearly everyone considered his policy a failure.[14] After the liberation the administrators' policy was to be formally evaluated and the government would decide what measures to take.

Purge Legislation

The Dutch government-in-exile in London was faced with the extremely complicated task of preparing for the punishment of collaborators. This not only meant the harsh punishment of Dutch National Socialists, but also the removal of all non-Nazi mayors, aldermen, and civil servants who had failed to fulfill their patriotic duties during the occupation. The latter task was deemed at least as important as the former for the reconstruction of postwar society. But for the London government, it was difficult to grasp the extent of bureaucratic collaboration. The only information it received was from obsolete newspapers and refugees who provided accounts of the situation in the occupied area. One of these refugees, a lawyer from the town of Dordrecht named Jaap Burger, arrived in the spring of 1943. He was employed as a cabinet minister to help prepare for the government's return to the Netherlands after liberation.[15] Broadcasting from London, the government radio station, Radio Orange, backed the Dutch resistance view that the local government apparatus was hopelessly compromised. The resistance demanded a rigorous purge after the liberation and claimed that they had a right to assume the posts that would be left vacant after such a purge, because of their patriotic service to the nation. In the alternative public opinion circuits that developed in resistance circles, the issue of the purges grew to be connected with the idea of a postwar political mission of the movement as a whole. It was widely believed in these circles that the only way to overcome the weaknesses and fragmentation of prewar society was to promote a sense of national unity and vigor by putting the men (and women, to a certain degree) of the resistance in charge. This reasoning would be the central argument that the resistance contributed to the debate on the purges, as it especially related not to the outright Nazis, but much more to the old and obsolete representatives of the ancien régime that had shown an utter lack of fighting spirit in the face of Nazism.

In these discussions, Burger tried to foster understanding for the position local administrators were still in. He also took the then controversial view that a resistance fighter who managed to steal identity papers and ration cards from a city hall during the occupation would not necessarily make a good mayor after the liberation. Burger managed to steer the debate in a new direction by appealing for a "synthesis" after the war. In his view, the existing administrative apparatus should be revived by employing able and responsible representatives of the resistance. In his capacity as minister of the interior, Burger was to take responsibility for the passing of legislation to purge the civil service. This Purge Act of 1944 provided for the sacking of civil servants who had been disloyal to the Kingdom, the queen, or the government.[16] This clause was aimed at purging not only National Socialist civil servants, but also those who could not "on the basis of their position during the occupation, be expected to loyally contribute to the restoration of Our Fatherland."[17] This meant that not only national socialists were subject to discharge, but also those who had failed in their duty through cooperation with the enemy or through misjudgment.

The Purge Act divided the purge into two phases. According to an agreement with the Allied command, the Netherlands was to be ruled for a transitional period by an interim military administration (known as the Netherlands Military Authority or NMA). During this period, which technically lasted until the end of 1945, the military administration would see to the purge. In this "first phase," NMA representatives had to suspend civil servants who were clearly pro-German and withhold their pay. Otherwise, when a civil servant's attitude during the occupation was criticized, he was suspended but allowed to continue drawing a salary pending the results of an investigation. In London, the government had been keeping track of the sympathies of key civil servants and mayors, so that after liberation, personnel decisions would be well founded. When this method failed to supply adequate information, the authorities carried out a local investigation. The "second phase" of the purge would begin once the civilian government was back in power. The civilian authorities would then have to decide whether the decisions made in the first phase should be made permanent. Many people felt strongly that the government should act swiftly to make good on its promise of a rigorous purge of both local administration and society in general. Provisional measures would be needed to prevent the purge from becoming a lengthy and obscure process. In some areas, the purge actually did become a drawn-out, complex procedure; in the southern part of the Netherlands, some areas took over a year to complete the first phase of the purge.

The problems can be attributed to three causes. First of all, the government in London still had insufficient information on how the Dutch administrators had functioned under the German regime. So the government was unable to give the military authorities adequately specific guidelines on whom to suspend. Secondly, the sanctions prescribed by the Purge Act were too black and white. In the first phase, after all, civil servants could only be suspended. But there were many doubtful cases where suspension seemed too harsh a measure, which meant that the civil servant in question was left in office. The resistance sometimes complained about these decisions, which led to general frustration. Some controversial mayors and civil servants were simply deposed by local resistance members. They were arrested and in some cases kidnapped. And military administrators were sometimes left with no choice but to formally seal such faits accomplis. A third reason for the difficulty was that the Netherlands was liberated over such a long period, from September 1944 until May 1945. During this long, multiphased liberation, the legal government first remained in London and later moved to liberated Eindhoven. The military administration had the status of acting governmental authority, but could not get a grip on the course of events. It had to work by trial and error, which was made more difficult by the organized resistance. A powerful force in the liberated area, the resistance was particularly intent on influencing the purge of collaborators. At the same time, the military adminsitration had too little staff to control the situation. Therefore, the military authorities decided to cooperate with the organized former resistance, and to appoint resistance representatives to local and regional advisory committees working on the purge.

Even before the liberation was completed, in May 1945, the purge had fallen into chaos and needed to be brought under control. The exclusion of National Socialist mayors and other civil servants went on in rather uncomplicated ways: as demonstrated in the opening lines of this chapter, they were removed from their offices and put behind bars to await trial. In the meantime, many who had not been NSB members were criticized nevertheless as having been too lenient toward the Nazis. In a number of places resistance groups also called for the replacement of those mayors whom they considered too much out of touch with local interests and sensitivities, or simply incompetent or too old. Such people could no longer function in office as a result of this pressure. Positions often were at stake as part of the local, factional infighting in which resistance groups of conflicting backgrounds clashed. Even an important town such as Nijmegen for a short time had three contestants who were appointed mayor at the same time by different authorities. Elsewhere, private conflicts were translated into the political terms of the day and thus gave way to purging procedures. To solve such problems, the purge legislation had to be expanded and refined. Disciplined leadership was also necessary to prevent the purge from getting bogged down in arbitrariness and local controversy. The crisis in the purge contributed to a political crisis in the Dutch government. In February 1945, as a result of his moderate stand, Jaap Burger lost his position as minister of the interior. His place was taken by Louis Beel, who immediately opened a "battle for control of the purge," a prolongued struggle that he would eventually win. During the occupation, Beel had been a high-ranking civil servant in the city of Eindhoven, the home of the Philips Works, but resigned in 1943 because he could not accept the appointment of a Nazi mayor. At the liberation of the southern part of the country, he became an advisor to the resistance movement and consequently for the military authorities.

Beel's first decision upon taking office was to expand and revise the Purge Act. In terms of criminal law, he widened both the definition of the offenses and the punishments. Both of these measures had been appealed for by the resistance movement in the liberated part of the Netherlands. The 1944 Purge Act provided only one sanction, namely a dishonorable discharge and automatic loss of pension. There was a group of people who had lost the public's confidence, but who might not deserve the severity of this measure. Which is why, between March and October 1945, Beel issued a few new decrees detailing lighter disciplinary measures, such as reprimands, transfers, and so on. He issued a separate regulation for those who had acted in good faith and had yet failed to fulfill their duties and thus lost the public's confidence—a regulation relevant to the purge of mayors. According to this measure, "Decree F-221,"[18] the minister could decide to force a resignation while acting outside the scope of the Purge Act. This discharge could be either honorable or dishonorable, and depending on circumstances, it could revoke one's claim to redundancy payments, pension, and transfer. This refinement of the purge legislation paved the way for far more complex casuistry and jurisprudence than had previously been thought possible. This was another reason why the second phase of the purge had to be strictly controlled. Beel withstood the acid test, taking control of the entire process by setting up additional procedures and continually consulting the resistance. Shortly after the German capitulation of May 1945, Beel terminated the first, military phase of the purge. In fact, this was a premature move, but the minister felt that many local hearings had degenerated into fruitless hairsplitting and factional infighting. He disbanded the advisory committees and, in so doing, removed the resistance's influence upon the purge. In March 1945, he announced a plan to turn over management of the purge to a new, independent department in his ministry: the Central Bureau for the Purge of the Civil Service. The minister put this department in charge of drafting final measures for the purge. It had access to what were now more complete files and to new documentation committees. The Central Bureau was operational as of September 1945 and soon had more than one hundred staff.

Beel had implemented two principles crucial to the transition from the first to the second phase. First of all, he saw to it that the sanctions were, legally speaking, "measures" rather than "sentences." These punitive measures were actually in line with existing disciplinary statutes for civil servants. Formally, the civil servants could only be tried on two charges: having had incorrect political sympathies or having failed in political judgment. A separate criminal proceeding called the Special Administration of Justice (*Bijzondere Rechtspleging*) was provided for civil servants who had committed specific collaboration-related crimes while in office. Secondly, Beel made sure that the purge was not achieved through unbiased judgment. There was great political pressure from forces who wanted the second phase carried out by an independent arbitration court for civil servants. But Minister Beel, as the highest representative of executive power in this field, was a party to the purge and was adamant that he remain so. Hence, the final say went to the highest authority: the crown, or for local administrators, the minister of the interior. This reflects the main objective sought in purging the civil service: that in the interest of reconstruction, the government should quickly regain a loyal, trustworthy, and efficient civil service that had the full confidence of the public. This sounds like a nicely worded slogan intended to build a rhetorical bridge between the government's priorities and the ambitions of the resistance. And indeed, this was exactly how it was used. At the same time, it was also the basic principle of the civil service purge of 1945–47. The minister chose to apply a disciplinary procedure, sometimes enabling the question of someone's administrative quality to outweigh his or her conduct during the occupation. This also made the rulings more systematic and allowed outside influence, particularly from pressure groups in the resistance, to be excluded.

The Purge of Mayors, in Practice

In the summer of 1945, a new Dutch government was formed that was to take the measures necessary for rebuilding the nation. Part of this process was to settle the problem of collaborators, which threatened to get completely out of hand. Upon liberation, some 120,000 to 150,000 people were arrested on suspicion of National-Socialist sympathies and imprisoned in more than 100 different internment camps. Tens of thousands of people stood to lose their jobs and positions in society because of collaboration. The wave of arrests and purges was an understandable result of the desire to ruthlessly punish the enemy's henchmen. However, it quickly became clear that this effort was hindered by the very enormity of the problem. It was this that led the new prime minister, Willem Schermerhorn, to speak of a "cancerous tumor in our nation."[19] With these figures, it is no wonder that the purge lasted until the end of 1947 and that the collaboration-related criminal proceedings were not over until the early 1950s. These criminals were dealt with quite harshly; about fifty thousand collaborators were given prison sentences, many of them very long, and the death sentence was handed down in 152 cases. Forty of these were carried out.

In the new cabinet, Beel returned as minister of the interior, and thus he maintained responsibility for the purge of civil servants, some thirty thousand in all. The procedure, designed in 1944, had a top-down approach. First the highest-ranking officials would be purged, followed by midlevel civil servants and last of all other government personnel. Reports on the progress of the purge show how difficult it was to purge a municipality's personnel while the mayor was still under investigation. The first problem to arise was the case of the provincial governors. Seven of the eleven governors had been replaced by Nazis. After the liberation, the replacements were immediately suspended and arrested. The government decided that the remaining four, all of whom had stayed in office during the entire occupation, would be suspended pending an investigation of their policies. The four reacted indignantly and initially refused the orders issued by the military authorities to step down. Minister Beel had to meet with them personally to convince them to comply. He set up separate investigative committees that were to advise him on what measures to take. In the end the minister decided that three of the four would receive an honorable discharge outside the scope of the Purge Act. Frederiks, the secretary-general for the interior, was suspended, too, pending investigation by a special committee. The minister would not make a final decision on this matter until January 1946. Frederiks publicly defended himself in a sharply worded pamphlet entitled *In Defence Of.*[20] He argued that he had tried, to the best of his ability, to lead the loyal corps of mayors. The mayors themselves published pamphlets in which they passionately defended themselves against investigations of their wartime activities. By September 1944, as was stated before, 327 National Socialist mayors had been installed, out of a total of more than 900 mayors. By January 1946, after more than a year of purging and six months into the second phase, 345 mayors had been formally laid off, most of whom were NSB members. At that same moment, 153 mayors were awaiting a decision on whether they could return to office. By April the number of mayors sacked had risen to 418, and by the end of 1947, the total was 509. All told, 950 cases were heard.[21]

Two very important principles underlying the purging of the mayors were swift handling of cases and uniformity of standards. Unfortunately, these proved to be mutually exclusive priorities. A nationwide fair application of identical standards would have required an even progress in assembling investigative dossiers. This failed in the first phase because of local infighting. The most important resistance group, the National Organization for Assitance to People in Hiding, had drawn up a detailed questionnaire concerning the policy of mayors during wartime. This was filled in by the group's local leaders. The questionnaire had no formal status, but was accepted by many investigative committees appointed by military authirities as a sound basis for starting dossiers. In other cases, dossiers contain much less precise evidence and sometimes nothing more than anonymous letters of complaint from local citizens. Another problem was that in a few provinces a conflict of competence broke out between the provincial governors and the Central Bureau for the Purge of the Civil Service. Under normal circumstances, provincial governors have a big say in a minister's decision to appoint or discharge a mayor. For the sake of the purge's uniformity and methodology, however, such decisions were temporarily subjected to the Central Bureau's guidelines. The governors, who were self-confident, apolitical, and often of nobility, considered it undignified to be made the executors of a ministerial purge policy. They felt that they alone were best qualified to take the appropriate measures on the basis of their own personal knowledge of local circumstances and their contact with the people. As a rule, they wanted to give the benefit of the doubt to all non-Nazis who were under investigation for losing public confidence.[22] The minister, however, supported the Central Bureau and thus preserved the pivotal role it played in the purge.

When defending their wartime policy, a number of mayors referred to the government instructions from 1937. They used this document in particular when defending their decision to stay in office as long as possible. The minister and the Central Bureau felt it necessary to investigate whether indeed the mayors had acted correctly according to the 1937 guidelines. Therefore, mayors who simply referred to the Instructions to justify having stayed in office were not necessarily off the hook. One of the officials who experienced this firsthand was Frederiks. His defense was based on the argument that by staying in office, he had prevented an assumption of power by the NSB and had, in so doing, protected the population from great evil. First the investigative committee, and later the minister, dismissed this assertion. They acknowledged the courage and determination with which Frederiks had done his job. However, they concluded that he had failed to take a principled stand against the nazification of policy. Beel therefore gave him an unsolicited honorable discharge pursuant to Decree F-221. In a written statement, Beel argued that in effect, Frederiks' policy had "undermined" the spirit of resistance. He had "acted in good faith, but failed, thereby losing the confidence of the public and of his boss, the minister." Beel insisted on a strict judgment of the former chief bureaucrat's policy even later, when faced with intense lobbying from political and bureaucratic circles. The decision, after all, was a matter of great principle for the purge of civil servants. One could hardly discharge lower-ranking bureaucrats on the basis of Decree F-221 if the secretary-general himself had been allowed to stay on.

Between November 1945 and June 1946, the Central Bureau set guidelines based on the practice of purging, determining which sanctions were appropriate to which forms of bureaucratic collaboration.[23] The severest punishment remained dishonorable discharge with loss of all benefits and pension, pursuant to the Purge Act. This measure had to be consistently applied to National-Socialists and also to those who had behaved so badly that their policy could be characterized as political disloyalty. According to the guidelines, there were several specific acts that were supposed to be punished with this measure. Among them was selecting men for forced labor on German defense works such as airfields or antitank ditches. Another was handing the German authorities the names of people who had taken part in the strikes of May 1943. The measure was also applied to mayors who were too cooperative in the persecution of Jews. Discharge based on Decree F-221 was the measure applied for those who had failed to take a stand or who had committed other, less serious mistakes that had lost them the confidence of superiors, colleagues, or the public. In theory, this type of discharge was not defamatory, but merely a conclusion that there was insufficient confidence for further service. In practice, however, it was widely seen as a punishment and a loss of honor. This perception was strengthened by the clause in Decree F-221 that stated that as an additional sanction, the designation "honourable" could be revoked, as could benefits and pension.

This jurisprudence naturally helped standardize the proceedings. However, it did not change the fact that the purge's methodology required an individual investigation of the context in which reprehensible acts had been committed to find any mitigating or incriminating circumstances that would influence the severity of the disciplinary measure. The Central Bureau's dossiers indicate that especially in the case of mayors, such "compensatory and exculpatory factors" had a significant affect upon judgments.[24] The resistance had continually appealed for a particularly harsh judgment of mayors, because of their special, responsible role. This argument, however, could also be used to justify a milder purge of mayors. After all, they had been placed under heavier pressure than most other administrators. Based on this view, some argued for the retainment of mayors, who, on the basis of the jurisprudence mentioned above, would be eligible for no more than automatic discharge.[25] The Central Bureau investigated 950 mayors in all.[26] This led to 509 discharges, 435 of them under the Purge Act. Of this last category, mostly pro-Nazi mayors, 342 had already been formally sacked by 1 January 1946. By the end of April, nearly four months later, this number had risen to 379, and another 56 mayors were discharged under the Purge Act between May 1946 and the autumn of 1947. Discharges under Decree F-221, due to loss of confidence, were less numerous but far more complicated. As a result, these cases, which eventually led to disciplinary action for 74 mayors, took far longer to complete. By 1 January 1946 only three such decisions had been handed down. By the end of April that number had climbed to 39. On 24 April 1946 there were still about 210 cases pending. To recapitulate, nearly a year after the German surrender, about 20 percent of the municipalities were still awaiting a final decision on the position of their mayor. This was not necessarily a problem, if for instance the suspended official had been replaced by an acting mayor who functioned to everyone's satisfaction. In up to sixty municipalities, however, there were sharp differences of opinion, and local lobbies both for and against the purge tried to influence the minister's decisions.

Conclusion: Restoration of Confidence?

The Netherlands was hit hard by the war. The Nazi terror had taken away and murdered more than 100,000 Jews and killed several thousand political prisoners and activists of the resistance. Moreover, especially during the final year of the conflict, some 20,000 perished because of suffering and starvation, while destruction of the economy and infrastructure left the prospect for a rapid recovery rather bleak. The purge was part of a wider operation to reconstruct and modernize the administrative apparatus, especially to make it a loyal, energetic force capable of leading the reconstruction of society. The overall goal was to determine the outcome of the process. The purge of mayors was an extensive and time-consuming operation. In a majority of municipalities, it created few or no problems. As a rule, Nazi mayors were rapidly replaced by those who had been sacked by the Germans or by trusted newcomers. Still, there remained a public perception in the liberated Netherlands that the purge of mayors had at least partially failed. This notion resulted from the publicity and public debate that surrounded problem cases and local controversy. This hindered restoration of the public's confidence in the administrative apparatus. This sentiment was aggravated by the circumstance that the purge proceedings were held behind closed doors, obscuring the arguments upon which decisions were based. The refinement of purge legislation, whose supporters nominally included the resistance, made it possible to weigh all aspects of a case, not only locally but also centrally. This process of weighing cases was, however, inaccessible to the public, provoking suspicion. This distrust was deepened by seemingly inconsistent cases that received a great deal of publicity and fed a notion that the purge was spoiled by the opportunism and machinations of old-boy networks.

Despite the thoroughness of the bodies involved, the purge did not completely undo the nazification policy of the German occupiers. The nazification of personnel was no problem; it was reversed by consistently sacking all mayors who had been installed by the occupier. In fact, this measure was also applied to a number of mayors who had merely been tolerated by the occupier because of their cooperativeness. However, the purge could not adequately erase the nazification of policy and remove all those who had been made coresponsible. This was the result of a collective political and administrative powerlessness that stemmed from government guidelines; neither the instructions from 1937, nor the guidelines issued by the government-in-exile had given administrators enough basis for their conduct. At the onset of the occupation, Dutch administrators failed to fully recognize German political goals. The Dutch civil servants failed to develop a common strategy against the nazification of policy, and they withdrew into a formal stance. The postwar order did not manage to fully condemn this conduct. If it had, hardly anyone could have retained their position.

When looking back at the purge, it can be concluded that during the occupation, a dual crisis of confidence had emerged in relation to the civil service and to mayors in particular. On the one hand, confidence was lacking between the civil service and the legal government, as represented by the minister of the interior. And on the other hand, a similar crisis arose between the civil service and the public, especially as represented by the resistance. This dual crisis set the stage for the purge that had to be carried out immediately after the war. It is to the credit of Minister Burger that he pointed out the difficulty of judging civil servants and proposed the idea of synthesis. As long as the war lasted, the opinions of both sides coincided. This was logical, because the government admired the resistance, identified with it, and wanted its support. But this changed after the liberation. The new government immediately asserted the primacy of the reestablished order and return to the rule of law. Minister Beel deserves credit for firmly taking responsibility for the second phase of the purge. He saw that the military authorities were not able to define a firm course that could put an end to local controversies and maximalist claims by resistants. Connected with the resistance and a *homo novus* as he was, he quickly displayed the characteristic attitude of the elite that was to shape the postwar recovery: Beel shifted the priorities toward normalization and reconstruction as consistently as possible. These priorities were to take shape in the purge by means of the minister's tight control of procedures and jurisprudence. The executive power made it a top priority to restore confidence between itself and the civil service. This was the main goal and as such it was part of an integral policy of reconstruction of society. This would be a bitter disappointment to those in the resistance who were aspiring to take over administrative positions as a recognition of their national merit and ideals.

In the longer run, during the first ten years after the liberation, a process of gradual renewal of local government was initiated. The word *modernization* would not exactly represent what was happening, although at the time it was often used to rouse enthusiasm for the reconstruction of the civil service. Local government was not restructured that much: procedures, decision making, or democratic control were not fundamentally adapted. What happenend was rather a renewal in the field of staffing, a rejuvenation by means of absorption of young, energetic, and able men (at the time almost exclusively men!) often with a resistance background, but in general firmly rooted in civil society as a whole. They were to fill the open spaces that resulted from the purge and consequently were the ones who realized a more profound synthesis between resistance and society as a whole. These people reinvigorated local government, exploring new fields of activity and new ideas about the tasks to set for government in general and local government in particular that had originated during the years of crisis, occupation, and war. As a matter of fact, the objective of restoration of public confidence rather quickly became a secondary goal, although everybody understood that a minimum of public confidence is necessary for any bureaucratic apparatus to function.

Notes

1. "The Netherlands" is the official name that covers the whole territory of the Kingdom with the same name (Capital: Amsterdam); abroad, the name "Holland" is often used to indicate the same. This, however, only indicates the two traditionally dominant coastal provinces on the North Sea.

2. This chapter is based mainly on my dissertation: Peter Romijn, *Snel, streng en rechtvaardig: Politiek beleid inzake de bestraffing en reclassering van "foute" Nederlanders, 1945–55* [Swift, Severe, and Fair Justice: The Poblem of Collaboration and Collaborators in Dutch Politics, 1945–55] (Houten: 1989) and also on a current research project into the nazification of the administration in the Netherlands during the German occupation.

3. E. H. Kossmann, *The Low Countries 1780–1940* (Oxford, 1978), 567–74.

4. Kossmann, *Low Countries*, 574; Louis de Jong *Het Koninkrijk der Nederlanden in de Tweede Wereldoorlog* (The Kingdom of the Netherlands during the Second World War) vol 1, chapter on *een conservatief land* (a conservative country).

5. Cf., Jan T. Gross, *Revolution from Abroad: The Soviet Conquest of Poland's Western Ukraine and Western Belorussia* (Princeton, N.J., 1988).

6. Peter Romijn, "Die Nazifizierung der lokalen Verwaltung in den besetzten Niederlanden als Instrument bürokratischer Kontrolle" in: Wolfgang Benz,

Johannes Houwink ten Cate, Gerhard Otto, eds., *Die Bürokratie der Okkupation: Strukturen der Herrschaft und Verwaltung im besetzten Europa* (Berlin, 1998), 110.

7. In a number of cases, a single mayor served several small municipalities.

8. J. in 't Veld "De Gemeenten" [The Municipalities], J. J. van Bolhuis et al., *Onderdrukking en Verzet* [Repression and Resistance], (Arnhem, 1948–55), vol. 4, 453–54.

9. This was done on the basis of the German order, no. 152/41 dated 12 August 1941.

10. The secretary-general played a crucial role in the process of appointing mayors and he had stayed in close contact with them prior to the war; at the onset of the occupation, he had been in office for nearly ten years.

11. Peter Romijn, "De Oorlog 1940–45" [The War 1940–45], in J. C. H. Blom, R. Fuks-Mansveld en I. Schöffer, eds., *Geschiedenis van de joden in Nederland* [History of the Jews in The Netherlands] (Amsterdam, 1995), 313–50; 428–35.

12. Romijn, "Die Nazifizierung der lokalen Verwaltung," in *Die Bürokratie der Okkupation*, 117–19.

13. Quoted in Romijn, *Snel, streng en rechtvaardig*, 34.

14. Ibid., 128–40, on the special procedure against Frederiks.

15. On 11 August 1943 Burger was appointed minister without a portfolio and was put in charge of preparing for the return to the Netherlands. From 31 May 1944 until 31 January 1945, Burger was minister of the interior.

16. 1944 Purge Act, *Staatsblad* no. E 14, dated 13 January 1944, replaced in 1945 by the new 1945 Purge Act, no. F 132, dated 13 August 1945.

17. Romijn, *Snel, streng en rechtvaardig*, 46.

18. Decrees, *Staatsblad* F-70 (March 1945) and F-221 (October 1945).

19. Prime minister's radio address, dated 27 June 1945, in *Keesings Historisch Archief*, vol. 1945, 6345–49.

20. K. J. Frederiks, *Op de Bres, 1940–45* [In Defence Of] (The Hague, 1945).

21. Romijn, *Snel, streng en rechtvaardig*, 141; the figures in this paragraph were found in the Purge Archive of the Department of the Interior in The Hague.

22. Romijn, *Snel, streng en rechtvaardig*, 144.

23. Ibid. 145; circular from the Central Bureau dated 16 November 1945 present in the Purge Archive of the Ministry of the Interior.

24. Minutes of the Central Bureau's meetings dated 13 and 27 July 1945, in Purge Archive of the Ministry of the Interior.

25. W. Derksen and M. L. van der Sande, *De burgemeester, van magistraat tot modern bestuurder* [The Mayor: From Magistrate to Modern Administrator] (Alphen aan de Rijn, 1984), 69–70.

26. Here, too, it is evident that during the occupation mayors could serve more than one municipality.

SARAH FARMER

Postwar Justice in France: Bordeaux 1953

IN THE early morning of 12 January 1953, a train pulled into the station at Bordeaux carrying a group of men accused of participating in the massacre of the 642 inhabitants of the French town of Oradour-sur-Glane on 10 June 1944. For eight years the families of the victims had been demanding that the killers be tracked down and punished for their crimes. The survivors of the massacre wanted vengeance: justice should be done swiftly, efficiently, and with appropriate severity. Now, as the case came to trial, it had become clear to the French public that the task of dispensing justice would be difficult, divisive, and in some cases impossible. Many of the officers who could have been held responsible had died on the Normandy front. Others had gone into hiding in Germany, or were otherwise unavailable to be tried.[1] And most troublesome of all, investigations after the war had revealed that among the sixty-six soldiers and officers still alive who could be identified as having belonged to the SS company that had committed the atrocity, fourteen were French, from Alsace. Among them was one volunteer; the others had all been drafted into the German forces in late 1943 and early 1944, only to be transferred to the SS a few weeks later. Their sympathizers referred to them as *malgré-nous* (in spite of ourselves) rather than the more neutral *incorporés de force* (forcibly incorporated). As their defenders were quick to point out, eight of them had been under eighteen years of age at the time they were drafted. These were the men, along with seven German soldiers who had been in prison since the end of the war, who were brought before the military tribunal in Bordeaux in 1953.

In postwar France the crime of which they were accused had come to stand for the ultimate victimization of innocent French people during the occupation. On 10 June 1944, SS troops encircled the town of Oradour-sur-Glane in the rolling farm country of the Limousin region of west-central France. They rounded up Oradour's inhabitants on the marketplace and divided the men from the women and children. The men were marched off to barns nearby, lined up, and shot. Soldiers locked the women and children in the church, shot them as well and then set the building and the rest of the town on fire. Those residents of Oradour who had been away for the day, or who had managed to escape the roundup, returned to a blackened scene of horror, carnage, and devastation.

This massacre emerged almost immediately after the war as the pre-eminent example of French suffering at the hands of Germans. In 1946 the French parliament passed a special law classifying Oradour as a historic monument and mandating that the vestiges of the old town be preserved for eternity. The law also provided for construction of a new town overlooking the ruins of the old one. Oradour became France's "martyred village" par excellence.

But with the trial at Bordeaux, Oradour, which had figured as a symbol of Nazi barbarism and French innocence, suddenly became the source of a bitter *guerre franco-française*. The trial provoked an intense if brief national crisis. The turmoil and the lasting bitterness it brought about showed that the French system of justice could not resolve the legacies of the German occupation.

In 1953 the people of Oradour were still preoccupied with the events of June 1944. The rest of the country, however, was seeking to put the past to rest. The trial took place during the last stage of a long national debate over how severely collaborators during the occupation should be punished. While the people of Oradour were unwilling to forget what had happened to them and who was responsible, the French Parliament was more interested in promoting reconciliation at home by wiping out the wartime records of many of its citizens.

The debate over collaboration and punishment began before the war ended. At the start of the purge trials in October 1944, Albert Camus and François Mauriac argued it out, Camus writing in *Combat* and Mauriac in *Le Figaro*.[2] Mauriac, expressing de Gaulle's concern for moderation and conciliation, desired that sentences not be harsh. Camus argued that forgiving collaborators meant sacrificing the ideals for which resisters had died, as well as betraying the dead by allowing their executioners to go free. In Parliament, the same moral arguments were brought by the opposing sides to the debates on amnesty legislation that took place in 1950 and 1952. All political parties in the French Parliament were caught up in the controversy. The stakes were enormous, as Henry Rousso has remarked, "because [the debate took place] at the crossroads where the law, ethics, and memory meet. 'Juridical forgetting' [*Oubli juridique*], by the very terms of the law, could singularly modify the perception of the Occupation; notably by the shroud of silence it imposes on verdicts that have been handed down."[3]

The debate over creating new laws and modifying sentences had been overtaken to some extent by events. French prisons were being emptied of convicted collaborators. The postwar presidents (de Gaulle, Gouin, Bidault, and Auriol) had all used their presidential power to shorten or suspend prison sentences and to release prisoners. Of the 40,000 people who had been arrested for collaboration at the liberation, only 13,800 were still in jail in December 1948. In October 1949, 8,000 remained. In 1951, on the eve of the first amnesty, only half that number were still in custody.[4]

After two months' consideration, with a vote of 327 to 263, the National Assembly enacted the first amnesty law, promulgated on 5 January 1951. It benefited those who had been punished for a crime first defined just after the liberation: *l'indignité nationale*, or "civic unworthiness," which encompassed violations of moral, patriotic values.[5] Those deemed guilty of this crime had been punished by *dégradation nationale*.[6] The amnesty law granted clemency to those who had received dégradation nationale as a chief penalty, reduced the list of punishments it included, and provided for the early release of some prisoners. Clemency was not, however, extended to people who had been judged by the High Court (Pétain, cabinet officers, and colonial governors), nor to those who had informed or tortured, or to those who had worked for the German police.[7]

Eighteen months later a second, broader amnesty bill was introduced. After a year of maneuvering and debate, the final bill passed on 24 July 1953. This time, dégradation nationale was abolished altogether as a chief penalty. Those who had been stripped of voting rights had them restored, and objects of the administrative purge were given back their pension rights. All but the most flagrant collaborators were released from prison. The first amnesty law had reduced the number of collaborators jailed from 4,000 to 1,570. When the second law had taken full effect, in 1956, only 62 of those jailed in 1945 remained in custody.[8]

A Conflict of Regions

Until the trial at Bordeaux, debate over the treatment of French citizens accused of wartime crimes had been discussed in terms of individual crimes and punishments. But during the trial at Bordeaux, the conflict over the culpability of soldiers at Oradour became a conflict between regions; the trial pitted against each other two French provinces with very different experiences of the war and the occupation.

In the days preceding the trial, Alsatian politicians and veterans' associations rallied to the defense of the *malgré-nous* and to plead for understanding of Alsace's special situation during the war. Despite the armistice agreement in which Germany promised to respect France's sovereignty, the Germans had annexed, de facto, the departments making up the regions of Alsace and Lorraine. In August 1940 they had appointed a

Gauleiter for each of the two French provinces.[9] The institution of German civil, racial, and penal codes soon followed. In January 1942 membership in the Nazi youth organizations became obligatory for everyone between the ages of ten and eighteen. Both men and women were compelled to work in Germany as part of the *Reichsarbeitsdienst*. And then on 25 August 1942, the *Gauleiter* decreed that military service in the German armed forces was obligatory for all men born between 1920 and 1924. Those who refused were often sent to the "security camp" (*Sicherungslager*) at Schirmeck in the eastern foothills of the Vosges. Others saw their families forcibly resettled in the Reich.[10] By the end of the war, though an estimated 40,000 young men had escaped to other parts of France, or deserted, 160,000 men from Alsace and Lorraine had been mobilized. At the end of the hostilities, 25,000 were officially counted as dead, 22,000 were missing, and approximately 12,000 still remained in Russian prisoner-of-war camps.[11]

Whatever compromises they had made while serving in the army of the enemy, the *incorporés de force* were not caught up in the toils of postwar justice. At the liberation the provisional government of the French republic had passed a war crimes law, but it applied only to "nationals of enemy countries or non-French agents in the service of enemy interests." It made no provision for the legal pursuit of French citizens by the military tribunal.[12] Thus, although a number of the Alsatians who took part in the killing at Oradour had been interviewed in English prisoner-of-war camps and, at the end of the war, made depositions to French authorities, only two Alsatians had been jailed along with the German soldiers who had been caught.[13] The others were considered only witnesses and were allowed to return home. It seemed likely that these men would never be held accountable for their actions at Oradour.

La Loi spéciale

All this changed in 1947 when, at the commemorative ceremonies of 10 June at Oradour, President Vincent Auriol revealed that the French government had designed special legislation "aimed specifically at the authors of this odious crime which we commemorate today. . . ." The proposed legislation would consider any member of a criminal unit (and the SS had been deemed such in the Nuremberg trials) as a coauthor or an accomplice in any crimes the group had committed.[14] Fifteen months later, the Parliament unanimously passed the law of 15 September 1948, which introduced a new notion into French penal law—the concept of collective responsibility of groups that committed war crimes.[15] The legislators' intent was clear: since individual participation would be difficult to establish in most cases, the presumption of collective guilt of criminal organizations would allow all members to be charged with a crime committed by a unit to which they had belonged. In other words, anyone who on 10 June 1944 had been a member of the Third Company of the regiment *Der Führer* of the division *Das Reich* could be presumed guilty. "The law of collective responsibility," as it became known, went against the principles of established law; now, in the case of war crimes, the burden of proof shifted from the prosecution to the accused, who would have to prove their innocence.

The third article specifically addressed those not included in the war crimes law of 28 August 1944—that is, French citizens. They could now be included in prosecution by the French military court.[16]

The Alsatian public and their representatives in Parliament considered it an outrage that in Bordeaux the Alsatians had been charged under a retroactive law, and that they would now sit in the dock side by side with the accused Germans. With the trial impending, the regional press and politicians from all parties rallied to defend Alsace from what they considered an accusation against the entire province.[17] The intensity of local feeling took outside observers by surprise. One journalist from Paris reported: "I was in Alsace a few days ago. One is stupefied by importance that the Oradour affair has taken on. One Alsatian clearly told me: 'Watch out! Don't take this lightly; the Oradour affair, for us, is a new Dreyfus affair.'"[18] These considerations were of little interest to the people of the Limousin, who remained unmoved by Alsatian pleas for special understanding. As the trial approached, the opposing parties became only more deeply entrenched. At the opening session, the judge who presided over the trial declared, "This trial is, and will remain, a trial of Nazism."[19] But instead Oradour, a symbol intended to unify the French in the contemplation of Nazi barbarism, turned the French against the French. In an atmosphere heavy with tension and acrimony, the trial in Bordeaux began.

The Trial

On the afternoon of 12 January the accused and their lawyers appeared for the first time in front of the military tribunal. From their bench, the judges (six active officers and a presiding civil magistrate) looked down on the row of the accused. The absence of any high-ranking officers made them appear all the more like ordinary individuals: "They are above all common folk," wrote Jean-Marc Théolleyre, correspondent for *Le Monde*. "All—their names matter little under the circumstances—

practice manual professions: machinist, postman, worker, mason, driver, farmer, cowherd, etc."[20]

Over the next few days the court heard arguments in which lawyers for the Alsatians gave long exposés about the situation of Alsace during the war. They protested the provisions of the law of collective responsibility, which placed their clients side by side with the German defendants.[21] But the court would have none of it and the trial finally proceeded to an interrogation of the accused.

While the presiding judge tried to move the trial forward, the parliamentary deputies from Alsace managed to have the law of collective responsibility brought up for debate before the National Assembly. The representatives from Alsace used this forum to argue passionately for reestablishing the principle of individual responsibility and for returning the burden of proof to the prosecution in the case of Alsatians. Once again, the representatives asserted that Alsatians had little in common with the accused Germans, and even claimed that they shared the victimization of Oradour: "How much we would have liked to mix our tears with theirs in common suffering from an evil which, in truth, far from dividing us, unites us in blood, humiliation and infinite sadness." Others argued that to try the Germans and French together was, in effect, a ratification of the Nazi annexation of Alsace. Always they invoked the political imperative of integrating Alsace into the national union. On 27 January, while witnesses from Oradour were testifying in Bordeaux, the National Assembly voted 365 against 238 to exempt the Frenchmen from the law of collective responsiblity.[22] The next day, the first article of the law of 15 September 1948—the article that established the notion of collective responsibility itself—was quietly abrogated.[23]

The Alsatians were gratified. Elsewhere, there was indignation. President Vincent Auriol was disgusted with what he considered the pusillanimous conduct of the assembly: "It is the most saddening thing to have occurred while I have been in office."[24] In the courtroom in Bordeaux, the president of the National Association of the Families of the Martyrs of Oradour-sur-Glane threatened to boycott the trial. But the president of the military tribunal expressed once again his determination to let nothing impede the trial. In a final comment, brandishing a little red law book, he remarked that if necessary, "the good old penal code" would suffice to prosecute: "Since this was written, no one has come up with anything better."[25]

As the trial continued, the defense presented witnesses from the Alsatian resistance to testify about the overwhelming difficulties of defying the German occupying power. Another spoke of the near impossibility of desertion. Joseph Rey, mayor of Colmar, questioned how much heroism one can expect of teenagers.[26] While this testimony increased awareness in the "interior" of the infernal situation of Alsace, the witnesses from Oradour, when they finally took the stand, presented the inconsolable anguish of those who suffered as individuals.

The starkness and simplicity of survivors' testimony made a striking and dramatic contrast to the legal arguments and tactics that had so far characterized the proceedings. First, men and women from outlying hamlets described seeing the Germans arrive and the horror and carnage they had found in the ruins after the massacre. But by all accounts, the sole survivor among the women and children who were burned in the church made the greatest impact on the court:

> What great writers achieve by the power of art: a stripping away, concision, the power of sober lines and density like marble, Mme. Rouffanche, a peasant of the Limousin, achieves effortlessly. . . . A perfectly sober account, and, in that, overwhelming, reduced to the essential facts. . . . She holds herself dignified and austere, dressed in clothes of deepest mourning. . . . Her face under her black hat is white as chalk. . . . Her voice, without the least trace of easy sentiment, reaches us clear and implacable. She is Nemesis, calm and inexorable.[27]

In her final words to the court, she spoke with "the intense illumination of a visionary":[28] "I ask that justice be done with God's help. I came out alive from the crematory oven, I am the sacred witness from the church. I am a mother who has lost everything."[29]

Though the the presiding judge expressed his hope that the suffering on both sides might become "an element unifying French people who suffered under the same doctrines and the same men," the days shared in the courtroom did little to increase mutual understanding. Alsatians continued to view the proceedings as a trial of the entire province. The Limousins resented the testimony on behalf of Alsace that cast the *malgré-nous* as victims.[30]

The Limousin's legacy of resistance contributed to the alienation of the two regions. Certainly it increased the desire of the Limousins to see the Alsatians punished. It also contributed to the Communist party's position on the trial. Besides being a stronghold of Communist-led resistance during the war, the Limousin had been a center of rural Communism ever since the founding of the Party in 1920. Since the end of the war, the Communists had taken a dominant and often polemical role in commemorating the massacre. In choosing sides in the trial at Bordeaux, Communist sympathy and political acumen led the Central Committee to defend the Limousin at the expense of their Alsatian supporters, who had never been very large in number.[31]

Whereas the Limousin as a region rejected the arguments in defense of the Alsatians, the families of the victims perceived them as a personal affront. Back home, the people of Limoges rallied in support of Oradour. On the evening of 3 February, forty thousand *Limogeauds* filed past a catafalque in an expression of sympathy and solidarity for the families of the martyrs of Oradour. While church bells tolled and sirens rang, all business as well as public transportation in the city came to a standstill. After listening to declarations demanding the punishment of the perpetrators of the massacre and the extradition of General Lammerding, an enormous cortege marched to the city's World War I memorial before silently dispersing.[32]

On 12 February the court heard the last of the closing arguments. The courtroom emptied and the judges went into conference to conduct the sentencing. Finally, after thirty-two hours of deliberation, the judges pronounced their sentences at 2:10 A.M. on Friday, 13 February. The highest-ranking German received the death penalty. One German soldier who had proved his absence from Oradour on 10 June 1944 was freed. The court condemned the four other Germans to sentences ranging from ten to twelve years of hard labor. The Alsatians received somewhat lighter penalties. The one volunteer in the group was sentenced to death.[33] Nine Alsatians were given sentences ranging from five to twelve years of hard labor. The remaining four were sentenced to a range of five to eight years in jail. All except one, who had already served most of his sentence, immediately requested an appeal.

Within hours the morning editions of newspapers announced the verdict throughout France, and by 8:30 in the morning the newsstands in Alsace were sold out. In the streets of Strasbourg, the verdict was the only subject of discussion.[34] The *Nouveau Rhin Français* reported similar consternation in Mulhouse.[35] Throughout the province, Alsatians vehemently objected. In Paris an Alsatian deputy in Parliament entered a request at the National Assembly for an inquiry into the "condition and atmosphere in which the trial of Oradour took place," the verdict itself, as well as the "moral repercussions for the youth of Alsace" and "the future of the province."[36]

Citizens who sympathized with the *malgré-nous* did not wait to vent their dismay and anger. In Strasbourg flags hung in mourning could be seen along a main thoroughfare near the cathedral.[37] Later in the day posters went up in every commune in the Haut-Rhin, emblazoned with a message from the department's association of mayors: "We don't accept it." At six o'clock in the evening church bells tolled for fifteen minutes throughout the Haut-Rhin.[38] The veterans association of the *malgré-nous* of the Bas-Rhin made the most inflammatory gesture. They plastered kiosks in Strasbourg with yellow signs listing the names and sentences of the *malgré-nous*. These posters were identical in color, format, and lettering to those that had been put up by the Nazis to announce death sentences against Alsatian resisters.[39] As night fell, silent men and women with drawn faces stood grouped around these signs.[40]

The next morning, while the Alsatian members of Parliament were meeting in Strasbourg to draw up strategies of protest, Deputy Pierre Pflimlin received a telegram in which the minister of defense made it clear that the government would facilitate parliamentary efforts to grant amnesty to the Alsatians.[41] Thus, the possibility arose that in the Oradour affair, the legislature would once again intervene in a judicial matter in order to ease the political crisis.

Pleven's telegram immediately brought some calm to Alsace. But local politicians kept up the pressure with dramatic ceremonial gestures. On Sunday the mayor of Strasbourg led six thousand people on a march from the town hall to the Place de la République, where the familiar white stone sculpture of the city's monument to the dead of World War I loomed under a black shroud.[42] At the same time, in large Alsatian towns, demonstrators gathered at their own World War I memorials, which were similarly veiled in protest.[43]

The design of the monument in Strasbourg made it a particularly powerful site for the expression of distress over the latest eruption of the *drame d'Alsace*. The monument depicts a piéta figure supporting two dying soldiers on her lap—sons of Alsace who fought in the opposing armies of France and Germany. Two nude male figures, sculpted in the style of Rodin, clasp each other's hands in the last moments before death. This group of figures faces in the direction of the old town where the silhouette of the spires of the Cathedral of Strasbourg pierce the skyline. In keeping with the sober mood of the statue, there are no heroic inscriptions or names of individuals on the monument. Instead, a simple inscription is carved on the base: A NOS MORTS 1914–1918.[44]

The government was so concerned by the unrest in Alsace that it gave its support to yet another *loi d'exception*. This bill proposed amnesty, full and complete, for those who had been "forcibly incorporated into the German armies." In order that the amnesty would be interpreted as a gesture from the entire nation toward Alsace, the draft legislation was proposed by eight deputies from "provinces of the interior" who represented all political parties except the Communists. On the morning of 17 February the president of the *Conseil des Ministres*, René Mayer, went to the Palais-Bourbon to prepare the way for the debate and vote, which would take place the next day. "The government is uttering a solemn appeal to the unity of the nation," he told the Chamber of Deputies. "The mourning and the trials of our diverse provinces should bring us to understand each other, not to tearing each other apart."[45]

In the Limousin, those who had attended the trial had not been surprised by the verdict, but they had taken the news bitterly. The families of the victims found the sentences scandalously lenient. There was no middle ground; the only sentence acceptable to them would have been the death penalty for all who participated in the crime. Not surprisingly, the proposed amnesty completed the outrage. In the regional Socialist Party paper, *Le Populaire du Centre*, Deputy Jean Le Bail railed against the bad faith of his Alsatian colleagues in the assembly. He pointed out that during the debate over the abrogation of the law of collective guilt, they had insisted that they were not trying to subvert justice, but wanted only to do away with an unjust law. That had been achieved. Now they were proposing yet another exceptional measure to skirt the judgment of the court.[46]

Aside from the vociferous complaints of the Limousin and the Communist Party, it was in the newspapers born of the clandestine press of the resistance that one detects discomfort with the arguments made by the defense and the subsequent protests in Alsace. Though one could certainly make a case that Alsace had suffered exceptionally during the occupation, the proposition that French citizens could have been forced to act "in spite of themselves" raised troubling questions about how the French were to judge any act of collaboration. To those who had fought in the resistance, the logic of the Alsatian defense led in the direction of accepting the notion that for other French citizens as well, resistance had not been possible.

President Vincent Auriol was apparently troubled by such thoughts on 18 February when, five days after the verdict had been handed down, he received a delegation of Alsatian deputies. This meeting took place only hours before the National Assembly was to vote on the legislation to grant amnesty to the Alsatians. First, Auriol commented on the conditions that had permitted the passage of the original war crimes law of 1948, which had proved untenable: "everyone was like me, under the impression of those little white coffins; doubtless the horror of the drama got the better of them." But, he went on to remind them, none of them had opposed the law at the time: "You made the law of 1948, you accepted the judgment in advance." Auriol indicated that he was willing to provide some sort of clemency for the Alsatians to resolve the painful situation. Something would have to be done to appease Alsace.[47] He did not approve, however, of the proposed amnesty, which would have had the effect of expunging the court's conviction. Nine years after the end of the war, Vincent Auriol, who had been a *grand résistant* and colleague and personal friend of Léon Blum, remained committed to the ideal of resistance and was uneasy with a gesture that appeared to absolve the *malgré-nous*.[48] Notes in his diary make plain that Auriol would have been happier with a presidential pardon (granted on an ad hoc, case-by-case basis) than with the amnesty voted by Parliament, which was a sweeping decision by society to wipe the slate clean.

In the the parliamentary session of 18 February, deputies from the Limousin passionately warned their colleagues of the serious threat the bill posed to the principle of the separation of powers: "If the lawmaker now takes it upon himself to annul the judgment before the ink has dried, where are we going, in what sort of state are we?" asked the Socialist deputy André Bardon. He went on to question whether the proposed bill, coming so quickly after the court's judgment, could claim the moral legitimacy of a true amnesty: "They are saying to us: 'amnesty.' Amnesty, according to the Greek etymology, is forgetting, it is the law of forgetting. Amnesty is a gesture that one makes only with a cool head. What forgetting is there in our hearts?. . . Not exhibiting the character of a true amnesty, it shreds the pronouncement of conviction."[49]

The proponents of the amnesty did not engage in a discussion of the legal ramifications of an amnesty, but instead sought to frame the debate by what they considered the overriding consideration at hand: the exigencies of national unity. "The country is a mother," cried President of the Assembly Edouard Herriot. "She cannot let her children tear each other apart on her breast." The minister of defense asked the deputies to consider the problem apart from the juridical issues: "The decision by politicians should be taken on a totally different level than that of the judges, a level that is not that of judicial reasoning, but that of the national interest and of the unity of the French community."[50] Even General de Gaulle, despite his essential role in establishing Oradour as a national symbol, also appealed for understanding of the Alsatians in the interest of national unity.[51]

In the end, it seemed that the Assembly deemed the alienation of a poor, rural, leftist region to be less of a threat to national unity than continuing unrest in populous, prosperous Alsace. Three hundred nineteen deputies—the great majority from the *Mouvement Républicain Populaire* (MRP) and *Rassemblement du Peuple Français* (RPF)—approved the amnesty; all the Communists, three-quarters of the Socialists, a third of the Radicals, and a dozen isolated members from other parties—211 in all—voted against the bill. Eighty-three deputies abstained.[52] Three days after the vote of the assembly, in the early morning hours of 21 February, the thirteen Alsatians walked through the gates of the military prison in Bordeaux. They quickly climbed into four waiting vans that drove northeast, through the dark and fog. By the early afternoon they had arrived home in Alsace where they were received by their families with relief and joy.[53]

While the newspapers in Alsace published pictures of the *malgré-nous* reunited with their wives and children, in Oradour those who had lost their families in the massacre reeled with shock, anger, and despair. The National Assembly that had voted seven years before to make Oradour a national symbol had now turned its back on the 642 "martyrs." For the people of Oradour, this amounted to a second martyrdom—this time at the hands of their own countrymen. In the face of this blow, the people of Oradour used their only means of retaliation; they acted to reclaim the commemorative site for themselves alone. On 20 February a delegation of the National Association of the Families of the Martyrs of Oradour-sur-Glane, led by André Desourteaux, returned to the prefect the Cross of the Legion of Honor. They also gave back the bronze plaque presented in the name of the republic by President de Gaulle.[54] The next day, the mayor of Oradour returned the *Croix de guerre* that the community had received in 1948.

In the Limousin and throughout France the Communist Party called for protests against the amnesty. Although the Communists dominated the active protest, there was also sharp disapproval of the amnesty among veterans of the Resistance in general—particularly in regions of France where there had been widespread resistance. At the other end of the spectrum, unapologetic supporters of Vichy demanded a sweeping amnesty, "one and indivisible," for "victims of the purges."[55] For its part, the German government, which had approved of sentencing that did not distinguish by nationality, was dismayed that only Alsatians had been absolved.

In the end, the president of the Republic pardoned the two men condemned to death. By 1958, five years after the trial, all prisoners had been freed. This fit into the larger pattern of leniency for collaborators. In all of France in 1958, only nineteen people accused of collaboration remained in jail. Twenty years after the liberation, in 1964, there were none.[56]

Calm returned to Alsace immediately after the amnesty, and the ferment died down in the rest of the country. In Oradour the shock and bitter disappointment still endure. For many old-timers of Oradour, recollections of 1953 are as gloomy as those of 1944. Dr. Robert Lapuelle, who took up a medical practice in the new town of Oradour in 1949, remembers: "So, to this sentiment of very great pain and of survival there was added a sentiment of injustice, abandonment, and, at times, revolt."[57] The sense of betrayal occasioned by the vote for amnesty led the community of Oradour to turn inward and reject relations with the state. They no longer invited government officials to participate in the yearly commemorative ceremony in the ruins on 10 June. The families of the victims caused the most consternation by posting signs at the entrances to the ruins listing all the deputies who had voted to grant amnesty to the Alsatians. The alienation and anger of the old-timers of Oradour had an enormous impact on both the commemoration of the massacre and the evolution of the new town. To this day, many of those who lived through the shock of the amnesty divide Oradour's postwar into two periods: "before Bordeaux" and "after Bordeaux."

The trial in Bordeaux showed that the system of justice could not resolve the bitter legacies of the Occupation. The system's task in a liberal democracy such as the Fourth Republic, was to adjudicate the particular cases of the individuals accused, not to deliver "the verdict of history." The duty of the court was to consider these cases within the confines of the law, regardless of political or emotional pressures. The trial at Bordeaux remains a striking example of the tension between the state's responsibility to provide justice to individuals and the necessity of maintaining social and political order. By intervening in the judicial process, the National Assembly gave more weight to national unity than to punishing a war crime or assuaging the families of the victims. In 1953, by granting amnesty to the Alsatians in the interest of national unity, France's elected representatives delayed once again France's reckoning with its wartime past.

Notes

1. The commander of the SS Division Das Reich, which had carried out the crime, was known to be living in Düsseldorf (in the British-occupied zone), but the British proved unresponsive to French demands for his extradition. In February 1953, during the trial, a delegation of the French government, on an official visit to London, asked that Lammerding be extradited. The delegation included the *Président du Conseil* and the Minister of Foreign Affairs. Vincent Auriol, *Journal du Septennant,* eds. Pierre Nora and Jacques Ozouf, 7 vols. (Paris: Librairie Armand Colin, 1970–71), 7: 55. Requests were also made to the British High Commission in Germany, which stated that the case was "under study" and that they were awaiting instructions from London. They added that as of 1 September 1948, the British were extraditing only Germans accused of homicide as defined by German law. In 1985 journalist Jean-Marc Théolleyre added further information: with the onset of the Cold War, the Americans protected Lammerding (as they did many former Nazis, including Klaus Barbie) in exchange for intelligence information. Jean-Marc Théolleyre, *Procès d'après-guerre* (Paris: Éditions La Découverte et Journal Le Monde, 1985), 39–40.

2. *Combat*: 20, 25 October 1944; 5, 11 January 1945. And *Le Figaro*: 8 September 1944; 13, 19, 22–23 October 1944; 2, 7–8, 12 January 1945. See also

Tony Judt, *Past Imperfect: French Intellectuals, 1944–56* (Berkeley: University of California Press, 1992), 68–72.

3. Henry Rousso, *Le Syndrome de Vichy, 1944–48* (Paris: Éditions du Seuil, 1987), 62.

4. Peter Novick, *The Resistance versus Vichy: The Purge of Collaborators in Liberated France* (London: Charles and Windus, 1968), 187–88. Novick's study, for years the only detailed analysis of the purges, was not translated into French until 1985—a telling indication of the taboo nature of the subject in France. The Comité d'histoire de la deuxième guerre mondiale launched an extensive survey, under the direction of Marcel Badot, of the purges (legal and extralegal). The results from the study of seventy-three departments refine and confirm Novick's. See Marcel Baudot, "L'Épuration: Bilan chiffré", *Bulletin de l'Institut d'Histoire du Temps Présent* 25 (September 1986): 37–53. For a recent consideration of the purges and an evaluation of statistics, see Henry Rousso, "L'Épuration en France: une histoire inachevée," *Vingtième siècle* 33 (January–March 1992): 78–105. For a detailed analysis of the purge of the civil service, see François Rouquet, *L'Épuration dans l'administration française* (Paris: CNRS Éditions, 1993).

5. Special *chambres civiques* were instituted to deal with cases of national indignity. *The Resistance*, Novick, 152–53.

6. The American observer Janet Flanner noted in 1945: "National degradation . . . consist[s] of being deprived of nearly everything the French consider nice—such as the right to wear decorations, the right to be a lawyer, notary, public-schoolteacher, judge, or even a witness, the right to run a publishing, radio or motion-picture company or bank." Janet Flanner, *Paris Journal, 1944–65* (New York: Atheneum, 1965), 15.

7. Novick, *The Resistance*, 188.

8. Ibid., and Rousso, *Le Syndrome*, 64.

9. Josef Bürckel, the *Gauleiter* of Vienna, was named civil adminstrator for Lorraine and the Sarre-Palatinate. Robert Wagner, the *Gauleiter* of Baden, extended his control to Alsace.

10. Though rarely mentioned by the defenders of the *malgré-nous*, the Germans also set up the concentration camp of Struthof in Natzwiller, eleven kilometers from Schirmeck, in the mountains. Whereas Schirmeck was a "reeducation camp" for recalcitrant Alsatians, Struthof was a full-fledged concentration camp complete with a gas chamber and Nazi doctors who performed experiments on prisoners. Although some of the inmates of Schirmeck were sent to their deaths at Struthof, the concentration camp was destined for French resisters and Jews from all over Europe. Whereas those sent to Schirmeck served a sentence and were then released, the people sent to Struthof were worked to death or exterminated. In discussing the sufferings of Alsace and the *malgrés-nous*, almost no mention was made of these people. In portraying their own sufferings, it would seem that the *malgrés-nous* had no interest in evoking those who were perhaps greater victims of the Nazis.

11. Mairie-Joseph Bopp, "L'Enrôlement de force des Alsaciens dans la Wehrmacht et la SS," *Revue d'histoire de la deuxième guerre mondiale* 20 (October 1955): 42.

12. *L'Ordonnance du 28 août 1944 relative à la répression des crimes de guerre.*

13. These two were Georges René Boos, who admitted to volunteering for the SS, and Paul Graff, who was the only one to actually confess to having killed someone in Oradour.

14. AN 4 AG3. Rélatif au voyage du président Auriol à Oradour-sur-Glane 10 juin 1947. Speech of the president of the republic.

15. The exact wording: "For crimes which come under the ordinance of 28 August 1944 on the punishment of war crimes, when these crimes can be attributed to the collective action of a group or military formation that belongs to an organization declared criminal by the international military court [which was the case for the Waffen SS] . . . then all individuals belonging to this formation or this group may be considered coauthors, unless they can bring proof of having been forcibly drafted and also proof that they did not participate in the said crime." *Loi No. 48–1416 du 15 septembre 1948 relative à la repression des crimes de guerre.*

16. Under this article French citizens would not be prosecuted by virtue of collective guilt, but rather as "personally coauthors or accessories." The trial at Bordeaux was not the first time the law had been applied. In 1949 the military court at Metz used the law to convict Germans who had massacred civilians at Ascq on 1 April 1944. *L'Aurore,* 7 Janvier 1953.

17. The Communist Party in Alsace was the notable exception from the general sympathy for the *malgrés-nous.* Since the end of the war, the PCF had been calling loudly for the punishment of the soldiers who had taken part in the massacre. Furthermore, the Limousin region (though not Oradour itself) had been a center of Communist resistance. With the affair of the malgré-nous, Alsatian Communist leadership was caught between regional loyalties and party policy. But they soon fell into line. Throughout the trial, the Alsatian Communists defended the interests of the Limousin victims. As a result, the Communist Party in Alsace would see its regional following drop precipitously.

18. "*L'Aurore,* 25 December 1952.

19. *Le Monde,* 18 and 19 January 1953.

20. Ibid., 13 January 1953.

21. The Limousin press lamented the emphasis of the opening days of the trial: "[T]otal confusion does not cease to reign: speeches follow up speeches, squabbles multiply between the lawyers for the Germans and the lawyers for the Alsatians and we are still at the same point: the trial hasn't moved one step forward. To be sure, it is a question—too much of one in my view—of Alsatian patriotism, of Nazi barbarism. . . . The misfortune in all this . . . the victims of the massacre seem to be relegated to the background." *Le Populaire du Centre,* 14 January 1953.

22. This debate revealed and exacerbated another regional conflict. The department of the Moselle, part of the Lorraine, had also been annexed and had seen its young men forcibly drafted. But there had been no *mosellans* in the company that committed the massacre at Oradour. More to the point: forty-four refugees from the Lorraine town of Charly had been killed at Oradour. Raymond Mondon, mayor of Metz and a deputy from the department of the Moselle,

opposed modifying the law of 15 September 1948. His colleague, Jules Thiriet, evoked the 300,000 *lorrains* who were expelled from the department in 1939 and the sufferings of Charly, which had been renamed Charly-Oradour. He too voted against the resolution to exempt the *malgré-nous* from the law of collective responsibility.

23. *Journal Officiel*, séance du 18 fevrier 1953, 1114.

24. The president recorded his sentiments in his diary: "The trial of Oradour continues. The Chamber is in a panic. It sufficed that there was a groundswell of feeling in Alsace for the deputies who voted for the law of 1948 to immediately want to abrogate it now. It is the most saddening thing to have occurred while I have been in office. In 1948 one passed a law to give satisfaction to the population of Oradour. At that moment, indignation was such that one ceded to it and voted for an absurdity. But see now that it's Alsace that's protesting and immediately the Chamber backtracks. It's enough in this Assembly that someone sneezes for everyone to run for cover. There is no longer any democracy and fear weighs on all these mediocre people. It's saddening. It's obvious that one of these days I'll have to say it. But I can't say it being here [in my current position]." Vincent Auriol, *Journal du Septennat, 1947–54*, 7 vols. (Paris: Librairie Armand Colin: 1971), 7: 38.

25. *Le Figaro*, 29 January 1953. President Auriol approved of the judge's sangfroid: "President Saint-Saens is a remarkable man, who has proved his independence by twice rejecting motions to sever [motions to try the Alsatians and Germans separately] and he appeased the people of Oradour who wanted to leave saying that the tribunal would continue to act as it had in the past; up until now he has ruled in accordance with French laws, normal laws, the good old penal code which was created by men who knew what they were doing. No one has brought this out, but I have the intention of telling him that he has all my sympathy." Auriol, *Journal du Septennat*, 7:38.

26. *Le Monde*, 1–2 February 1953.

27. *Le Figaro*, 2 February 1953.

28. *Le Monde*, 3 February 1953.

29. *Le Figaro*, 2 February 1953.

30. AN F715431, Renseignements généraux, Gueret, No. 367/C3. "According to them [the people of the Creuse], the Alsatians who invoke physical and moral constraints to justify and camouflage their acts, did nothing to attenuate the barbarity. . . . Furthermore, reading the summary of the proceedings shows, according to the *creusois*, the duplicity of the Alsatians who pose as victims. . . ."

31. AN F7 15431. Renseignements généraux, Colmar, S.L.I. no. 179/53, 28 janvier 1953.

32. *Le Figaro*, 4 February 1953.

33. Boos's case had been separate from the other Alsatians from the very beginning of the trial. As a volunteer in the SS he was not tried for war crimes, but for treason.

34. Cited in "Après le verdict de Bordeaux", *Franc-Tireur*, 14 February 1953.

35. *Le Nouveau Rhin Français*, 14 February 1953.

36. *Le Figaro*, 14 February 1953, *Les Dernières Nouvelles d'Alsace*, 14 February 1953.

37. *Le Franc-Tireur*, 14 February 1953.

38. *Paris-Presse l'Intransigeant*, 15 February 1953.

39. *Le Monde*, 15 February 1953.

40. *Le Figaro*, 14 February 1953. Only one violent incident was reported: in the early afternoon someone drove by the office of the Communist Party paper, *L'Humanité de l'Alsace-Lorraine*, and hurled bricks through the window. *L'Alsace*, 14 February 1953.

41. *Le Monde*, 15 February 1953.

42. *Le Figaro*, 16 February 1953.

43. *L'Aurore*, 16 February 1953.

44. Paul Ahne, "Le Monument aux Morts de Strasbourg," *Archives Alsaciennes d'Histoire del'Art, 1936 Extrait* (Librairie Istra: Strasbourg, 1936), 167–75.

45. *Le Figaro*, 18 February 1953.

46. *Le Populaire du Centre*, 17 February 1953.

47. The Paris correspondent of a Swiss newspaper neatly summed up the situation: "Let's put it clearly: the question posed to France today is to choose between the natural desire to satisfy the families of the victims of Oradour, who want justice rendered to their dead, and the danger of seeing the province of Alsace, which is dear to her [France], separate itself and thereby bringing about the rebirth of autonomist tendencies that manifested themselves in the interwar years. If the verdict at Bordeaux was absolutely equitable, if the truly guilty ones had been punished, one wouldn't hesitate to respond. But given that doubts remain for certain of the condemned men, there is every reason to believe that Alsace will receive the appeasement it demands." James Donnadieu, "Les Réactions de l'Alsace," *Le Journal de Genève*, 17 February 1953.

48. Auriol, *Journal*, 7: 707, n. 30. See also Auriol's memoirs of the war years: *Hier et Demain*, 2 vols. (Paris: Charlot, 1945).

49. *Journal Officiel*, séance du 18 February 1953, 1112–13.

50. *Journal Officiel*, séance du 18 February 1953, 1123.

51. "What French person will not understand the inflamed suffering of Alsace? In this serious affair what we have to avoid, above all, is that after having lost so many of her children assassinated by the enemy in the tragedy of Oradour, in addition France lets a bitter wound be inflicted on the national unity." Charles de Gaulle, *Discours et messages, dans l'attente, fevrier 1946–avril 1958* (Paris: Librairie Plon, 1970), 563–64.

52. The breakdown was as follows: of the 319 who voted for the amnesty: 80 members of the RPF (out of the 85); 77 MRP (out of 89); 37 Radical-Socialists (out of 75); 36 Independent Farmers Party (out of 47); 35 Independent Republicans (out of 55); 23 ARS (dissidents from the MRP) out of 32; 14 Independents d'outre-mer (out of 15); 9 UDSR (the party of Minister Pleven (out of 23), and 8 Socialists. Of the 211 who voted against the law: 96 Communists plus 4 Progressives affiliated with PCF; 76 Socialists (out of 105); 21 Radical-Socialists (out of 75); 4 ARS (out of 32); 3 RPF (out of 85); 3 Independent Peasants Party (out of 47); 2 MRP (out of 89); 2 USDR (out of 23). Fifty-five deputies abstained, 28 did not cast any ballot, and 13 deputies were not not present at the vote. "Wie die Kammer abstimmte," *L'Alsace*, 20 February 1953.

53. "Wie die '13' heimkehrten," *Les Dernieres Nouvelles d'Alsace*, 24 Feb-

ruary 1953; "Die Heimatkehr der '13' ins Elsass," *Le Nouveau Rhin Français*, 24 February 1953.

54. *Le Populaire du Centre*, 21 February 1953.
55. "Pour une amnistie une et indivisible", *Rivarol*, 27 February 1953.
56. Novick, *The Resistance*, 188.
57. Dr. Robert Lapuelle, interview by Sarah Farmer, March 1988.

MARK MAZOWER

The Cold War and the Appropriation of Memory: Greece after Liberation

> He was struck by the war not as a historical,
> geopolitical fact but as a multiplicity, a near-
> infinity of private sorrows, as a boundless grief
> minutely subdivided without diminishment
> among individuals who covered the continent
> like dust, like spores whose separate identities
> would remain unknown. . . . For the first time he
> sensed the scale of the catastrophe in terms of
> feeling: all those unique and solitary deaths, all
> that consequent sorrow, unique and solitary
> too, which had no place in conferences, head-
> lines, history, and which had quietly retired to
> houses, kitchens, unshared beds, and anguished
> memories. . . . What possible good could come
> of a Europe covered in this dust, these spores,
> when forgetting would be inhuman and danger-
> ous, and remembering a constant torture?
> —*Ian McEwan,* Black Dogs

EVERYWHERE IN Europe the obsessions and polarities of the Cold War era imposed themselves upon people's understanding and memory of the Second World War, but in few if any countries can they have done so with greater force or speed than in Greece. Well before the Truman Doctrine revealed Greece's importance as a locus for the Cold War, perhaps even before the December 1944 fighting between the British and EAM/ELAS (the left-wing resistance movement), the conflict between communism and anticommunism had overlaid and superseded the struggle against Fascism.

In this essay I aim to elucidate the ways in which Cold War attitudes shaped and influenced official and unofficial memories of 1940–45. What were the Greek state's policies toward war criminals, collaborators, and the resistance? What, too, of the more personal experiences of former collaborators and *résistants* themselves? What was the interplay between political and historiographical debates about the war? One underlying problem concerns the relationship between memories of the war, the Cold War, and reformulations of Greek nationalism. This is linked to the issue of reconciliation: when and how, if at all, was reconciliation achieved (at least as an act of official policy) in Greece? To what extent did this involve a redefinition of historical events, and who gained and who lost as a result of this redefinition? I offer some thoughts on these issues by way of conclusion.

During the last months of the German Occupation a bitter and potentially lethal debate took place behind the scenes between Security Police (SiPo/SD) Chief Walter Blume and Foreign Office representative Hermann Neubacher. Blume proposed that as the Germans withdrew from Greece they should carry out what he called the "Chaos Thesis": this would have involved arresting and executing every member of the political elite who was suspected of having ties to the British. Neubacher countered that it was better to ignore the Athenian politicians' pro-British sentiments so long as they were willing to work with the Germans against EAM/ELAS. At the very last moment Neubacher's line prevailed and Blume was withdrawn from Greece.[1]

Neubacher's success ensured the survival of a basically pro-British elite of anticommunist politicians, fearful of the power of EAM/ELAS and linked informally to some of the politicians who had held power during the Occupation. At Liberation, Prime Minister George Papandreou openly declared that "traitors of the Fatherland" would be punished. A law for the prosecution of collaborators was published in the *Government Gazette* on 6 November 1944. However, following the *dekemvriana* (the fighting in Athens in December 1944 between the British and EAM/ELAS), the atmosphere changed. With the Left weakened by its defeat at the hands of the British, ELAS was disbanded and EAM limped on, impotent to do more than watch as provisions for a purge of the civil service were turned against its own supporters. Official Greek policy toward those who had collaborated with the Axis turned out to be milder and more hesitant than perhaps anywhere else in Europe.

Collaborationist ministers, whose trial opened in February 1945, were heartened by the Government's anti-Left line. Rex Leeper, the British ambassador, reported that the accused adopted "a defiant and almost menacing tone," while the public prosecutor was "thrown so much on the defensive as to become almost plaintive." At one point it seemed as though the defendants might actually be acquitted; in the event, only Tsolakoglu, the first quisling premier, was sentenced to death. This was eventually commuted to a life term.

When the infamous General Alexandros Lambou, wartime head of the special security police, went on trial in the summer of 1945 it was far from a foregone conclusion that his defense plea—that he had been defending the state against Communism, not deliberately helping the Germans—would be rejected. In the courtroom, national guardsmen and defense lawyers threatened the judges. Lambou was sentenced to death— hundreds of Athenians, after all, had been eyewitnesses to the executions he had personally overseen during the roundups one year earlier—but the majority of his codefendants received only short prison terms. Leeper— no sympathizer of EAM—wrote that these verdicts had aroused "great indignation."[2]

In March 1945 prominent EAM members among the faculty of the University of Athens were dismissed. Over the following months large numbers of civil servants were also fired, ostensibly on economic grounds but in fact for political reasons.[3] EAM supporters were also systematically screened out of the new national guard. Through October and November 1944, they had begun to be conscripted into the guard while members of the collaborationist security battalions remained in detention until such time as they could be individually screened. When the *dekemvriana* erupted, however, many battalionists were released to fight for the Papandreou government, and within a year there were hundreds of former battalionists in official positions; at the same time, screening procedures were turned against anyone suspected of having fought in EAM/ELAS. Appointees to the army officer corps included 228 security battalionists and 221 former ELAS officers; the latter were kept inactive by the general staff until retirement.[4]

The sharp shift to the Right led, especially in the provinces, to a wave of right-wing violence. According to EAM, the year following February 1945 saw over 1,200 of its supporters murdered by paramilitary gangs or the national guard and over 6,600 assaults. Reports from all over the country indicate that despite the fact that "a very large part of the population is weary of all this strife and dispute," anti-Communist violence was, if anything on the increase through 1945. In Lamia, national guardsmen came to the EAM/KKE (Greek Communist Party) headquarters, took the furniture, burned the papers, destroyed pictures of Stalin and Roosevelt, billeted their own personnel in the building, and forbade its use by EAM/ KKE. In Volos, men who had collaborated with the Gestapo arrested former ELAS officers in the street. In Patras former *andartes* (guerrillas) were arrested for singing ELAS songs.[5]

Over eighty thousand people were prosecuted during 1945, the overwhelming majority belonging to the Left. The judges, many of whom had served through the Occupation, sentenced suspected leftists harshly. In comparison, wartime collaborators escaped lightly. Government figures showed that only 2,896 of 16,700 prisoners held in September 1945 were convicted of collaboration; by January 1951 they numbered only 1,275 out of 28,000 prisoners. The proportion of those convicted for collaboration to those imprisoned for their part in the resistance was roughly one to ten in the late 1940s.[6]

When the Greek regent, Archbishop Damaskinos, was reproached by the British for the high number of prisoners, who included men congratulated by the Allies for their wartime services, Damaskinos replied that the numerous atrocities committed by the communists during and immediately after the war had poisoned the atmosphere in Greece. Some people had to be imprisoned for their own safety, lest they fall victim to private vendettas. Public opinion, he argued, would not stand for a general amnesty.[7]

Undoubtedly, personal feelings were running high; EAM/ELAS had, after all, carried out a large number of "executions" of their own before and after Liberation. The real stumbling block for those inclined to leniency, however, was not Greek public opinion but the security apparatus and, in particular, the lack of discipline of the new national guard. After the 1946 elections, Greek politics shifted rightward and the Tsaldaris government turned a blind eye to the activities of the guard, the army, and the police. Incoming MPs included men who openly declared their support for the wartime quisling governments. The new vice-premier was one of several leading figures in the new administration to have played a key role in the formation of the wartime security battalions. Over one thousand former battalionists received commissions in the new Greek army while, according to EAM, over 80 percent of the 3,500 held on charges of collaboration had been acquitted by the middle of 1946, while another 11 percent were released before trial.[8]

The KKE's response to renewed official persecution was twofold. On the one hand, suspected leftists fled to the hills and formed bands that launched attacks against the gendarmerie and government supporters. Limited in scale at first, these attacks spread across much of Greece during 1946. The other element in KKE strategy was a highly publicized policy of calling for reconciliation. Zachariades, the Party general secretary hoped to use limited violence to pressure the government into conceding a general amnesty together with the convocation of an all-party conference that would restore to the Left a modicum of political respectability.[9]

Predictably, perhaps, the idea of reconciliation in any form appears to have alarmed the Right more than did the prospect of left-wing violence. EAM publicized a leaked memorandum from Public Order Minister Theotokis in which he ordered his subordinates to instruct the public about "the dangers of reconciliation." Theotokis warned that the KKE had successfully arranged several "spectacular festivals of reconciliation" in which "peasants gave their hand to the communists in their village and even threw their kitchen knives into the bonfire as a sign of reconciliation." Noting that young royalists had gone on excursions at the invitation of EPON, the Communist youth movement, the minister warned that "every effort must be made to make nationalist citizens and organizations realize that they must abstain at all costs from such a movement. Such activity must be considered as suspect, and people who take part must be kept under surveillance."[10]

Theotokis was under growing pressure from members of the extreme Right such as Napoleon Zervas, formerly chief of the British-sponsored resistance movement EDES and now leader of the National Party. Ambitious to become minister of public order, Zervas berated Theotokis for softness toward the KKE, forcing a censure vote against the government that was only narrowly defeated. Zervas's own political career was to be cut short in 1947 following revelations at Nuremberg (at the Trial of the Southeastern Generals) of his wartime contacts with the Wehrmacht. But both before and after the referendum in September 1946, which brought the king back to Greece, pressure from the Right continued to mount, plunging Greece into the last and most bitter round of the civil war.[11]

———————

Parliamentary government never quite collapsed during the Greek civil war. It survived with the aid of draconian emergency decrees, martial law, and an official ideology that equated sympathy for the Left with Slavo-communism. Nationalism and anticommunism went hand in hand. In 1947 loyalty certificates were brought in based on the example provided by the Truman administration. But where the U.S. legislation had invoked "reasonable grounds for the belief that the person involved is disloyal to the government of the U.S.," the Greek legal formula simply targeted those "imbued with antinational convictions." When the Makronissos camp was opened in 1949 as part of the Diomidis government's Measures of National Reeducation, it was designed to house those suspected of "antinationalist tendencies" and to obtain their recantation.[12]

Attitudes to the wartime resistance were often the acid test of a suspect's political reliability. Laws depriving those convicted of antinational behavior of both property and citizenship included in their terms of reference those who "since the start of enemy occupation had contributed in any way to the struggle of the rebels against the State." At the court-martial of Stavros Dimitrakos, for example, one of the many young men accused of subversive activity in the late 1940s, the presiding judge focused on his wartime activities and his current attitude toward them. Dimitrakos, a thirty-five year-old civil servant, had helped EAM/ELAS in 1943 by passing them maps of German aerodromes for the use of the British in the Middle East:

> *Judge*: Did you believe that ELAS was cooperating with the Middle East, and do you today?
>
> *Dimitrakos*: I have no reason to suppose otherwise.
>
> *Judge*: You have retsina in your eyes!

As Dimitrakos went on to describe his work for the divisional staff of an ELAS unit, the judge intervened: "You ought to be ashamed!" To express positive views about EAM/ELAS was to "make propaganda for Markos" (commander of the rebel Democratic Army of Greece).[13]

Courts-martial, loyalty oaths, expropriation of property, and the withdrawal of Greek nationality remained the lot of former *andartes* for years after the civil war ended. The effects spread beyond the individuals directly concerned to include entire families and communities, and this disruption of the family offered one of the main lines of attack upon official policy in the 1950s. At a time when the nationalist credentials of the Right could not be openly challenged, those concerned at the scale of political repression focused instead on its impact upon the home.

In campaigning publicly for the release of political prisoners, Greek women played a prominent part. While the men who ran ex-ELAS combatants' organizations were quickly targeted and jailed, their womenfolk proved more troublesome for the authorities. In the Panhellenic Union of Families of Exiles and Prisoners, founded in 1949, they campaigned for "our sacred right to look after our children, husbands, and brothers" and against government efforts to "stifle the mother, the wife, and the sister." It was two remarkable British women—Marion Pascoe and Diana Pym— who were instrumental in the formation of the British lobby group, the League for Democracy in Greece. And when prominent female Communist cadres put their name to appeals for the release of individual prisoners, they typically idenitified themselves as "Katina Zevgou, mother of a soldier killed in 1940," or "Paraskevi Koutouliki, mother of a man killed during the national resistance struggle."[14]

The family problems they highlighted were real enough. Not only had families lost their main breadwinner; other relatives, too, had access to work, pensions, and higher education barred. Borders divided spouses. Children suffered from psychological problems and there were cases of suicide—historically rare in Greece. Appealing to the West in 1960, the Panhellenic Union wrote that "we believe it is not only our tormented families, but all the people of Greece who desire to forget a period of upheaval and the return of our country to normality and serenity."[15]

218 TRIALS AND POLITICAL EXPEDIENCY

By the early 1960s this sense of sheer exhaustion was echoed more widely in the public campaign for a general amnesty. What people felt privately is harder to gauge. The few letters that survive suggest that a desire to put an end to the privations and disappointments of the postwar period had not entirely extinguished a sense of pride in what people had achieved during the war itself. A teenage girl called Nausicaa wrote to an English pen-friend in 1955 that "since 1944 till today we have not had a proper home"; her father had been killed by collaborators in 1944, and other male relatives had fought with ELAS; she and her sister had fled their village and made their way to Athens. But she writes as though her duty was to identify with EAM, too: "about my beliefs never be in doubt since from the moment that I understood things I have always tried with all my heart to help our struggle . . . since 1943 when the Germans were still here . . . I did what I could." Her father's "struggle" had become hers, and in 1955 she still uses the old EAM first person plural.[16]

Another example is the letter of a certain George Kandris who wrote from jail in Crete in 1962 to British officers he had met during the war:

> Dear Fellow-fighters,
> Perhaps you do not remember me for in any case many years have passed since then; so please allow me to remind you about that time. I am called George Kandris and I was a fighter in the National Resistance, 1941–1944. . . . As you will remember, throughout the summer and autumn of 1943 we were kept busy marching night and day to the mountain villages with the radio equipment of various missions. You will remember the mountain villages of Gouras, Kalyvia, Sivistra, Zarouchla, Groza, Grechi, Skotini, Kandila, Mazi, Doulia, Vrousti and also the distant Kryavrysi. . . . Now that I have reminded you of all these details, you cannot but remember me. I am Lykourgos. Together with you I spent many months of an heroic and critical period for humanity when our two peoples were struggling for the common Allied cause. Eighteen years have elapsed since then. I do not know what these years have been like for you though I hope they were years that were both creative and happy for you and your families. Unfortunately, this cannot be said for me. . . . For all these years I have really been buried alive . . . for eighteen years I have been eating the bitter bread of prison. I fought for Freedom but I have seen no freedom.[17]

One reads here the intense and passionate accumulation of detail, necessary for Kandris to reveal himself, but also clearly a source of pride after eighteen years. One senses the tension between memories of a time of dangerous but exciting physical activity and the subsequent years of being "buried alive." And in the final lines one can discern the overwhelming sense of injustice and weariness that was driving forward the campaign for an amnesty. One might add only that it is not known whether his letter ever reached those it was intended for. The Captain

Peter Fraser he wrote to was by this time a prominent Oxford classicist, engrossed in the *Oxford Dictionary of Greek Proper Names*, which was to make his reputation. Like several other Oxford dons who had served in the same area as Lykourgos—Eric Gray, Antony Andrewes—Fraser has never discussed his wartime experiences publicly.

In a typically wide-ranging talk for the BBC Home Service delivered in November 1945, A. J. P. Taylor surveyed the impact of the war across Europe. Attacking the contemporary intellectual tendency to divide the continent in two, he argued that apart from the Soviet Union and Great Britain every state in Europe shared two things—defeat and occupation by the Germans. The result had been to discredit pre-1939 forms of government across the continent, while the Right had virtually ceased to exist as a political force. Liberation "has turned into something like revolution—except in Greece where we prevented it."[18]

Prompted by the *dekemvriana*, a heated debate about Greece took place in Britain. Churchill, of course, had regarded ELAS as "miserable banditti" and had been in no doubt that his prompt action in December 1944 had forestalled a long-planned Communist coup d'etat. At the time, this was not as widely held a view as it later became. In April 1945 he shocked even the Foreign Office with his comment that "the collaborators in Greece in many cases did the best they could to shelter the Greek population from German oppression."[19]

More typical of British public opinion was the torrent of criticism that greeted Churchill's defense of his policy at the end of 1944 and that continued as it became clear that the new Labour government would not diverge sharply from its predecessor's line. Analyses of British policy toward the wartime resistance were at the heart of the debate. Many journalists and public figures saw it as tantamount to supporting fascism. In Parliament, the most damaging critic was a Labour MP called Lyall Wilkes, who wrote two articles for the *New Statesman and Nation* in which he drew upon his own experiences with SOE in the Peloponnese to cast doubt upon the government's commitment to see collaborators punished.[20]

As Wilkes was an MP, he could not be prevented from speaking out; but Whitehall was increasingly concerned to shape the debate, and other insiders with expert knowledge of what had actually happened during the war fell foul of its informal but effective modes of censorship. The case of Brigadier Myers, the first head of the British Military Mission to Greece, makes this clear enough. In 1943 Myers had been unceremoniously removed from his position as Mission head at the behest of the Foreign Office for revealing the strength of antimonarchist sentiment within Greece. When he tried to publish his own version of what had happened during the war, numerous obstacles were placed in his way. His first type-script ("The Crisis in Greece: A Review of Its Causes") submitted to the Foreign Office for vetting in 1945 was promptly "lost."[21]

In 1947 he tried again. The relevant files indicate an interesting episode in the official management of history. First, the Foreign Office solicited a rival account from Myers's successor C. M. Woodhouse. "It was partly in anticipation of the appearance of [Myers's] book," minuted one official, "that Colonel Woodhouse was himself induced to write his own account of all these matters and was given special facilities in the Foreign Office library for the purpose of doing so." That Woodhouse had been granted these "facilities" was not to be publicly disclosed.[22]

At the same time, Myers's manuscript was passed over to David Balfour, who had served with Rex Leeper, the British ambassador to Greece. Balfour was "uneasy" about publication and wrote down a long list of textual changes that Myers was to be asked to make.[23] Coincidentally, Balfour was also asked to vet yet another account of the war submitted at around the same time by his former boss, Rex Leeper. To this Balfour simply made a few corrections and suggested to Leeper that he show the manuscript to Churchill, as the former prime minister was writing up his own record of wartime Greece. Balfour thought it would be better if the two accounts meshed.[24]

Although the Foreign Office files are silent about what happened next, we can guess. Myers's manuscript was blocked; as *Greek Entanglement* it only saw the light of day in 1955 in an expurgated form; it was only issued in a fuller, revised version in 1985. Woodhouse's *Apple of Discord* was published in 1948 and quickly became regarded as an authoritative analysis of wartime British policy. Leeper's *When Greek Meets Greek* appeared in 1950 and preserved a discreet silence about the author's disagreements with Churchill, particularly at the start of the *dekemvriana*. As Churchill himself had done in 1944, Leeper now justified British policy on the grounds that EAM/ELAS had been a Moscow stooge and therefore not genuinely Greek, a Cold War interpretation of wartime politics in Greece that was to remain standard until the 1970s.

If the official management of history revolves essentially around the two poles of censorship and celebration, we might, in pursuit of the latter, track down the debates surrounding the erection of war monuments and cemeteries in postwar Greece. One example might be provided by the 1952 Commonwealth War Memorial that turned away from the bitterness of Liberation to the relatively uncontentious start of the war—when Britain and Greece stood gloriously together against the Axis—to commemorate the ties binding the two countries at the very moment when British influence there was on the wane; one might explore the village memorials raised at the sites of mass executions and ask, for example, why the annual commemoration of the massacre at Kalavryta became a national event while that at Komeno, which had attracted national attention in 1945 and 1946, disappeared from the public arena and is unknown to most Greeks today.

In general, however, the point needing emphasis is how few organized acts of celebration or commemoration there were before the fall of the junta opened the floodgates. Through the 1950s, the Greek state remained faithful to a Cold War vision of the war, unwilling either to praise the resistance or to condemn collaborators. Silence and repression were the main elements of its policy. Even Karamanlis, who was in power from 1955 to 1963 and saw himself as a modernizer, remained unwilling to push against the anticommunist norms of the civil war years. Indeed in some respects his modernization project served to reinforce them.

The classic instance of this—and a cause célèbre at the time—involved the arrest in 1957 of a middle-aged German tourist called Max Merten. Merten, it transpired, had headed the wartime military administration of Thessaloniki and was heavily implicated in the deportation of the city's Jewish population to Auschwitz. He was on his third visit to Greece when he was arrested and must have been somewhat surprised to have been charged as a war criminal.

His arrest came as Greece was soliciting German economic support and Greek "guest" workers were flooding into the Federal Republic. In March 1959 Merten was sentenced to twenty-five years imprisonment by an Athens military tribunal. But after only eight months, and following considerable pressure from Bonn, he was extradited to West Germany. At the height of the furor, the Greek Parliament passed a law suspending all future legal proceedings against German war criminals, amid claims that a German loan had been the sweetener for this.[25]

All this was bad enough, but worse was to follow. Waiting to stand trial in West Germany, Merten made sensational allegations against members of the Karamanlis administration. He claimed that during the war the undersecretary of defense had sent Greek hostages to be shot, while Makris, the interior minister, was said to have accepted—together with Karamanlis himself—the gift of an abandoned Jewish shop that they resold. He revealed that Makris's wife had worked as his secretary during the war and threatened to produce a photo showing her, Makris, and Karamanlis together in Thessaloniki in 1943.

The more outlandish of these accusations were soon exposed and nothing ever emerged directly to implicate either Makris or Karamanlis himself. But enough was true—Makris's wife had worked for Merten, Jewish shops had been sold off to prominent Greek notables, Themelis the undersecretary for defense had been a regional prefect during the occupation—to make clear how inadequately the Karamanlis administration had distanced itself from wartime collaborators. Merten's allegations turned out to be a storm in a teacup but they caused acute and in some respects lasting embarrassment. Karamanlis preserved a discreet silence—his wartime activities were later passed over hurriedly by Woodhouse, his biographer—while Makris mounted an extremely unconvincing defense of his position in Parliament. "How could an affair so petty in itself assume such large dimensions that it overshadowed in this country for the time being everything else? How could such squalid allegations, virtually unsupported by any evidence, have been allowed to create a major political incident?" asked the British ambassador in Athens. "The issue of wartime collaboration is one on which the Greeks are still rather surprisingly sensitive."[26]

This sensitivity became even more evident when, in the early 1960s, the first challenges emerged to prevailing taboos. The origins of this shift are complex and would repay much closer analysis than can be offered here. They encompassed the dramatic socioeconomic change that was turning Greece from a rural into an urban society, the passing of generations, and the influence of broader political and cultural trends occurring internationally. Public pressure mounted on the Karamanlis government in its last years to revise existing civil war legislation; it bore fruit in the policies of the center-left Papandreou government of 1963. But the dogged resistance to such changes was equally clear—in the way Karamanlis tried to deflect such pressure, and in the obstacles that confronted his more progressive successor.

To start with Karamanlis and the question of legal reform, the 1952 constitution had supposedly replaced the provisional statutes of the civil war period with a modern framework of safeguards for civil liberties and rights; in practice, however, the "special legislation" of 1946–51 remained in force, a sort of "paraconstitution" that existed alongside and often superseded the actual one. Part of Karamanlis's modernization project involved tidying up this unsatisfactory state of affairs. In 1962 the Council of State admitted for the first time that the legal fiction of a state of "permanent civil war" was outdated. From the Left there were calls for the emergency decrees of the late 1940s to be explicitly abrogated, in particular Law 509, which criminalized the Communist Party.[27]

Karamanlis refused to accept this, however, and the new legislation that eventually replaced Law 509 actually extended its definition of seditious activity. Even the Greek judiciary, not noted for its liberal sentiments, regarded this with unease. When twenty-eight leftists were put on trial under the new statute for "having propagated slogans of dissolved parties and organisations"—in other words, having sung resistance songs at a celebration of the twentieth anniversary of the liberation of Athens—

the presiding magistrate refused to accept the constitutionality of the new legislation. Another judge insisted that a magazine editorial exalting the resistance movement did not constitute propaganda of "illegal" activities by EAM since insofar as EAM had contributed to the resistance against the Axis, these activities could not be regarded as illegal. These were straws in the wind, indicating the emergence of new attitudes across quite a broad spectrum of public opinion.[28]

Yet the old ways died hard. To publish an editorial in 1966 entitled "The Resistance Lives" was still an act of defiance and considerable courage. The 1963 Papandreou government displayed its progressive credentials by releasing most remaining political prisoners and encouraging public discussion of the war, but this made it dangerously radical in the eyes of powerful elements in the state apparatus. Acts of public commemoration and celebration became the sites of angry exchanges and bitter confrontations.

In November 1964, for example, the first celebration took place to mark the anniversary of the blowing up of the Gorgopotamos viaduct in 1942. This operation had been undertaken by a combined force of different resistance groups, including ELAS, under the aegis of Britain's Special Operations Executive (SOE). To the Right, the unfamiliar presence of representatives of EAM/ELAS at the ceremony was an affront scarcely mitigated by the fact that they were not allowed to form part of the official party standing close to the monument. Nothing could more aptly symbolize the Papandreou government's hesitant stance than the fact that although the leftist delegates had been kept with the public behind a police cordon, they were allowed at the conclusion of the official ceremony to step forward with their resistance banners and to lay a wreath. Nor could there have been a more dramatic expression of the Right's outrage than the bomb explosion at the site that immediately followed their action and killed fourteen people.[29]

The aftermath of this tragedy was grotesque. Those responsible for the bomb blast were never traced. But several resistance leaders who had tried to calm the large crowd were arrested on charges of sedition; they were accused of having shouted wartime slogans and sung resistance songs and of having illegally laid wreaths alongside those of government officials. Although the charges were absurd, several former EAM/ELAS dignitaries were found guilty, and while some were released on appeal, others—notably the seventy-six-year-old General Avgeropoulos—remained in jail.

Avgeropoulos had fought in the Balkan Wars and had been a divisional commander in ELAS. After the war he had been jailed until 1952 and had then entered Parliament as a left-wing deputy. "I do not feel I committed any offense," he protested at his trial. "The resistance song

'To arms, to arms!' was a national, not a class song, calling on the en-
slaved people of Greece to fight for freedom. . . . It should be taught in
school."

Another of those jailed, Kostas Tassopoulos, argued similarly. He was
secretary of the Panhellenic Union of Fighters of the National Resistance,
a powerful lobby-group for ex-andartes, and had suffered miserably since
the war—driven from his village by right-wing bands in 1945, his vineyards, olive groves, and farm burned down; jailed with his wife in 1948
and not released until 1960, by which time he had contracted TB. Denying all the charges brought against him, Tassopoulos said that it was time
that in Greece the "national resistance" was recognized and not brought
before the courts.[30]

The Left was moving from calls for an amnesty—more or less won
under Papandreou—to reaffirmations of its own patriotic and nationalist
credentials. No doubt, this strategy was partly at least dictated by the
Cold War itself, which made it hazardous to claim legitimacy for a project
with an explicit class basis. But it also reflected older hesitancies in Greek
political culture about the possible divisiveness of class-based politics—
hesitancies that EAM/ELAS itself had countered during the Occupation
by stressing its nationalist pedigree.[31]

In the early 1960s, then, the battle between Right and Left for the nationalist mantle was finely poised. The future seemed to lie with the Left,
but present power was in the hands of the Right. What the outcome might
have been had the argument continued to run through democratic institutions is not easy to say. For what, of course, precipitated the Left's eventual victory was the junta's seizure of power in 1967.

Politically there could be no doubt where the colonels stood in relation to
the war. They were determined to turn the clock back to the late 1940s.
Former resistance fighters released in the early 1960s were rearrested and
detained. A decree made men who had served in the quisling security
battalions eligible for state pensions. Yet at the same time the regime arrested large numbers of royalists and other conservative opponents. Their
criticism was encapsulated in Seferis's 1969 protest, broadcast outside
Greece, in which he stated that: "A regime has been imposed on us . . .
that is entirely opposed to the ideals for which our world fought during
the last war." Thus Left and mainstream Right were slowly being pushed
together. The wartime resistance against the Germans became an inescap-
able analogue to the campaign against the junta.[32]

The historiographical repercussions were also considerable. The
junta's emergence—with the discreet acquiescence of the United States—
called into question the entire Cold War rationale for Allied intervention
in Greek affairs at the very time when the Vietnam War was prompting
similar concerns more widely.[33] Rather than seeing British and U.S. pol-

icy as having saved Greece from Communist tyranny, a new generation
of historians now suggested that at the least the nature of communist
control of EAM/ELAS needed further investigation and at worst that
Anglo-American imperialism had strangled a genuinely popular radical
movement at birth. Critical analyses of British and U.S. diplomacy took
advantage of newly released archival material to fit Greece into the
emerging revisionist consensus.[34]

Both historiographical and political trends were thus moving in the
direction of a redefinition of the resistance along the nationalist lines
mapped out by the Left in the early 1960s. The Right now stood accused
of subordinating Greece to foreign powers (a charge to which even Karamanlis, with his stress upon the Common Market, and particularly
Germany, was vulnerable). Andreas Papandreou created his Panhellenic
Liberation Movement and started to map out the path for a left-wing
nationalism that would bring his PASOK Party to power in 1981. Resistance to the junta, he wrote in 1970, "is increasingly taking on a character
of *national liberation.*"[35]

It is scarcely surprising, then, that upon the fall of the junta in 1974 Papandreou was among the most enthusiastic advocates of an official recognition of EAM/ELAS. EAM/ELAS was coming to stand for a broad,
popular center-left constituency that PASOK and the newly legalized
Communists competed to woo. The pro-Moscow Communist Party announced that it planned to broaden its appeal by reaching out to the "EA-
Mogenous" (i.e., those with EAM "in the family"). But it was PASOK
that grabbed the EAM inheritance for itself.

In the flood of memoirs by former *andartes* that appeared following
the junta's demise, the Communist Party came in for growing criticism.
Former Party members like Thanasis Hadzis (general secretary of EAM)
and Giannis Ioannides (deputy general secretary of the Party) revealed the
disputes and hesitancies within EAM/ELAS. The critique of the Party's
Stalinism was accompanied by a trend among many memoirists to paint
the war as a "national liberation struggle" in the colors of 1821. An article in the pro-PASOK daily *Eleftherotypia* about the ELAS supremo Aris
Velouchiotis was entitled simply, "He Belongs to the Nation," and went
on: "Was Aris Marxist? Not impossible! Was he socialist? Perhaps so.
Was Aris on the Left? So be it. . . . In a few more years, when the glorious
and unforgettable generation of the Resistance crosses over to the other
side, no one will remember whether Aris was a bad Marxist or a moderate communist or if he succumbed to 'rightist or leftist deviations.' In the
national soul and memory he will remain as a bold, freedom-loving slayer
of tyranny who combined the '41 with '12 and '21."[36]

Marxist critics denounced this indifference to ideology and the arousal
of "nationalist bravado." PASOK remained unabashed. As the bandwagon rolled on, Papandreou talked about giving back "the People" its

"national memory" as a vital step toward creating "national unity." Georgios Karras in the Marxist *Politis* noted with concern the creation of a sense of external threat that made national unity seem desirable. A PASOK journalist wanted recognition for the resistance on the grounds that "today so many dangers and threats to our national sense of unity surround us." There was nothing to choose between this and the statement of a representative of the cross-party campaigning movement, the United National Resistance, who claimed at a ceremony at Mauthausen in 1980 that recognition of the resistance would lead to a "national unity of spirit . . . that is vital especially in the current international situation if the country is to confront the dangers that threaten it."[37]

By Papandreou's electoral victory in 1981, there was broad acceptance of the need to revise attitudes toward EAM/ELAS. Most on the Left were too grateful for Papandreou's commitment to question his motives very closely. When PASOK introduced its 1982 "Law for the Recognition of the Resistance of the Greek People against the Occupation Troops, 1941–44" there was spirited opposition from some conservative MPs—New Democracy was split between the moderates who were prepared to support the bill provided it drew a sharp distinction with the civil war period, and the extremists who rejected any reference to the war at all—but not enough to threaten the bill, which went through with Communist support. "PASOK is for EAM but not for those who fought in it," noted Karras dryly. "It is for the 'national' EAM, its own EAM, the EAM of us all—in other words, an EAM that never existed." But what else would do if Papandreou was to present himself to the Greek public as "a national leader, defending national unity"?[38]

Who gained and who lost as a result of this redefinition of the activities of the wartime resistance? Those who gained are obvious enough: they include—PASOK apart—the thousands of former *andartes* who were now able to claim state pensions (as well, perhaps, as numerous others who filed claims with less justification). They also included a number of pioneers in the movements for women's liberation and for educational reform, whose wartime achievements were recognized by PASOK during the 1980s.

The question of those who lost is more complex. The first camp comprises those on the Right who, like Opposition leader Averoff, were opposed to any recognition of the resistance on the grounds that this was "antinational and immoral," giving in effect a "pardon to the Communist Party." Averoff, after all, as defense minister between 1975 and 1981, had continued to grant state pensions to former security battalionists. Yet by the 1980s he was an old man and represented what appeared to be a vanishing mentality. It lingered on in the memoirs of rightist *an-*

dartes like Vasilis Baltoyianni; friends praised his book when it appeared in 1986 and bemoaned the fact that "the distortion of the history of national resistance in Greece for party purposes has reached a climax."[39]

The second group of critics lay at the opposite end of the political spectrum. Many Marxists were incensed by PASOK's easy dismissal of the political dimension of EAM/ELAS. Karras argued that a genuine acknowledgement of what had happened in Greece during the war would have involved facing up to the history of a "conflict between two radically different 'resistances.'" If this had failed to happen, it was because the Left was exhausted and sought simply to escape persecution while since 1974 the bulk of the Right was ready to accept EAM's contribution against the Germans. Recognition—as it had occurred under PASOK— had "destroyed another recognition of EAM that, however much it borrowed from the fighters of '21, was the product of society and social configurations—the creation of its own contradictions. This is the EAM that the Law embraces to conceal."[40]

This percipient observation highlights vast lacunae in the existing resistance historiography. Virtually the entire discussion had revolved around Cold War themes. First had come the portrayal of EAM/ELAS as a Russian instrument, often incorporating a rather paternalistic social model that depicted basically well-meaning, "pure" but ill-informed rank-and-file Greeks being led astray by "unGreek" party members. Then the pendulum had swung back to show a "popular" EAM brutally suppressed by Western imperialism. By the 1980s a more sophisticated view was emerging, but it still focused on questions of high policy and Anglo-Greek relations. In all this, questions of the impact of Axis policy in Greece remained largely untouched. So too did the social dimensions of resistance and the wartime period generally. The nature of EAM/ELAS as a mass organization—its structure and efficacy as an instrument of power—lay unresearched, and the flood of memoir literature provided nothing to rank with, say, Djilas's *Wartime* as an aid to understanding these issues. The importance of wartime regional and localist impulses was also unappreciated. In their small way, these historiographical deficiencies undoubtedly helped smoothed the path for PASOK's easy nationalistic appropriation of EAM/ELAS.[41]

The third group is that which from our current perspective seems most important. It should hardly surprise us that "non-Greek" elements of the wartime record that threatened to disrupt PASOK's nationalistic nostrums were ignored or suppressed. During the war, for instance, EAM/ELAS had given considerable support to Greece's Jews, helping many escape and encouraging others to enlist. Many Jews had played a prominent role as guerrilla officers. Although the 1980s saw a revival of interest and research in these questions—chiefly in the United States—PASOK's

hostile relationship with Israel created a hostile atmosphere inside
Greece. The Jewish Museum of Greece, established in the late 1970s and
fully functioning with U.S. support by the early 1980s was repeatedly
hindered in its efforts to obtain full legal status in Greece, and President
Sartzetakis only agreed to sign the necessary decree near the end of the
decade.[42]

Reference to other wartime ethnic divisions, complexities, or sources
of tension still remains more or less taboo. Most egregious in this respect
has been the complete lack of any discussion of the fate of the Albanian
Cham community that was driven out of northwestern Greece at the end
of the war by Zervas's nationalist EDES. Hundreds were killed and some
fifteen thousand driven north. Their villages were burned down and
EDES notables installed themselves on formerly Muslim estates.[43]

More contentious still is the issue of the Slavic-speaking population of
northern Greece. Many villagers from the Florina and Kastoria areas had
fought for EAM/ELAS, or for Bulgarian-backed militias, or both; many
had fought against the government during the civil war in the hope of
obtaining some form of autonomy from Athens. During the 1940s at least
thirty thousand fled to Yugoslavia, while others were expelled or forcibly
relocated by the Greek authorities, who had been attempting to suppress
all signs of the existence of a Slavic-speaking community since the 1920s
if not earlier.[44]

Many Slavic-speaking exiles left family, land, and property behind in
Greece. In this respect, their position was little different from the thousands of other former *andartes* who lived in exile behind the Iron Curtain,
waiting for a general amnesty to be proclaimed. When this was introduced, however, under PASOK, its nationalist premise became clear: former *andartes* were only allowed back to Greece if they declared themselves "Greek by race" [*ellines to genos*]. Gennimatas, who as PASOK
interior minister orated eloquently on the need for reconciliation, made it
clear that Slav speakers would not be readmitted to the country unless
they made the requisite declaration. The Resistance—in other words—
had been entirely Greek and had to be commemorated in such terms.[45]

Let us conclude by exploring some of the general implications of the
changing memories of the war in Greece. Given the events of December
1944 and then of the civil war itself, memories of the war inevitably fell
under the shadow of the Cold War. It is perhaps tempting to see the postwar period as dominated by the struggle of Left and Right, until the fall
of the junta created the conditions for an emergent nationalist consensus
that would grow in intensity once the Cold War ended. On reflection,

however, the contest over the memory of the war had been about nationalism from the very beginning. In the late 1940s and 1950s, the Right had successfully claimed the nationalist mantle. But if the Right had accused EAM/ELAS of subservience to Moscow, the Left had managed by the 1970s to attack the Right for tying Greece to the United States, the European Community, and Western capitalism. PASOK's ingenuity lay in combining anticapitalism with anticommunism. With the Left worn out by decades of repression and the Right shocked and defensive in the wake of the junta, the path was open for reconciliation. This form of reconciliation, however, smoothed away the memories of social division and skated over equally dark areas of ethnic complexity. According to a prominent PASOK MP: "The laurels of the National Resistance do not belong to individuals and groups. They belong to the Nation, to the Whole, to the unconquerable soul of the Greek."[46] If this be the voice of reconciliation, it seems unlikely to presage peace.

Notes

1. Allow me to refer to my *Inside Hitler's Greece: The Experience of Occupation, 1941–44* (New Haven, 1993), ch. 21.

2. P. Papastratis, "I ekkatharisi ton dimosion iperesion stin Ellada tis paramones tou emfyliou polemou," in L. Baerentzen et al., eds., *Meletes yia ton emfylio polemo, 1945–1949* (Athens, 1992), 47–66; FO 371/48263 R 5857/4, Leeper-FO, 19 March 1945; FO 371/48286 R20169/4, Leeper-FO, 22 November 1945. There is no serious study of war crimes trials in Greece; see, however, N. Karkanis, *Oi dosilogoi tis katochis* (Athens, 1985).

3. Papastratis, I ekkatharisi, 57–65.

4. D. Close, "The Reconstruction of a Right-Wing State," in Close, ed., *The Greek Civil War, 1943–1950: Studies of Polarization* (London and New York, 1993), 156–65.

5. FO 371/48271 R 9355/4, "Situation in Greece: Regional Surveys, 13–19 May 1945"; FO 371/48271 R 10009/4, "Situation in Greece: Regional Surveys, 31 May 1945"; FO 371/48263 R 5860/4, "Situation in Greece: Regional Surveys, 21 March 1945."

6. "Reconstruction," 164–65.

7. FO 371/48279 R 15383/4, Bevin-Caccia (Athens), 7 September 1945; FO 371/48284 R 20262/4, Leeper (Athens)—FO, 30 November 1945 on the case of Thomas Venetsanopoulos, "one of many outstanding in Greece where people who undoubtedly did good work for the Allied cause are nevertheless accused of crimes against the Greek penal code . . ."; see also H. Richter, *British Intervention in Greece: From Varkiza to Civil War* (London, 1986), 193–97.

8. Modern Greek Archive, King's College, London (hereafter MGA)/INFO IV, "EAM 1945–47."

9. Alexander, *The Prelude to the Truman Doctrine: British Policy in Greece,*

1944–47 (Oxford, 1982) 206–07; J. Iatrides, ed., *Ambassador MacVeagh Reports: Greece 1933–1947* (Princeton, 1980), 694–98.

10. MGA/INFO I, "Civil War: Partsalides Case," Theotokis memo of 31 July 1946.

11. Alexander, *Palude*, 208–09.

12. N. Alivizatos, *Les institutions politiques de la Grèce á travers les crises, 1922–74* (Paris, 1979), 383.

13. Ibid., 383–88; Dimitrakos transcript in MGA/INFO III, "Courts-Martial, 1946–73."

14. FO 371/101802 Athens-London, 13 March 1952; R. Furness, "The League for Democracy in Greece, 1945–50," Master's thesis, King's College London, 1992.

15. MGA/INFO XII, "Prisoners and families," 18 April 1960.

16. MGA/INFO XI, "Prisons, 1945–67: Individual Dossiers," text of a letter from Nausicaa, 19 February 1955 to George Anglos.

17. MGA/INFO XI, "Prisons, 1945–67: Individual Dossiers," text of a letter from George Kandris (Lykourgos).

18. Text found in MGA/INFO I, 'BBC': talk delivered on 14 November 1945.

19. Cited in Papastratis, "I ekkatharisi," 51–52.

20. *The Times*, 20 October 1945; Richter, *British Intervention in Greece*, 230–31, 329.

21. FO 371/48275 R 12880/4, 27 July 1945.

22. FO 371/67129 R 5872/5872, minutes of 14 April 1947.

23. Ibid. Balfour minutes of 2 October 1947.

24. FO 371/72334, "Publication of Book on Greece by Sir Rex Leeper."

25. FO 371/153018, Allen (Athens)—London, 4 October 1960.

26. In the absence of any serious examination of this episode, see FO 371/153018, especially R 91661/3, "Merten Affair," 18 October 1960; also C. M. Woodhouse, *Karamanlis: The Restorer of Greek Democracy* (Oxford, 1982), 16–22.

27. N. Alivizatos, "Les Institutions," 431–48.

28. Ibid., 446–48.

29. MGA/INFO VI, "Gorgopotamos."

30. Ibid.

31. On interwar hesitancies concerning class-based politics in Greece, see my *Greece and the Interwar Economic Crisis* (Oxford, 1991), 294–96.

32. Seferis in R. Roufos, "Culture and the Military" in R. Clogg and G. Yannopoulos, eds., *Greece under Military Rule* (London, 1972), 157.

33. Note that serious scholarly discussion of the war was impossible in Greek universities before 1974. The debate referred to here took place outside Greece. Standard Cold War accounts of wartime Greece include: D. George Kousoulas, *Revolution and Defeat: The Story of the Greek Communist Party* (London, 1965); E. O'Ballance, *The Greek Civil War* (London, 1966); B. Sweet-Escott, *Greece: A Political and Economic Survey, 1939–53* (London, 1954); F. Voigt, *The Greek Sedition* (London, 1949); S. G. Xydis, *Greece and the Great Powers* (Thessaloniki, 1963). Among the key British firsthand accounts, R.Capell, *Simiomata: A Greek Note Book 1944–45* (London, 1946); G. Chandler, *The Divided*

Land: An Anglo-Greek Tragedy (London, 1959); R. Leeper, *When Greek Meets Greek* (London, 1950); E. C. W. Myers, *The Greek Entanglement* (London, 1955); C. M. Woodhouse, *Apple of Discord: A Survey of Recent Greek Politics in Their International Setting* (London, 1948); a curious subgenre are the reports on aspects of the antipartisan war in Greece commissioned by the U.S. Army to serve as aids to U.S. antipartisan policy. These include: R. M. Kennedy, *German Antiguerrilla Operations in the Balkans, 1941–44* (Washington, 1954); H. Gardner, *Guerrilla and Counterguerrilla Warfare in Greece, 1941–45* (Washington, 1962). The way wartime Greece was used as a model for U.S. counterinsurgency is discussed in M. McClintock, *Instruments of Statecraft: U.S. Guerrilla Warfare, Counterinsurgency, Counterterrorism, 1940–1990* (New York, 1990), 71–73; and D. M. Schafer, *Deadly Paradigms* (Princeton, 1990).

34. The revisionist literature includes H. Richter, *1936–1946 Griechenland zwischen Revolution und Konterrevolution*, 2 vols.(Frankfurt, 1973); J. L. Hondros, "The German Occupation of Greece," Ph.D., Vanderbilt University, 1969 (published in 1983 as *Occupation and Resistance: The Greek Agony, 1941–44*); H. Fleischer, "Griechenland 1941–44: Kampf gegen Stahlhelm und Krone," Ph.D. Free University, Berlin (published in 1986 as *Im Kreuzschatten der Mächte*, 2 vols.); D. Eudes, *Les Kapetanios* (Paris, 1970); L. Wittner, *American Intervention in Greece, 1943–49* (New York, 1982); J. Iatrides, *Revolt in Athens: The Greek Communist "Second Round"* (Princeton, 1972); Iatrides, ed., *Greece in the 1940s: A Nation in Crisis* (Hanover, N.H., 1981). This literature should be seen in the context of a contemporary tendency to stress foreign intervention in Greek affairs more generally: see T. Couloumbis, J. Petropulos, and H. Psomiades, *Foreign Intervention in Greek Politics: A Historical Perspective* (New York, 1976).

35. A. Papandreou, *Democracy at Gunpoint* (New York, 1970), 333.

36. Th. Hadzis, *I nikifora epanastasi pou chathike (1941–45)*, 3 vols. (Athens, 1977–79); G. Ioannides, *Anamniseis* (Athens, 1979); Elefantis reviewing Boukouvalas's *To Andartiko Ippiko tis Thessalias* in *O Politis* 22 (November 1978); *Eleftherotypia*, 8 July 1979.

37. See G. Karras, "Lithi alalazousa," *O Politis* 53 (August–September 1982), 16–20; Enomeni Ethniki Antistasi 1941–44, *1941–81: Saranta chronia tis Ethnikis Antistasi* (Athens, n.d.).

38. Ibid.

39. M. Ploritis, *Nea Politika*, i (Athens, 1990), 169–74; V. Baltoyiannis, *Ethniki Antistasi EOEA-EDES* (Athens, 1986), 477.

40. Karras, "Lithi alalazousa."

41. The most nuanced and balanced interpretations of Anglo-Greek relations include P. Papastratis, *British Policy toward Greece during the Second World War 1941–44* (Cambridge, 1984); G. Alexander, *The Prelude to the Truman Doctrine: British Policy in Greece, 1944–47* (Oxford, 1982); H. Vlavianos, "The Greek Communist Party: In Search of a Revolution," in T. Judt, ed., *Resistance and Revolution in Mediterranean Europe, 1939–48* (London, 1989), 157–213. The neoconservative impulse reflected at one level by J. Loulis, *The Greek Communist Party, 1940–44* (London, 1982) and at another by N. Gage, *Eleni* (London, 1982) failed to make much impact. Studies of the social and ideological

aspects of the resistance are slowly appearing. Two superb new works are R. van Boeschoten, *From Armatolik to People's Rule* (Amsterdam, 1992) and, especially, G. Margaritis, *Ap'tin itta stin exormisi* (Athens, 1993).

42. N. Stavroulakis, "The Jewish Museum of Greece from Its Inception until the Present Day," *Bulletin of Judaeo-Greek Studies* 12 (Summer 1993): 26–35.

43. There is still to my knowledge no reliable study of this subject. See, however, the detailed EAM memorandum in MGA/INFO VIII "Zitima Tsamourias" (n.d.); also K. Cooper, *The Uprooted* (London, 1979), 75–89.

44. For a relatively moderate Greek view, see E. Kofos, "National Heritage and National Identity in Nineteenth- and Twentieth-Century Macedonia," *European History Quarterly* 19 (1989): 103–43; cf., A. Karakasidou, "Politicizing Culture: Negating Ethnic Identity in Greek Macedonia," *Journal of Modern Greek Studies* 11:1 (May 1993): 1–28. Valuable primary sources include A. Rossos, "The Macedonians of Aegean Macedonia: A British Officer's Report, 1944," *Slavonic and East European Review* 69:2 (April 1991): 282–307; FO 371/95163, Athens—London, 7 August 1951. John Koliopoulos is currently completing a study of Western Macedonia during the Occupation that should shed light on this subject.

45. Karakasidou, "Politicizing culture," 12; H. Poulton, *The Balkans: Minorities and States in Conflict* (London, 1991), 180.

46. S. Kostopoulos, *PASOK. 2 Chronia*, ii (Athens, 1983), 170.

The People's Courts and Revolutionary Justice in Hungary, 1945–46

FOLLOWING WORLD WAR II, the Hungarian "people's courts" pronounced sentences over approximately 27,000 persons accused of war crimes, crimes against the state, or crimes against humanity. Up to 1 March 1948 their verdicts included 322 death sentences of which 146 were executed.[1] Until the end of 1946, four former prime ministers, one deputy prime minister, two ministers of the interior, a minister of finances—who had held that post in eight consecutive governments—and six other former cabinet members were sentenced to death and executed. Seven former government members were given life sentences, of whom five actually died in prison.[2]

This chapter will deal with the great political trials in Hungary without touching on such postwar punitive measures as police internment, which affected 40,000 people before 1949; the expulsion to Germany of between 180,000 and 200,000 German Hungarians; and the activities of the so-called denazification commissions, which resulted in the dismissal of 62,000 public servants.[3] As these figures indicate, well over 300,000 Hungarian citizens, or about 3 percent of the country's total population, suffered some kind of punishment during the immediate postwar purges. Considering that those involved were mainly adult males, we can say that about one in ten adult male Hungarians was subjected to a punitive measure. It should be noted, however, that in Hungary—unlike in Italy, for instance—there were no lynchings of putative collaborators and war criminals.

Hungary suffered perhaps the greatest defeat of any of the nations involved in the First World War. At the Trianon Peace Treaty in 1920, the victorious entente powers legitimized the forcible loss to its neighbors of two-thirds of Hungary's territory, which meant, among other things, that three million ethnic Hungarians became subjects of the so-called successor states. Following a bourgeois-democratic and a communist revolution, a counterrevolutionary government was helped to power by the entente. During the twenty-five-year reign of Regent Miklós Horthy, the main foreign political aspiration of the successive governments was territorial revision. Political leaders whose ideology consisted mainly of conservatism, antiliberalism, anti-Semitism, and irredentism were able to stand up against both extreme leftist and extreme rightist pressures. Between 1938 and 1941, they also suceeded in taking back a major part of the country's territorial loss virtually without the use of force. However, these successes were made possible only with the help of Germany and Italy. At the end of June 1941, Hungary joined Germany in the war against the Soviet Union; this fatal decision made by Regent Horthy and Prime Minister László Bárdossy, was especially senseless because Germany had not requested active Hungarian participation in the "anti-Communist crusade."

In 1943 Miklos Kállay's government cautiously tried to withdraw from the Axis powers, but the attempt was cut short on 19 March 1944 when German troops occupied Hungary. The lives of the approximately 800,000 Jews living in Hungary were immediately imperiled. Unconstitutional anti-Jewish laws, adopted between 1938 and 1942, had already deprived the Hungarian Jews of most of their civil rights, and in the August 1941 mass killings at Kamenets-Podolsky in Galicia, as well as killings in the northern Yugoslav city of Novi Sad (Ujvidék in Hungarian) in January 1942, about 20,000 Hungarian Jews died. Also, before 1944 approximately 25,000 Jews who had been drafted into forced labor service by the military died at the eastern front, as incidentally did 100,000 Hungarian soldiers. After March 1944, however, the pro-Nazi government of General Döme Sztójay placed its entire administrative apparatus, including police and gendarmerie, at the disposal of SS Obersturmbannführer Adolf Eichmann and his "Jewish experts." This resulted in the deportation of 430,000 Jews, most of them to Auschwitz, between 15 May and 7 July 1944. When Horthy put a stop to the deportations, he spared the lives of most Budapest Jews. At the end of August 1944, the regent appointed General Géza Lakatos prime minister with the aim of preparing a separate armistice. On 15 October Horthy announced to the public that he wished to sign a separate armistice agreement, whereupon the German army helped the fascist Arrow Cross movement of Ferenc Szálasi to power.

The cabinet ministers, legislators, and judges originating from the small antifascist parties and appointed by the Soviet Red Army following Hungary's liberation in the winter and spring of 1945 took it for granted that the leaders of the previous system—from Ferenc Szálasi down—would be tried, sentenced to death, and executed. The "judge is the Hungarian people," people's Judge Ákos Major said in one of his speeches. Szálasi and his ilk were to be punished so as to provide "moral amends for all Hungarians of honest intentions."[4] After the execution of the former prime minister László Bárdossy of 1941 fame, and before the trial of the former prime minister Béla Imrédy, it was made clear by Minister of Justice István Ries, a Social Democrat, that the trials of the principal war criminals were primarily a political and not a legal affair. Those found guilty could not expect justice, only retribution, Ries said.[5] Or as a legal expert stated at the time, the point was not "to try and punish . . . the principal war criminals . . . for simple breaches of the law" but "to retaliate against them for the political mistakes they made and that nearly ruined the nation."[6] The National Council of People's Courts (Népbíróságok Országos Tanácsa, in Hungarian) stated in the reasons adduced to the death sentence of Minister of Justice László Budinszky that it was "twenty-five years of an oppressive ruling system that had brought the country to the brink of destruction."[7]

The "tortured, humiliated and plundered Hungarian people," as Sándor Szalai, the political prosecutor in the Bárdossy trial put it, can be satisfied through the rejection, expulsion, and annihilation of the leaders of the counterrevolutionary system.[8]

The daily papers printed articles rich in invectives regarding the first group of principal war criminals handed over to the Hungarians by the American occupation forces in Germany and Austria. One journalist lamented that the press was allowed to see only Szálasi, Imrédy, and László Endre, the latter the secretary of state for the interior in the Sztójay government: "We won't be able to see the others," he reported. "However, there will be enough time for that when they will be called on to account to the people's court for the destruction of the nation's capital, the collapse of our bridges, and the ruin of our railways and economy. Like a modern-day Tartar invasion, these people devastated our thriving towns and villages."[9]

Many journalists wrote disparagingly of the principal war criminals. According to a columnist for a bourgeois radical weekly, they were characterized by "a pathetic lack of talent, an incredible lack of cultural refinement and education," and by "ostentatious ignominy," as well as "shameful cowardice."[10] In reality, former prime ministers Bárdossy and Imrédy, former minister of culture Bálint Hóman, former minister of justice László Budinszky, and many other principal war criminals were intelligent, well-educated, and well-informed people. About former Minister of Commerce Antal Kunder, another journalist commented: "despite the fake and ridiculous pride he had forced himself to exhibit, this piece of shit was visibly wetting his pants with fright."[11] The respected democratic journalist Béla Zsolt reported that former prime minister Béla Imrédy was "wriggling like a grey lizard under the weight of evidence" in the people's court, and that Imrédy was a "a spindly gnome, fumbling about in terror," "a wretched beast," and "a pitifully despicable figure."[12] Ferenc Szálasi reminded one communist editorialist of a "country bank teller turned into a pitiful embezzler."[13] No doubt a very grave political responsibility rested on the shoulders of László Bárdossy for having waged war on the Soviet Union on the side of Nazi Germany; still, it was artistic license alone that enabled a people's judge to argue in court that the former prime minister "committed a serious crime and a breach of the constitution without precedent not only in Hungarian but in that of the whole world."[14] The harsh personal language used by journalists, people's judges, and people's prosecutors alike made it possible for Ferenc Szálasi, the Arrow-Cross "leader of the nation," to declare, from a high moral pedestal, that "the prosecution presented no evidence in court; it only abused my person. This has made my task easier for I am not ready to discuss my own case."[15]

When these articles and declarations were published, the so-called people's courts had already been in operation for several months in Hungary. The fourteenth paragraph of the armistice agreement proclaimed, in ccordance with the declarations of the Allied powers in London on 13 January 1942, and in Moscow on 30 October 1943, that "Hungary will cooperate in arresting the persons charged with having committed war crimes. It will either extradite them to the governments concerned or will pass judgment on them."[16] Law VII, 1945, published on 16 September 1945 gave statutory force to the decrees previously passed by the Council of Ministers regarding the indictment of war criminals.[17] Deliberately discarding the principles of *nullum crimen sine lege and nulla poena sine lege*, the Hungarian legislators stated in the first section of Law VII, 1945, that war criminals could be indicted even if at the time they committed their crime, their actions were not liable to prosecution according to the laws then in vigor. Special sections of the law were devoted to indicting those charged with joining and participating in the war, "active participation in the activities of the Arrow Cross party, and gaining power or membership in the government of Ferenc Szálasi." Prosecution was conducted by people's prosecutors appointed by the minister of justice; he could revoke the appointment at any time. The people's courts were actually party courts since, at first, the Bourgeois Democratic Party, the Independent Smallholders Party, the Communist Party, the National Peasant Party, and the Social Democratic Party each delegated a member to the council of people's courts. The heads of these courts were all trained professional judges. The people's judges, delegated by the antifascist parties, were later complemented by the people's judges delegated by the National Trade Union Council. Verdicts were handed down in the people's courts by a majority of votes; an appeal was only possible if the majority of the judges found the convict worthy of mercy. As an appellate forum, the Council of People's Courts operated with the same party composition, and if the defendant or his counsel wished to appeal a death sentence, he could do so by addressing the president of the republic. Death sentences had to be approved by the Allied Control Commission (ACC) representing the armed forces occupying Hungary. The main concern of the ACC, however, was to make sure that those who had been sentenced to death were not needed as witnesses in the great Nuremberg trials.

Retroactive legislation and jurisdiction were a general practice throughout Europe at the time. What Bárdossy and Imrédy and fellow members of the same cabinet asked for, however, was to be taken to a court made up of parliamentary members. This would have been in accordance with Hungarian Law III, 1848, defining the responsibilities of the ministers by which they were made accountable for their deeds. Although it was not mentioned in Law VII, 1945, this earlier law was still in force. The people's court dismissed these requests, however, stating in its four-page rejection of Imrédy's request: "The parliamentary court is qualified to pass judgement over political criminals guilty of crimes of a national character. The defendants here charged with war crimes, and crimes against the people, attacked and endangered not only the constitution and political system of their own country but international law and the peace of civilized humanity as well."[18]

For the most part, the press followed with indignation and incomprehension the cases of acquittals or relatively mild verdicts passed by the people's courts and especially by the National Council of People's Courts. As early as the fall of 1945, the communist daily *Szabad Nép* furiously attacked the Council of the People's Courts for deviating "far from its initial aim. The professional judges sitting in the Council have completely forgotten that they are the people's judges. The people do not play around with documents; they do not look for mitigating circumstances in the case of war criminals but demand merciless retaliation against those who are responsible for their misery, suffering, and humiliation."[19] People's Prosecutor General János Szűcs voiced his dissatisfaction with the proceedings at a press conference only a short week before the Bárdossy trial. According to Szűcs's data, until 20 August 1945 the people's courts had brought in 3,893 verdicts, of which only 64 were death sentences. The rest included 46 life sentences, 2,377 prison sentences, and 1,014 acquittals. Szűcs called the results "not at all satisfactory" in the struggle against reactionary forces, and he alluded to the discontent of foreign observers.[20] According to Judge Ákos Major's memoirs, Gábor Péter, the communist head of the political police, who by then had acquired great power, firmly demanded that the people's judges enforce "revolutionary legality" over the "marshland of . . . traditional . . . legal practices."[21]

Minister of Justice István Ries encouraged the judges to use a firmer approach by suspending and relieving a number of them, as well as some of the members of the Council of People's Courts.[22] One evening during the Bárdossy trial Mátyás Rákosi, first secretary of the Communist Party, sent for the judge and council president Ákos Major and warned him against arguing with Bárdossy, especially over the Trianon Peace Treaty. The latter was increasingly regarded as a taboo subject.[23] In his prison diary, Szálasi noted that his number one defense counsel, Sándor Zboray, had been summoned to the Ministry of Justice before the last day of the trial and told that only Imre Latkóczky, the second defense counsel, would be allowed to deliver the plea for the defense.[24]

Those who made the decrees and laws regarding the people's courts, as well as the people's judges themselves, were not only subjected to the pressure of the media and the politicians but had to act with an eye on the peace negotiations in Paris. Sándor Szalai attacked Bárdossy in a rage saying that during his defense, the former prime minister had paid no attention to the fact that "the opinion of the world about our people will largely depend on our proving that it had been dominated by a clique."[25] In their verdicts, the people's judges often implied that the Hungarian public was innocent and had repudiated its leaders with horror during the Second World War.[26] The presiding judge of the Council of the People's Court, Béla Ernő Bojta, pointed out in the legal justification of the death sentence pronounced on Szálasi and accomplices: "A recommendation for acquittal would be an assault not only on the Hungarian people but also on international interests, because the accused are not only war criminals from a Hungarian point of view but also from the point of view of the world. Thus it would be especially harmful to our international reputation if those who had prepared and executed the coup of October 15 [1944] were pardoned."[27] In the legal justification of the death sentence pronounced on Minister of Industry Emil Szakváry, the Council of People's Courts stated that it may well be assumed that no true Hungarian would have accepted a position in the Szálasi government.[28]

The illusions of the people's judges were, however, soon dispelled by the decision makers in Paris who restored the pre-1938 frontiers. In any case, the main concern of those involved in setting up the trials of the principal war criminals in the fall of 1945 was the order in which these great historicopolitical proceedings should take place.

In the spring and summer of 1945, when all that the Hungarian government knew about the principal war criminals was that they were being held in British or American captivity, the plan was already clear: Szálasi and all members of his government would be taken to court together;

consequently, theirs would be the first in a series of great trials. In the court building on Markó Street, an announcement by the People's Court of Budapest, posted on 3 August 1945, set the date of the trial of Szálasi and accomplices for 3 September 1945.[29] In reality, however, the first batch of principal war criminals did not arrive in Budapest until 3 October 1945.

During the course of the entire summer, evidence was diligently collected to support the testimonies of witnesses for the prosecution in the first and most important trial, that of Ferenc Szálasi and his accomplices. On October 6, the correspondent of *Kis Újság* still believed that the trial of the members of the Szálasi government would commence in the Municipal Theater on October 15, the first anniversary of the Arrow Cross takeover.[30]

On the same day, however, the communist daily announced the government's latest and final decision: the first defendant to appear in the dock alone would be László Bárdossy, and his trial would begin on October 29.[31] In his memoirs, Ákos Major did not even attempt to explain why the great trials began with the most difficult case—that of Bárdossy.[32]

The decision was most probably a result of Hungarian domestic politics, more precisely the Budapest municipal elections on October 7 and the national elections on November 4. On the eve of the Budapest municipal elections, it was announced that the great trials would begin not with that of Szálasi, the object of general contempt who had been able to grab power only with German military assistance, but with that of László Bárdossy, who had been legally appointed prime minister, and who was believed to be an irreproachable gentleman whom both the bourgeoisie and petite bourgeoisie generally believed to be innocent. Perhaps the communist and Social Democratic leaders already guessed that they would be defeated in the elections. For this reason, they may have wished to show the public that they were ready to use any and all means at their disposal to annihilate their enemies and adversaries. As the editorial of the communist *Szabad Nép* put it: "fate ordered that this criminal be tried on the eve of national elections. The horrors revealed during the hearings should serve as an alarm signal to the inhabitants of the country: it will show them what political reaction is about; what means the reactionaries have at their disposal, and what crime against himself is committed by the one who follows in the footsteps of the leaders of the former regime."[33]

Fate, of course, did not order the date of the trial; the change in timing was a political decision. Even though he was aware that it was impossible to prepare for a trial of such importance in two or three weeks, Ákos Major accepted the job of presiding over the trial. By the eve of the elections to the national assembly, Bárdossy had already been sentenced to death, and almost ten days later the trial of former prime minister Béla Imrédy began.

In the years 1945 and 1946, fourteen great political trials were held in Hungary. At first glance, it becomes obvious that no logic (or anything that could be considered logical even today) motivated those who prepared the trials. Typically, for the great political trials the defendants were treated as stand-ins for the absent principal culprit. This was the case with the political trials held in Moscow in the 1930s, where the Bolshevik defendants had to account for the absent Trotsky's devilish plans. It was also the case later in Hungary, especially at the trial of László Rajk, who was a stand-in for the main culprit, Marshal Tito. Demanding that Regent Miklós Horthy be extradited and that his trial be conducted in a people's court should have been the logical outcome of these trials but, for reasons that still remain obscure, this never happened.

Only four members of the Szálasi cabinet stood with Szálasi before Council President and Judge Péter Jankó, (the "bloody judge" of the Rajk trial in 1949). Of the fourteen Arrow Cross ministers, only Béla Jurcsek was not in jail in Budapest at that time; he had committed suicide in Austria in April 1945. Although there was a certain logic to the Endre-Baky-Jaross trial, the three persons most reponsible for the Hungarian Holocaust, Lieutenant Colonel László Ferenczy and a few other gendarmerie officers who had also played an important part in the deportation of the Jews from the provinces in 1944, could easily have been included in the same proceedings. Confusion and insufficient preparation of the trials were common. In the case of the rabidly anti-Semitic Arrow Cross press chief Mihály Kolosváry-Borcsa and three other defendants, the Council of People's Courts declared that originally the office of the people's prosecutor had submitted a separate indictment for each defendant: "none of the acts made subject of the indictment have been committed by the defendants together or in common, thus the combining of the cases and a common trial was completely unjustified."[34]

In his memoirs, Ákos Major himself admitted that he and his colleagues had been unable to prepare László Bárdossy's trial with the thoroughness it would have required. Moreover, Major said that he could have exposed Bárdossy's argument defending his territorial revisionist policy more convincingly had he himself not been convinced of the "historical necessity" of this policy.[35]

In addition, the most important historical files and documents necessary (in principle and in practice) for the great historicopolitical trials were missing. The people's prosecutors and people's judges repeatedly stated that the defendants had acted openly and that everything was known about their actions. But it would have been possible to verify exactly what the ministers had said at an important meeting of the Council of Ministers only if the court had been in possession of the records. The business of collecting and perusing the minutes of the meetings of the Council of Ministers, as well as the more important documents of the ministries of foreign and internal affairs at the trials, began only in the spring of 1946. There is no evidence to prove that the people's courts in Hungary were familiar with any of the German ministerial files and documents used so extensively at the Nuremberg trial.

The unpreparedness of the representatives of the people's prosecution is easily proven by the papers relating to the preparation of the trial of Ödön Mikecz, who was minister of justice from 9 March 1938 to 6 November 1938. On 25 September 1945 the head of the Budapest People's Prosecution ordered his subordinates to "investigate and to establish" how long the suspect had served as state secretary and how long as minister of justice. Rather than issuing such an order, it would have been sufficient to check the relevant volumes in the directory of public officials that was available in all the larger libraries. These directories contained data about the exact position of each public official, retrospectively, for several decades. Ödön Mikecz was acquitted by the people's court largely because of his advanced age. (He was fifty-one years old in 1945 and died in Budapest in 1965.) In fact, he played an important part in the preparation of the first anti-Jewish law. On the other hand, László Radocsay, who was minister of justice from 9 November 1939 to 22 March 1944, and who was responsible for at least three anti-Jewish laws, was conspicuously missing from the series of great political trials. Radocsay died in Budapest in 1968 at the age of ninety.

A list of factual errors, mistaken quotations, and many instances when the people's judges lost their tempers, whether deliberately or unintentionally, during the great trials would be quite long. Often defendants charged with principal war crimes were asked to give sworn evidence against other principal defendants. Reviewing the sentence of former Prime Minister Béla Imrédy, the Council of People's Courts remarked: "The court of first instance made a mistake in ordering the witnesses Kálmán Rátz, Csaba Gaál, József Gera, and Ferenc Szálasi to swear to their testimonies as there are criminal proceedings against each one of these persons and they themselves are suspected of having committed war crimes."[36] In another statement the Council warned the people's courts of first instance not to forget to include the confiscation of property in their verdicts in the cases of the principal war criminals.[37]

In the great trials, Edmund Veesenmayer, Hitler's minister plenipotentiary to Hungary, and Otto Winkelmann, head of the German police and the SS forces in Hungary, were regularly heard as witnesses. They refused to say anything of importance, particularly regarding the role they played in the deportation of Hungarian Jews. However, even the Council of People's Courts considered it a violation of criminal procedure that in the trial of former Minister of Justice and Culture István Antal the people's court had been satisfied with Veesenmayer's testimony as recorded in the prosecutor's office, even though there was no reason the witness should not have been heard in court.[38] The defendants complained repeatedly, and justifiedly, that the people's court refused to hear the witnesses the defendants had called on, it being argued in court that the facts were well known.

During the course of the trials, the judges attempted to give their assessment of history. The reading of these historicizing arguments reveals not only the factual historical errors the judges made but also their political bias. According to the explanation given for Bárdossy's death sentence, the fate of Hungary was decided in the spring and summer of 1919, when it became obvious that Hungary could not remain a democracy: feudalism would continue to prevail with the help of foreign arms. Further, the survival of feudalism in 1919 was held responsible for the territorial dismemberment of Hungary.[39] In reality, in the spring and summer of 1919 Hungary was governed by a communist Republic of Councils that could hardly be called democratic. As for the future borders of Hungary, they were decided by the Entente Powers several months earlier, a decision that was not influenced by internal Hungarian political developments. In their arguments, the people's judges tried to overturn the unhistorical charge against democracy and communism previously voiced by counterrevolutionary propaganda. During Miklós Horthy's reign, it was customary for the government to claim that Hungary had been subjected to the disastrous Trianon Peace Treaty as a punishment for its liberal Jewish-Bolshevik revolutions.

In vain did Bárdossy and Imrédy point to Hungary's historical and geographical position and to wartime German pressure. We may voice some reservations even in connection with the main charge evoked by the people's judges in 1945–46. Bárdossy, Imrédy, and even such ministers who held expert nonpolitical departments—including Szász and Kunder—were rebuked for having been unable to foresee that Germany could not possibly win the Second World War. In other words, the principal charge against the defendants was that as responsible statesmen they had made a mistake. However, in the spring of 1941, Stalin himself, as well as Churchill and many military experts, believed that the Red Army had little chance against the Wehrmacht. Mutatis mutandis: how many Western or Eastern experts were able to foresee, between 1958 and 1988, that the Soviet Union and its Eastern European empire would crumble after 1989?[40]

Another absurd charge was that the Germans invaded Hungary on 19 March 1944 because Imrédy had suggested to Veesenmayer, in a private conversation in the fall of 1943, that the Germans should try to persuade Regent Horthy to appoint a government that would serve German interests more eagerly.[41] The verdict also marshaled as evidence against Imrédy his "immense desire for power and aspiration for rank"— the fact that in January 1935 he resigned from his post in the government as minister of finances at the suggestion of Prime Minister Gyula Gömbös and that he accepted the presidency of the Hungarian National Bank. Imrédy tried in vain to refute the accusation by arguing that the minister of finances is superior, in both rank and in influence, to the president of the Hungarian National Bank.[42] Equally in vain did he claim before the people's court that Hungary's joining the Anticomintern Pact under his prime ministry did not signal an inevitable step down the road leading to war against the Soviet Union. After all, in 1939 Germany and the Soviet Union were allies.[43]

The only charges that the people's prosecutor were able to bring against Fidél Pálffy were that he was an extreme rightist; that he wrote anti-Semitic and prowar articles, and that he accepted the agricultural portfolio in Szálasi's cabinet. Although the people's judges still claimed, in the fall of 1945, that each and every member of the Szálasi cabinet was equally guilty, two Arrow Cross ministers, Emil Szakváry and Vilmos Hellebronth, were not executed. There must have been two main reasons behind the execution of Pálffy: his trial was among the first held and his relationship with Szálasi was ideologically closer than that of Szakváry or Hellebronth. One might add that had he not descended from a great historic family and had he been tried in the second half of 1946, after the people's judges' thirst for blood had been quenched, he may well have received only a life sentence.

It may be worth pointing out here that the people's courts in Hungary sentenced at least two dozen journalists to shorter or longer periods of imprisonment. Among the charges brought against those who were sentenced to death was that they had written prowar and anti-Soviet articles. In this regard Béla Imrédy justifiedly cited the example of László Ravasz, a bishop of the Reformed Church, whose printed commentaries between 1939 and 1942 could have been the basis for a death sentence in 1945. Yet Bishop Ravasz acted as one of the prosecution's star witnesses at the great trials and he himself was never tried.[44]

The main charge against Szálasi and accomplices was their preparation of the Arrow Cross coup and the actual assumption of power. As it

became clear during the trial, the Arrow Cross takeover had been organized primarily by Emil Kovarcz, yet he was brought to Hungary from
Germany only after Szálasi and his codefendants had been executed. The
people's judges were unwilling to believe that Szálasi and his party had
not been given any money or other material support by the Germans
before September 1944.

Remarkably, almost nothing important concerning the Jewish policy
of the Szálasi regime was discovered during the Szálasi trial. In his testimony, Miksa Domonkos, one of the leaders of the Hungarian Jewish
Council in 1944, repeated only what every contemporary knew—namely
that after the Arrow Cross takeover, the Arrow Cross militia, and other
such people who had managed to get hold of arms, killed and robbed
the Jews of Budapest indiscriminately. The people's court, however, was
unable to establish the role of the Arrow Cross ministers in the atrocities.
In reality, they had done almost nothing one way or another. Moreover,
the establishment of the ghetto in Budapest was listed among the main
charges against Szálasi, yet confining the Jews to a ghetto instead of deporting them actually contributed greatly to the survival of about
150,000 in Budapest. Szálasi had several reasons for creating the Budapest ghetto. First of all, he wanted desperately to get official recognition
of his regime by the neutral states. Secondly, he was under constant pressure by the diplomats of these states, especially the Papal Nuncio Angelo
Rotta and his colleagues, the Swedish Minister Carl Ivan Danielsson and
the Swiss Consul Carl Lutz, to spare the lives of the Jews. The death
marches of the Hungarian Jews had shocked not only the diplomats but
many Hungarians as well. At the end of 1944, the German authorities,
following a Himmler order, stopped the death factories; they were interested in deporting only able-bodied Jews from Budapest.

In 1945–1946, there were heated arguments between the people's
judges, certain people's courts, and the Council of People's Courts. Emil
Szakváry was given ten years "only" by a people's court of the first instance because he successfully argued, among other things, that he had
not participated in the elaboration of the so-called Arrow Cross national
development plan, and he had regularly protested the persecution of the
Jews in the Council of Ministers. In spite of all that, the Council of People's Courts sentenced Szakváry to life imprisonment.[45] Former Minister
of Justice László Budinszky was first sentenced to death by the people's
court, then the people's judges unanimously recommended him for
mercy. In the end, though, he was sentenced to death by the Council of
People's Courts. Subsequently, and against the wishes of the Social Democratic president of the Council of People's Courts and the Communist
judge, the other judges, representing the Smallholders Party, the Peasant
Party, and the Bourgeois Democrats recommended mercy for Budinszky,

claiming that he had tried to relieve the Arrow Cross terror, had protected the independence of the judges, and had freed several people from Gestapo captivity. The president of the Republic, Zoltán Tildy, a former leader of the Smalholders Party, turned down Budinszky's appeal for mercy on March 7.[46] In the case of Bálint Hóman, three people's judges recommended ten years of imprisonment, three voted for a life sentence. Finally, it was the vote of the presiding judge that decided the vote for a life sentence.[47]

The great historical trials did not serve the didactic or propaganda aim of "educating the nation," that had originally been intended. According to Minister of Justice Ries, these trials were necessary to help "the misled and stupefied public opinion of the country learn the history of twenty-five years of Hungarian fascism."[48] In vain did the people's judges explain, while justifying their verdicts, that once the counterrevolutionary order had taken power in 1919, its fall and the catastrophe of war were unavoidable. Today we can confirm what many individuals saw as early as 1945–46, that such reasoning failed to convince the nation.[49] Only the people's judges at the Sztójay trial had the courage to declare that whereas they were able to assess politically the events as well as the facts emerging from the charges, they lacked the perspective necessary for an overall historical evaluation.[50] Giving the reasons for its sentence, the Council of People's Courts was quick to warn the people's judges of the Sztójay trial: "one should avoid, by all means the kind of admission that the historical perspective necessary for a rightful assessment of the events tried here is lacking." The Council went on to remind the people's judges that they had been delegated to the people's courts by political parties, all of which shared the conviction that the catastrophe was caused by the previous system.[51]

According to plans worked out at the beginning of 1946, the material of the trials was to become a compulsory subject at school and/or universities.[52] However, until as late as the beginning of the 1980s, even such pro-Communist historians who were considered most reliable, had great difficulties in obtaining permission to look into the materials of the people's courts, which were kept in the archives of the Ministry of the Interior. Meanwhile the number of documents shrank significantly.

In 1945–46 the public gained relatively little information from the press regarding the great trials. In 1946 accounts of the great trials in the daily papers became shorter and shorter. The public itself showed interest only in the trials of the major war criminals. The trial of the less known journalist Ferenc Rajniss was conducted in front of empty seats.[53] During the Endre-Baky-Jaross trial a large crowd filled the main hall of the Music Academy where the trial was held despite the freezing cold of the unheated court room.[54] The ones there were primarily Jews.

War criminals who were shot dead or hanged in 1945–46 belonged to three categories: former government ministers, Arrow Cross mass murderers, and former guards or officers in the *munkaszolgálatos* (Jewish forced labor) units. Jews who had survived the war, forced labor, deportation, and the concentration camps now appeared in great numbers, motivated by the desire for revenge. Contemplating the audience at the the Endre-Baky-Jaross trial, the Communist journalist Géza Losonczy noted bitterly "the complete uninterestedness and indifference that the majority of the non-Jewish public manifests toward the case," although, as Losonczy hastened to point out, this was not a trial on behalf of the Jews: "This is a trial of the Hungarian people against its executioners, a trial of the Hungarian nation against its infamous traitors."[55] Losonczy's argument did not seem to convince many people. As Ákos Major described in his memoirs, the activities of the people's courts in January–October 1945, when they sentenced only a few "petty" mass murderers to death, created the impression among nine million Hungarians that the people's courts were there to compensate for, or to retaliate on behalf of, the Jewish victims.[56]

In a study published in 1948, the writer and political sociologist István Bibó discussed in detail one of the most serious problems of the entire system of people's courts—namely the participation of Jewish survivors in the impeachment and trial of war criminals. As Bibó correctly stated: "so many Jews or persons affected by the anti-Jewish laws played a part in various phases of the investigation and litigation or as judges that there is an empirical basis for the view that the essence of the whole process of retribution is that now the Jews pass judgment over the Hungarians as a revenge for the past when the Hungarians passed judgment over the Jews. For this we should reckon with serious repercussions."[57] In his memoirs written in political exile, the democratic politician Dezső Sulyok, who had been prosecutor in the Imrédy trial, claimed that in the Bárdossy trial Sándor Szalai had made Hungarian history after 1919 appear as if it had consisted of a single colossal crime committed by the Hungarian people against the Jewish ethnic minority.[58] In reality, in the Bárdossy trial the Jewish question was not given as much publicity as it may well have deserved, while Sándor Szalai did his best to clear the Hungarian people of any conceivable suspicion.

Besides the understandable thirst for revenge, there was another reason for the massive participation of Hungarians of Jewish origin in the trials of the war criminals: many such professional judges who had not been compromised in the counterrevolutionary system were reluctant to participate in the activities of the people's courts. But the Jews' thirst for revenge manifested itself in other ways as well. Although the daily press gave scant coverage of these events, it eagerly reported those instances in which crowds of Jews attacked war criminals, gave them a heavy beating, wounded them, or tried to lynch them.[59] This was what happened to László Endre and László Baky who were nearly lynched by the crowd after the second day of their hearing.[60]

Epilogue

Much was expected from the great historical trials. As one of the contemporary journalists explained, the organizers expected a catharsis, a purification; they hoped that "the whole nation would watch with baited breath." Nothing came of all that. The only consequence of the executions was that "the severe verdicts of the people's courts recruited more loyal supporters of democracy even from the ranks of those who had been indifferent before than the number of grateful devotees won over by the generous distribution of political rights."[61] The people were more interested in such things as the unscrupulous ambition of the communists; the "salami policy" whereby the Communists gradually crushed the Smallholders Party (which had easily won the November 1945 elections), the soaring inflation; and food rationing. Neither did it prove beneficial to the dignity of the people's courts when the people's prosecutors were accused of corruption and arrested. The chief prosecutor, Sándor Molnár, stated sadly in February 1946: "In vain did we search out all the honest and democratically inclined lawyers and ask them to assume the role of prosecutor; our efforts yielded no results. Thus we were obliged to employ people almost without any selectivity, who later considered their position as a profitable and flourishing sinecure. They squandered their power and influence. The devil take the hindmost of such people."[62]

Sensing the indifference of public opinion after mid-1946, the Council of the People's Courts, which had been much more "bloodthirsty" than the people's courts, now reprieved one principal war criminal's death sentence after another. The reasons for the relatively lenient sentencing of Emil Szakváry become clear from the chief judges' explanation of this: "The Council feels that by inflicting such severe punishments, it has served the principle of retaliation in that full justice has been done to the aggrieved Hungarian people."[63] At the end of December the Council changed András Tasnádi Nagy's death sentence, meted out by the court of first instance, to life imprisonment on the basis that "with the imposition of a number of severe punishments and with the full consolidation of democracy, the retaliatory character of the punishments laid down in the original law should now be shifted to a classical level where prevention precedes retaliation."[64]

On the first day of the Bárdossy trial, Ákos Major declared that the great trials taking place before the people's courts "would be a test of great significance for the Hungarian people's democracy."[65] It is not the historian's task to decide whether the Hungarian people's democracy failed the test. But the historian may remind the reader that there have been trials ever since the age of the Jacobin dictatorship in France where the defendants were sentenced not for what they had done but for who they were by virtue of their social origin and class membership. The historical responsibility of the Hungarian principal war criminals is beyond question. What is questionable, however, is whether the people's courts were sufficiently equipped to establish their criminal responsibility.

Notes

1. Tibor Zinner, "Háborús bűnösök perei: Internálások, kitelepítések és igazoló eljárások 1945–1949," *Történelmi Szemle* (Budapest, 1985), 133–40. See also Tibor Lukács, *A magyar népbírósági jog és a népbíróságok 1945–50* (Budapest, 1979); and Ákos Major, *Népbíráskodás-forradalmi törvényesség* (Budapest, 1988).

2. The data compiled from József Bölöny, *Magyarország kormányai 1848–1975* (Budapest, 1978), and the files of the people's courts.

3. Zinner, *Háborús bűnösök perei*, 119, 123. For more details about the deportation of the Germans, see Ágnes Tóth: *Telepítések Magyarországon 1945–1948 között* (Kecskemét, 1993).

4. István Kelemen, "Szálasiék tetemrehívása" *Haladás* (6 October 1945), 8.

5. István Ries, "A népbíróság védelmében," *Népbírósági Közlöny* (8 November, 1945).

6. A lecture without a date or a signature written most probably by István Ries with the title: "A népbíróságról és az esküdtszékről" (Documents of the trial of Béla Imrédy) Budapest Főváros Levéltára—Budapest Municipal Archives (hereinafter BpFL); Népbírósági iratok (hereinafter Nb). 3953/45., 3d vol.

7. Magyar Országos Levéltár hereinafter OL); Documents of the National Council of the People's Courts (hereinafter NCPC), Documents of the trial of László Budinszky 1149/46.

8. *Bárdossy László a népbíróság előtt*, citing the indictment by Sándor Szalai. Edited, with introduction and explanatory notes written by Pál Pritz (Budapest: 1991), 203. György Marosán, the prosecutor of the Sztójay trial, said in his indictment: "it is the duty and obligation of every political system, especially if it is to serve the interest and development of the Hungarian people, to weed out and to eliminate from the body of the people all those who had sinned against the people and the country or are likely to do so in the future." The Documents of the Sztójay trial in the Szálasi trial papers, BpFL, 19.430/14 c., p. 904. d. 265.

9. Sándor Mátrai, "Második felvonás az Andrássy út 60-ban" *Kis Újság* (5 October 1945): 1.

10. "Visszhang" (Echo), unsigned, *Haladás* (20 October 1945), 6.

11. Dezső Király, "Pillanatképek a nagy perről," *Haladás* (24 November 1945): 7.)

12. Béla Zsolt, "Pillanatfelvétel Imrédyről," *Népbírósági Közlöny* (17 November 1945): 5.
13. *Szabad Nép* (7 February 1946): 1.
14. Cited by Pritz, *Bárdossy László*, 104.
15. Ferenc Szálasi's last plea, in: *A Szálasi per*, Elek and László Karsai, eds. (Bp. 1988), 657.
16. In the 2/1994 (January 14) resolution of the Constitutional Court, 43–44.
17. In PM Decree of the People's Jurisdiction 81/1945 (25 January 1945); PM d. 6750/1440 (16 August 1945).
18. The No. 3953/1945 verdict of the PC. Imrédy Béla halálos itéletének indoklása, Belügyminisztérium Történeti Irattára (The Historical Archives of the Ministry of the Interior, hereinafter BMTI) V. 55.184/a., 25–26.
19. "Mi a NOT—népbíróság vagy a fasiszta urak felmentője?" *Szabad Nép* (9 November 1945): 2.
20. A press conference given by people's prosecutor Szűcs, *Szabad Nép* (23 October 1945): 2.
21. Major, *Népbíráskodás*, 147.
22. *Szabad Nép* (9 January 1946): 1.
23. In Pritz, *Bárdossy László*, 164.
24. Karsai, *A Szálasi per*, 656.
25. In Pritz, *Bárdossy László*, 203.
26. The motivations of the verdict passed by the people's court in Béla Imrédy's trial, BMTI V. 55. 184/a. The motivations of the verdict passed by the people's court in László Budinszky labeled Italian and German fascism outright as "alien to the Hungarian soul" (BpFL V.—19.618., 265. d.).
27. Documents of the Szálasi trial, NOT 1923/1946. (BpFL V. 19.430/3.b.,—19.618/48.,258.d).
28. The motivations of the verdict in Emil Szakváry's trial, OL—NOT 4432/1946.
29. Elek Karsai, *Itél a nép* (Budapest, 1977), 14–15.
30. *Kis Újság* (6 October 1945): 1.
31. *Szabad Nép* (6 October 1945): 2.
32. Ákos Major recalls wrongly that "the first timetable" of the trials of the principal war criminals at the people's court was only announced on October 19 (Major, *Népbíráskodás*, 192–93.) Pál Pritz, who edited the material of the Bárdossy trial for the press, did not deal with the question of why the series of historical trials was begun with that of Bárdossy.
33. *Szabad Nép* (30 October 1945): 1.
34. Documents of the trial of Mihály Kolosváry-Borcsa and his accomplices. BMTI V. 99.145; NOT 4732/1946.
35. Pritz, *Bárdossy László*, 133.
36. Documents of the Imrédy trial. NOT 304/194, BpFL, Nb. 3953/1945/2.
37. Documents of the trial of László Budinszky OL-NOT 1149/1946.
38. Documents of the trial of István Antal OL-NOT 3678/1946.
39. Pritz, *Bárdossy László*, 242–43.
40. In his introduction to the Bárdossy trial Pál Pritz, choosing his words very cautiously, does not say whether or not he considers the death sentence of the

former prime minister justified. However, in an interview he gave following the publication of his book, he clearly said yes to the question whether he agreed with Bárdossy's death sentence (*Magyar Hírlap*, 21 December 1991: 6).

41. Documents of the Imrédy trial. BpFL, Nb. 3953/1945.

42. In the reference literature dealing with the subject, Elek Karsai agrees with the view of the people's court (Karsai, *Itél a nép*, 73).

43. Documents of the Imrédy trial. The motivations of the verdict, BpFL, Nb. 3953/1945. Imrédy was even charged with ordering air raid practices on the night of 14 October and 9 December 1937.

44. Documents of the trial of Béla Imrédy. BpFL, Nb. 3953/1945/3.

45. Documents of the trial of Emil Szakváry. OL-NOT 4432/1946; Nb. 968/1946. Szakváry was freed from prison on 1 November 1956, then emigrated.

46. Documents of the trial of László Budinszky. BMTI 101.531/1. Nb. 3449/1945; NOT 1149/1946.

47. Documents of the trial of Bálint Hóman. BpFL Nb. 864/1946.; NOT 1149/1946.

48. István Ries, "A népbíróság védelmében," *Népbírósági Közlöny* (8 November 1945): 1.

49. The motivations of the verdict passed by the people's court in Béla Imrédy's trial saw the history of the era of the counterrevolution as a tragic and fatal tree "planted by Gyula Gömbös, watered by Béla Imrédy, and harvested by Szálasi" (BMTI V. 55.184/a./2.a.).

50. Documents of the trial of Sztójay. BMTI, V. 101.501.

51. Ibid., NOT 3845/1946.

52. *Kis Újság* (6 January 1946): 3.

53. *Kis Újság* (1 December 1945): 3.

54. *Kis Újság* (18 December 1945): 1.

55. Géza Losonczy, "Antiszemitizmus és antibolsevizmus a Népbíróság előtt, *Szabad Nép* (23 December 1945): 1.

56. Major, *Népbíráskodás*, 186.

57. István Bibó, "Zsidókérdés Magyarországon 1944 után" *Válogatott tanulmányok 1945–49* (Budapest, 1986, v. II), 772.

58. Dezső Sulyok, A magyar tragédia in Béla László Horváth, *Hóman Bálint utolsó évei 1945–51*, 199.

59. On 18 October 1945 *Világ* reported that a few people who had served in the military labor service during the war recognized their Arrow Cross henchman in Budapest and attacked him and stabbed him several times. Their victim was taken to the hospital in a very grave condition. Reporting from the trial of another Arrow Cross henchman, on 21 October 1945, *Szabad Nép* wrote that when the people's court announced the verdict (eight years), the angry spectators attacked the man and tried to lynch him. The guards had to fire in the air to disperse the crowd. At the trial of Arrow Cross henchman Géza Huver the spectators beat up Mrs. Huver and her son with sticks and umbrellas because they had made loud remarks about the witnesses (*Világ*, 17 November 1945, 2.) In another trial where military labor servicemen were involved, the former labor servicemen present at the trial seriously injured, then denounced to the authorities, one of the witnesses

of the defense who was immediately arrested by the people's prosecutor (*Világ*, 21 November 1945, 3).

60. See more details in, Karsai and Molnár, eds., *Az Endre-Baky-Jaross per* (1994), 2.

61. "Szálasiék az akasztófán," *Haladás* (14 March 1946), 1.

62. Sándor Mátrai, "A férgese most hullik el," *Kis Újság* (2 February 1946): 4.

63. Documents of the trial of Emil Szakváry OL-NOT 4432/1946.

64. Documents of the trial of András Tasnádi Nagy OL-NOT 7764/1946.

65. Pritz, *Bárdossy László*, 75.

The Politics of Retribution: The Trial of Jozef Tiso in the Czechoslovak Environment

THE DECADE between 1938 and 1948 was the most fateful in the history of Czechoslovakia, encompassing truncation, dissolution, occupation, war, liberation, radical social reform, and absorption into the communist bloc. It commenced with the infamous Munich agreement of September 1938, which ceded large portions of Czechoslovakia to Nazi Germany and left the state militarily crippled and internally divided. In the wake of the Munich accords, the Czechoslovak central government gave the Slovak province wide-ranging autonomy, in the hope that this might preserve its citizens' loyalty to the unitary state. Whatever gains were achieved by this, however, were soon lost less than six months later. Hitler had decided to remove Czechoslovakia from the map, and, as a lever toward this end, he presented an ultimatum to the Slovak autonomous leadership: either Slovakia would declare its independence and become subservient to the Third Reich, or it would be crushed by the Nazi armed forces with the rest of Czechoslovakia. The Slovak leadership, under Jozef Tiso, made the decision to declare an independent Slovak Republic on 14 March 1939. The following day, that state came into existence, and the two western Czech provinces were occupied by German armies and reconfigured as the "Protectorate of Bohemia and Moravia." For the following five years Czechoslovakia existed as two separate states: a Nazi-occupied and increasingly terrorized Czech one, and a nominally independent but increasingly dependent Slovak one.

In the wake of liberation in April and May of 1945, Czechoslovakia was reconstituted as a parliamentary democracy within its pre-Munich frontiers.[1] In the less than three years that the reborn state experienced before the communist takeover, its leaders attempted to tackle a number of difficult tasks simultaneously. They strove to reorder the internal workings of the state to satisfy Slovak aspirations, a task that should have been eased by the expulsion of Czechoslovakia's three million ethnic Germans, who would no longer clamor for rights and privileges equal to those of the Slovaks. Further, they undertook a wide-ranging socialist economic reform that quickly placed 62 percent of the work force in the state sector. All banks, insurance agencies, natural resource extractors, and other "key industries" were nationalized. In accomplishing this, the state traveled a great distance toward its primarily ally in foreign policy, the Soviet Union. It was hoped that Czechoslovakia would be able to maintain a free and independent existence by establishing economic, social, and political systems that would be looked on favorably by the Soviets. These hopes foundered in February 1948, when a government crisis resulted in the Communist Party's assumption of total power and the end of Czechoslovak democracy for over forty years.

In the historiography of this fateful decade, there is a notable lacuna in the serious study of the wartime Slovak state.[2] More interesting, perhaps, is the effect the nationalism, clericalism, and anticommunism that marked the state's six-year existence had on the renewed Czechoslovakia's slide into communist dictatorship. In the immediate postwar years, the "Slovak question" that had plagued the Czechoslovak Republic since its founding called desperately for a solution that would satisfy the national aspirations of the Slovaks on the one hand, and Czech demands for a unitary state on the other. In the less than three years between the final liberation of the state and the communist assumption of total power in February 1948, the course toward the reaching of a mutually acceptable form for Czech-Slovak relations was gravely damaged by the political maneuvering that surrounded the long trial of the former president of the wartime Slovak state, the Roman Catholic priest Jozef Tiso.

Before beginning, however, a few words about what this contribution is about and particularly what it is *not* about are in order. The following will concern itself particularly with the political motives, maneuverings, and considerations surrounding the Tiso trial and the carrying out of the sentence of death levied against him.[3] First and foremost, it is not intended to examine and pass judgment on the Slovak state and its legitimacy, practices, legality, or morality. The long-running polemic between Slovak émigrés defending the state against all charges and the Czechoslovak communist regime condemning it with equal vehemence lies outside the scope of the present study.[4] Second, the related question of Tiso's guilt or innocence, as well as juridical questions and the precise course of the trial will remain almost entirely outside the purview of this examination.

In contrast to these issues, concentration will be placed on the political surroundings of the trial and Tiso's execution, because of the importance placed on these by three interlocking sets of political actors in the course of their political struggles. The first of these is the conflict over the appropriate division of powers between Slovak political forces and the central government in Prague. The second is the heightened conflict between the Communist Party of Slovakia (CPS) and the noncommunist Democratic Party (DP) over political leadership in Slovakia. The final pairing is the political contest being carried out across the republic between communism (represented by the CPS and the Communist Party of

Czechoslovakia [CPCz]) on the one hand, and noncommunist forces and particularly conservative Roman Catholicism (represented by the DP and the Czech People's Party) on the other. The first two of these struggles were carried out largely in the environment surrounding the trial itself, while the third came into play over the question of granting Tiso clemency. Nonetheless, the political moves made to ensure a "correct" final result to the Tiso trial influenced the course of all three struggles, having ramifications outside of Slovakia as well as internally.

Prelude: The Czech Trials

Any attempt to understand the implications of the trial of the former Slovak Republic's government must take into account the preceding trial of the leaders of the government of the wartime "Protectorate of Bohemia and Moravia," the results of which caused tremendous conflict within the National Front coalition. The trial commenced on 29 April 1946 and concerned itself with the activities of five defendants: Jaroslav Krejčí (chairman of the Protectorate government), Richard Beinert (minister of the interior), Adolf Hrubý (chairman of the only party permitted in the Protectorate), Jindřich Kamenický (minister of railroads) and Josef Kalfus (minister of finance). Even before the trial had begun Justice Minister Prokop Drtina, a member of the Czech National Socialist Party (the CPCz's primary electoral competitor), came under pressure from the CPCz to demand the death penalty in a number of these cases. The communists were supported in this aim by diplomatic pressure applied by the USSR, including that of the Soviet ambassador, who "expressed himself very directly: At least three of the accused should be condemned to death." In the event, the government closed its case on 27 June and asked the court for the levying of the death penalty in the cases of Krejčí and Hrubý and twenty years imprisonment for Beinert, while leaving the punishments of Kalfus and Kamenický to the discretion of the judges.[5]

In the month between the end of arguments and the handing down of verdicts, it became increasingly clear that neither the National Court nor public opinion supported the harshness of the demanded penalties. As Karel Kaplan notes, "The discussion of the members of the cabinet signaled that their original ideas about the guilt and punishment of the Protectorate ministers diverged from the ideas and evaluations of the majority of citizens who had lived in the occupied lands."[6] When the verdicts were handed down on 31 July, they proved even lighter than expected and caused a brief but acrimonious confrontation between Czech communists and noncommunists. No death sentences were given, only Hrubý was sentenced to life imprisonment, and Kalfus was found guilty but not sentenced at all.[7] Justice Minister Drtina immediately began receiving telegrams of protest calling for the revision of the verdicts, overwhelmingly originating in organizations controlled by the Communist Party.[8] A furious battle developed in the party press and the government between communists calling for a revision of the verdicts that would be more in accordance with "the will of the people" and noncommunists demanding that the independence of the judiciary be protected. Prime Minister Klement Gottwald (CPCz) instructed Justice Minister Drtina to look into the possibility of reopening the case or revising the verdicts, which he did, drawing the conclusion that it would be legally impossible without important new evidence being produced.[9]

In terms of the Tiso trial, three important features of the trial need to be pointed out. First, during the course of the government's discussions of the trail of the Protectorate ministers, members of the Slovak DP remained silent: for them "The Protectorate government was at base a Czech affair."[10] Second, the communists uncompromisingly maintained a harder line than either the public or the other governing parties. The general public mood of agreement with the verdicts, despite the communist-organized protest campaign, was recognized by the noncommunist parties and helped guide them in their confrontation with the communists. Third, the Czech parties were very concerned about the effect that the lightness of the sentences would have on the Tiso trial, which was then being prepared and which began three months after Drtina's report ended any possibility of revision.

The Setting: The Slovak Political Environment

The situation in Slovakia was much different from that obtaining in the Czech lands at the conclusion of the war. Part of this was historical, as the Slovak portion of the country was on the whole less developed, being less industrialized, more sparsely populated, and less educated, as well as being more intensively Roman Catholic. The war had brought even further divisions between the two parts of the country, however. While damage to the Czech lands was relatively slight, there was extensive destruction throughout Slovakia. Much of this was a result of the 1944 Slovak National Uprising, the largest operation of its type in Europe (mobilizing perhaps eighty thousand men and women). The extent of the uprising did not mean, however, that the Slovak Republic had no popular legitimacy. In contrast to the Protectorate of Bohemia and Moravia, the Slovak state commanded reasonable support. Even many important figures of the uprising had no regrets regarding its establishment, but opposed its political orientation and its increasing subservience to Germany.[11] Perhaps most important, the mere existence of the Slovak state had given a great boost to Slovak self-confidence by proving that Slovaks could administrate a state without Czech tutelage and providing an experienced and nationally conscious managerial elite. In essence it acted, as Carol Leff has pointed out "as a watershed, enhancing the general level of national consciousness and permanently weakening, if not destroying, a collaboration with Prague based on ardent assimilationism."[12]

In an attempt to recognize the sympathy for some measure of self-government among the Slovak population and reconcile it to the renewal of Czechoslovakia, the wartime exile government proposed a wide-ranging reorganization of internal relations in its first programmatic proclamation upon returning to native soil. This denominated the Slovaks "a nationally sovereign nation" and declared that the government would strive "to create a Czech-Slovak relationship on the foundation of 'equal among equals' in order that true brotherhood between the nations will be felt."[13] In the months immediately after liberation, one of the greatest supporters of this conception was the chairman of the CPCz, Klement Gottwald. In several speeches, he called the document the "Magna Charta of the Slovak nation," and maintained that "In a word, the Slovaks will have the full possibility and the full right—not in promises and in words but in reality, not in the future but already now in the present—to be lord and master in their native land."[14] The anchoring of these vague ideas in the law of the state, and the precise content of the division of powers between Slovak organs and the central government, was left for the elected representatives who would assume office after the elections of May 1946, and the outcome of those elections affected their content drastically.

The two main Slovak actors in the election would be the CPS and the DP, for they were the only two parties permitted to organize in the months following the liberation.[15] The CPS ran into many problems campaigning in Slovakia. Although it could draw on its record in the uprising, the structure of Slovak society made it difficult for the party to gain membership. Although the party was more resoundingly working class (63 percent) than its sister CPCz, it was hampered by the small number of industrial workers in the land, and further by their dispersal among the numerous reconstruction projects.[16] The CPS also encountered serious problems in gaining support among a large agricultural population that was by nature resistant to communism and particularly concerned about the future of their holdings in any communist-sponsored land reform project. While the CPCz had gone far in securing widespread support for measures that had a major impact on the Czech lands in the months after liberation, the internally disunited CPS was seen as "lagging behind" particularly in view of the fact that Slovakia had been liberated earlier. This caused a major shakeup in its leadership and policies that resulted in its subordination to decisions made by the CPCz. These, however, often failed to take into account the vast differences between the social and economic conditions in the Czech lands and those of Slovakia, thus harming the CPS's electoral prospects even further.[17]

In contrast, the DP had less trouble gaining a receptive audience for their message. The party relied on rural voters, who composed about 80 percent of its membership, and cultivated a distinctly moderate program that resurrected the (now banned) Agrarian Party message from the prewar period. Through their control of almost the entire administrative machinery in the agricultural sector, they were able to keep land reform to a minimum and by doing so could both calm wealthier peasants' fears and claim responsibility for everything good that happened in the run up to the elections. In the wake of the banning of the parties that had participated in the Slovak state, the DP acted as "yet another of the historic holding companies for Slovak politics in times of political flux."[18] Because of this very fact, however, the DP was marked by internal inconsistencies, as the divisions Catholic/Protestant, progressive/agrarian, and "Czechoslovakist"/separatist were represented in all possible combinations. Nonetheless, the party could rely on the inherent anti-Communism of the rural population and on the Roman Catholic Church, "which was often [Slovak villagers'] most effective contact with the outside world."[19]

In the months immediately preceding the election, all of the noncommunist Czech parties tried to establish sister parties in Slovakia, and the DP tried to expand into the Czech lands. Their relative success tells us much about the relationship between the Czech and Slovak parties, which was to be crucial in the battle to gain clemency for Tiso. The DP announced its intention to attempt to organize across the republic in an editorial in its daily organ, Čas. By doing so, it hoped to gain the votes of the former supporters of the interwar republic's largest party, the Agrarians, as well as of Slovaks living in the Czech lands. Unfortunately for the DP, every other political party in the central government opposed the move. It was opposed by the CPS and CPCz largely because they wanted to maintain their position as the only group to receive delegates from both lands, by the People's Party because it had been the Agrarian Party's largest competitor for rural (especially Moravian) votes and therefore stood to gain the most from its proscription, by the Czech National Socialists because they too estimated they would pick up votes from ex-Agrarians, and by the Social Democrats because they were in a period of close cooperation with the communists. With the exception of the People's Party, all also expressed concern about the DP's lack of enthusiasm for the Czech-and communist-led program of social revolution, and harbored suspicions about its ties to former supporters of the wartime Slovak state.[20]

In contrast to this rejection, when the Czech Social Democrats attempted shortly thereafter to create a sister party in Slovakia by revoking their wartime merger with the CPS, they were not opposed by the DP although one of its founders was the DP vice-chairman.[21] The resulting "Party of Labor" was the third party to emerge in postwar Slovakia. Slovak members of the Czech National Socialist Party withdrew their attempt to found a "Party of State Unity" in Slovakia at the last minute, and the attempt of the People's Party to organize in Slovakia similarly disintegrated.[22]

As can be seen from the attempts of Czech parties to change Slovakia's party-political structure, all parties saw the tremendous potential support that could be mustered by attempting to take advantage of the internal inconsistencies of the DP. The greatest plum to be won in this maneuvering was the support of the politically Catholic and nationalist L'udáks, and particularly that of its leadership, the clergy.[23] These former supporters of the Slovak state would undoubtedly be a major force in the upcoming elections, and attempts were made to woo them away from giving their votes to the DP (as their home of last resort in the face of the CPS and the Party of Labor). These attempts centered on a group of disgruntled deputies from within the DP and eventually forced that party to take active measures aimed at securing the support of Catholic circles for the party.

The first attempts to create a party for the adherents of political Catholicism in Slovakia began already in July 1945.[24] The CPS, surprisingly, had no objections to these strivings, hoping to make up for its weakness in the land by supporting any new bourgeois party because it would have to stand "at least a millimeter" to the left of the DP. Even more surprising, CPS leaders met with leaders of the Catholic hierarchy and disaffected Catholic members of the DP, aiming to create a Catholic party that would work with them. These plans ultimately crumbled when the Catholics asked the CPS to write a sample program for a possible party. The program was a virtual copy of the CPS's, revealing how little the communists understood the mentality of the new party's potential supporters, and the disgruntled Catholics ended their discussions with the CPS and drifted back to the DP.[25]

Much more serious were the plans of another group of Catholic DP representatives disturbed by the stance of the DP. This was an odd collection composed of two distinct parts, although sharing a Catholic orientation. One faction was committed to the unity of the Czechoslovak state and had the blessing of President Edvard Beneš and the party closest to him, the Czech National Socialists.[26] The other, larger wing was far more conservative, having close ties to separatist groups and the Catholic hierarchy. The leadership of this latter wing was given the task of creating the program for the nascent "Christian Republican Party," which it presented to the National Front government on 13 March 1946. The party was granted preliminary approval, conditional upon it changing its name[27] and stating its positions on four fundamental issues, the first two of which were its positions toward the Czechoslovak Republic and toward the planned trials of Tiso and other representatives of the Slovak state. Their response was to change the party's name to the inoffensive "Freedom Party" and to issue a vague statement supporting the policies and direction of the National Front, ensuring its approval above the protests of the DP.[28]

Before the Freedom Party could gain official recognition, however, the DP leadership recognized that it would gravely damage their chances at gaining the support of political Catholicism by default, and took steps to reconcile itself with the right wing of the splinter group. DP representatives had been meeting with the right-wing renegades since January, but had been unable to convince them that they would be better served by remaining inside the party. When the Freedom Party seemed sure to gain recognition, the DP stepped up its activities and convinced the conservative Catholic wing that it could gain what it wanted within the party. There were several reasons the two could reach agreement. From the point of view of the renegades, there were only two months left until the elections—little time for building a Slovakia-wide organization and finding financing for it—and there were ongoing disputes with the more progressive "Czechoslovak" wing about the true character of the party. Even if the conservatives and clericals were to control the Freedom Party's program and win a substantial number of votes with it, there was the danger that—as a party without leadership from former participants in the uprising, and with a conservative program—they would be branded "reactionary" and marginalized in both the Slovak and central governments. In contrast, the DP could offer an established campaign organization with a party that had leaders of the uprising among its most visible figures. From the point of view of the DP, winning over the supporters that political Catholicism could muster meant a guarantee of electoral success.

In view of these considerations, the right wing of the Freedom Party returned to the DP after the signing of the "April Agreement" on 30 March 1946, two days before the official recognition of the now rump Freedom Party. The agreement, which was never fully published in Slovakia, contained points concerning the reorganization of the DP leadership to include more right-wing Catholic figures, the ratio of Catholics to

Protestants to hold office in DP-controlled organizations, and a guarantee of support for church schools, which had been under CPS attack for some months. In addition, there has been very wide speculation that the DP leadership promised to see that Jozef Tiso received a light sentence, if there were no way to keep him from being tried at all.[29]

In return for this distinct nod toward conservative Catholic circles, the DP was rewarded with a virtual flood of support from all levels of the Catholic hierarchy. The enthusiastic Catholic supporters followed a general line that included explaining the meaning of the agreement, warning that Roman Catholicism was under attack (with special reference to communist atheism and the question of church schools), rejecting the Freedom Party, and exhorting the public to vote for Christianity and democracy. Notably, important features of the Catholic hierarchy's electoral campaigning were "anticommunism . . . anti-Czech and anti-Soviet agitation . . . and speeches in defense of Tiso." The pressure also included articles in the influential *Catholic News* and stern warnings from the pulpit that the election was a choice between Christianity and the devil. Although it was only in rare instances that priests and representatives of the Roman Catholic laity commanded their listeners to vote for the DP, the point of this "electoral orgy" could not be missed.[30]

This pressure from Catholic circles, in combination with the DP's solid organization, left the result of the election in little doubt. As the table below shows, the DP won a convincing victory, receiving the blessing

Party	Percentage	Mandates
DP	61.43	43
CPS	30.48	21
Freedom Party	4.20	3
Party of Labor	3.11	2
Blank	0.78	0
Total	100.00	69

of over three-fifths of the Slovak electorate. They showed remarkable strength across all demographic categories. The DP won almost all of the votes of the supporters of the (previously very large) banned parties, and showed disproportionate strength also among the Roman Catholic population. In contrast, the CPS did better than its average only in the regions where the uprising had taken place (which were also more highly industrialized than average) and among Protestants.[31]

Four important conclusions can be drawn from the preelection political maneuvering and the results of the elections. First, the Czech bourgeois parties all recognized the importance of the mass of anticommunist voters in Slovakia. Rather than attempting to support the DP, however, they regarded it with suspicion and attempted to cut into its share of the Slovak vote through the formation of sister parties in Slovakia on the one hand, and by keeping the DP from campaigning in the Czech lands on the other. Second, even though Vílem Prečan's orthodox communist study notes that the size of the DP victory cannot be attributed solely to the votes of L'udáks,[32] there can be little doubt that the *extent* of the surprising victory won by the DP was largely due to the supporters of political Catholicism.[33] Third, the L'udák, Slovak separatist aspect of the victory should not be underplayed. The Freedom Party, which also campaigned on an explicitly Catholic program but stressed the unity of the Czechoslovak Republic, received only negligible support. Finally, the L'udák electorate showed an internally consistent ideology: it was anticommunist, anti-Czech (both for nationalist reasons and because the Czechs were seen as allies of communism), and Catholic.

The election results in Slovakia were the cause of much concern in communist ranks, particularly as the CPCz had emerged with 40 percent of the Czech vote, making it almost twice as large as its nearest competitor. CPCz Chairman (and new Czechoslovak Prime Minister) Klement Gottwald summed up the communist view:

> We didn't expect anything terrific, but that it would fall apart in this way we had no idea. . . . It is a fact that the old [L'udák] reaction rushed into the Democratic Party. . . . That the Democratic Party is so strong in Slovakia distorts the picture that we have across the republic. Our Slovak comrades say that in Slovakia even the bishops declared themselves for the "democrats" and that priests from the pulpits called for voting for the Democratic Party. . . . What to do now to secure Slovakia for the republic and for democracy? [34]

At a joint session of the Presidia of the CPCz and the CPS, it was decided that the best strategy was to launch an all-out attack on the DP. This would center on two main goals: the limitation of the power of the DP through limiting the power of Slovak institutions, and the securing of a severe verdict in the Tiso case.[35]

In the first of these aims, the fact that only one year before Gottwald had proclaimed the beginning of a new era in Slovakia with the Košice Program's "Magna Charta" obviously did not concern his comrades in the CPS. They proclaimed "the necessity of a new agreement between the Slovak National Council [the main administrative body in Slovakia] and the government."[36] In order to achieve this, the communists had to secure the support of the Czech bourgeois parties. This was to prove easier than it might seem, because the Czechs were both not very well informed about the course of events in Slovakia and predisposed to believe that Slovakia "was a playground for reactionary, anti-state elements."[37] Evidence of this can be seen in the condescending attitude throughout the only Czech book devoted to current events in Slovakia during the period in question, Josef Dvořák's *Slovak Politics Yesterday and Today*. In it, the author proclaims the Czechs and Slovaks one nation and condemns the Catholic Church, tacitly comparing it to fascism.[38] The results of the elections certainly reinforced the impression among the Czech parties—only one of which did not explicitly call itself a "socialist" party—that the DP was a "reactionary" force whose power needed to be limited.[39]

The National Front government met three times in quick succession after the elections. In these the Czech bourgeois parties made a show of defending some measure of Slovak autonomy, before plunging into agreement with the communists: "The original tendencies of the Czech National Socialists and [People's Party representatives], just like [the Social Democrat] Majer to defend 'Slovak interests' to a certain degree were coy. . . . The decisive actor was not class solidarity with the Slovak bourgeoisie, but Czech chauvinism."[40] The result of these discussions was the "Third Prague Agreement." Among other limitations, the agreement subordinated Slovak local authorities and administrations to their central government equivalents, required legislation approved by Slovak representatives to gain approval from Prague, and allowed the central government to suspend acts of the Slovak administration "even though this goes beyond the content of their legal power."[41] In short, the document reduced the Slovak institutions to "little more than a regional administrative unit of the Prague-centered government."[42]

The Trial in Its Environment

The CPS could not "underestimate the immense importance" of Tiso's prosecution because, in the words of one CPS leader, "With this trial we are going to liquidate the whole reactionary Slovak past and the betrayal of the Slovak bourgeoisie and Slovak reaction."[43] There can be no doubt that after the elections the communists in both halves of Czechoslovakia engaged in all out war against the "reactionary, *Ľudák*" DP. Their goal, which they hoped to bring to victory in the battle over Tiso, was to split the more moderate "uprising" faction of the DP (which also contained many Protestants) from the conservative, Catholic *Ľudák* section of the party.[44] The supposed existence of the "secret promise" in the April Agreement by the DP to this conservative wing to ensure a light sentence for Tiso was to be the lever for splitting the party. By ensuring the levying and carrying out of the death penalty against Tiso, the communists hoped either that conservative Catholics would lose faith in the DP and abandon it for the CPS (which would have proven itself a more effective political actor), or that the two wings of the DP would fall into internal confrontation, disaffecting many of its voters. For this reason, "Of the political struggles with the forces of political Catholicism in Slovakia in 1946–47 the battle for the condemnation of Tiso and the execution of the proper punishment—the death penalty—was perhaps the most tenacious, [because] the consolidation of political relationships and the strengthening of the unity of the republic were dependent to a great extent on the result."[45]

Support for Tiso before the Trial

The Tiso case generated much interest even before the actual trial began. Tiso had fled with the German army to Austria, where he broadcast a speech to his homeland filled with expressions of anticommunism and Slovak nationalism that was to remain in the minds of communists and Czechs alike in the coming two years: "In the face of the assault of the Bolshevik army we understand our duty to defend for the Slovak nation its greatest treasure—the idea of the state independence of Slovakia. . . . We will work—you at home and us abroad—for as long as world opinion does not look positively on the natural striving of the Slovak nation for Slovaks to be the exclusive rulers of their home."[46] He was turned over to Czechoslovak authorities by allied troops at the end of October 1945. Tiso was flown to Bratislava, and photographs of him returning in handcuffs were displayed publicly by the communist-dominated National Committee in Bratislava. This caused the first of a long series of protest actions, when the display cases were smashed and the photographs inside them destroyed, apparently by a group of students. The next day an underground leaflet campaign in his defense commenced, which was quickly followed by the "Cross Action," in which people would wear small crucifixes on the lapels of their coats to show sympathy for the ex-president.[47]

Immediately after Tiso had been forcibly returned to Czechoslovakia, steps began to be taken by political circles in Slovak society to protect Tiso, as well as by the Church both inside and outside Slovakia. The first intercession on behalf of Tiso came, surprisingly, from the British ambassador in Prague, Philipp Nichols, who asked Justice Minister Drtina to recommend clemency should Tiso be condemned to death, because he feared that the execution of Tiso would "deepen [Slovak] mistrust and opposition toward the Czechs." He was followed shortly by Jozef Lettrich, the chairman of both the DP and the Slovak National Council, who Drtina promised to recommend lessening Tiso's sentence to life imprisonment should the Slovak National Council recommend such a step to him after the trial.[48] One month later, the Vatican asked that Tiso be held in a monastery rather than in prison until his trial and that the trial not be held in public, warning of the "danger of nationalistic disturbances."[49] Both of the Vatican's requests were eventually declined.

The mixture of Catholic and Slovak politics came to the fore in January 1946, when a group of Slovak bishops sent a letter to President Beneš. In it the bishops tactfully attempted to defend Tiso against the charges made against him, excusing him for acting in the interests of "the lesser evil." More important for our view of the political aspects of the trial, the bishops maintained that they had not written the letter because Tiso was a Catholic priest, but because "the solution of his personal question will have extensive influence on the thinking and behavior of part of the Slovak nation toward the renewal of the Czechoslovak Republic and its representatives." In light of this, they argued, it would "very much serve the peace of the nation if the case of Dr. Jozef Tiso were handled in a considerate way and not with ruthless harshness."[50] This concern for—or veiled threatening of—worsening relations on the part of Slovaks toward Czechs, and often of Slovak Catholics toward Slovak Protestants, became the primary argument for treating Tiso lightly. The CPS, however, rejected the intervention of the bishops into the affair and went so far as to request the Vatican to replace those church officers who had signed the letter, as they were "persons unacceptable to today's political regime."[51]

In the run up to the 1946 elections, the activity of Tiso supporters notably increased. "Long live Dr. Tiso" was written on walls and along streets throughout Slovakia, and praise of Tiso and the Slovak state interrupted a number of political meetings. Even more worrying for the CPS was the establishment of an underground "United Workers Union" in February, which published and distributed pamphlets containing calls for the "liberation" of Tiso from prison and the renewal of the Slovak state. They also called the communist-dominated Headquarters of the Slovak Trade Unions "a violent, totalitarian organization . . . completely under the thumb of the Communist Party," a political force whose worldview "is absolutely materialist and atheistic."[52] The stress these documents placed on Slovak independence, Christianity (understood as the Roman Catholic Church), and anticommunism had much resonance among the Slovak population, and Tiso was portrayed as the incarnation of these virtues. After the signing of the April Agreement, the expression of these sentiments became much closer to *Salonfähig*, as the *L'udáks* were in the ascendant. The anti-Czech and anticommunist tone of church religious and lay representatives in the period immediately preceding the elections has already been noted, as have the results of those elections, to which Tiso's response was "Glory to God, we won."[53]

Some example of the feeling among nationalist and Catholic— although attempting to separate the two is usually not particularly useful—groups in the wake of the elections can be seen in the disturbances surrounding the Bohemia/Moravia-Slovakia football match played on 30 May 1946, a scant four days after the elections. This classic example of bad timing (and bad choice of location—it was played in Bratislava) became an opportune venue for displays of resurgent Slovak nationalism. Before it even began, crowds gathered in front of the building of the DP daily, *Čas*, sang the hymn of the Slovak state, and called for Tiso's release.[54] Weak officiating at the match angered the crowd, after which developments took their own course: "After a wave of anti-Czech and anti-state shouting and the throwing of various objects, the crowd broke onto the field, wanting to insult the Czech players. A brawl broke out, into which soldiers, called by General Širica, mixed. Only through the use of strengthened units of the National Security force and fire department hoses did they succeed in regaining order."[55]

This outbreak of national chauvinism, coming on the same day that the CPCz and CPS had decided to launch war on the DP, shocked the communists into two responses. First, they organized, primarily through their control of the unions, a work stoppage the following afternoon. Factory workers and employees of state institutions met on Bratislava's main square, where they were joined by representatives of the communist-dominated uprising organizations. As a sign of how seriously the CPS took the matter, both Gustáv Husák and Štefan Bašt'ovanský (the party's general secretary) joined the communist head of the trade union movement on the dais. Although the crowd that was assembled numbered an impressive thirty thousand, this represented less than one-fifth of the population of the city, a far smaller proportion than the communists were normally able to muster in Prague.[56] Second, the union of printers refused to print the DP's primary organ, *Čas*, for four days, accusing it of creating the conditions for the events at the football match by being "oriented against the government program, against the unification of the trade unions, against the consolidation of relations . . . and serving the enemies of the nation and state."[57]

In the five months between these events and the beginning of the trial, the leaflet campaign in Tiso's defense continued, although its leaders continually warned against further public demonstrations.[58] More important, it was accompanied by maneuverings on a higher political level. The communists had wanted the trial to take place before the elections, hoping that by achieving a harsh verdict they could break the back of Slovak political Catholicism, but this proved unworkable due to the large number of witnesses who needed to be interviewed. Thereafter the conflict turned to the makeup of the National Tribunal that would oversee the case. The presidency was given to Igor Daxner, a Slovak communist and a Protestant, which raised howls of protest from Catholic representatives and even Protestant groups that continued through the first day of the trial, when the last of their objections was overruled.[59]

Despite the unfavorable composition of the tribunal, Catholic circles anticipated an acceptable result from the trial. They believed that Tiso would be found guilty and probably sentenced to death, but equally believed that he would be granted mercy by President Beneš and would be allowed to spent the remainder of his days in a monastery. To this end, the chairman of the DP, Jozef Lettrich, reports that he interceded with Beneš "to assure a Presidential reprieve for Tiso, if he were to be sentenced to death. Both before the trial and after it had started, the President promised to reprieve the death sentence."[60] They argued, as noted above, that Tiso should gain clemency because, in addition to the fact that he was a priest (and therefore regarded as almost infallible by Slovakia's rural Catholic population), executing Tiso would have the following negative consequences: (1) it would harm Czech-Slovak relations at a fragile time in their development, and perhaps lead to an outbreak of violence; (2) it would increase tension between Catholics and Protestants in Slovakia, and (3) it would create a martyr for the cause of Slovak nationhood. In the last of these they were supported by the most important Czech Catholic journal, which drew on Czech history to make its point.[61] In addition, Tiso's defenders found reason for hope in the lightness of the sentences given the members of the Czech wartime government described above. Going into the trial it is reasonable to assume that "60%–70% of the population [was] convinced that the trial will end well and that Tiso will not be condemned."[62]

The Trial

In preparation for the trial, the central government braced for a wave of demonstrations. It placed state security organs and army units on a higher state of alert and considered "the eventual use of Czech organs" despite the constant calls to the population by Catholic religious and lay leaders to avoid any provocation.[63] Even the CPS leader Gustáv Husák was forced to admit that the Catholic hierarchy had successfully acted to prevent the lower clergy from inciting the faithful.[64] As one of the results of the postelection Third Prague Agreement, Slovak-only army units had been disbanded, and during the reshuffle Slovak units were transferred to the Czech lands, and Czechs were sent to Slovakia. This was accomplished in time for the beginning of the Tiso trial, in what one DP representative called "a political resettlement of the army." In support of them, two hundred members of the central government's National Security Corps who had served in Slovakia before the war were sent from Prague to monitor events, and more than 150 were moved into the courthouse and surrounding buildings in order to ensure trial security.[65]

The communists were also busy in the days before the trial commenced. The resistance organizations, which were under communist control, held a mass meeting two weeks before the trial began. This concluded with a resolution in which they called for "the rapid carrying forward of the trial with the traitors to the Slovak nation Dr. Tiso, et.al. Let a hard and just sentence be given and carried out, as the honor of the nation demands and its greatest traitor deserves." This resolution was followed by others from local organization spread over the ensuing three months.[66] In addition, the Central Committee of the CPS met with its CPCz counterpart about the trial, deciding that the communists "must devote all necessary attention to its course, correct political guidance and successful conclusion," because "it will have a marked influence on the intraparty relations of the DP."[67]

When the trial finally began, on 2 December 1946, it commanded the interest of all Slovakia. It was broadcast live on the radio for the first day, but then the communists succeeded in having coverage suspended, after ensuring that the public had heard the reading of the charges against Tiso. Thereafter the public had to be content with following the events in the press, and the leading Catholic weekly registered a marked increase in subscriptions.[68] Presiding judge Daxner controlled the distribution of tickets to the trial, and according to one source, "even the newspapers had to be cautious in giving accounts of it because any journalist who proved too indulgent to the cause of the accused found himself barred from the courtroom; such was the fate of Mr. Pakan, editor of the *Times* (*Čas*), official newspaper of the Democratic party."[69] There was also significant interest from the foreign, especially Catholic, press with newspapers from several countries sending reporters to Bratislava. In the courtroom, the proceedings were translated simultaneously into Russian, French, English, and German for the journalists and diplomats from the USSR, Poland, Romania, Great Britain, and France.[70]

The trial ran for seventy-one days, until 19 March 1947, and included the testimony of dozens of witnesses. The court record ran to some 8,000 pages, weighing (with supporting documents) 700 kilograms, and the verdict alone totalled 255 pages. Tiso was charged with crimes under four main rubrics: (1) splitting the Czechoslovak Republic in 1938–39; (2) the Slovak fascist regime and support for the Nazi war effort; (3) the crushing of the Slovak National Uprising; and (4) crimes against humanity.[71] In this list of some seventy punishable acts, a few points are worthy of note. First is the stress placed on the crimes against Czechs and the Czechoslovak state. Coming first in the sets of charges (although probably because they were arranged roughly chronologically), Tiso's role in the (first) breakup of Czechoslovakia was the most important in the eyes of the Czechs.[72] Even in the list of Tiso's crimes against humanity, thievery from Czech citizens constituted the first two charges, followed only then by charges related to the deportations of the Slovak Jews. Second is the emphasis on "preparations for aggression against the first socialist state in the world, against the USSR" in the section on aiding the German war effort, which included charges of "entry into the Pact Against the Comintern" and "propaganda throughout the war against the USSR, in which the fabrications were expressed that the USSR threatens all of civilization and Christianity."[73] It seems evident from even the reading of the charges that there was no small measure of Czech national pride at stake in the case and that at least part of this was based on the communist and more "progressive" Czech political representation's desire to show its faithfulness to its great ally, the Soviet Union.

As we are concerned here with the political aspects of the trial, there is no need to go into great detail about the trial's development. Nonetheless, a few words are in order about some individual features. Perhaps the most exciting moment of the trial came when Archbishop Kmet'ko was called to testify by the prosecution. First, he entered the courtroom and shook hands with the defendant, drawing a rebuke from Chief Justice Daxner, and then proceeded to defend Tiso on all charges, admitting only that he perhaps should have stepped down from his post when the transport of the Jews commenced.[74] In Tiso's testimony, the complicated nature of his relationship to the Germans was revealed, as well as his Slovak nationalism and his complete rejection of communism (of the roughly three thousand political prisoners in wartime Slovakia, over half were communists).[75] Tiso's defense consisted of either claiming that he was unaware of events that were transpiring, or that he was acting in the interest of Slovakia by attempting to protect the nation from a greater evil by doing the lesser.[76] In his closing speech, Tiso expressed no regret, saying that he would do everything the same if he had to do it over again, and gave vent to expressions of Slovak nationalism and anticommunism. On 19 March 1947, the prosecutor demanded the death penalty for Tiso, and the panel of judges retired for a month to consider their verdict.

Maneuvers before the Handing Down of the Verdict

During the trial, although Slovakia remained largely calm as a result of constant reminders from the Catholic leadership to avoid "provocations,"[77] neither Tiso's supporters nor opponents were idle. In the following, only the most important events from the viewpoint of politics and interest-group pressure will be considered. These events have to be seen in the context of a larger atmosphere of tension, and of two sets of ongoing events. The first was a series of meetings of the communist-controlled resistance organizations, trade unions, and so on that produced a stream of largely identical resolutions calling for a "just" and "rigorous" verdict against the "great traitor" Tiso. The second was an ever increasing wave of petitions, letters, telegrams, circulated fliers, and slogans painted on walls, which spread over the land. The petitions, letters, and telegrams were of two types: those sent by official organs that stressed the consolidation of political relations in Slovakia, religious tolerance, and cooperation between Czechs and Slovaks, and those sent by individuals that simply asked the recipient to help in the Tiso affair.[78] The slogans, often repeated in anonymous leaflets, were more blatant and in addition to anti-Czech, anti-Semitic, and anticommunist content proclaimed "Long live Tiso," "Release Tiso," "Who murders Tiso, murders the Slovak Nation," and so forth. Some were tied to more political issues, such as "We want Catholic schools," and "We gave you [the DP] our vote, get Tiso out of the clink for us," which obviously referred to the "secret clause" in the April Agreement. Prečan reports that although the security organs arrested dozens of people for propagating these slogans, not one was convicted, which seems to indicate some sympathy for Tiso among the local judiciary.[79] Again, as in the L'udák preelection campaigning, there was both an explicit and implicit web of relationships between anti-Czech (Slovak nationalist), anticommunist, and Catholic rhetoric.

The largest display of support for Tiso occurred on 19 March, the name day for those, like Tiso, bearing the name Joseph. Post offices were flooded with cards, telegrams, and packages for the prisoner that to the outrage of local communists were often delivered even though postage had not been paid.[80] The only public demonstrations in support of Tiso during his trial also took place this day. The largest of these took place in Piešt'any, a medium-sized town northeast of Bratislava. A group of 80–100 women set out from church services on the outskirts of town toward the center. Along the way their ranks swelled to between 1,200 and 1,500 people, overwhelmingly women but also including some soldiers,[81] singing national and religious hymns and clamoring for Tiso's release. A delegation of them met with the head of the County National Committee and called for Tiso to be set free, while another delegation was sent to Bratislava to congratulate Tiso on his name day. The demonstration was broken up by members of the security forces, and twelve women and three Catholic religious functionaries were arrested. Similar demonstrations took place that day and the day following in at least three other towns in the same region.[82]

There was a serious response to these events both on the part of the CPS and in the deliberations of the central government. Resistance organizations orchestrated a demonstration in Bratislava that attracted ten thousand participants and speakers from all political parties. The DP representative, while apparently not condemning the Piešt'any demonstration or Tiso directly, maintained that his party stood for a united Czechoslovakia.[83] In the wake of this demonstration the Catholic hierarchy, which had consistently warned against taking their struggle to the streets, attempted to paint the demonstrations as part of a plot to discredit the church. This obvious attempt at damage control fit well with their larger strategy of painting a picture of Slovakia in which, as one headline put it, "Dark Forces Are Striving to Expel the Church and Religion from the World and Life."[84] In the meeting of the central government, the Czech parties were quick to condemn the Piešt'any events, and larger components of the State Security Forces and even army units were placed at the disposition of the Slovak commissioner of justice.[85] The CPS was especially keen on the introduction of increased central government power in Slovakia, hoping by this to weaken the forces of political Catholicism generally, and of the DP particularly. To this end they urged the government "to intervene with full weight into Slovak affairs and to force respect for government power."[86]

These expressions of public sympathy for Tiso were followed by renewed attempts on the part of leading figures in the DP and the Catholic hierarchy to ensure presidential clemency in the case of a guilty verdict and the levying of the death penalty. During the month-long hiatus between closing arguments and the handing down of the verdict, Slovak bishops and representatives of the DP began to apply pressure on President Beneš. On 21 March a DP leader met with the president, and after telling him that he had "an uncommon opportunity to tie contentious Slovak Catholicism to him by an act of mercy" tacitly attempted to make a deal with him: "The bishops offer a calm Slovak people."[87] The following week, the Slovak bishops convened in Trnava for a conference that resulted in the dispatch of a letter to the president in which essentially the same offer was made. The bishops warned that the execution of Tiso "would shake Slovakia to its foundations, and we do not know when it would be possible to overcome the breach caused by it," and counseled that "the granting of clemency to Dr. Jozef Tiso would certainly strengthen Slovak Catholics' faithfulness to the state."[88] The bishops' letter was accompanied by further apostolic and DP directions to the Slovak people "not to demonstrate and not to come into confrontation with governmental offices."[89]

Endgame: The Decision over Clemency

The guilty verdict and the levying of the death penalty were handed down on 15 April 1947, commencing a series of complex maneuvers on both the Slovak and Czechoslovak levels. Before moving into the sphere of high politics, however, a discrepancy in dates needs to be addressed. The verdict was announced a week before the intended time, and it is impossible not to see the hand of communist maneuvering in this. Those supporting Tiso anticipated a guilty verdict and, as we have seen, were maneuvering to secure presidential clemency. On 2 April, the communist presiding judge, Daxner, had promised to inform Lettrich, who was both the head of the DP and the chairman of the Slovak National Council, of the verdict before it was due to be handed down on 22 April. Instead, Daxner announced on 14 April that the verdict would be announced the following morning and refused Lettrich's plea to know the verdict beforehand, a move that took Tiso's supporters by surprise and disrupted the timing of their plans. According to information gleaned from the minutes of a Ministry of Justice meeting, the sudden change in the date for announcing the verdict was a result of the "engagement of G. Husák and V. Široký," the two leading figures of the CPS.[90] In addition to throwing Tiso's supporters off balance, the communists desired an earlier date for the handing down of the verdict for another reason. The Czech trial of the head of the former "Protectorate of Bohemia and Moravia" government, Rudolf Beran, had been taking place simultaneously with that of Tiso. Given the light sentences given to other members of that government, CPS leaders required that "at any price the verdict in the trial of Beran not be given before the verdict against Tiso," lest it become a precedent. This proved to be a wise calculation, as Beran was sentenced six days after Tiso to the comparatively light sentence of twenty years' imprisonment.[91]

According to the laws governing mercy pleas, the course of events would conform to a strict plan. First, the defendant needed to officially petition for mercy, a step that was taken immediately in Tiso's case. Second, the National Tribunal was obligated to make its recommendation, which was against the granting of clemency. Then the Slovak commissioner of the interior, a DP representative, made his recommendation in favor of a reduction to life imprisonment. From this point the official organs had forty-eight hours to decide on the request, with two stages left in the process. The first was a formal vote in the executive committee of the Slovak National Council, and the second was the decision of the president of the Republic, Edvard Beneš.

Neither of these last two crucial steps in the process was carried out in as straightforward a manner as the legal schema indicates. In the five-member executive committee of the Slovak National Council, the DP held a three-to-two advantage, so there was wide expectation that the committee would recommend the granting of clemency and a reduction of the sentence to life imprisonment with an eye toward transfer from prison to a monastery at some time in the future. When the issue came to a vote, however, a DP representative named Polák abstained, leaving the committee deadlocked. Although no concrete evidence for Polák's decision has yet been brought to light, two possible explanations exist. The less likely possibility is that he was collaborating with the communists, since he joined the CPS after the communists' assumption of power in February 1948. More likely, however, is that he was caught between two ultimately irreconcilable forces within the DP. As a DP representative, his party allegiance led him toward voting for clemency, but he was also the president of the Union of Soldiers of the Slovak National Uprising, a group firmly committed to Tiso's execution.[92] The committee argued until the time constraint forced them to pass the appeal for clemency on to the president without a recommendation in either direction.

Here the "Tiso question" took another turn, for although constitutionally the responsibility for deciding on the granting of clemency lay with President Beneš alone, he decided to refer the case to the Czechoslovak National Front government.[93] In a letter to the prime minister, the CPCz's Gottwald, Beneš discerned two separate issues at stake. After vehemently condemning Tiso and applauding the work of the tribunal, Beneš delimited what he called the "human" issue, on the basis of which he was *"willing to grant [Tiso] clemency."* Second, however, was the constitutional and political question, and this is where the National Front ministers were brought in:

> According to the wording of the still valid constitution, my granting of clemency requires the countersignature of a responsible minister. Since the Tiso case is undoubtedly one of a political character, the government as a whole will pass a resolution on the granting or non-granting of clemency. I must therefore wait to see the resolution of the government in this matter, and the recommendation signed by the Minister of Justice and submitted to me. If this recommendation will read in favor of the granting of clemency, I repeat what I have just said, *that I will grant clemency to the condemned Tiso in accordance with the government* resolution.
>
> If, however, clemency is not recommended, there is for me, as I said, a constitutional question. Should I give clemency to Tiso, who has been sentenced to death, and thereby stand against the standpoint of the government (or of its majority)? By this there would be created a situation in which there is a discrepancy between the president of the republic and the government. This could have marked political consequences for the future development of political events in the state and could lead to a governmental or even to a constitutional crisis. . . . That is why I consider it necessary in the interests of the state and the calm development of the republic *that in this question full unity is observed between us.*[94]

By presenting his arguments but at the same time assuring them that he would act in accord with its decision, Beneš in effect handed over his decision to the National Front government. A shrewd tactician, Beneš could calculate the votes in the government and surmise that clemency would not be recommended. This is fully in accord with Prečan's judgment that, despite the promises to the DP's Lettrich, "[f]or Beneš the condemning of Tiso was such a personal matter and such a matter of prestige" that the granting of clemency was unlikely.[95]

The special meeting of the government took place on 17 April in an atmosphere marked by increased activity on both sides. The tide of telegrams and visits reached flood proportions, as both sides attempted to influence the decision. A total of 150 telegrams were received in the president's office from resistance organizations, local communist organizations, and so on demanding that the sentence be carried out. Three hundred fifteen telegrams were received on Tiso's behalf, including ones from each of the Slovak bishops and representatives of the Protestant and Eastern Orthodox leadership.[96] In concert with this, the Vatican sent a representative to discuss the matter with the president's office, but refused to intercede to a large extent in defending Tiso's life.[97]

The course of the extraordinary meeting of the government was predicated on the agreement between the DP leader Jozef Lettrich and Justice Minister Drtina, who represented the Czech National Socialist Party. Drtina had promised Lettrich that if Tiso were sentenced to death and the Slovak National Council recommended the granting of clemency, he and his party would recommend that the government grant clemency.[98] In the meeting, Drtina found himself in a difficult position, as the Slovak National Council had passed the request for clemency on to the government without recommendation. Drtina proposed that the matter be sent back to the Slovak National Council, and the government wait for it to reach some sort of a decision. The sharp debate that took place over this suggestion revealed just how divided the government was: the CPCz, CPS, and Social Democrats stood on one side, and the DP, Czech National Socialists, and (Roman Catholic) People's Party on the other. A vote on returning the matter to Slovakia was finally taken that progressed along these party lines and failed thirteen votes to ten.[99] In the wake of this, Drtina felt that he had fulfilled his promise to Lettrich, and when the vote on whether to recommend clemency was taken, the National Socialists voted against clemency, leaving the DP and the People's Party alone in recommending clemency. President Beneš accepted the recommendation against granting clemency, and, despite a frantic series of last-minute phone calls to Beneš by Lettrich, Tiso was executed on the morning of 18 April 1947.[100]

In the intragovernmental debate there was universal agreement that Tiso was guilty as charged and that the sentence of death was correct. The source of contention lay in the political decision on whether to carry it out or not, a decision seen as over "the fate and future of Slovakia." More important, it reveals crucial facets of both the troubled nature of Czech-Slovak relations in the immediate postwar period, and of the changes in the Czech—as the dominant nation—conception of the state's character. On the first of these, both sides agreed that the goal was to strengthen Czech-Slovak unity, although they each advocated a different path toward this end. The DP, and to a large extent the Czech People's Party, stressed that clemency should be granted primarily to strengthen Slovak loyalty to Czechoslovakia and avoid creating a martyr to Slovak nationalism, for "[i]f you leave a seed on the surface, it shrivels and nothing grows from it. If, however, it is planted into the soil, then it germinates and a plant can grow." The communists and Social Democrats saw the granting of clemency as both a backing down to Slovak nationalism and a clear blow to the unity of the state.

Most notable is the concern expressed by many Czech ministers that the deadlock of the Slovak National Council represented an attempt "to pass the responsibility for the decision to the Czechoslovak government, on which the odium should fall." They suspected that a judgment against clemency was designed to cause, in the words of one noncommunist minister, "gossip that the Czechs are evil and did not grant clemency" such that Slovaks could "abuse the government decision to blacken the Czech nation." This Czechocentrism was also evident in the comments of one communist minister, who seemed to endorse the already rejected notion that the Czechs and Slovaks were one nation. Similarly, the only of Tiso's crimes that was mentioned by all the Czech parties (with the notable exception of the People's Party) was the breaking up of the state, which had made him the "most vile enemy of the state and the [Czech] nation." In response to this, one DP minister warned his Czech colleagues not to repeat the mistakes of the interwar republic, in which politicians "saw Slovakia as they wanted to see it and not as it really was." In the postwar, he continued, it was important to realize that "The majority of Slovaks, even if it is the worse part of the population, see in Tiso only the former head of the state and a popular figure." In order to successfully reconstitute the state, a gesture had to be made to this majority, and the DP minister argued for a strategy of "[c]lemency for Tiso, but act[ing] sharply against the Tisoites."

The second most notable feature of the government debate was the role played by socialism and the world's leading force for socialism, the USSR. As we have already seen, in addition to the nationalist suspicions Czechs had of Slovaks, the Czech political class had taken measures curbing Slovak self-administration after the convincing DP victory in the 1946 elections largely because of fears that the region was a refuge for "reactionaries." These fears revealed themselves in two specific ways. The first was the Czech ministers' (in this case a Social Democrat's) concern that "What would the millions of Soviet citizens say . . . if Czechoslovakia were to give clemency to one of the main criminals? What moral authority would our alliance with the Soviet Union have in the future?. . . [O]ur granting of clemency would discredit us in the eyes of our allies, the Slavic states. We would be especially seriously discredited in the eyes of the Soviet Union."[101] To this, the DP responded that the USSR had not complained after the light sentences given to the members of the Czech Protectorate government, which brought the fire of Klement Gottwald, who replied that the Protectorate had never sent soldiers to fight against the USSR, which he saw as the "sacramental" difference.

Perhaps the most surprising statement in the entire meeting came from a leader of the Communist Party's most serious opponent in the Czech lands, the National Socialist Party. Just before the final vote was taken, Hubert Ripka pled with the ministers of the DP and the Czech People's Party to at least abstain from voting, such that the recommendation against the granting of clemency could be seen as unopposed. His argumentation sounds as if drawn from a handbook on communist rhetoric. He warned that there were "forces that are working, in various parts of the world, for disruption in Slovakia and through this for a disruption in the entire republic." For him, the struggle against the "enemy ideology" would be continuous, and vigilance must be maintained because "these forces will always look for the weakest points, in order to attempt to cause disruption." The only minister who responded to the stunning plea directly could only express the hope that regime was secure enough in itself that it "would not have to fear ideological opponents."[102]

In conclusion, three main points can be made based on the deliberations of the government. First, the argument made by Catholic political and religious leaders fell on deaf ears among the Czech government ministers. In addition to their traditional Czech anti-clericalism, these ministers saw Tiso's position as a priest as far secondary to his position as a traitor to the idea of a unitary Czechoslovak state. Second, there was no small measure of Czech national pride tied up in the decision not to grant clemency. This is not to say that it was a matter of revenge or that it was the Czechs who condemned Tiso. Rather it is to point out that in the eyes of the noncommunist ministers from whom he might have gained support, his main crime lay in leading the secession of Slovakia from the Czechoslovak Republic in 1939. Finally, the conservatism of the DP made its position in favor of the granting of clemency weaker because the Czech parties (with the exception of the People's Party) decidedly conceived of themselves as socialist. For them, carrying out the death sentence had implications—both for the securing of an as yet vaguely defined socialism in Czechoslovakia as a whole and for proving the state's loyalty to the Soviet Union—that could not escape either the Czech or the Slovak political elite.

All three of these divergent aspects between Czech and Slovak thinking in the Tiso case were only made more explicit by Tiso's final statement. In his short "message to the Slovak nation," he again played the religious, national, and anticommunist cards. He urged Slovaks to maintain the principle *"For God and for the Nation,"* which he regarded "the explicit command of God." In conjunction with this, he declared that he considered himself "first of all a martyr to God's law," by which he implied that he was being punished for serving God and the Slovak nation's interests. Finally, he maintained that he was also "a martyr in the defense of Christianity against bolshevism, against which our nation must defend itself in all possible ways." In this short statement, then, Tiso cast in a positive light the attributes of anticommunism, Slovak separatism, and Catholic conviction that had made him anathema to the Czech political elite, but that had been the coin of the successful DP election campaign.[103]

Conclusions

The threat of a potentially violent response to Tiso's execution never materialized. Although a few scattered demonstrations were reported, public acts were limited to the ringing of church bells, the lighting of candles, and the holding of special masses and prayer vigils.[104] Although the exact extent and scale of disapproval is impossible to assess, this outward calm does not mean that there was no disappointment, and the constant efforts of DP leaders and the Roman Catholic hierarchy to maintain public calm should be seen as largely responsible for the maintenance of public order. Nonetheless, some forty thousand subscribers to the DP daily, *Čas*, canceled their subscriptions within days of the execution and some younger members of the party called for its representatives to withdraw from the government. In response, the party attempted to counter the disappointment of this section of its supporters in two ways. First, they attempted to publish an article in *Čas* defending their actions in the Czechoslovak government debate. This issue of the paper was confiscated in many areas as provocative, and the party was forced to inform its supporters of its position through the printing and distribution of a special leaflet. Only on 27 April could the *Catholic News* publish—under the title "They Condemned and Hung Dr. Jozef Tiso"—the comments of the Vatican's *Osservatore Romano* condemning the execution.[105] Second, using their majority in the Slovak National Council, DP members succeeded in passing a resolution ousting Presiding Justice Daxner from his position at the

National Tribunal. His ouster was only temporary, however, as it was overturned in a session of the Czechoslovak government shortly thereafter. This was done despite the fact that the decision lay fully in the competence of the council, and only served to widen the gap between the DP and the Czech noncommunist parties.[106]

For the communists, the execution of Tiso and the maintenance of Daxner's position were hailed as great victories. The course of events admittedly did not cause the open rupture between the "uprising" and "*L'udák*" wings of the DP that the communists had hoped for. It had, however, weakened the party and revealed that pressure, if applied in such a way as to assure the support of the Czech bourgeois parties, could yield even larger political gains in Slovakia. One month after Tiso's execution, the CPS threatened to withdraw from the Slovak National Council, claiming that the DP had extensive ties with underground, "antistate" organizations and that the situation threatened national security. In conjunction with concerted attacks on the two general secretaries of the DP, the CPS used the state security forces to concoct an anti-state "conspiracy" in Slovakia, as a result of which a wide-ranging anti-DP purge of the administrative apparatus was begun in September 1947.[107] In the wake of the Cominform meeting of that month, the CPS declared a crisis in Slovakia and called for the exclusion of the DP from the Slovak National Council, citing its unreliability and presenting largely fabricated evidence of its involvement with "conspirators." Although they were unsuccessful in completely removing the DP from the council, with the help of the Czech bourgeois parties they achieved its reorganization such that the DP lost the majority it had gained through the ballot box.

Looking back at the whole range of developments associated with the trial and execution of Jozef Tiso, a number of important conclusions can be reached. On the Slovak level, the victory the CPS won in the struggles over Tiso and Daxner, as we have seen, encouraged it toward even more aggressive and confrontational tactics. The success of these—largely a result of Czech noncommunists' unwillingness to support the DP but also of demoralization and conflict in the DP ranks—culminated in the ease with which the communists could remove the DP from the Slovak National Council in February 1948. Second, the conclusion cannot be escaped that among a certain proportion of Slovaks the Czechs and the communists were considered responsible for the judicial murder of the primary symbol of Slovak national consciousness and the sharp curtailment of Slovak self-administration. After 1948, and in light of the way the communists had risen to total power, the categories of "Czech" and "communist" became conflated in the minds of many Slovaks. Still today, there are many who, with not unsubstantial justification, maintain that communist dictatorship was forced on them against their will by Prague.

On the Czechoslovak level, there were two primary results of the machinations surrounding the developments in Slovakia. In the short term, the Tiso case revealed a rift between the DP and Czech noncommunists, severely hindering the possibility of creating a common front to oppose communist strivings for total power. As Paul Zinner has noted, the tension brought by the Tiso trial "retarded—if it did not altogether prevent—efforts by democratic parties to work out a joint, comprehensive program of action."[108] The communists undoubtedly learned from the postelection decision to limit Slovak autonomy and the debate over the Tiso case that the Czech bourgeois parties could be seen as allies on issues concerning Slovakia, a realization they promptly exploited. It was only after the disastrous events surrounding the Czechoslovak rejection of Marshall Plan aid that the Czech National Socialist Party at least "better understood the necessity" of striving for "coordination" with the DP. As the Slovak "conspiracy" became more and more transparently a fabrication, Czech noncommunists hurried to forge links with the DP, as they began to perceive the communist threat as more dangerous than the rightist one emanating from Slovakia.[109] This is not to imply that had Czech noncommunists acted more quickly Czechoslovakia could have kept itself out of the Soviet orbit, as noncommunist forces had managed to substantially close ranks before the February 1948 crisis. The question remains, however, whether resistance to communist domination would have been stiffer had the noncommunists been able to act in a concerted fashion before the state was on the brink of dictatorship.[110]

The second was a deepening of the mutual mistrust between Czechs and Slovaks. From the Czech side, the DP and Catholic support for Tiso, matched by a not inconsiderable level of public sympathy for his case, caused grave concern. At the very least it reinforced a perception of persistent Slovak unreliability toward the Czechoslovak Republic and raised the specter of an intractable fascism on Czechoslovak soil. From the Slovak side, the conscious erosion of Slovak self-administration in the months after the 1946 elections was a direct result of Czech and communist collaboration that touched a raw nerve. It smacked of Czech condescension and particularly rankled Slovaks whose self-confidence and self-esteem had been raised by the experience of managing their own state through six years of turbulence and war. The limitations on Slovak autonomy, in the words of Joseph Rothschild, "reimposed a chronic strain on Czech-Slovak relations that was later to yield a bitter harvest in the 'spring year' of 1968. Compounding this source of bitterness was the treason trial . . . of Monsignor [sic] Josef Tiso."[111] For both sides, the trial and execution of Tiso provided an enduring symbol for both Czechs and Slovaks of Slovakia's national strivings and its anticommunist, even reactionary, political base, one which diverged widely from conditions in the Czech lands.

The cause of Roman Catholicism, politically viewed, also suffered from the execution of Jozef Tiso. Beyond the obvious weakness shown by the failure to defend Tiso's life, the church placed itself irreconcilably on the side of the implacable enemies of communism. After the communist takeover, it was to pay a heavy price for this in both the Czech lands and Slovakia. The communists, with the support of Protestant churches, launched an attack on both the church as an institution and individuals within it, such that the result by 1953 was "a shattered and crippled church." In the most serious two show trials, in 1950 and 1951, three Slovak bishops were given essentially life sentences, and a set of eight Czech religious officials was sentenced to a total of 142 years imprisonment, while a further one was sentenced to life.[112]

Finally, one of the crucial lessons to understand from the limitation of Slovak self-administration and the condemnation of Tiso and the wartime Slovak Republic by both the immediate postwar regime and especially under communist rule is that it did not eradicate Slovak nationalism or the image of Tiso from the minds of many Slovaks. Since the "velvet revolution" of 1989, a group of radical Slovak nationalists have kept Tiso's name in the media, attempting to claim at least part of his heritage, rehabilitate his reputation, and resuscitate respect for the state he led. Some measure of the controversy that Tiso still generates can be seen in the schizophrenia of the contemporary Slovak population. Since 1989, a majority of Slovaks have regularly viewed both the wartime state and the uprising against it positively, and Tiso's name has appeared on lists of both the most adored and most despised of Slovak historical figures. While the schizophrenia can be explained by the postcommunist resurgence of Slovak national feeling—"Slovaks did it, therefore it was good"—in such conditions one can expect the debate over Tiso and his heritage to continue far into the future.

Notes

1. This with the exception of the most easterly portion of the prewar state, Sub-Carpathian Ruthenia, which was ceded to the Soviet Union.
2. The only serious scholarly work available in English is Jelinek.
3. Although he was tried together with two other high-ranking representatives of the wartime Slovak state, Tiso was viewed as the symbol of the state, and was the focus of the political machinations surrounding the trial.
4. See, for example, the following unrepentant disquisitions by Slovak émigrés in America: Stephan Blasko, *Slovakia in Blood and Shackles* (Passaic N.J., 1954; Josef Paučo, *Christian Slovakia under Communism* (Valparaiso, Ind., 1959; M. Šprinc, *Slovenská republika, 1939–49* (Scranton, Pa., 1949); Josef Paučo, ed., *Dr. Josef Tiso o sebe* (Passaic, N.J., 1952); Josef Kirschbaum, *Slovakia: Nation at the Crossroads of Central Europe* (New York, 1960); and Konstantin Čulen, *Po*

Svätopukovi druhá naša hlava [After Svätopluk Our Second Leader] (Middletown, Pa., 1947). Czechoslovak publications of the same period include Tibor Halečka, *Ľudáctvo a náboženstvo* [Populism and Religion] Martin (1957); Maria Sedlaková, *Krycie meno Jozef: O zločinoch príslušníkov POHG. Reportáže, proces, dokumenty* [Code Name Josef: On the Crimes of the Members of the POHG.] (Bratislava, 1959); Andrej Siracký, *Klerofašistická ideologia ľudáctva* [The Clerico-Fascist Ideology of the Ľudáks] (Bratislava, 1955); and Imrich Stanek, *Zrada a pad: Hlinkovšťi seperatisté a tak zvaný slovenský stát* [Betrayal and Fall: The Hlinka Separatists and the So-Called Slovak State] (Prague, 1958).

5. Drtina II/1, 189–92. Citation 191. Drtina notes an important distinction in that the Soviets demanded a certain number, while the Communists did not, and indicates that there would have been even less than two demands for the death penalty had it not been for Soviet pressure. All translations in this piece are by the author.

6. Kaplan (1992), 11, and Document 4. The Czech National Socialists and People's Party appeared more aware of this divergence. The first postwar government was drawn entirely from the ranks of the wartime exiles, rather than from the ranks of those who had remained in the country during the occupation.

7. Beinert was given three years, Krejčí twenty-five and Kamenický ten. See Foustka 640–1.

8. Drtina suspects that these were prepared in advance, as many came on the day of the verdict's announcement. Of the 318 protest documents, 139 were from Communist Party organizations and 134 from Communist-dominated factory organizations. Drtina II/1, 195.

9. Kaplan (1992) Documents 10 and 11.

10. Drtina II/1, 188

11. See, for example, the CPS leader Laco Novomeský's comment in 1968 that "We were never opposed to a Slovak state as an autonomous home of the Slovak people. On the contrary, we engaged in conflict—occasionally armed conflict—precisely because it was not autonomous but, from the very beginning, only a product of Nazi machinations and, to the very end, tied to its fascist origins. In other words, we were opposed to the fascist state *as it existed*, not *because it existed*." Liehm, 111.

12. Leff, 186.

13. Article Six of the Košice program. See *Program* 13–4.

14. Gottwald (1955a), 365, 379. During the period of the Nazi-Soviet Pact, the Communist representation in Moscow argued that "The slogan 'The Renewal of Czechoslovakia' today hides imperialistic and anti-Soviet plans," and that communist strategy should be "Among Czechs to fight for the renewal of national and state freedom. Among Slovaks to fight for the full sovereignty of the present Slovak state." Cited in Falt'an, 116. Even after the end of the Pact, the CPS was slow to resurrect the demand for the reconstitution of the state. This stands in marked contrast to the London exile group headed by President Edvard Beneš. Beneš' demand for the repudiation of Munich and all that followed had the effect of annuling the Slovak autonomy agreement (October 1938), and statements by his colleagues supporting the idea that the Slovaks had "stuck a knife in the back

of the Czechs" point out the differences in the ways in which the entire Slovak question was viewed in London and Moscow. See, for example, *Dokumenty*, Documents 124 and 157.

15. This was the result of an agreement in the exile government that excluded parties deemed to have collaborated with the Germans during the war. There were only four permitted parties in the Czech lands: the CPCz, the Czech National Socialists, the Social Democrats, and the People's Party. Therefore, the Communists were the only political force allowed to campaign across the nation.

16. Jarošová et.al., 18 and 42. Only 9.5 percent of the economically active population was employed by industrial concerns having more than fifty workers. Kaplan (1968), 131.

17. M. R. Myant reports that the change was done in the absence of the CPS chairman, and that Viliam Široký was "sent as the representative of the [CPCz] Central Committee to take over the leading position in the [CPS]." Myant, 99.

18. Leff, 95.

19. Myant, 94. Already in August 1945 Gottwald pointed to the influence of the clergy as especially baneful in his admonishment of his Slovak colleagues. Gottwald (1955b), 107–108.

20. *Čas.* 21 October 1945. See also Vartíková (1962), 88–9.

21. This despite the minuscule support the party would have, as witnessed by the fact that the Bratislava district committee of the new "Party of Labor" (it was forbidden to call itself "Social Democratic") could muster only 206 members more than five months after its inception. See Pleva, 96–98. Although it was made explicit the party would not directly compete with the CPS, the communists naturally saw that it would weaken "the unity of the working class" and accused the instigators of serving only their own ends. The DP remained out of this fray because it was concerned with its attempt to extend itself into the Czech lands. See Vartíková (1962), 89–94.

22. On the "Party of State Unity," see Vartíková (1968), 72–73, 75. They apparently withdrew when the leadership of the Czech Socialists decided to support the foundation of a Catholic-based party. Prečan, 98. On the People's Party, see Prečan, 83.

23. *Ľudáks* were former supporters of Hlinka's Slovak People's Party (Hlinkova slovenská ľudová strana), the interwar Catholic Slovak Party that was the state party during the wartime Slovak Republic.

24. Prečan 81. In view of the election returns, it is interesting to note that Msgr. Forni, a Vatican representative sent to observe the situation in Czechoslovakia, completely misjudged the situation in the country. He estimated that the Czech land, with its numerous middle class, were immune to "communist influence," while less developed Slovakia was ripe for "devouring by communism." In light of this, he recommended against the creation of a Catholic party in Slovakia, slowing the early stages of this plan. See Prečan, 84–85.

25. For details of this fascinating episode, see Kaplan (1993a), 58, or the same author's article in *Studie* (Rome) 6:54 (1977): 453–56.

26. The Czech National Socialists' decision to back this wing had led to the disintegration of the attempt to form the "Party of State Unity."

27. In the name, "Christian" was seen as violating the prohibition against

confessional parties, and "Republican" as recalling an interwar conservative party that had been banned.

28. The story of the Christian Republican Party can be found, with substantial variation, in Prečan, 97–99 and Vartíkova (1968), 75–77.

29. A text purporting to be the "minutes" of the agreement appeared in the United States in the émigré Slovak newspaper *Slovák v Amerike* on 10 December 1946. Although extensive, it contains no mention of a deal concerning Tiso. The article is reprinted in Prečan, appendix 9. On the Agreement, see Prečan, 100–08, Vartíková (1962), 105–08, Falt'an, 220, or Kaplan (1987), 56.

30. See Prečan, 109–24. The citations are from pages 109 and 115.

31. According to Kaplan and Sláma, the DP "could bring in almost all of the voters of the Agrarian Party and also ca. 70 percent of the voters of the former Hlinka Party," i.e., *Ľudáks*. Kaplan and Sláma, 69.

32. Prečan argues that the remainder was made up of "honorable working people, convinced democrats and patriots, who had not yet found the way to the Communist Party and had only one real choice." Prečan 127.

33. The leading Czech National Socialist, Hubert Ripka, viewed the DP victory as "Against all hypotheses" and attributed it to the April Agreement, while Drtina called the result a "surprise." Ripka, 58; Drtina II/1, 167.

34. Gottwald (1957), 80–81, 85.

35. Jaroš and Jarošová, 191–92.

36. Gustav Husák and Laco Novomeský, in Jaroš and Jarošová, 157.

37. Kaplan (1987), 91. Eva Hartmannová has pointed out the lack of interest in developments in Slovakia in the pages of the leading noncommunist weekly. Hartmannová, 105–08.

38. See Dvořák, esp. pp. 74–75 and 78–81.

39. See, for example, the Czech National Socialist internal memo that went so far as to claim that "The struggle over Slovakia will not be carried out between Prague and Bratislava, but Prague and Rome. A settlement with Rome, which would call for extreme concessions, would be the most reliable path to the liquidation of the Slovak question." *Cesta*, 178.

40. Barto, 162. This carefully researched work also contains several fascinating quotes from various Czech noncommunist leaders revealing a remarkable degree of condescension toward, and frustration with, the persistent "Slovak problem." See esp. pp. 161–69 and 196–97.

41. For the text of all three agreements, the comparison of which reveals the depth of the shift in power toward the center, see Rákoš and Rudohradský, 550–57.

42. Rothschild, 92.

43. Viliam Široký at a meeting of the Central Committee of the CPS, 16 December 1946. Vartíková (ed.), 500–01.

44. In communist terminology, the communists went on the offensive in the Tiso case because "the tempo of differentiation in the DP did not correspond to the needs of revolutionary development of Slovakia." Jaroš and Jarošová, 191.

45. Prečan 131. Similar comments are to be found throughout both the communist and the noncommunist literature. See, for example, Huml's comment

that the trial "creates a dividing line in the development of Slovak society," or Vartiková's judgment that it was a "watershed." Huml, 125; Vartíková (1962), 109.

46. Huml, 127.

47. Pleva, 94–95. Prečan, 134.

48. Drtina II/2, 295–98.

49. Kaplan (1992), Document 14.

50. Ibid., Document 16.

51. Vartíková (1968), 73.

52. On the slogan painting, see Prečan 136. On the United Workers Union, see Jarošová, Škurlo, and Vartíková, 105.

53. *Národná obroda* (29 May 1946), cited in Prečan, 126.

54. Jarošová, Škurlo, and Vartíková, 109.

55. Pleva, 109–10

56. The figure appears in Jarošová, Škurlo, and Vartíková, 109. The population of Bratislava (without suburbs) in 1946 was 154,226 (Pleva, 92). When one takes into account the traditional communist strategy of busing in protestors from surrounding towns, the figure loses some of its immediate impact.

57. Pleva, 111.

58. See, for example, *Čas.* (1 December 1946), cited in Jaroš and Jarošová 192–93.

59. The vice presidency was given to Ľudovit Benada, a Czech, and member of the CPCz Central Committee. The DP argued that Daxner was not an unbiased observer and raised questions about his health, while Protestants were worried about the potential negative effects on relations between Protestants and Catholics. See Kaplan (1992), Document 20. These objections are maintained to this day by several Slovak émigré writers. For example, see Vnuk passim.

60. Prečan, 140. Lettrich, 244.

61. The Czech Catholics used the example of the Czech Bohemian nobles executed on Old Town Square after the Battle of White Mountain in 1621: "If he [Ferdinand II] had not hung them, we would look at them today as average enough politicians. Certainly they would not belong in the national Pantheon. However, because they fell on the gallows, they became heroes and martyrs. History supposedly does not repeat itself, but we can and should learn from it." They also noted the importance of priests in Slovakia, questioned Daxner's independence, and argued that "The future development of our relationship with the Slovaks will depend on [the trial] to a marked extent." ak. [Adolf Kajpr] "Začátek procesu" [The Beginning of the Trial] *Katolík* 9:28 (1946), 1.

62. This was reported to Beneš' office 4 December 1946. See Kaplan (1992), 28. The commissioner of the interior in Slovakia Ferjenčík reported the optimism springing from the Czech trial on 28 November 1946. See Kaplan (1992), Document 23.

63. See Ibid., Document 22.

64. See Ibid., Document 27.

65. Ludvík Svoboda, the minister of defense, was the originator of the idea of transferring the divisions. Although his post was supposed to belong to a non-party expert, Svoboda was firmly in the Communists' hands, having requested

membership in the CPCz during the war. At that time Gottwald turned him down, noting that he could best serve the party by remaining outside it, since he would then fulfill the political requirements of the ministerial position and could give the Communists an added vote in the cabinet while also overseeing the military for the party. Vondrášek, 331–32.

66. Vartíková (1962), 167. The Union of Slovak Partisans, Czechoslovak Legionnaires, Union of Soldiers of the Uprising, and the Union of Anti-Fascist Prisoners and Workers in Illegality took part. On other resolutions, see Huml, 135.

67. Barnovský, 308.

68. "Získali jsme 7000 nových odberateľov" [We Have Received 7,000 New Subscribers] *Katolické noviny* 62:10 (9 March 1947): 4.

69. Mikus, 176.

70. Daxner, 169.

71. The complete list of individual charges can be found in Daxner, 141–67.

72. See Drtina II/2, 297, or Vaško, 149, for example.

73. Daxner, 153–59 passim, here 141, 158–59.

74. *Katolické noviny* published Kmeťko's entire testimony (numbers 5–9, 1947), while limiting itself to short excepts from the testimony of others.

75. Vaško, 150–51. The most interesting account of the trial is *Proces*.

76. The constant intoning by the defendants that they were acting in the interests of Slovakia drew criticism even from the leading Czech journal *Katolík*, which pointed out that Hitler could have said the same thing regarding Germany. They argued that the biblical rule of "Do unto others" should be the rule for conducting international relations. See ak. [Adolf Kajpr] "Všechno pro zájem Slovenska" [Everything for the Interests of Slovakia] *Katolík* 9:31 (1946): 6. This prompted a sharp reply from its Slovak equivalent, *Katolické noviny*, which raised the Czechs' ongoing expulsion of almost three million Germans from the land, asking if it conformed with the rule *Katolík* recommended. See "Český 'Katolík' a Slovensko" [The Czech *Katolík* and Slovakia] *Katolické noviny* 62:2 (1947): 3.

77. For information on some of these, see Jaroš and Jarošová, 193, 200, or Vaško, 156.

78. Prečan, 148–49.

79. Kaplan (1992), Document 28, passim, Huml, 136; Pleva, 127–28, Vaško, 154. The last of these rhymes in the Slovak language: "Dali sme vám svoje hlasy, prepusťte nám Tiso z basy!" Prečan 146. Although the level of pamphlet, etc. activity rose across Slovakia, the places with the highest incidence were Spišská Nová Ves, Senica and Trnava. Vondrášek 334. Prečan cites one of the pamphlets as representative, which should give some idea of the general tone: "We have been living through a terrible tragedy for the Slovak nation in the past days. A Jewish-Bolshevik clique with Daxner at its head wants to condemn Dr. Jozef Tiso and the rest of the Slovak politicians to death . . . the Slovak nation will not allow the first president of the Slovak Republic to be hung in disgrace. And you, the so-called representatives of the nation. . . . Do you think you you can satisfy your blood-thirsty Bolshevik appetites with the blood of the Slovak people? . . . remember that the statement of the American senator Capehart—'We must fight against

communism wherever we encounter it'—holds today for the entire civilized world." Prečan 144–5.

80. Prečan, 142–43. Mikus reports that a postmaster in Bratislava was relieved of his duties for allowing several thousand telegrams and letters to be delivered to Tiso. Mikus, 180.

81. Vondrášek, 334.

82. Huml, 136; Prečan, 145; Vartíková (1962), 167–68; Mikus, 180–81; Pleva, 128. The other towns named were Nové Mesto nad Váhom, Chynorany, and Ostratice, in each of which there were over six hundred participants. See Kaplan (1992), Document 29. The deputation sent to Bratislava was turned back after reaching the city.

83. Vartíková (1962), 168–69.

84. A quick glance through the pages of *Katolické noviny* suffices to show the volume of articles discussing attacks on the church, especially in reference to the conflict over church schools. The cited article is "Temné sily sa usilujú vyhnat' Cirkev a náboženstvo zo světa a života." *Katolické noviny* 62:8 (1947): 3.

85. Kaplan (1992), Document 29.

86. Jaroš and Jarošová, 195. They may have been alarmed by the spreading of insubordination even into the ranks of the communist-controlled trades union. For example, in one union election the communist candidate failed to even make it to the second round and many of the ballots were turned in blank with "Long Live Tiso!" written on them. See Jaroš and Jarošová, 198.

87. Prečan, 147

88. See Kaplan (1992), Document 30.

89. Vaško, 155–56.

90. Kaplan, 23. Lettrich had asked to know in advance because the Slovak National Council would bear the political responsibility for the verdict. Daxner justified his change of mind about informing Lettrich on the grounds of judicial independence. Daxner, 172; Kaplan (1992), Document 32.

91. The quotation is from CPS leader Husák's letter of 3 March 1947 to Gottwald, cited in Barnovský, 312.

92. On possible motives for Polák's surprising vote, see Barnovský, 313, and Drtina II/2, 302, who thinks that perhaps Polák was "bought" by the CPS and that he had already decided at that time to betray the DP in favor of the CPS.

93. The Second Prague Agreement, from April 1946, specifically states that "The president of the republic grants clemency also in Slovakia." (Article 1, Paragraph b) Rákoš and Rudohradský, 552. This is not to say whatsoever that Beneš acted unconstitutionally, for he could consult with whomever he wished, but only to point out that the ultimate responsibility for the decision rested with him alone.

94. Kaplan (1992), Document 38. Emphasis in the original.

95. Prečan, 156–57. On the relationship between Beneš and Tiso, see Kolář.

96. Prečan 152–53, 158. The weight of numbers in Tiso's defense is misleading, because most of the telegrams supporting him were sent by individuals.

97. In fact, the Vatican's distancing of itself from Tiso after the 1946 elections reached its peak here. Monsignor Forni informed Beneš's secretary of three important facts damaging to Tiso's request for clemency: (1) he was there only as a

representative of the Holy See, not of the pope directly; (2) Tiso was no longer a monsignor, as his mandate had not been renewed by Pius XII, and (3) the Vatican would refuse any direct political intervention, because the Holy See had requested that Tiso step down from his presidency during the period of the final solution, which he did not. Kaplan (1992), Document 37.

98. Drtina II/2, 298.

99. The minutes of the meeting are presented in Kaplan (1992), Document 39. Drtina ascribes the failure of the resolution to the absence of the People's Party minister Monsignor Šrámek, but his one vote obviously would not have changed the outcome. Drtina II/2, 303.

100. According to a report of unassessable reliability made by a state security spy in the DP, Lettrich was the leader of a minority in the DP that wanted to save Tiso's life. The majority argued that if he were executed he would be seen as a priest first, and his political influence would wane with the passing of time. If he were only imprisoned, however, his political importance would continue into the unforeseeable future. Barnovský, 313.

101. Kaplan (1992) Document 39.

102. Ibid.

103. Tiso's statement can be found in Mikus, 182.

104. The largest event seems to have been a meeting of eight hundred people at the cemetery in Martin. Pleva, 128.

105. *Osservatore Romano* reported that "it is certain that the granting of clemency would have effectively led to the strengthening of ties between Czechs and Slovaks. The nation is exhausted from war, hatred and division. The carrying out of the punishment certainly weakened markedly the chances for the calming of spirits in the Czechoslovak Republic." *Katolické noviny* 62.17 (1947): 3.

106. This obvious attempt at revenge drew no support from Czech political representatives who saw it as transparent meddling with judicial independence. See Daxner, 174–75.

107. It should be noted that it was at this time that such "conspiracies" were being "discovered" in Poland, Romania, and Bulgaria. In these cases, however, the "conspiracies" were on the part of the political opposition, while in Slovakia (as in Hungary) it was a leading member of the coalition government.

108. Zinner, 189.

109. The National Socialists agreed at a meeting in Karlovy Vary in late 1947 to open discussions with the leadership of the DP. Ripka, 112–13; Drtina II/2, 341–42.

110. Interestingly, however, the government vote on whether to return the Tiso verdict to the Slovak National Council fell along the same party lines— CPCz, CPS, and Social Democrats on one side, and Czech National Socialists, the Czech People's Party, and the DP on the other—as the division of ministers was in the government crisis of February 1948. In this way the events surrounding the Tiso trial foreshadowed the communist takeover and raise the question of whether the noncommunists understood the consequences of this earlier measure of strength.

111. Rothschild, 92.

112. The citation is from Kaplan (1993b), 182. On the trials, see Ministerstvo, (1950, 1951).

References

Barnovský, Michal. "K niektorým otázkam súdneho procesu s Jozefom Tisom" [On Some Questions of the Legal Trial of Jozef Tiso]. In *Pokus*, 308–20.

Barto, Jaroslav. *Riešenie vzťahu Čechov a Slovákov (1944–48)* [The Management of the Relationship of the Czechs and Slovaks (1944–48)]. Bratislava: Epocha, 1968.

Cesta k únoru: Dokumenty [The Road to February: Documents]. Praha: Academia, 1963.

Daxner, Igor. *Ľudactvo pred národným súdom 1945–47* [The Ľudáks before the National Tribunal 1945–1947]. Bratislava: Slovenská Akademie vied, 1961.

Dokumenty z historie československé politiky 1939–43 [Documents from the History of Czechoslovak Politics 1939–43]. Praha: Academia, 1966.

Drtina, Pavel. *Československo můj osud* [Czechoslovakia My Fate]. Vol. 2. Books 1–2. Praha: Melantrich, 1992.

Dvořák, Josef. *Slovenská politika včera a dnes* [Slovak Politics Yesterday and Today]. Praha: Knihovna Národního osvobození, 1947.

Falťan, Samo. *Slovenska otázka v Československu* [The Slovak Question in Czechoslovakia]. Bratislava: Vydavateľstvo politickej literatúry, 1968.

Foustka, Radim. "Národní očista v letech 1945 až 1946" [National Purification in the Years 1945–46] *Československý časopis historický* 3 (1955): 626–42.

Gottwald, Klement. *Spisy XI: 1943–45* [Writings XI: 1943–45]. Praha: Státní nakladelství politické literatury, 1955a.

———. *Spisy XII 1945–46* [Writings XII: 1945–46]. Praha: Státní nakladelství politické literatury, 1955b.

———. *Spisy XIII 1946–47.* [Writings XIII: 1946–47]. Praha: Státní nakladelství politické literatury, 1957.

Hartmannová, Eva. " 'My' a 'Oni': hledání české národní identity na stránkách *Dneška* z roku 1946" ["Us" and "Them": The Search for the Czech National Identity in the Pages of *Dnešek* in 1946] In *Strankami soudobých dějin: Sborník statí k pětašedesátinám historika Karla Kaplana* [Through the Pages of Contemporary History: *Festschrift* for the Sixty-Fifth Birthday of the Historian Karel Kaplan]. Praha: Ústav pro soudobé dějiny, 1993, 93–109.

Huml, Vladimír. *Slovensko před rozhodnutím* [Slovakia before the Decision]. Praha: Naše vojsko, 1961.

Jaroš, O., and V. Jarošová. *Slovenské robotníctvo v boji o moc (1944–48)* [The Slovak Working Class in the Struggle for Power (1944–48)]. Bratislava: Vydavateľstvo politickej literatúry, 1965.

Jarošová, Viera, Ivan Škurlo, and Marta Vartíková. *Odbory na ceste k februáru (1944–48)* [The Trade Unions on the Road to February (1944–1948)]. Bratislava: Práca, 1967.

Jelinek, Yeshayahu. *The Parish Republic: Hlinka's Slovak People's Party, 1939–45.* East European Monograph Series 14. Boulder, Colo.: East European Quarterly, 1976.

Kaplan, Karel. *Znárodnění a socialismus* [Nationalization and Socialism]. Praha: Academia, 1968.

Kaplan, Karel. *Dva retribuční procesy: Dokumenty a komentáře* [Two Retribution Trials: Documents and Commentaries]. Praha: ÚSD, 1992.

——. *Nekrvavá revoluce* [The Bloodless Revolution]. Praha: Mladá fronta, 1993a.

——. *Stát a církev v Československu 1948–53* [The State and the Church in Czechoslovakia 1948–53]. Brno: Doplněk, 1993b.

Kaplan, Karel, and Jiří Sláma. *Die Parlamentswahlen in der Tschechoslowakei 1935–46–1948: Eine statistische Analyse* [The Parliamentary Elections in Czechoslovakia: A Statistical Analysis] Veröffentlichungen des Collegium Carolinum 53. München: R. Oldenbourg, 1986.

Kolář, Michal. "Edvard Beneš a Josef Tiso." In *Pokus*, 345–49.

Leff, Carol Skalnik. *National Conflict in Czechoslovakia*. Princeton, N.J.: Princeton University Press, 1988.

Lettrich, Jozef. *History of Modern Slovakia*. New York: Praeger, 1955.

Liehm, Antonín. *The Politics of Culture*. Peter Kussi, trans. New York: Grove, 1973.

Mikus, Joseph. *Slovakia: A Political History 1918–50*. Marquette Slavic Studies 5. Milwaukee, Wisc.: Marquette, 1963.

Ministerstvo spravedlnosti: *Proces proti vatikánským agentům v Československu Biskup Zela a společníci* [The Trial of the Vatican Agents in Czechoslovakia (Bishop Zela and Accomplices)]. Prague: Ministerstvo spravedlnosti, 1950.

Ministerstvo spravedlnosti: *Proces proti vlastizradným biskupom J. Vojtaššákovi, M. Buzalkovi, P. Gojdičovi* [The Trial of the Traitorous Bishops Jan Vojtaššák, Michael Buzalka, and Pavel Gojdič]. Bratislava: Ministerstvo spravedlnosti, 1951.

Myant, M. R. *Socialism and Democracy in Czechoslovakia*. Cambridge, England: Cambridge University Press, 1981.

Opat, Jaroslav. *O novou demokracii* [On the New Democracy]. Praha: Academia, 1966.

Pleva, Ján. *Bratislava na prelome rokov: Príspevok k jej dejinám* [Bratislava at the Turning Point of the Years: A Contribution to Its History]. Bratislava: Vydateľ'ské stredisko Zs KNV, 1966.

Pokorný, Ctibor. "Der Kommunismus und die Slowakei" [Communism and Slovakia] In *Die Slowakei als mitteleuropäisches Problem in Geschichte und Gegenwart* [Slovakia As a Central European Problem in History and the Present] Veröffentlichungen des Collegium Carolinum 15. München: Robert Lerche, 1965.

Pokus o politický a osobný profil Jozefa Tisu [An Attempt at a Political and Personal Profile of Jozef Tiso]. Bratislava: Slovak Academic Press, 1992.

Prečan, Vilém. *Slovenský katolicizmus pred Februárom 1948* [Slovak Catholicism before February 1948]. Bratislava: Osveta, 1961.

Proces s dr. J. Tisom: Spomienky obžalobcu Antona Rašlu, obhajcu Ernesta Žabkayho [The Trial of Dr. J. Tiso: The Memoirs of the Prosecutor Anton Rašla and the Defender Ernest Žabkay]. Bratislava: Svedectvá, 1990.

Program první československé vlády národní fronty Čechů a Slováků přijatý 5. dubna 1945 v Košicích [The Program of the First Czechoslovak Government of the National Front of Czechs and Slovaks Adopted 5 April 1945 in Košice]. Praha: Rudé právo, 1955.

Rákoš, Elo, and Štefan Rudohradský. *Slovenské národné orgány 1943–68* [Slovak National Organs, 1943–68]. Bratislava: Slovenská archívna správa, 1973.

Ripka, Hubert. *Únorová tragedie* [The February Tragedy]. Brno: Atlantis, 1995.

Rothschild, Joseph. *Return to Diversity: A Political History of East Central Europe since World War II.* Oxford, England: Oxford University Press, 1989.

Vartíková, Marta. *Roky rozhodnutia: K dejinám politického boja pred Februárom 1948* [Years of Decision: Toward a History of the Political Struggle before February 1948]. Bratislava: Vydavateľstvo politickej literatúry, 1962.

Vartíková, Marta. *Od Košic po február* [From Košice to February]. Bratislava: Obzor, 1968.

Vartíkova, Marta, ed. *Komunistická strana Slovenska: Dokumenty z konferencií a plén 1944–48* [The Communist Party of Slovakia: Documents from Conferences and Plena 1944–48]. Bratislava: Pravda, 1971.

Vaško, Václav. *Neumlčena, Kronika katolické církve v Československu po druhé světové válce* [Unsilenced: A Chronicle of the Catholic Church in Czechoslovakia after the Second World War]. Vol. 1. Praha: Zvon, 1990.

Vnuk, František. "Retribučné súdnictvo a proces s Jozefom Tisom" [Retributory Justice and the Trial of Jozef Tiso]. In *Pokus*, 287–309.

Vondrášek, Václav. "Činnost ilegálního podzemí na Slovoksku v době Tisova procesu" [The Activity of the Illegal Underground in Slovakia in the Period of the Tiso Trial]. In *Pokus*, 330–35.

Zinner, Paul. *Communist Strategy and Tactics in Czechoslovakia, 1938–48.* London: Pall Mall, 1963.

Part IV

EPILOGUE

The Past Is Another Country:
Myth and Memory in Postwar Europe

> Fifty years after the catastrophe, Europe
> understands itself more than ever as a common
> project, yet it is far from achieving a comprehen-
> sive analysis of the years immediately following
> the Second World War. The memory of the period
> is incomplete and provincial, if it is not entirely
> lost in repression or nostalgia.
> —*Hans-Magnus Enzensberger*

FROM THE END of World War Two until the revolutions of 1989, the
frontiers of Europe and with them the forms of identity associated with
the term "European" were shaped by two dominant concerns: the pattern
of division drafted at Yalta and frozen into place during the Cold War,
and the desire, common to both sides of the divide, to forget the recent
past and forge a *new* continent. In the West this took the form of a movement for transnational unification tied to the reconstruction and modernization of the West European economy; in the East an analogous unity,
similarly obsessed with productivity, was imposed in the name of a shared
interest in social revolution. Both sides of the divide had good reason to
put behind them the experience of war and occupation, and a future-
oriented vocabulary of social harmony and material improvement
emerged to occupy a public space hitherto filled with older, divisive, and
more provincial claims and resentments.

In this chapter I want to propose some reflections on the price that was
paid for this deliberate and sudden unconcern with the immediate European past and its replacement by "Euro-cant" in its various forms. I shall
argue that the special character of the wartime experience in continental
Europe, and the ways in which the memory of that experience was distorted, sublimated, and appropriated, bequeathed to the postwar era an
identity that was fundamentally false, dependent upon the erection of an
unnatural and unsustainable frontier between past and present in European public memory. I shall suggest that the ways in which the official
versions of the war and postwar era have unraveled in recent years are

indicative of unresolved problems that lie at the center of the present continental crisis—an observation true of both Western and Eastern Europe,
though in distinctive ways. Finally I shall note some of the new myths and
mismemories attendant upon the collapse of Communism and the ways
in which these, too, are already shaping, and misshaping the new European "order."

The Second World War was a very particular, and in certain respects
novel experience for most Europeans. It was in the first place horribly,
unprecedentedly destructive, especially in its final months. In particularly
badly hit countries like Yugoslavia, something like 66 percent of all livestock, 25 percent of all vineyards, most railway rolling stock, and all
major roads were destroyed. Western countries, too, suffered terrible material loss—during the fighting of 1944–1945, France lost the use of some
75 percent of its harbors and rail yards and half a million houses were
damaged beyond repair. Even unoccupied Britain is calculated to have
lost some 25 percent of its entire prewar national wealth as a result of
the war.[1]

But the scale of material destruction pales in comparison with the
human losses, in Central and Eastern Europe in particular. There is no
need here to go through the familar statistics of death, suffering, and loss.
On the one hand the human cost has to be calculated on an industrial
basis, so efficient was the machinery of extermination elaborated and operated by Germans and their associates; on the other hand, the war saw
an unanticipated return to older terrors—in the weeks following the Soviet army's capture of Berlin some 90,000 women in the city sought medical assistance for rape. In Vienna the Western allies recorded 87,000 rape
victims in the three weeks following the arrival of the Red Army. From
the Volga to the Elbe, the Second World War constituted an experience
whose special combination of efficiency, fear, violence, and deprivation
was comparable to nothing in local memory (though Armenians and
Spaniards had been afforded a brief foretaste in earlier years).

And yet . . . the Second World War was not the same for everyone.
Some places had quite a "good" war, at least until the very last months.
Bohemia and Moravia, for example, did relatively well under Nazism,
favored for their natural and industrial resources, their skilled and pliant
workforce, and their proximity in manner and outlook (if not race) to
their German neighbors. Most Czech workers and peasants were coddled
by the Germans, securing high wages, full employment, good rations, and
so forth; only resisters, communists, and Jews, here as elsewhere, were
seriously at risk and exposed to the constant threat of harassment, loss,
and deportation. Slovaks and Croats finally got their own "independent"
states, albeit run by collaborators, and many were pleased with the
achievement. Germans and Austrians suffered badly only toward the lat-

ter part of the war, their economies sustained until then by the forced extraction of materials and labor from the occupied territories. Even France, perhaps especially France, did not do so badly—most of French wartime losses and some of the worst acts of collective punishment came only after the Allies landed (which accounts for mixed French memories on that subject). Overall, it was clearly not good to be a Jew, a Gypsy, or a Pole in World War II; nor was it safe to be a Serb (in Croatia), a Russian (until 1943), or a Ukrainian or German (after 1943). But if one could stop the clock in, let us say, January 1944, most of occupied Europe would have had little of which to complain in contrast with what was about to come.

Another way of putting this is to say that most of occupied Europe either collaborated with the occupying forces (a minority) or accepted with resignation and equanimity the presence and activities of the German forces (a majority). The Nazis could certainly never have sustained their hegemony over most of the continent for as long as they did had it been otherwise: Norway and France were run by active partners in ideological collaboration with the occupier; the Baltic nations, Ukraine, Hungary, Slovakia, Croatia, and Flemish-speaking Belgium all took enthusiastic advantage of the opportunity afforded them to settle ethnic and territorial scores under benevolent German oversight. Active resistance was confined, until the final months, to a restricted and in some measure self-restricting set of persons: socialists, communists (after June 1941), nationalists, and ultramonarchists, together with those, like Jews, who had little to lose given the nature and purposes of the Nazi project. Such resisters were often resented, opposed, and even betrayed by the local population either because they brought trouble by attracting German retaliation, or because the indigenous ethnic and political majority disliked them almost as much as the Germans and were not unhappy to see them hunted down and removed.

Not surprisingly, then, the war left a vicious legacy. In the circumstances of the liberation, everyone sought to identify with the winners—in this case the Allies and those who had sided with them before the final victory. Given the nature of the war, which by its end had mutated into a whole series of brutal local civil wars, it was for most Europeans a matter of some urgency that they emerge on the correct side. This in turn entailed distinguishing and distancing oneself from those who had been the enemy (within and without), and since the actions of this enemy had been without precedent in their brutality and scale, there was universal agreement that it should be punished. Even those like Albert Camus, who came to doubt the possibility of identifying "war criminals" with any accuracy or justice, recognized the emotional and political necessity of such a judicial purge and retribution. The question was who and how.[2]

At this point we leave the history of the Second World War and begin to encounter the myth of that war, a myth whose construction was undertaken almost before the war itself was over. Everyone had an interest in this affair, the context of which ranged from private score settling to the emerging international balance of world power. Indeed, it was the years 1945–1948 that were the moment not only of the division of Europe and the first stage of its postwar reconstruction but also, and in an intimately related manner, the period during which Europe's postwar memory was molded.

There is space here to note only briefly the factors that contributed to the official version of the wartime experience that was common European currency by 1948. Of these I shall list just the most salient. The first was the universally acknowledged claim that responsibility for the war, its sufferings, and its crimes lay with the Germans. "They" did it. There was a certain intuitive logic to this comforting projection of guilt and blame. After all, had it not been for the German occupations and depredations from 1938 to 1945, there would have been no war, no death camps, no occupations—and thus no occasion for the civil conflicts, denunciations, and other shadows that hung over Europe in 1945. Moreover, the decision to blame everything on Germany was one of the few matters on which all sides, within each country and among the Allied powers, could readily agree. The presence of concentration camps in Poland, Czechoslovakia, and even France could thus readily be forgotten, or simply ascribed to the occupying power, with attention diverted from the fact that many of these camps were staffed by non-Germans and (as in the French case) had been established and in operation before the German occupation began.[3]

Moreover, this focus on Germany made it possible to resolve by neglect certain tricky subjects such as the postwar status of Austria. Beginning with the Moscow Declaration of 1943, Austria was established as the "first victim" of Nazi aggression, something that suited not only Austrians but also the prejudices of someone like Churchill, for whom Nazism was a natural extension of Prussian militarism and expansionist ambitions.[4] If *Austria* was guiltless, then the distinctive responsibilities of non-German nationals in other lands were assuredly not open to close inspection. Hence the achievement of Nuremberg, where *German* guilt was in turn distilled into a set of indictments reserved exclusively for German *Nazis*, and then only a select few. This was a matter of some concern to the Soviet authorities involved in the war crimes trials; they wished to avoid any discussion of broader moral and judicial questions that might draw attention to the Soviet Union's own practices before and during the war. That the Nuremberg trials served an important exemplary and jurisprudential function is beyond doubt; but the selectivity and apparent hypocrisy with which the Allies pursued the matter contributed to the cynicism of the postwar era while easing the consciences of many non-Germans (and non-Nazis) whose activities might easily have been open to similar charges.

Next there was the issue of denazification. Within a very short time after the liberation it became clear that Germany (and Austria) could not be returned to civil administration and local self-government, even under Allied supervision, if the purging of responsible Nazis was undertaken in a sustained and consistent manner. Moreover, the local Social-Democratic and Christian Democratic parties in both countries could not be expected to ignore the votes of former Nazis once these were allowed to reenter public life; thus the 1948 amnesty in Austria, which returned full civil rights to some 500,000 former registered Nazis, inevitably resulted in a sort of instant amnesia, whereby all sides agreed that these men and women were henceforward no different from the rest. Even the remaining "more incriminated" Nazis, some 42,000 of them, were nearly all amnestied within the following seven years, as the Western Allies sought to minimize the risk of alienating Austrians and Germans from the Western bloc through any excessive emphasis on their past and its price. In a process that would have been all but unthinkable in 1945, the identification and punishment of active Nazis in German-speaking Europe had effectively ended by 1948 and was a forgotten issue by the early fifties.

The association of wartime responsibility with Germans, and of Germans with Nazism, sat all the more comfortably with non-German nations in that it provided a context and an excuse for a "final solution" to the nationality problem in continental Europe. Woodrow Wilson and the Treaties of Versailles notwithstanding, the sixty million Europeans living under an "alien" jurisdiction in 1914 had not all achieved self-determination after World War I: there were still some 25 million persons living in "someone else's state." The Nazi occupation had gone some way to resolving this perennial European problem by killing most of the Jews and some of the smaller stateless groups. After the war, the liberated states took the occasion to further this process by removing the Germans themselves. As a result of the shifting of Poland's frontiers agreed on at Potsdam, the expulsion of the *Volksdeutsche* from the Balkans, and the collective punishment visited upon the Sudeten Germans, some 15 million Germans were expelled in the postwar years: 7 million from Silesia, Pomerania, and East Prussia; 3 million from Czechoslovakia; nearly 2 million from Poland and the USSR; and a further 2.7 million from Yugoslavia, Romania, and Hungary. After some 2 million died in flight or during the expulsions, the majority ended up in Western Germany (especially Bavaria), where as late as 1960 some 28 percent of the federal government employees were *Vertriebene* (expellees).[5]

Beyond its significance for postwar German domestic politics (which were considerable), this process had a marked impact on the states whence these Germans came. Poland and Hungary (as well as Western Germany itself) now became ethnically homogenous states as never before. Others felt free to indulge in further exercises in ethnic purifiation: the Czechs, especially, took the opportunity to expel or transfer hundreds of thousands of ethnic Hungarians from Slovakia (in some cases forcing them to occupy the vacated Sudeten regions), the liberal Beneš announcing the day after his country's liberation that Czechs and Slovaks "did not want to live" in the same state as Germans and Hungarians.[6] It might be thought that such actions, and the sentiments they reflected and aroused, would have caused misgivings in a Europe so recently liberated from similarly motivated collective miseries brought upon the continent by the occupier. On the contrary: a clear and quick distinction was made between the sorts of collective violence and punishment visited on these lands by German war criminals, and the mass, racially motivated purges represented by these expulsions and undertaken by freely elected or newly liberated national authorities.

Two sorts of memories thus emerged: that of things done to "us" by Germans in the war, and the rather different recollection of things (however similar) done by "us" to "others" after the war (taking advantage of a situation the Germans had obligingly if unintentionally made possible). Two moral vocabularies, two sorts of reasoning, two different pasts. In this circumstance, the uncomfortably confusing recollection of things done by us to others *during* the war (i.e., under German auspices) got conveniently lost.

It was in these circumstances that the "resistance" myth emerged. If there was to be a reference point in national memory for the years between 1939 and 1945, it could only be the obverse of that now firmly attached to Germans. If Germans were guilty, then "we" were innocent. If guilt consisted of being German or working for Germans and their interests—and it could hardly be denied that in every occupied country such persons had been present and prominent—then innocence had to mean an anti-German stance, after 1945 but also before. Thus to be innocent a nation had to have resisted and to have done so in its overwhelming majority, a claim that was perforce made and pedagogically enforced all over Europe, from Italy to Poland, from the Netherlands to Romania. Where the historical record cried out against this distortion—in France, in Italy where the anti-Fascist resistance came late and was confined to the North, in the Netherlands where grossly exaggerated accounts of heroic farmers rescuing downed British airmen became part of the postwar national mythology—national attention was consciously diverted, from the very first postwar months, to examples and stories that were repeated and magnified ad nauseam in novels, popular histories, radio, newspapers, and especially cinema.

It is understandable that former collaborators, or even those who simply sat it out, should have been happy to see the wartime tale thus retold to their advantage. But why did the genuine resisters, who in most cases were also those in power in the immediate postwar years, agree to retouch the past thus? The answer is twofold. In the first case, it was necessary somehow to restore a minimal level of cohesion to civil society and to reestablish the authority and legitimacy of the state in countries where authority, trust, public decency, and the very premises of civil behavior had been torn down by totalitarian government and total war. Thus De Gaulle in France, De Gasperi in Italy, and the various communist-dominated National Front governments in Eastern Europe all found it necessary to tell their citizens that their sufferings had been the work of the Germans and a handful of traitorous collaborators, that they had suffered and struggled heroically, and that their present duty, the war now over and the guilty suitably punished, was to address themselves to postwar tasks, place their faith in constitutional regimes, and *put the war behind them*. Seeing little option but to concur, the domestic resistance movements abandoned their plans for radical domestic renewal and went along with the priority accorded to the search for stability, even if (as in the Italian case) it entailed signing the Rome Protocols of November 1944, which effectively secured the continuity of the Fascist state apparatus into the postwar era.[7]

Secondly, the communists, whose agenda was of course distinctively different from that of their allies in the domestic resistance, nevertheless had reasons of their own to recast the wartime record of their fellow citizens in their own heroic image. In the West, they could hope to capitalize on their war record by claiming to have spoken for the nation in its time of trial, and thus seek the authority to speak for it still. For that reason the Parti Communiste Français (PCF) in France or the Partito Communista Italiano (PCI) in Italy had no objection to exaggerating the resistance record of the French or Italians, so long as they could themselves inherit the benefits of this illusion at the voting booth and in the national memory. It was thus ironically appropriate that it should be Togliatti, the Italian communist leader, who drafted the 1946 amnesty that ended the foreshortened and selective postwar Italian purges.

In the East, where communism everywhere except in the special cases of Yugoslavia and Albania had returned to the country not through the heroic efforts of the local resistance but in the baggage train of the Red Army, the communists had an interest in flattering the recalcitrant local population by inviting it to believe the fabrication now deployed on its behalf by the USSR—to wit, that Central and Eastern Europe was an

innocent victim of German assault, had played no part in its own downfall or in the crimes perpetrated on its territory, and was a full partner in
the work of liberation led by Soviet soldiers abroad and Communist partisans at home. This story, which found its way into forty years of school
texts in the "Peoples' Democracies" was actually even less credible than
the fibs being told in Paris and Rome, and few in Central and Eastern
Europe believed it, even among those who had strong motives to do so.
But since no one had an interest in denying it—and within two years to do
so was anyway no longer possible—the story took root.

Moreover, the communists' emphasis in Eastern Europe on identifying
and punishing those few "traitors" who had betrayed the otherwise heroic local people offered them the occasion to indict, try, and imprison or
execute a lot of people whom they feared might impede their path to
power. Thus in January 1945 "Peoples' Courts" were set up in Hungary
to try war criminals. Initially these functioned with reasonable integrity,
but later the crimes of "sabotage" and "conspiracy" were added to their
remit with somber consequences; something similar happened in Romania and especially Bulgaria, where the Fatherland Front settled postwar
scores with thousands of real or potential political rivals, making no distinction between pro-German, pro-Western, and anticommunist candidates for punishment, all in the name of the nation and its wartime sufferings. Meanwhile the construction of war memorials was undertaken, all
of them with the same pedagogical message: the Second World War had
been an "antifascist" war in which the Nazi Germans had served capitalist and imperialist ends and been opposed by the undifferentiated "people" whose lands they occupied. Atrocities were described as perpetrated
by "fascists" (foreign and domestic) against the local population, and no
mention was *ever* made of the sufferings of national, ethnic, or religious
minorities, whether at the hands of Russians (of course), the local population, or even the Germans themselves. This process reached its purest
form in the officially approved version of the wartime experience and
postwar character of *East* Germany, a land of workers and peasants hitherto oppressed by and now liberated from a handful of Nazi capitalists
from the West.

That is why, in East and West alike, the process of punishment and
purge that was supposed to hand down justice upon criminals and collaborators in the postliberation era was so partial and aborted. The issue
was of course inherently complicated and paradoxal: how do you punish
tens of thousands, perhaps millions of people for activities that were approved, legalized, and even encouraged by those in power (in the case of
Vichy France, the heirs to a constitutionally elected parliament)? But how
do you justify leaving unpunished actions that were manifestly criminal
even before they fell under the aegis of "victors' justice"? How do you

choose whom to punish and for which actions? Who does the choosing? At what precise moment is a purge sufficient to meet elementary demands for justice and revenge, and not yet so divisive as to damage still further an already rent social fabric? The point I wish to make here is simply that under almost any conceivable good-faith response to these questions, the postwar response proved tragically inadequate.[8]

Most of the acts of retributive punishment that took place in this period happened before the countries in question had been liberated, or else at the very moment of that liberation, as German authority lapsed and new powers had yet to be installed. Of the approximately ten thousand summary executions in France that marked the transition from Vichy to the Fourth Republic, about a third were carried out before D-Day and a further 50 percent during the battles of the following weeks. Similarly in Italy, most of the twelve to fifteen thousand persons shot for fascist or collaborationist activities at this time were dealt with before or during the weeks of final liberation. In other words, the majority of the most severe "punishments" meted out for wartime activities were completed *before* formal or official tribunals had been set up to pass judgment.[9] The same is true in Eastern Europe (Yugoslavia included) where partisan score settling was the primary form of semiofficial retribution for collaboration and war crimes.[10]

Thus at least two of the functions of retributive jurisprudence—the administration of natural justice and the canalization of private violence—had been co-opted and largely dispatched before legitimate postwar institutions came into force. What remained were the establishment of public security to protect new political institutions, symbolic acts of justice to legitimize the new authorities, and public words and deeds designed to shape and circumscribe the moral regeneration of the nation. Here the postwar European experience of justice was universally unsuccessful and inadequate. Of denazification I have already spoken. But even when it came to dealing with serious criminals, the exercise was halfhearted. The Austrian and French instances are exemplary (the Eastern European experience was distinguished by the abuse of court procedures already noted). In Austria, 130,000 persons were investigated for war crimes; of these 23,000 were tried, 13,600 found guilty, 43 sentenced to death (about the same number as were condemned to death in Denmark), and 30 executed. In France, 791 death sentences were carried out of the 2,640 passed by the courts. More telling were the overall figures: whereas in Norway, Belgium, and the Netherlands the number of persons sentenced for collaboration varied between 40 and 64 per 10,000 inhabitants, in France the numbers were just 12 per 10,000.[11]

In both France and Austria, then, the emphasis was clearly placed upon the need to reduce to the minimum the number of convictable and convicted persons, reserve for this select few a sort of symbolic and representative function as criminals and traitors, and leave the rest of the social fabric untouched or, where this was not possible, repair the damage as soon as possible through a process of benign collective neglect.[12] It should also be noted that in many countries those who were in the end punished were more likely to have been chosen for the egregious nature of their activities—the record left by their writings—or for their prewar prominence than for the extent or consequencs of their actions, a basis for selection that did not pass unnoticed and helps account for the public skepticism of the era.[13]

In Italy, where the matter was further complicated by the need (or, rather, the inability) to come to terms with not just war and occupation but twenty years of domestic fascism, the purges and retribution that followed the initial bloodletting of the liberation were almost cynically inadequate. Membership in the Fascist Party having been obligatory for Italian civil servants, it was simply not possible to undertake a thorough and consistent purge of the government and administration of the country. Instead, nothing was done. As late as 1960, 62 of the 64 prefects of the Republic had been functionaries under fascism, as was also true of *all* 135 police chiefs! Whether something different was possible in the difficult circumstances of Italy, France, or Austria in 1945–47 is unclear.[14] But what *is* clear is the result of these murky transactions: for most of the population, and especially for those whose own wartime record was ambivalent, the apparently random and ultimately benign exercise of justice after the war made it all the easier to forget, and to encourage others to forget, the circumstances and actions that had marked the fascist and occupation years.

The last point to note in the context of the postwar years concerns the international arena. With the exception of a series of imposed agreements with minor belligerents, signed in Paris in 1946, the Allies never resolved their postwar dealings with former enemy states by any final peace treaty. In contrast with the experience after World War I, the Second World War petered out in a string of ever more contentious and unproductive meetings of foreign ministers, culminating in those of 1947 and 1948 in Paris, Moscow, and London that saw an end to the wartime Allied collaboration and the onset of the Cold War. The main issue was of course disagreement over the division of Germany; the formal creation of the Federal Republic and its Eastern doppelgänger in 1949 was thus the effective end of the immediate postwar era, with the Western Allies nonetheless waiting until July 1951 to declare that their "state of war" with Germany was now over. The significance of the absence of any peace treaty of the kind traditionally signed after major European conflicts was this: World War II lost its original and particular meaning as a struggle between Germany and the Allies and became instead a sort of bloody prelude to other arrangements and new confrontations, a situation that produced different configurations and thus further confused an already obscure memory of the war itself.

Thus Western Europeans, having begun the postwar era by thrusting all responsibility for the war on Germany, found themselves in a short period of time having to think of Germany, or at last some part of Germany, as an ally. In Eastern Europe a war of national liberation from Germans became the overture and starting point to a domestic revolution that forced inhabitants of the region to describe the wartime years in a way that made no sense and could only be achieved by an act of voluntary amnesia. It was necessary to forget everything one had known not only about Germans and Russians and Americans, but also about one's neighbors, one's friends, and even oneself. A peace treaty would not of course have changed this outcome very much if at all. But it would have ended the Second World War and thus given it a distinctive framework, in time and in memory. Until such a treaty came along, Europeans (governments and peoples alike) postponed any collective effort to come to terms with the memory of the war it would have rounded out. When it never happened, they simply left the matter unresolved, buried, neglected, and selectively forgotten.

Up to this point, I have treated the experience of Eastern and Western Europe as one. Despite the obvious differences in the wartime and postwar history of Europe's two halves, in the respects relevant to this paper they had much in common. But from 1948 their histories diverge in ways that are also directly pertinent to the theme of memory and national mythology. Only in the later process of recollection and awakening do their paths again converge. From 1948 the Western nations of Europe waved good-bye to the immediate past and embarked on the "European adventure" to which their national energies and prospects have been officially attached ever since (with the exception of Britain, for whom the story begins distinctly later, for reasons not unconnected with its good fortune in missing the sorts of experiences continental Europeans were in a hurry to forget). In the course of this newfound Europeanism, Western Europeans settled for some twenty-five years into a comforting "collective amnesia" (the phrase is Enzensberger's), resting their half of the continent on a number of crucial "foundation myths."[15]

These myths were in essence the obverse of the wartime and postwar histories noted above. They required common acceptance of the claim that Nazism was a strictly German phenomenon, that Western Germany had been effectively denazified, and that those who ought to be punished had been, with certain notorious individual exceptions. France's Vichy interlude was treated as an aberration in the national history, brought

about by the circumstances of war and occupation and foisted on an unwilling country by the treasonable activities of a minority. Italy's experience with fascism was left largely unrecorded in public discussion, part of
a double myth: that Mussolini had been an idiotic oaf propped into
power by a brutal and unrepresentative clique, and that the nation had
been purged of its fascist impurities and taken an active and enthusiastic
part in its own liberation. Norway, Denmark, the Netherlands, and Belgium were accorded full victim status for their wartime experience, and
the active and enthusiastic collaboration and worse of some Flemings
and Dutch stricken from the public record. Austria, returned to full independence in the 1955 State Treaty, extracted from the Allies an agreement
to relieve it of any responsibility for its years under Nazi rule and thereby
relieved its citizens in their turn of any last remaining need to remember those years or the enthusiasm with which *all* sides (many Social-
Democrats included) had greeted the idea, if not the reality, of Anschluss.[16] Sweden and Switzerland, too, managed to share in this Era of
Good Feelings, of Franco-German reconciliations and economic mira-
cles, purged of any vague abiding memories of Sweden's economic dealings with wartime Germany and the Swiss insistence on distinguishing
Jews from non-Jewish Germans and returning the former to the Nazis
whenever they attempted to make their way across the border.[17]

It is not easy today to recall this particular Europe, the one that held
sway from the Marshall Plan to the early seventies. It, too, is another
country. It was characterized by an obsession with productivity, mo-
dernity, youth, European economic unification, and domestic political
stability. Symptomatically, it was largely the creation of politicians
who came from the geographical margins of their respective nations—
Schumann, De Gasperi, and Adenauer—and who encouraged their more
typical countrymen to think beyond their traditional terms of national
and local reference.[18] While the accumulation and relatively radical redistribution of wealth and services displaced national traumas and unhappy memories, the idea of "Europe" was refurbished as a substitute for
the sorts of national identitifications that had caused such wounds in the
recent past. I say "refurbished" because the notion of a united Europe
was not new. The very phrase "Etats-Unis d'Europe" was first used in the
Paris journal *Le Moniteur* as early as February 1848, and the concept of
a European identity had in fact flourished in certain circles during the
interwar decades and in the war itself. But the problem was that it was the
Right, specifically the fascist Right, that had played with the idea at that
time, contrasting a new European order with the anarchic and febrile
democracies of the liberal era and proposing it as a bulwark against the
imperialist challenge of the "Anglo-Saxon-Jewish plutocracies" that
threatened the old continent from the West and the "Judeo-Communist-

Slavic" danger from the East. Thus, after 1945 "Europe," too, remained to be invented, benefiting from a line drawn across the past and dependent for its credibility on a refusal to acknowledge its own provincial, defensive, and exclusive roots.

———————

The revenge of history has been slow, and remains partial. For many years the teaching of modern history in West Germany did not pass beyond Bismarck, and it is well known that the French government refused for more than a decade to allow Marcel Ophuls's film *Le Chagrin et la Pitié* to be shown on national television. But in both France and Germany a new generation began to ask embarrassing questions, prompted in Germany especially by the series of trials of concentration camp administrators held in the years 1963–65. These, together with the trial in Jerualem of Adolf Eichmann, in turn prompted the passage in France, on 26 December 1964, of a law making crimes against humanity imprescriptible.[19] Despite this evidence of a growing concern with the crimes committed in France under the auspices of the German occupation, it was often left to foreign scholars to raise and investigate the hard questions; the "Vichy syndrome" described so well by Henry Rousso (himself born in 1954), which can stand for similar historical mystifications throughout Western Europe, has only really begun to unravel in the last few years.[20]

The forms of that unraveling have been various. In France, and to a lesser extent in the Netherlands and Belgium, it has been the work of professional scholars working in relative obscurity, their conclusions and evidence surfacing into the public realm only when a particularly egregious case—those of René Bousquet, Maurice Papon, and Paul Touvier in France being the best known—caught the headlines.[21] In Germany the *Historikerstreit*, a much publicized argument among professional historians over the proper way to interpret and contextualize the Nazi years, did not so much reveal new material about Nazism (for the reasons noted earlier, the sins of the Germans had been widely advertised) as open for the first time a discussion of the relative status of Nazism in the context of other contemporary state crimes, notably those of Stalin's Soviet Union.[22] In Austria it took the presidential candidacy and election of Kurt Waldheim to shake the nation (or some of it) from its historical complacency— the widely held opinion that 1945 was "Year Zero" in Austrian history, with all that preceded it dismissed as being of no consequence.[23]

The common theme of these uncomfortable revelations and discussions has been the degree of *refoulement*, of public and private denial, upon which democratic Western Europe was reconstructed. Older Europeans still cling to this alternative past—polls in France suggest that the majority of persons over fifty would rather the matter just went away and cannot wait for Touvier and his like to die and be buried along with their crimes. They see little benefit in rehashing the atrocities committed by Vichy even when they themselves bear no possible personal responsibility for them. In Austria the Waldheim experience has exacerbated the generation gap: in a March 1988 poll, Austrians under thirty were evenly divided on the question of whether Austria was a victim of the Anschluss or its accomplice, whereas for those over fifty the status of victim was selected by nearly twice as many as those who assigned blame.

A further element in the opening up of the past has been the steady decline of Communism. Once the French and Italian communist parties lost their stranglehold on some of the electorate and much of the political imagination of their countries, it became easier to ask hard questions about their role in the resistance and the real dimensions of the latter itself. Now that everyone is jumping on this bandwagon and a virtual subdiscipline of critical resistance historiography has emerged, it is sometimes difficult to remember that until just recently the dispassionate analytical studies of historians like Claudio Pavone or Henry Rousso would have been unthinkable—and in certain circles unpublishable. It is a curious irony that it should be the decline of the antifascist *Left* that makes it possible to acknowledge the true dimensions of domestic fascism and collaboration in an earlier era. Yet there is some logic in this: few in France wished to acknowledge the elements of continuity between Vichy and the preceding and subsequent republics, both because of the implicit downgrading of the "break" of 1945 and the apparent "normalizing" and relativizing of the Vichy years that such an acknowledgment might entail.[24] Similar constraints impeded close attention to continuities in modern Italian history, not to mention the sort of study of Mussolini's true place in the Italian imagination recently published by Luisa Passerini.[25]

Because so much of this troubled and troubling renegotiation with the past is directed toward the public rather than the scholarly community (few of the debates alluded to above have added much to our knowledge of past events any more than the seminal impact of the *Gulag Archipelago* depended on the new information it imparted, which was minimal), it has had its most important impact only in the countries directly concerned. Foreign, especially British and American, interest has been occasional, selective, and perhaps just a little *schadenfreudlich*. But even in France, Italy, and Western Germany the impact of the newly acknowledged past, bubbling its half-digested way back into the throats of politicians and journalists whose real attention is elsewhere, has been as nothing compared to the dramatic implications of the recovery of memory in Central and Eastern Europe.

If the problem in Western Europe has been a shortage of memory, in the continent's other half the problem is reversed. Here, there is too much memory, too many pasts on which people can draw, usually as a weapon against the past of someone else. Whereas the West European dilemma was confined to a single set of unhappy memories located in the occupation years 1940–44/45, the East Europeans have multiple analogous reference points: 1918–21, 1938, 1939, 1941, 1944, 1945–48, 1956, 1968, and now 1989. Each of these moments in time means something different, and nearly always something contentious and tragic to a different nation or ethnic group, or else to succeeding generations within the same group. For Eastern Europeans the past is not just another country but a positive archipelago of vulnerable historical territories to be preserved from attacks and distortions perpetrated by the occupants of a neighboring island of memory, a dilemma made the more cruel because the enemy is almost always within: most of these dates refer to a moment at which one part of the community (defined by class, religion, or nationality) took advantage of the misfortunes of another to help itself to land, property, or power. These are thus memories of civil wars, and in a civil war the enemy is still there once the fighting stops—unless some external agency has been so helpful as to impose a final solution.

The coming of communism seemed to put an end to all this. Soviet power appropriated national myths for its own ends, banned all reference to uncomfortable or conflictual moments save those that retroactively anticipated its own arrival, and enforced a new "fraternity" upon the Eastern half of Europe. But it did not just abolish the past, of course, it also reinvented it. We have already seen how and why communist regimes inflated the myth of wartime antifascist resistance. More subtly, the communists deemphasized the revolutionary nature of Nazi occupation—the fact that Eastern Europe's social revolution, completed under the Soviet aegis after 1947, was in fact begun by the Germans, sweeping away old elites, dispossessing a large segment of the (Jewish) urban bourgeoisie, and radically undermining faith in the rule of law. But the historical reality, that the true revolutionary caesura in modern Eastern Europan history came in 1939 and not 1945, could not be acknowledged. The continuities between Nazi and Soviet rule were necessarily denied, and the alternative myth of revolutionary *postwar* transformation took their place.

From Bulgaria to Poland this process was more or less similar. In East Germany a special national history was conceived, whose emphases varied with the needs of Soviet foreign policy, but whose consistent impact on the local population was disastrous. After an initially aggressive pursuit of denazification, the communists reversed their strategy and announced to the East Germans that their own history was unsullied. Meanwhile, significant numbers of low-ranking Nazis pursued their careers in the police and in bureaucracy under the new regime. East Germans, all too knowledgeable about their real past and the initially violent way in which the Russians had extracted revenge for it, were now invited to sit back in officially mandated approval while the essential characteristics of the Nazi state apparatus were reconstructed before their eyes. The consequences of what Peter Schneider has called the "double zombification" of East Germany are now clear to all.[26]

The silence that fell across Eastern Europe was unbroken for forty years. The revolts of 1956 and the reforms of 1968 did not crack this frozen past; on the contrary, the memory of them, and the fact that it could not be acknowledged except mendaciously, added to the strata of public mythology. In private many people of course scorned the official version of the past; but having only their personal or communal recollection to put in its place and pass on to their children, they contributed inadvertently to the double crisis of history that now afflicts Eastern Europe. On the one hand cynicism and mistrust pervade all social, cultural, and even personal exchanges, so that the construction of civil society, much less civil memory, is very, very difficult. On the other hand there are multiple memories and historical myths, each of which has learned to think of itself as legitimate simply by virtue of being private and unofficial. Where these private or tribal versions come together, they form powerful counterhistories of a mutually antagonistic and divisive nature.

In the present situation there are certain chronically intertwined themes that are reshaping and further distorting the Eastern European past. The first is guilt over the communist era itself. No matter how many times people proclaim that "they" did it to "us," the fact is that very few people could or did object to communist power (in some places, notably Czechoslovakia, it was even initially welcomed in free elections by a large minority of the electorate). It was in the nature of "real existing socialism" in Eastern Europe that it enforced the most humiliating, venal kinds of collaboration as a condition for rendering daily life tolerable. And most people, sooner or later, collaborated: intellectuals, priests, parents, managers, workers, shoppers, doctors, and so on. It is not for any real or imagined crimes that people feel a sort of shame at having lived in and under communism, it is for their daily lies and infinite tiny compromises. Until the coming of *Solidarity* this pattern was unbroken, and even the uniform heroic picture of Polish resistance in the eighties is not without its self-serving mythological dimension. In Czechoslovakia, just 1,864 persons in a population of 15 million signed Charter 77. Even in June 1989, with the repressive apparatus relatively relaxed and well into the Gorbachev era, only 39,000 signed "A Few Sentences," the first manifesto of what would become Civic Forum.[27]

It is this sense that whole nations share a dirty little secret that accounts for the obsession—in eastern Germany, in Czechoslovakia, and to a lesser extent elsewhere—with retribution, purification, and purge. The analogy with 1944 in France is striking. There is an epidemic of finger pointing and blame, with all opinions represented, from those who wish to restrict guilt, indictment, and punishment to a representative or egregious few, to those who would have whole nations atone for their past. What is getting lost in all this is any dispassionate appreciation of the communist era in Europe. Few dare to point out that Communist rule differed from previous regimes in most of the region mostly by virtue of its cynical exploitation of national resources for a *foreign* (Soviet) interest. As governments, regimes, and elites, post-Stalinist Communists were not always so very unlike what had gone before—and will thus have to be absorbed and included in any undertanding of the history of these lands. They cannot just be written out and written off.

Here, too, the analogy with Vichy, or with Italian Fascism, is perhaps appropriate. The Soviet-imposed regimes of Eastern Europe are part of their respective national histories; they continued in certain local traditions, pursued preestablished patterns of economic policy, and have contributed to the postcommunist character of their societies. As with Pétain and Mussolini, so with the puppet authorities of the "Peoples" Democracies": however tempting it may be, they cannot be eliminated from their country's history, nor "bracketed" from it, as an alien and passing aberration. In addition, the arrival of the Red Army saved what remained of certain minorities (Jews, notably); this was an important strand in the arguments of some of the protagonists in the German *Historikerstreit*; but in a region where anti-Semitism remains endemic it is hardly a popular argument in defense of regimes that were often themselves charged (in private) with being the work of Jews. My point here is not to attempt any sort of a balance sheet for Soviet rule, but to note that the communist experience did not come from nowhere, did not disappear without leaving a certain record, and cannot be written out of the local past, as it had earlier sought to extrude from that past those elements prejudicial to its own projects.

The mismemory of communism is also contributing, in its turn, to a mismemory of anticommunism. Marshal Antonescu, the wartime Romanian leader who was executed in June 1945, defended himself at his trial with the claim that he had sought to protect his country from the Soviet Union. He is now being rewritten into Romanian popular history as a hero, his part in the massacre of Jews and others in wartime Romania weighing little in the balance against his anti-Russian credentials. Anticommunist clerics throughout the region; nationalists who fought along-side the Nazis in Estonia, Lithuania, and Hungary; right-wing partisans who indiscriminately murdered Jews, communists, and liberals in the vi-cious score settling of the immediate postwar years before the commu-nists took effective control are all candidates for rehabilitation as men of moderate and laudable convictions; their strongest suit, of course, is the obloquoy heaped upon them by the former regime.[28]

As to the issue of retribution and rehabilitation, here, too, the histori-cal record is hostage to contemporary sentiment. The "lustration" project in Czechoslovakia, intended to deprive of their civil rights all who had the slightest association with the former ruling party, was the most extreme option, pernicious in its application of collective responsibility and op-portunistic in its appeal to the right-of-center parties who saw in it a chance to embarrass their leftist and liberal opponents in national elec-tions. Bulgarians established "civic tribunals" to pronounce a sort of public "degradation" on those convicted of active collusion in past crimes. Even the Hungarians were in angry dispute: there was a running argument over whether to indict Andras Hegedus, a man who took the wrong side in 1956 and abetted the fall and murder of Imre Nagy, but who some see as having rehabilitated himself by his later conversion to "reform communism."

The most telling crisis of all concerns the theme of restoration of prop-erty. In most of Eastern Europe there has been, or is about to be, legisla-tion to restore land and buildings to those who lost them in 1948. But this raises hard questions. Why 1948? Just because it was the communists who at that point began a program of expropriation? What of those whose homes, farms, and businesses were expropriated in the years 1945–48? Or the millions whose possessions were illegally taken dur-ing the war itself and, in the Czech and Slovak cases, after 1938? If the communist regime alone is to be treated in this way, what of those who benefited from the expulsion of the Sudeten Germans, the forced trans-fers of Hungarians in Slovakia, the deportation and murder of the Jews everywhere? Was illegal expropriation, collective punishment, and loss of material goods and livelihood wrong in itself or only if undertaken by communists?

The complication here of course is that there are many in all these countries who benefited from the sufferings of others in the years 1938–48. This is not something on which the communists laid any emphasis after 1948, and it is not something the beneficiaries, their heirs, and their fellow countrymen want to hear about today. It explains why so many Czechs and Slovaks resented Havel's apology to Germany for the expul-sion of the Sudeten Germans (almost his first public act upon entering the presidency), and it is also part of deeper complexes and silences about wartime and postwar collusion and worse in the treatment of minorities. The problem of Poles and Jews in Polish history, including the traumatic experiences of Jews in Poland *after* the war, is the most dramatic and best known of these issues, but it is far from unique.[29] Finally there is another, utterly unresolvable dilemma: what good does it do to restore *property* when you cannot return to tens of millions of people the loss of opportunity and liberty they suffered after 1948? Is there not something wrong in an outcome whereby the Schwarzenberg family gets back its palaces and long-departed emigrés are paid for a loss that their descendants have turned to advantage, while those who had nothing get nothing and watch bitterly as their own and their children's lost chances go for nought? It may or may not be just, but it certainly does not look very fair and it is politically most imprudent.

These and other ironies of present attempts to resolve unhappy memories help explain the resurfacing of older sentiments and allegiances in post-1989 Eastern Europe. This was in some measure predictable, of course. The communist era did not forge new ways of identifying and describing local and national interests, it merely sought to expunge from public language all trace of the old ones. Putting nothing in their place, and bringing into terminal disrepute the socialist tradition of which *it* was the bastard product, it left a vacuum into which ethnic particularism, nationalism, nostalgia, xenophobia, and ancient quarrels could flow; not only were these older forms of political discourse legitimated again by virtue of communism's very denial of them, but they were the only real terms of political communication that anyone could recall with roots in the history of the region. Together with religious affiliation, which in pre-1939 Eastern Europe was often itself the hallmark of nationality, they and the past they describe and represent have returned to haunt and distort postcommunist politics and memory.

This has to be understood on its own terms. Unlike France or Britain, for instance, the little nations of Eastern Europe have lived for centuries in fear of their own extinction. It is truly tragic that on those occasions when they were afforded a measure of autonomy or independence it was usually at the expense of someone else and under the protection of an authoritarian foreign interest. Many Slovaks today speak enthusiastically of Father Tiso, the Slovak leader hung in April 1947 for his collaboration and war crimes during the years of Slovak independence from 1939 to 1944. This helps explain both the Slovak drive for separation and the refusal by some Slovak representatives to vote ratification of the accords with Germany that declared Munich null and void. The cruel fact is that for many Slovaks, then and now, Munich *was a good thing*.[30]

Croats by contrast are largely unenthusiastic about the brutal rule of the Ustasha regime, which took advantage of the German-protected independent Croatian state to exterminate Jews and Serbs on a massive scale; but they can hardly be blamed for a degree of confusion when they are asked to disassociate utterly from that brief memory of autonomous national existence. Polish national sentiment can be an ugly thing, rooted in an unhealthy Catholic exclusivism. Jews and Ukrainians have good reason to fear it (as do Czechs, who know something of Poland's opportunistic land grab after Munich). But Polish memory has for two generations been force-fed a counterintuitive affection for Russian-imposed internationalism, and it would be surprising indeed were the nation to have turned directly from a "fraternal Socialist Europe" to the cosmopolitan (Western) Europeanism of optimistic dissident imaginings without passing through some such nostalgic engagement with a properly *Polish* past.

Of all the old languages that have rushed in to fill the space left by communist discursive power, anti-Semitism is the most striking. It is almost irrelevant that there are hardly any Jews left in contemporary Eastern and Central Europe.[31] Anti-Semitism in this part of Europe has long had a central political and cultural place; it is as much a way of talking about "them" and "us" as it is a device for singling out Jews in particular. What is striking, though, is the discomfort aroused by any suggestion that Eastern Europeans today need to come to terms with their *past* treatment of Jews. That particular past has been so profoundly buried, by communists and noncommunists alike, that attempts to disinter it are resented by everyone, including Jews. Indeed, the Jewish intelligentsia of Budapest and Warsaw (which includes a goodly portion of the dissident intellectuals of the past twenty years) does not like to be reminded, (a) that its own and its parents' recent past was closely tied to that of the communist movement, and (b) that Jews in Eastern Europe who survived the war and chose not to emigrate often made considerable efforts to hide their Jewishness—from their colleagues, their neighbors, their children, and themselves. They are often the first to insist that anti-Semitism ended in 1945—indeed they will sometimes claim that its earlier presence in countries like Poland, Czechoslovakia, Hungary, and even Romania was much exaggerated.[32]

The special difficulty of coming to terms with the treatment of Jews, especially during the war, is that it is hopelessly imbricated with other buried histories already mentioned. For some time now there has been an interesting debate among Hungarian historians over whether the extermination of the Hungarian Jews could have been prevented. Certain of the historians involved in this debate were Jews, from different generations. The older scholars (including Jews) were often very reluctant to concede that Hungarians could have done more to prevent the deportation of their Jewish community in 1944; what was at issue was less the fate of Hungarian Jews than the responsibility of Hungarians for their own dealings with the Nazis in the last stages of the war.[33]

Curiously, this syndrome has its close equivalents farther west. Post-war Austrians, Jews, and non-Jews alike, preferred to think of Hitler's Austrian victims as a single undifferentiated category: Jews, Social-Democrats (and Jewish Social-Democrats), Christian Socials, and so forth were conflated after 1945 into a single memory of the oppression of the Austrian nation by Prusso-German Nazis. In Austria as in her eastern neighbors, this misrepresentation of history and memory (which in 1945 was certainly recent enough) did little to help Jews melt back into the fabric of Austrian society. However, there are about ten thousand Jews in Austria today, but in an opinion poll taken in October 1991, 50 percent of respondents thought "Jews are responsible for their past persecution," 31 percent said they did not want a Jew as a neighbor and 20 percent said they wanted no Jews in the country.[34]

Farther west still, in France, returning Jewish survivors of the camps were tacitly invited to merge into the general category of "deportees." Only men and women deported for acts of anti-Nazi resistance received special recognition—indeed, in the 1948 parliamentary discussions of a law defining the status and rights of former deportees no one made any reference to Jews. It has taken some forty years for the distinctive experience of Jews in occupied France, and the manner in which Vichy singled them out for punishment, to become a central part of the debate over the memory of the occupation. In France, too, this neglect was in some measure the responsibility of the Jewish community, which sought to reclaim for itself an (invisible) place in the universal republic and had little interest in inviting further discrimination by arousing unpleasant memories—its own and those of its persecutors. This stance only began to alter with the next generation of French Jews, their consciousness "raised" by the Six-Day War of June 1967 and de Gaulle's ill-starred remarks. It is for this reason that the special responsibilities of the Vichy regime, which lie in its autonomous and thoroughly French reasons for seeking out and disadvantaging Jews in particular, were for so long shrouded in ambiguity.[35] If Helmut Kohl can today speak of the extermination of Jews as a crime "committed in the name of Germany" (and thus not by any particular Germans), it is not surprising that for the best part of half a century French politicians saw little reason to arouse any sense of guilt among the French for crimes committed "in their name."[36]

And now? Good-bye to all that? The revolutions of 1989 have forced open the East European past, just as the historiographical transformations in the West have removed decades-long taboos on parts of the wartime memory.[37] There will be infinite revisions and reinterpretations, but the recent past will never look the same again, anywhere. However, even the most superficial survey of the present scene reveals new myths and new pasts already in the making.

To begin with, there is something to be said, socially speaking, for taboos. In Western Europe, for forty years after the end of World War II, no respectable scholar or public figure would have thought to attempt a rehabilitation of fascism, anti-Semitism, or the hypercollaborationist regimes and their doings. In return for the myth of an ethically respectable past and an impeccably untainted identification with a reborn Europe, we have been spared the sorts of language and attitudes that so polluted and degraded the public realm between the wars. In Eastern Europe the brutal, intolerant, authoritarian, and mutually antagonistic regimes that spread over almost all the region in the years following World War I were cast into the dustbin of history. The many unpleasant truths about that part of the world were replaced by a single beautiful lie. For it must not be forgotten that Communism was constrained by its own self-description to pay steady lip service to equality, freedom, rights, cultural values, ethnic fraternity, and international unity. By its end few questioned the hypocrisy of the affair; but in public, at least, there were certain things no longer said and done that had once been the common currency of hatred throughout the area.[38]

These constraints are now loosened, if not altogether swept away. In the words of Bruno Mégret, Jean-Marie Le Pen's deputy in the *Front National*, "Nous sommes en train d'assister à la fin du monde reconstruit depuis Yalte. Toutes les idéologies, tous les tabous [*sic*] qui ont été fondés alors sont en train de tomber."[39] Monsieur Mégret knows whereof he speaks. His party has made no small contribution to the process. Without the loss of such taboos, could one really imagine that by October 1991 some 38 percent of Giscard d'Estaing's supporters and 50 percent of Jacques Chirac's would be "globally in agreement" with Le Pen's views? Only two years earlier the respective figures were 20 percent and 38 percent. Had anyone even thought to ask the question ten years ago the figures would have been negligible. The fact is that the selfsame myths that protected the French against the memory of Mégret's Vichyite forebears also acted as a sort of prophylactic against contemporary echoes of that past. It is a cruel and paradoxal truth that the work of historians like Henry Rousso, Jean-Pierre Azéma, and their colleagues has made it possible to tell the truth about the past—and thus allowed men from that past to tell their *own* truth in the present.

Hence, too, the circumstances in which Benito Mussolini's granddaughter Alessandra can get elected to the Italian parliament not long ago in part *by virtue of her name*,[40] something of which she need no longer feel ashamed, it being rather better established today that Il Duce was not so unpopular as people liked to think, and that his institutional legacy is with Italians still. So it is in Eastern Europe, where the helter-skelter rush to dismantle and deny communism and all its works has, as noted above, begun to legitimize the earlier doings of men who combined prewar or wartime anticommunism with attitudes and acts that were until just recently literally unspeakable.

What we are witnessing, so it seems to me, is a sort of interregnum, a moment between myths when the old versions of the past are either redundant or unacceptable, and new ones have yet to surface. The outlines of the latter are already beginning to form, however. Whereas for the purposes of European moral reconstruction, it was necessary to tell a highly stylized story about the war and immediate postwar trauma, the crucial reference point for Europe now will be the years immediately preceding the events of 1989. This is not to say that the earlier mismemories will henceforth be recast in tranquillity into objective and univerally recognized histories. As I have suggested, East Europeans in particular have not yet begun to sort through and understand the multilayered pasts to which they are the unfortunate heirs, including the past that began in 1948 and has just ended. The war and especially the postwar years are still largely unexplored territory in the historiography of this region (in any language), and Leszek Kolakowski is doubtless correct when he predicts that Eastern Europe is in for a painful *Historikerstreit* of its own. But the crucial new myths will be about something else.

Western Europe is already afloat in a sea of mismemories about its own pre-1989 attitude toward communism. Whatever they now say, the architects and advocates of a unified Europe à la Maastricht never wanted to include a whole group of have-not nations from the East; they had yet fully to digest and integrate an earlier Mediterranean assortment. The Soviet grip on Eastern Europe had the double virtue of keeping that region away from the prosperous West while at the same time allowing the latter the luxury of lamenting the very circumstances from which it was benefiting. In a like manner, the noncommunist European Left is already forgetting just how very defensive it had been for the previous two decades on the subject of Soviet rule. Between Willy Brandt's *Ostpolitik* and the fantasies of the extreme disarmers, the Western Left not only discouraged criticism of the communist regimes but was often quite energetic in their defense, especially in the later Brezhnev era. Even now there are suggestions of an attempt to cast perestroika as the missed occasion for a renewal and rebirth of the communist project, with Gorbachev as the would-be Bukharin of a different road to socialism. The history and memory of Western political and cultural attitudes toward the East is an embarrassing one; if Václav Havel and others do not allude to it as often or as acerbically as they once did, this is because they must needs look ahead and to their immediate interests. But they have not forgotten that the Western Left played *no* role in their own liberation, nor are they insensible to the manifest lack of enthusiasm displayed by French and other statesmen at the fall of the Wall and its consequences. If the West forgets its own immediate past, the East will not.[41]

But Eastern Europe, too, is in thrall to a freshly minted version of its own recent history. Of these the most disturbing may be, as I have already noted, a denial of the communist experience. That the years 1948–89 were an ugly parenthesis in the history of Central and Eastern Europe is of course true; their legacy is mostly ashes, their impact mostly negative. But they did not come from nowhere, and even ashes leave their mark. That is why the debates over collaboration and collusion in Germany, Czechoslovakia, and elsewhere are so crucial and difficult. But these very debates and the revelations surrounding them risk repeating the experience of the French postwar *épurations*: the whole episode was so shot through with private score settling and bad faith that within a few months no one any longer believed in the undertaking and it became difficult (and eventually unfashionable) to distinguish between good and evil in such matters. To avoid this result—to avert the danger of arousing sympathy for communist "victims" of revenge and public cynicism as to the motives of the revengers—some political leaders in the region have already begun to suggest that it might be best just to draw a veil over the whole uncomfortable communist episode.

But that same veil would also blur our understanding of the place of communism, for good or ill, in the modern transformation of Eastern Europe. This would be a mistake: communism in Eastern Europe has some achievements to its name, paradoxal though these may now appear; it industrialized certain backward regions (Slovakia being a notable case), and it destroyed old castes and structures that had survived earlier wars and revolutions—and they will not now return. Moreover, the communists pursued and accelerated programs of urbanization, literacy, and education that were sadly lacking in this part of Europe before 1939;[42] their drive to nationalize production and services was consistent in form, if not in manner, with a process that had begun in Poland and Czechoslovakia before 1939, was pursued by the Nazis, and maintained and extended by the coalition governments of the postwar years before the communists seized power. To insist, as many now do, that communism in Eastern Europe was an alien and utterly dysfunctional imposition of Soviet interests is as misleading as to claim that the Marshall Plan and Nato were forced upon an unwilling and supine Western Europe (one of the more enduring myths of an earlier generation of Western critics).

Finally, the very events of 1989 themselves may be about to enter the no-man's land of mythical and preferable pasts. It will be hard to claim that any of the liberations of Eastern Europe, even those of Poland or

Hungary, would have been possible without at least the benign neglect of the Soviet Union; indeed there is some reason to believe that in Czechoslovakia, and perhaps Berlin, the Soviets played an active part in bringing down their own puppet regimes. This is not a very appealing or heroic version of a crucial historical turning point; it is as though Louis XVI had engineered the fall of the Bastille, a course of events that would have had detrimental consequences for the identity of nineteenth-century republicanism in France. It is also a sequence of developments humiliatingly familiar in Eastern European memory, where the wheel of history has all too often been turned by outsiders. The temptation to tell the story in a different and more comforting way may become overwhelming.[43]

The new Europe is thus being built upon historical sands at least as shifty in nature as those on which the postwar edifice was mounted. To the extent that collective identities—whether ethnic, national, or continental—are always complex compositions of myth, memory, and political convenience, this need not surprise us. From Spain to Lithuania the transition from past to present is being recalibrated in the name of a "European" idea that is itself a historical and illusory product, with different meanings in different places. In the Western and Central regions of the continent (including Poland, the Czech lands, Hungary, and Slovenia but not their eastern neighbors), the dream of economic unity may or may not be achieved in due course.

But what will not necessarily follow is anything remotely resembling continental political homogeneity and supranational stability—note the pertinent counterexample of the last years of the Habsburg Monarchy, where economic modernization, a common market, and the free movement of peoples was accompanied by a steady increase in mutual suspicion and regional and ethnic particularism.[44] As for Eastern Europe, the "third" Europe from Estonia to Bulgaria, the idea of European identity there is fast becoming the substitute political discourse of an embattled minority of intellectuals occupying the space that in other circumstances would be taken up by liberal and democratic projects, and facing the same formidable opponents and antipathies that have weakened the latter on past occasions. At a time when Euro-chat has turned to the happy topic of disappearing customs barriers, the frontiers of memory remain solidly in place.

Notes

1. See figures given in Gerold Ambrosius and William H. Hubbard, *A Social and Economic History of Twentieth-Century Europe* (Cambridge, Mass., 1989), passim; Kenneth Morgan, *The People's Peace* (Oxford, 1990), 52.

2. For an extended discussion of Camus's shifting position on the dilemma of revenge and retribution in postwar France, see my *Past Imperfect: French Intellectuals 1944–56* (Berkeley, Calif., 1992).

3. In addition to the concentration camp established by the Nazis at Struthof in Alsace, there were several internment camps in southern France. Some of these had been set up in the last months of the Third Republic to handle Republican refugees from Spain; under Vichy they served as holding pens for Jews, refugees, and other undesirables prior to their deportation, in most cases, to the East. See Anne Grynberg, *Les camps de la honte: Les internés juifs des camps français, 1939–44* (Paris, 1991), as well as the haunting memoir by Arthur Koestler, *The Scum of the Earth* (London, 1955).

4. A view shared by De Gaulle, which helps explain his occasional inability to grasp the essential distinction, when it came to postwar retribution, between Prussian "barbarism" and Nazi genocide.

5. For a somewhat partial, but well-documented account of the expulsion of the Germans, see Alfred M. de Zayas, *Nemesis at Potsdam: The Expulsion of the Germans from the East* (Lincoln, Nebr., 1989).

6. On the unhappy history of post-war, precommunist Czechoslovakia's treatment of some of its national minorities, see Radomir Luza, *The Transfer of the Sudeten Germans: A Study of Czech-German Relations 1933–62* (New York, 1964); Petr Pithart, "Let Us Be Kind to Our History" in *Kosmas*, Winter 1984; and Kalman Janics, *Czechoslovak Policy and the Hungarian Minority 1945–1948* (New York, 1982).

7. See Paul Ginsborg, *A History of Contemporary Italy, 1943–88* (London, 1990), 53 ff.

8. I am thus inclined to agree with Henry Rousso, who has suggested that although the postwar purge in France can now be seen to have been tragically inadequate, its failure was probably inevitable under the circumstances. See Rousso, "L'épuration en France: une histoire inachevée, in *Vingtième Siècle* 33 (janvier–mars 1992): 78–106.

9. Ginsborg, A History, 64–70. On later charges leveled at the partisans for their acts of summary justice, see Luca Alessandrini and Angela Maria Politi, "Nuove fonti sui processi contro i partigiani, 1948–53," in *Italia Contemporanea*, 178 (1990): 41–62.

10. As in the case of the massacre of Hungarians in the Vojvodina by Tito's partisans, revenge for the Hungarian military's activities there in January 1942.

11. For the Austrian figures I am indebted to Dr. Lonnie Johnson of the *Institut für die Wissenschaften vom Menschen* in Vienna. For France, see the article by Henry Rousso cited in note 8, but also Marcel Baudot, "L'épuration: bilan chiffré" in *Bulletin de l'Institut d'Histoire du Temps Présent* 25 (Septembre 1986): 37–53.

12. In which the French at first proved remarkably adept. In July 1951 one observer wrote of their "alarming" success in putting Vichy out of mind. See Janet Flanner, *Paris Journal 1944–65* (New York, 1977), 153.

13. For the benign and limited character of the purge of economic collaborators, see e.g., Henry Rousso, "Les élites économiques dans les années qua-

rante," in *Le elites in Francia et in Italia negli anni quaranta* (Mélanges de l'Ecole française de Rome, tome 95, 1982–83).

14. In the Italian instance a further question arises, obscured by the aura surrounding the Resistance coalition. If Mussolini had chosen to keep out of Hitler's war, and had succeeded in remaining aloof, are there not some grounds for speculating that his regime may have survived into the postwar era? The comparison with Franco is not so implausible as it seems; the short history of the Italian nation-state had provided little occasion for the cementing of democratic or constitutional habits.

15. Enzensberger's phrase suggests a sort of passive collusion, an agreement not to discuss certain matters in public, as a result of which they become obscured in recollection. To the extent that historians contributed to this situation, they did so mostly through omission; the war years were too recent, and primary or official sources too scarce to permit of serious historical accounts of collaboration or resistance. As time passed and archives opened, some good scholarly studies were indeed undertaken, despite the problems of contemporaneity. But they were not necessarily read outside of a narrow circle of specialists. When their influence *was* finally felt, it was usually for reasons that had little to do with the formal conditions of academic production.

16. See William B. Bader, *Austria between East and West, 1945–55* (Stanford, 1966), and Robert E. Clute, *The International Legal Status of Austria, 1938–55* (The Hague, 1962).

17. See Rudolf Bindschedler, Hans Rudolf Kurz, Wilhelm Carlgren, and Sten Carlsson, *Schwedische und Schweizerische Neutralität im Zweiten Weltkrieg* (Basel, 1985), notably the contributions by Carlsson, Bindschedler, and especially Samuel Werenfels ("Die Schweizerische Praxis in der Behandlung von Flüchtlingen, Internierten und entwichenen Kriegsgefangenen im Zweiten Weltkrieg," 377–405). Also Sven-Olof Olsson, *German Coal and Swedish Fuel* (Göteborg, 1975).

18. A further shared characteristic of the community's founding fathers—their common Catholicism—may help account for initial suspicions and reticence on the part of Scandinavian and especially British politicians in the postwar years. I am indebted to Stephen Graubard for this observation. The British, of course, had many other reasons for seeking to remain aloof from European projects—see the interviews with senior British politicians and civil servants in Michael Charlton, *The Price of Victory* (London, 1983).

19. It should be noted, however, that France has never ratified the international and European conventions of 1968 and 1974, which make *war crimes* also imprescriptible. As a result, under French law it is only possible to prosecute someone for actions undertaken during the war if his or her handiwork falls under the at once restrictive and nebulous heading of "crimes against humanity."

20. Henry Rousso, *Le Syndrome de Vichy, de 1944 à nos jours* (Paris, 2d ed., 1990). Examples of the seminal contributions of foreign scholars include Eberhard Jäckel's *Frankreich in Hitlers Europa* (Stuttgart, 1966), of which a French translation finally appeared in 1988; Robert O. Paxton's *Vichy France: Old Guard and New Order* (New York, 1972); Dennis Mack Smith, *Italy: A Modern*

History (Ann Arbor, 1959) and *Mussolini* (London, 1981). Note, too, the work of Gerhard Hirschfeld. His *Nazi rule and Dutch Collaboration: The Netherlands under German Occupation 1940–45* (Oxford/New York, 1988), a translation of *Fremdherrschaft und Kollaboration. Die Niederlande unter deutscher Besatzung 1940–45* (Stuttgart, 1984), provided a much needed corrective to even the best Dutch historiography on the subject. See also Nanda van der Zee, "The Recurrent Myth of 'Dutch Heroism' in the Second World War and Anne Frank As a Symbol," in G. Jan Colijn and Marcia S. Littell, eds., *The Netherlands and Nazi Genocide* (Lewiston, N.Y., 1992), 1–14.

21. All three men have been "investigated" for their active roles in Vichy's treatment of Jews—and in each case the wheels of justice have turned with excruciating and suspicious slowness. The motive for this disinclination to raise again the old, uncomfortable issues is the same as it was in 1946; the undersecretary of state for justice in a socialist-led government, M. George Kiejman, declared on 19 October 1990 that "au-delà de la nécessaire lutte contre l'oubli, il peut paraître important de préserver la paix civile."

22. The German arguments raged not so much over issues of resistance and collaboration, which were marginal to the German experience, but rather around the problem of responsibility (and the limits of responsibility) for the policy of racial extermination. After four decades during which the subject was at once acknowledged and yet curiously undiscussed, some conservative scholars, taking advantage of the passage of years and the declining legitimacy of Soviet Communism, suggested that the time had come to "historicize" the Holocaust, to concede the comparability of Nazism and Stalinism and even to suggest that the Nazi policy of genocide was in some measure a rational and explicable response, however awful, to the threat posed to Germany by her totalitarian neighbour to the east. The moral and political shock waves of this historical dispute have been somewhat muted by the unexpected unification of Germany and *its* attendant moral dilemmas, but they remain potent and their implications endure. See Richard J. Evans, *In Hitler's Shadow* (New York, 1989); Charles S. Maier, *The Unmasterable Past* (Cambridge, Mass., 1988), and Peter Baldwin, ed., *Reworking the Past: Hitler, the Holocaust, and the Historians' Debate* (Boston, 1990), notably the contributions by Saul Friedländer, Hans Mommsen, and Hagen Schulze. See also the acerbic commentary by one of the participants in the argument, Hans-Ulrich Wehler, *Die Entsorgung der deutschen Vergangenheit: Ein polemischer Artikel zum "Historikerstreit"* (Munich, 1988).

23. For the Waldheim presidency and its ramifications in Austria, see the new book by Richard Mitten, *The Waldheim Phenomenon in Austria: The Politics of anti-Semitic Prejudice* (Boulder, Colo., 1992).

24. See the reflections on this theme by Rousso, Daniel Lindenberg, Stanley Hoffmann, and others in "Que faire de Vichy?" *Esprit* (mai 1992): 5–87.

25. Claudio Pavone, *Une guerra civile: Saggio storico sulla moralità nella Resistenza* (Turin, 1991); Luisa Passerini, *Mussolini imaginario* (Bari, 1991) and the editorial in *Italia Contemporanea* 181 (December 1990): 645–51, "Il nuovo processo alla Resistenza." See, in addition, Passerini's earlier work, *Fascism in Popular Memory* (Cambridge, 1987), a translation of her *Torino Operaia e Fascismo* (Bari, 1984). The steady disaggregation of the Resistance coalition in post-

war Italy, and with it the attendant foundation myth of the Republic, has also of couse affected the standing and support of the Christian Democrats. But it is the decline and fall of the ex-PCI that has done most to facilitate and even encourage public debate over the wartime experience of the country. For an authoritative instance of the traditional Communist position on the war and postwar years, see Luigi Longo, *Chi ha tradito la Resistenza* (Rome, 1975).

26. Peter Schneider's most recent work, *The German Comedy: Scenes of Life after the Wall*, was published in New York in 1991. On the way in which historians in the German Democratic Republic handled the issue of anti-Semitism, see K. Kwist, "Historians of the German Democratic Republic on Anti-Semitism and Persecution," in *Leo Baeck Institute Yearbook* 20 (1976) 173–98.

27. See Tony Judt, "Metamorphosis: The Democratic Revolution in Czechoslovakia," in *Eastern Europe in Revolution*, Ivo Banac ed. (Cornell University Press, 1992).

28. More problematic still is the case of someone like the Romanian writer Mircea Eliade, a liberal intellectual nowadays much admired for his prescient critiques of Stalinism in the fifties and after. It is all too easy to forget that before World War II, like much of the intelligentsia of Central and Eastern Europe, Eliade was a supporter of the extreme nationalist Right.

29. In the pogrom at Kielce on 4 July 1946, forty-one Jews died. There were many similar, lesser outbursts of anti-Semitism in postwar Poland. But there are some grounds for thinking that some atrocities (like the murder of two Jews at Kunmadaras in Hungary on 21 May 1946) were provoked by the Communist police, who had an interest in exacerbating already strained relations between Jews and non-Jews. See Alexander Smolar, "Jews As a Polish Problem," *Daedalus* 116 (ii) (1987): 31–73, and Yosef Litvak, "Polish-Jewish Refugees Repatriated from the Soviet Union to Poland at the End of the Second World War and Afterward," in Norman Davies and Antony Polonsky, eds., *Jews in Eastern Poland and the USSR, 1939–46* (New York, 1991). I am indebted to Professor Istvan Deák for his observations on this point.

30. The Treaty on Cooperation and Friendhsip between Czechoslovakia and Germany was signed on 27 February 1992 and ratified in the Czecho-Slovak Federal Assembly on 4 April 1992 by 226 votes to 144. Deputies from the Communist, Social-Democratic, and Slovak Nationalist parties voted against, the Slovaks objecting to the phrase that affirmed the "continuity of the Czechoslovak state since 1918."

31. Only in Hungary is the Jewish presence significant. It numbers about 100,000 persons, most of them in Budapest.

32. According to Joseph Rothschild, in interwar Eastern Europe "the only really potent international ideology . . . was anti-Semitism based on both conviction and experience," *East-Central Europe between the Two Wars*, (Seattle, 1974), 9. For some interesting remarks on the "hyperassimilationism of postwar Hungarian Jews (those who chose to remain), see Maria Kovacs, "Jews and Communists: A View after Communism," unpublished paper.

33. See Istvan Deák, "Could the Hungarian Jews Have Survived?," *New York Review of Books* 29, i (4 February 1982); Randolph L. Braham, *The Politics of Genocide: The Holocaust in Hungary* (New York, 1981); György Ránki, "The

Germans and the Destruction of the Hungarian Jewry," in Randolph L. Braham and Belá Vago, eds., *The Holocaust in Hungary: Forty Years Later* (New York, 1985); András Kovács, "Could Genocide Have Been Averted?" *Budapest Review of Books* 1, i (1991), 20–25.

34. On postwar Austrian handling of indigenous anti-Semitism and the memory of local enthusiasm for the Nazis, see Bruce F. Pauley, *From Prejudice to Persecution: A History of Austrian Anti-Semitism* (Chapel Hill, N.C., 1991), 301–10.

35. See Annette Wievorka, *Déportation et génocide: Entre la mémoire et l'oubli* (Paris, 1992), notably 19–159, 329–433; Serge Klarsfeld, *Vichy-Auschwitz: Le rôle de Vichy dans la solution finale de la question juive en France* (Paris, 2 vols., 1983).

36. Note that François Mitterrand avoided any official acknowledgment of Vichy's role in the deportation of Jews during his 1982 visit to the Yad Vashem memorial in Jerusalem, a silence that he maintained in spite of impassioned pleas from many quarters in French society. But France is not unique—historiographical and public interest in the circumstances of Jewish deportations in Belgium, Italy, and elsewhere is of very recent vintage. It is hard now to recall how small a part the extermination of Jews, and the sensitive issue of latent anti-Semitism, played in the political consciousness of Europe in the immediate postwar decades.

37. One of the more optimistic signs in Eastern Europe has been the organization or reorganization of centers for historical research, oriented in many cases to making good the damage done to historical studies in the region over the past forty years. In Prague, the *Pamatnik odboje* (Memorial of the Resistance), part of the former History Institute of the Czechoslovak army, now has a department, directed by Dr. Frantisek Janacek, devoted to the historical study of collaboration and resistance in Czechoslovakia during and after World War II.

38. The glaring exception, of course, was the ugly outbreak of officially condoned anti-Semitism in Poland in the years 1967–68. But for many people this has already been cosmetically reshaped as the work of a few hotheads in the political apparatus, with no support or roots in the party or nation at large.

39. 30 August 1991, cited in *Le Monde* of 31 August 1991.

40. And perhaps her looks . . .

41. Nor should it be forgotten that Socialists in Italy, especially, were happy to join with Communists in applauding the East-European show-trials of the forties and fifties, a subject over which they and their heirs now prefer to maintain a discrete silence. Even Aneurin Bevan in Britain's Labour Party was not exempt from temptation; in 1959, reiterating his faith in the future of the Soviet Union, he declared that "the challenge is going to come from those nations who, however wrong they may be—and I think they are wrong in many fundamental respects— nevertheless are at long last being able to reap the material fruits of economic planning and of public ownership." Quoted in Michael Foot, *Aneurin Bevan: A Biography, Volume II, 1945–60* (New York, 1974). All in all it is hard to dissent from the bitter conclusion of Paolo Flores d'Arcais: "nel comunismo la sinistra europea è stata coinvolta quasi tutta, direttamente o indirettamente. Per scelta, per calcolo, per omissione." See his editorial in *Micro-Mega* 4 (1991): 17.

42. In 1939, illiteracy levels were still 32 percent in Bulgaria, 40 percent in

Yugoslavia, and nearly 50 percent in Romania. See Barbara Jelavich, *History of the Balkans: Twentieth Century* (Cambridge, 1983), 242.

43. Witness the speech by Jozsef Antall, historian and prime minister of Hungary, on 11 January 1992, where he describes to his Hungarian audience the West's lack of appreciation for East-Central Europeans' heroic efforts on its behalf: "This unrequited love must end because we stuck to our posts, we fought our own fights without firing one shot, and we won the third world war for them." This stirringly revisionist interpretation of the Kádárist years is excerpted in *East European Reporter* V,ii (March–April 1992): 66–68.

44. See David F. Good, *The Economic Rise of the Habsburg Empire, 1750–1914* (Berkeley, Calif., 1984).

Contributors

István Deák, who is Seth Low Professor of History at Columbia University, was born in Hungary. His publications include, *Weimar Germany's Left-Wing Intellectuals* (Berkeley, Calif., 1968); *The Lawful Revolution: Louis Kossuth and the Hungarians, 1848–49* (New York, 1979); and *Beyond Nationalism: A Social and Political History of the Habsburg Officer Corps* (New York, 1990). István Deák has published widely on the revolutions of 1848; World War I in Central Europe; the rise of fascism; collaboration and resistance in Europe during World War II; and post–World War II political justice.

Jan T. Gross, Professor of Politics and European Studies at New York University, is the author of, among other works, *Polish Society under German Occupation, General Gouvernement, 1939–44* (Princeton, 1979), and *Revolution from Abroad: Soviet Conquest of Poland's Western Ukraine and Western Belorussia* (Princeton, 1988).

Tony Judt is Director of the Remarque Institute at New York University. His publications include *Marxism and the French Left* (New York, 1986); *Resistance and Revolution in Mediterranean Europe* (London–New York, 1989); *Past Imperfect: French Intellectuals 1944–56* (Berkeley, Calif., 1992); *Grand Illusion: An Essay on Europe* (New York, 1996); and *The Burden of Responsibility: Blum, Camus, Aron, and the French Twentieth Century* (Chicago, 1998).

Bradley Abrams is an Assistant Professor of East-Central European History at Columbia University. He is currently revising his dissertation, entitled " 'The Struggle for the Soul of the Nation': Czech Culture and Socialism, 1945–48," for publication, and commencing research on a project concerning Central European intellectuals and communism in the twentieth century.

Martin Conway is Fellow and Tutor in Modern History at Balliol College in the University of Oxford. He is the author of *Collaboration in Belgium: Leon Degrelle and the Rexist Movement 1940–1944* (New Haven, 1993) and of *Catholic Politics in Europe 1918–1945* (London–New York, 1997). He is currently preparing a study of the politics of liberation in Belgium after the Second World War.

Sarah Farmer is Associate Professor of History at the University of Iowa and author of *Martyred Village: Commemorating the 1944 Massacre at Oradour-sur-Glane* (Berkeley, 1998).

Luc Huyse is Professor of Sociology and Sociology of Law at the University of Leuven Law School (Belgium). He has written widely on postwar politics in Western Europe and is currently studying the role of courts during and after regime changes. He has done field research in South Africa, Ethiopia, and Burundi.

László Karsai is Associate Professor of History at József Attila University in Szeged, Hungary. His publications include the *Endre-Baky-Jaross per* (edited in collaboration with Dr. Judit Molnár, 1994) and the *Szálasi per* (edited in collaboration with Dr. Elek Karsai, 1988). The two books deal with the post–World War II trials of leading Hungarian officials responsible for the deportation of Jews to Auschwitz. László Karsai is preparing a documentary collection on the ghetto in Budapest in the winter of 1944–45.

Mark Mazower is Reader in History at the University of Sussex. He is author of *Inside Hitler's Greece: The Experience of Occupation, 1941–44* (New Haven, 1993) and *Dark Continent: Europe's Twentieth Century* (New York, 1999). He is currently writing a brief study of the Balkans in modern history and is working on a book about the city of Salonica and its Jewish community.

Peter Romijn is Director of Research at the Netherlands Institute for War Documentation in Amsterdam. He published a book in 1989 on the punishment and reintegration of collaborators in postwar Dutch society. He has also published studies on such topics as political justice and the Dutch administration's treatment of the Jews in World War II. He is preparing a monograph on local government as an instrument of nazification.

Index